# Awadh
# Symphony

# Awadh Symphony

*Notes on a Cultural Interlude*

## ASLAM MAHMUD

Introduction by *Shamsur Rahman Faruqi*

RUPA

Published by
Rupa Publications India Pvt. Ltd 2017
7/16, Ansari Road, Daryaganj
New Delhi 110002

*Sales centres:*
Allahabad Bengaluru Chennai
Hyderabad Jaipur Kathmandu
Kolkata Mumbai

ISBN: 978-81-291-4650-2

First impression 2017

10 9 8 7 6 5 4 3 2 1

The moral right of the author has been asserted.

Printed at

# Contents

# Preface

Born and brought up in Lucknow, for Aslam Mahmud, my Abba, Awadh has always been a subject very close to his heart—almost a part of him. A true Lucknowite at heart, imbued in Lakhnavi culture and customs, his deep interest in Awadh led him to acquire and read innumerable rare and valuable books on the rich symphony of art, monuments, cuisines, lifestyle and traditions that captivated him. The grand days of the past in the heartland of tehzeeb, Oudh or Awadh, has drawn the interest of many others like him. However Abba not only collected information and books for his own interest but desired to pen down the intricacies of Awadh's rich tapestry. This was primarily the reason why he wanted to come up with a go-to book on Awadh that would give the readers an overview of the life and times of the Nawabi era. For the past seven years I saw him working tirelessly on this book, referring and consulting numerous others from his personal collection as well as every possible source. He was excited as he was close to seeing his long-cherished dream turn into reality. However, God works in strange ways and, unfortunately, Abba could not live to see this book to its completion.

His untimely death was a setback not only for his near and dear ones but also for his dream project. His years of hard work and effort stared at us. How could one let go of something that was built with so much love and passion? It was a feeling of helplessness and despair. However, we derived our strength from the fact that such meticulous details and descriptions collected and compiled from numerous sources over the years into a book must reach the hands of the readers. In our quest for getting the book published, we were supported by none other than Mehra saab, Rajan Mehra, Chairman, Rupa Publications, Abba's friend and confidante over the years who was witness to Abba's years of hard work and always encouraged him to complete the book. We are grateful to Mehra saab for his guidance and support without which Abba's dream project would not have seen the light of day.

Though Abba had completed chapters of his book, he could not give them a final shape in his lifetime. My publishers and I have worked hard to remain as close as possible to retain his style without tweaking it too much. We have also standardized names of places and rulers according to the information available in books of antiquity in order to be as accurate as possible, both culturally and historically.

Finally, this book would not have been complete without the continued help and support of Shamsur Rahman Faruqi saab, who readily agreed to contribute an 'Introduction' to this book. The Introduction serves as the perfect jewel in the crown. He very kindly and graciously also looked into the dastangoi chapter and provided us with additional material on *Dastan-i Amir Hamza*.

My sincere thanks is also due to Saleem Kidwai saab for his inputs and guidance; Naiyar Masud and Azhar Masud saab for allowing us to glean required information to fill in the gaps in the narrative from their phenomenal work on chehra navisi and the street vendors of Lucknow titled 'Chehra Navisi' and 'Lakhnau ke Pheri Wale', respectively.

Last but not the least, special thanks to Abba's long-term loyal steno, Ovais Ahmad Siddiqui, for patiently and loyally helping him by typing the draft of the book and for being with him all these years.

I hand over the book to you, dear reader, and hope that you enjoy your journey through the mystical land of Awadh!

Tasneem Mahmud
Daughter-in-law of Aslam Mahmud

# Introduction

*Shamsur Rahman Faruqi*

*Where ever you look, it's like a scene of uproar, of commotion,*
*Is it a city, or is it a spectacular show?*
*Let the evil eye never touch such an urban habitation,*
*Because this city is the very purpose of Creation!*
*Lucknow is better than Delhi even, because*
*Someone's heart inclines to loving it.*

Mir Muhammad Taqi Mir (1723–1810),
'Celebrating a Marriage Together with the Festival of Holi', 1794

*Do the inimical heavens ever have the power to separate me from Lucknow?*
*Lucknow dies for me; I die for Lucknow!*
*Who could describe the grandeur of the King of Lucknow?*
*The bowl in the beggar's hand here is the wine cup of Jamshed,*
*the legendary king.*

Shaikh Imam Bakhsh 'Nasikh' (1772–1838)

India in the 1840s: the teeming, thriving, upward-looking city of Lucknow was a thorn in the English heart. Militarily and politically, Delhi had long since fallen on evil days. Shah Alam Bahadur Shah II, the least feeble of a feeble series of the last Mughals, came to the throne in 1759. He spent the first dozen years of his reign in practical exile. His successors were poets and scholars, but not kings. Siraj-ud-Daulah had been subdued and murdered in 1757. Tipu Sultan had perished at Srirangapatam in the last year of the eighteenth century. Murshidabad and Mysore now paid fealty to the English Company Bahadur. Hyderabad was, in effect, no more than a vassal. The Maratha had been declining steadily after the demise of Mahadaji Sindhia in 1794 and the decisive defeat in the battle of Delhi in 1803. The court at Poona now played no significant part in the political, military or cultural life of the Indian nation. The Sikhs of the Punjab were to be finally extinguished in 1849, but extensive areas of the Punjab had already been lost or ceded to the Englishman. But Lucknow, playful, frivolous, a military power manqué (Shuja-ud-Daulah and Emperor Shah Alam II had been decisively defeated by the English at Buxar in 1764, and the English forces had combined with a token army of Shuja-ud-Daulah to defeat and put to rout the valiant Rohillas in 1774; but Lucknow ceased to be a military power afterwards) continued to behave as if the balmy days of its spring would never cease to be.

Finally, English patience gave way to avarice. On 11 February 1856, Awadh was annexed and the king chose exile over resistance and bloodshed, leaving Lucknow forever.

Beginning from the mid-nineteenth century, Lucknow had bad press, especially among the English-influenced political chroniclers and historians. The English accounts trickled down quickly enough and effectively coloured the perceptions of ordinary Indians outside about Awadh. Both Indians and Europeans were nurtured on stories of Lucknow's misgovernment at the hands of the nawabs, their unbridled proclivity toward lechery, effeminacy, thriftlessness and exploitation of their subjects. Even among those who weren't hostile to Lucknow, its reputation for refinement and sophistication was mostly understood to mean the absence of 'manly' qualities like love of the martial arts, lack of inclination to deal with the problems of life, disregard for the practical side of things, absence of a sense of social responsibility; in short, a Lucknow gentleman was a beau who had a reputation for preciosity not only in his use of language but also in everything that he did. Premchand's short story *Shatranj ki Bazi* (1924, Urdu version 1928) and Satyajit Ray's film *Shatranj ke Khilari* (1978) say it all, in spades.

Efforts to redeem Lucknow's reputation and also—conscious or unconscious—efforts to run down the culture of Lucknow, therefore Awadh, continued side by side in the early twentieth century. Abdul Halim Sharar wrote his popular and adulatory *Guzashta Lakhnau* (*Lucknow of the Past Times*) during the 1920s; the book came out around 1924 (note the dates of the Premchand short story, 1924–28). It is still in print and an adequate English translation is also available with the title *Lucknow: the Last Phase of an Oriental Culture*, by E. S. Harcourt and Fakhir Husain. Both the Urdu and English versions are consulted by historians and aficionados alike, but the influence and reputation of Premchand's story and Satyajit Ray's film far exceed any penetration achieved by Sharar's book. (In fact, since the book is highly anecdotal, scholars have often pointed out that it is not authentic enough to be cited as history.)

In 1926 (again, note the date), Abdul Salam Nadvi, a reputed Islamic scholar and historian, published *She'r-ul hind* (*The Poetry of India*) a two-volume critical-historical account of Urdu poetry. It has become almost entirely superseded by subsequent scholarship, yet it left a pernicious legacy, which lives on. In Volume I of his fairly large account of Urdu poetry, Nadvi, quite casually and without laying any kind of theoretical or historical foundation, identified two 'schools' of Urdu poetry: Delhi and Lucknow. He coined the terms 'dakhiliyat' (internality) and 'kharijiyat' (externality) and pronounced that the poetry of the 'Delhi School' was marked by dakhiliyat and that of the 'Lucknow School' was characterized by kharijiyat. Without explicitly determining the 'Lucknow School' to be inferior to the 'Delhi School', he made it clear that dakhiliyat meant greater depth, more gravitas, more 'truth of thought and feeling', lesser degree of addiction to 'wordplay for its own sake', less concern with the carnal and the 'shallower' aspect of love. Lucknow was much possessed by the physical and the corporeal, a young upstart who didn't much care for the deeper and more 'inward' experiences of life, or the intellectual and spiritual side of things.

No one today subscribes to the 'Two Schools Theory' of Urdu poetry.

Yet the words dakhiliyat and kharijiyat have assumed almost canonical force in Urdu literary criticism. Another version of the two terms is 'Lakhnaviyat' (Lucknowness) for kharijiyat and 'Dihlaviyat' (Delhiness) for dakhiliyat. Lakhnaviyat and kharijiyat are spoken of with a distinct air of disapproval, but these terms are in popular use.

Doubtless, Lucknow has had its admirers and defenders too from the very time it began to earn its evil reputation. On the political side, there was the king himself who issued a Reply to the Company's *Blue Book on Oude*, published from Calcutta [Kolkata] in January 1857. The Reply was also presented to the British Parliament, but it seems to have invited no real discussion in or outside the Parliament. Hakim Masihuddin Khan, the king's envoy to London after the annexation, issued his own and perhaps more telling reply in the same year. Called *Oude: Its Princes and its Government Vindicated*, it was promptly banned by the English government. All unsold copies were seized and destroyed. Today, very few people have heard of Wajid Ali Shah's Reply, and perhaps none know of Hakim Masihuddin's book.

On the cultural-historical side, Abdul Halim Sharar's *Guzashta Lakhnau* remains the most popular, not least because of its anecdotal and narrative power. Much later, there was Mirza Jafar Husain's *Qadeem Lakhnau Ki Akhiri Bahaar* (*The Last Spring of Bygone Lucknow*). It was even more adulatory than Sharar's, and doesn't seem to have done much to dispel the common perception of Lucknow as a decadent society. A much stronger attempt was by Amarish Mishra in his *Lucknow: Fire of Grace, The Story of its Renaissance, Revolution and the Aftermath* (1999). Mishra also comes through as a cordial admirer of Lucknow, but his narrative is generally supported by facts and not just anecdotes.

Among modern Western scholars, Mike Fisher and Rosie Llewellyn-Jones have written important books on the cultural-historical aspects of Lucknow. Llewellyn-Jones on Wajid Ali Shah: *The Last King in India* (2014), is a particularly good example. But I am not aware of any book that deals with the nitty-gritty of Awadh culture, embracing all aspects of human activity from religious ritual to games and from the life in the closed environment of parda-nasheen women to the development of photography and print-making in the market place. The present book makes a valiant and largely successful attempt to fill the gap.

Aslam Mahmud was a senior civil servant in the Indian Railways who spent all his spare time in collecting and reading books. He was one of the few bibliophiles I knew who actually read all the books that he bought from all over the world. When I knew him first, many years ago, he was most interested in modern Western fiction and one could be sure of his having bought and read the latest of the novels from prominent modern authors in any Western language if it was available in English translation. Gradually he turned his attention to antiquarian books in English, and it was an easy transition for him to get into Urdu literature and Urdu's literary culture of the nineteenth century, and finally to concentrate on Awadh and its literary and social culture. Here again, he covered even the most arcane areas, like picture postcards, antiquarian photos, maps, poetry collections of obscure but culturally important poets. The present book is the fruit of his decades of labour. It testifies to his extremely wide and meticulous reading and painstakingly collected artefacts and documents concerning the culture of Awadh.

The title of the book is suggestive—Awadh from late eighteenth century to early twentieth century *was* an interlude. Lucknow was a nondescript city before Asaf-ud-Daula made it his capital, leaving Faizabad soon after he became the nawab wazir in 1775. The most prominent thing in Lucknow before 1775 was the haveli of Shaikh Abdur Rahim Bijnori who was deputed there by Akbar and who built the Machhi Bhawan and the Akbari Darwaza. The former, a famed building of the times, was demolished by the English in 1857. Akbari Darwaza (better known as Akbari Gate) remains, but shorn of its former glory. At the time of the death of Shaikh Abdur Rahim Bijnori, Lucknow was a middle-level provincial town and remained so for the next nearly two hundred years. Asaf-ud-Daula's shift of his capital to Lucknow inaugurated an era of unparalleled prosperity, sophistication and cultural achievement. Within just ten years of the move to Lucknow, the city could boast to be the site, in the form of the Bara Imambara (or the Asafi Imambara), of a unique building. It is now widely acknowledged as one of the largest vaulted and beamless buildings in the world. Fifteen metres tall, with a length of fifty metres and a width of sixteen, it is still unsurpassed as one of the chief architectural wonders of India. Built in the Mughal style, and designed by Kifayatullah, an architect from Delhi, the building helped Lucknow declare its coming of age as a seat of Mughal or Indo-Islamic culture.

In this book, Aslam Mahmud doesn't discuss the architecture of Lucknow, because this is one aspect of the culture of Awadh that has been studied in great detail and which has won admiration all round. (No one talks of 'decadence' in the context of Lucknow's architecture.) It is true that the monuments of Lucknow don't appear massive because stone is not their chief medium. But what is lacking in massivity is amply compensated by the lightness of touch. A comparison between Fatehpur Sikri's Buland Darwaza and Lucknow's Rumi Darwaza would be fruitful in this context. While the former gives the impression of living rock lifted from an ancient mountainside, the latter looks like the diadem of a queen.

Aslam Mahmud has rightly directed most of his attention to those aspects of the culture of Awadh that have often been neglected. He tells us about the fairs and bazaars, the speech of the common people, and the idiom of poetry. Then he enters the almost unknown and entirely unappreciated realm of dastan (oral romance) and the art of dastangoi (narrating the oral romance). It is a tragic fact of our culture that the dastan and its narrators sank without trace during the course of less than a hundred years. A performing genre, which the sixteenth-century Persian poet and critic Abdun-Nabi Fakhr-e Zamani described as superior to the calling of a poet, because a dastan narrator had to know poetry and much else besides, fell into disrepute and utter neglect over a few decades, thanks to the pervasive colonial discourse, which taught us that the datsan had no 'realism', no 'social relevance', and was 'pornographic' to boot. Aslam Mahmud has done well to provide comprehensive information about the state of dastan-composing and narrating in Lucknow in the nineteenth century.

Aslam Mahmud seems to have read every book and every essay relevant to his quest: a comprehensive and fact-supported picture of life as it was in Awadh during the days of its glory. From the dastan, he goes on to the marsiya, its poetry and recital. Even the detractors of Lucknow grant that the marsiya, or long narrative poem describing the valour, the suffering and the passion of Imam Husain, the Prophet's grandson, martyred in the battle of Karbala (now in Iraq) in 680 CE, reached unprecedented heights in Lucknow in the nineteenth century, heights that have never been approached, far less surpassed by later poets. Aslam Mahmud directs his attention also to the art of recitation of the marsiya, which had rigorous rules—care being taken to permit no hint of resemblance to acting—and which again became a discipline in itself. He gives a brief account of the origin of the tazia, and the construction of imambaras, as special places where the people congregated to hear discourses on the Imam and his family's excellence (faza'il) and their persecution and agony (masa'ib) during the month of Muharram (Imam Husain was martyred on the 10th of Muharram in 61 AH).

The account of Muharram observances as given by Aslam Mahmud—though he wasn't a shi'a—(nor am I, for that matter) is the most detailed that I have seen in English.

It should be noted here that the observance of Muharram throughout the territory of Awadh was an important feature of the people's lives, regardless of religion, or creed. It continues to be so today, except that the participation of Hindus has diminished somewhat, though not disappeared. Muharram thus provides a solid, living example of our Ganga-Jamuni culture.

Aslam Mahmud has some interesting, and to me, quite new details of the difference between the standard cuisines of Delhi and Lucknow. In fact, this whole field of the cuisine popular in pre-modern times is very nearly unexplored; the so-called 'mughlai' cuisine is not all that Mughal in its details and variety. Similarly, Mahmud's section on food taboos and the rules of eating is full of information not recorded elsewhere.

Of particular interest is the section on matters related to embroidery, gold work and dyeing; Aslam Mahmud's (re)search led him to the discovery of a practically unknown tract on the art of dyeing. Published in 1888, the author gives prescriptions for twenty-six vegetable colours used for dyeing clothes and dresses. Those who have good Urdu can identify a number of the twenty-six colours specified here. None can today actually identify all of them, and the English translations of the colour names given by Aslam Mahmud are just adequate to give a hazy idea of the actual tone and shade.

Contrary to popular perception, Lucknow excelled in outdoor games as much as it did in the indoor games like pachisi, chess, or that most difficult of games, ganjifa. While Aslam Mahmud gives an adequate account of these games, he stresses the fact that outdoor games were equally, if not more, popular in Awadh. He gives us the names and brief accounts of some of the outstanding sportspersons nurtured by Awadh. Apart from archery and firearms, wrestling, fencing, throwing the javelin, swimming and many arcane disciplines of unarmed combat flourished in Awadh. Mahmud gives the names not only of some of the sportsmen, but also of publications dealing with the martial arts.

A most important segment of the book is devoted to domestic and family life. The author dwells in detail on the purdah system and its social and legal implications. More informative are quotes from instruction books and guides to conduct and behaviour for both men and women. Nothing has come down from the pre-annexation period so it is difficult to hazard any details from there. In any case, Aslam Mahmud offers no opinions, far less, value judgements. His tone of voice throughout the book is unadulatory and non-judgemental.

Aslam Mahmud also discusses some little-known bureaucratic practices; for example, chehra navisi, or the recording of an employee's facial features and general appearance for purposes of identification. We occasionally come across the term in the poetry of the nineteenth century, but no details are available. The details that Aslam Mahmud has now itemized are much like the anthropometric system of recording details and measurements of various body parts called Bertillonage, invented in the late nineteenth century by the French criminologist Alphonse Bertillon. The chehra navis in Awadh didn't record head and body measurements, but his details were specific in many other ways. He took account of the eyebrows, shape of the ears, shape of the chin, and so on. We learn from Aslam Mahmud that chehra navisi was also used for recording identifying details of animals, especially horses and ponies.

This is not just a book: it's a guide to a past that was vibrant and intellectually and imaginatively affluent. It is not about the Awadh of modern anecdotal lore where the culture of Awadh is denigrated, or scoffed, or ignored. All of us owe a debt to Aslam Mahmud. It is sad that he didn't live to see the publication of this book, the fruit of a lifetime's labour of love.

# Customs and Traditions

$A$ wadh, considered to be the region in North India, with the city of Lucknow as its cultural centre, is home to some unique customs and traditions which have, over the years, defined the lives of its people and lies at the core of its rich cultural heritage. This section offers a glimpse into the lives of the people of Awadh and an understanding of their cherished customs and traditions.

The first chapter revisits some of the major ceremonial rituals, customs, manners, and traditions. It, in particular, provides an insight into the lives of Lakhnavi Muslims—their customs relating to birth and management of children, marriage and behaviour expected of Lakhnavi Muslim ladies. Etiquette required during meetings, norms of hospitality, salutations and the different types of fairs in the cultural life of the Lakhnavis in an earlier era finds prominent place in the chapter. Lakhnavi Urdu, which has contributed to the recognition of Awadh as the epitome of tehzeeb and the landmark Ganga-Jamuni culture which celebrates the spirit of unity in diversity—a hallmark of Awadh even today—finds mention in this chapter.

The second chapter details the art dastangoi, which originated in Delhi and later spread to Lucknow, Faizabad and Rampur. In this unique form of storytelling, the performer, always an expert orator, brings to life scenes from enchanting tales through the narration. This chapter also talks of the literary gem Dastan-i-Amir Hamza, which was published by the Naval Kishore Press, Lucknow. Dastangoi in recent times has been revived by Mahmood Farooqui along with Muhammad Qasim and found favour with young audiences at literature festivals across India.

Over the years certain customs have come to define the city of Lucknow. One *such instance is the first month of the Islamic calendar, Muharram, which marks the martyrdom of Imam Husain, grandson of Prophet Mohammed, in 680 CE. During the first ten days of Muharram, the city is witness to numerous assemblies held to commemorate the great sacrifice of the Imam. The third chapter in this section sheds light on the rituals and practices during this sacred month and how it has given shape to the recital of marsiyas (elegies)—a genre of Urdu poetry that expresses grief on the loss of a loved one. The greatest Urdu marsiya writers of all times—Mirza Salamat Ali 'Dabir' and Mir Babar Ali 'Anis'—worked in Lucknow in the nineteenth century and are remembered to this day for taking elegy writing to a different level. The chapter also explains the concepts of nauha (lamentation) and of soz (dirge), which were also part of the Muharram assemblies.*

# 1.

## Customs, Manners, Traditions and Ceremonies

The inhabitants of every region have their own customs and ceremonies, which are often unique to the locality. In Awadh, the Nawabi rulers were practising Shia Muslims, but there were also Sunni Muslims in sizable numbers. Practices whose observance and performance formed the cultural fabric of the society were mostly interfaith and followed without demur from any particular community. There were no biases even if some customs and traditions emanated from the long-standing Hindu culture. Strict Islam is very sparse in rites, commemorations and formalities. In fact, local rituals and practices are usually frowned upon. However, despite stringent regulations and the forbidding of unnecessary and inessential social activities, the majority of Muslims in Awadh (as elsewhere) adopted and engendered conventions and customs that had little to do with Islam but were only ritualistic and ceremonial, requiring time and money for their observance. The richer classes had money to spend on traditions and formalities and the poor sections imitated them within their means. Each class vied with the other in squandering money even if it meant borrowing and incurring mounting debts. Indeed, Awadh took the lead in celebrating many functions that had neither religious sanction nor social necessity. In these matters, everyone wanted to keep up with the Joneses.

## Customs

A rather good and detailed description of Lakhnavi Muslim customs (particularly inside the zenana[1]) can be found in the book *Observations on the Mussulmauns of India, Descriptive of Their Manners, Customs, Habits and Religious Opinions Made During a Twelve Years' Residence in Their Immediate Society*, by Mrs Meer Hassan Ali. The author, an Englishwoman, married a noble from Lucknow and spent a dozen years with him, carefully recording her observations on the manners, customs, habits and religious opinions of the Muslim community. This section reproduces some of the major customs of Awadh as meticulously recorded by her in the book.

Mrs Hassan Ali records that in her new home, she was struck by the following practices:

1.  The master and mistress of a family received the utmost veneration.
2.  The domestics were permitted to give their opinions.
3.  There was undeviating kindness to aged servants, no longer capable of rendering services.
4.  Attention was paid to the convenience and comfort of poor relatives, even if distantly related.
5.  Reverential homage was paid to parents.
6.  There was a strong belief in charity and almsgiving, such as clothing the naked, feeding the hungry, supporting the weak, consoling the afflicted, protecting the fatherless, sheltering the traveller and lending ear and heart to the distresses of the poor.

Mrs Hassan Ali also speaks of the custom of tying a band of ribbons, in the folds of which a coin was secured, to the upper right arm of a person going on a journey. This was known as Imam Zamin ka rupia or paisa, and was dedicated to Imam Zamin, the eighth Imam who was considerred the guarantor of the traveller in safety and success during the journey, as a protection from the dangers and difficulties on the way. This coin was expected to be given as alms later on. This custom is still in vogue in traditional Muslim families.

---

[1]The zenana is the part of the house where the female members of the family live.

According to Mrs Hassan Ali, another custom was that 'most of the respectable gentlemen' maintained an elephant for their own use and it was almost as common as keeping horses. If the royal procession passed, the elephant was made to kneel while the nawabs went by. The owner stood in his howdah, a seat for riding secured on the back of an elephant or camel, typically fitted with a canopy, accommodating two or more people. Others accompanying the owner dismounted and stood with heads bowed and hands folded.

The ruler of Awadh also presented his subjects with khilat, a dress or robe of honour, or any other object of value, which signified esteem. The personal rank and the degree of estimation in which the receiver was held defined the value and number of an individual's khilats. The khilats included swords and embroidered belts with enamelled or embossed scabbards, shields, dirks, chapkans (a close-fitting short coat), labadaas (quilted coats) trimmed with sable, ornamental turbans, shawls, lihaafs (heavy quilts), satin trousers and muslin shirts, etc. Often, the nawab presented one hundred and one pieces or less in a khilat. The investiture of khilats took place in the presence of the nawab with one of the articles being placed personally by the nawab upon the receiver. Each person receiving the khilat presented the nawab with a nazar (offering) according to his rank and the value of the khilat conferred.

Mrs Hassan Ali also made observations on the celebration of Basant, or the spring festival, in Lucknow. On that day, everyone wore yellow clothes, and anyone not wearing yellow was not admitted at court. Although Basant was a Hindu festival, everyone joined in the celebrations. This tradition goes back to the fourteenth century when Hazrat Nizamuddin Auliya and Amir Khusro started the practice of celebrating Basant in Basti Nizamuddin after the former saw Hindu ladies dressed in yellow (the colour of Spring) during that time. Besides Basant, Holi too was widely celebrated across the region and by one and all.

As the rulers of Awadh followed the Shia school of Islam, Nauroz (New Year) was celebrated and is still celebrated on the day of the vernal equinox, which is the 20, 21 or 22 of March in the Gregorian calendar. Even the appearance of the new moon was commemorated in some Muslim families. They dated the new moon from the evening it became visible and salutes were fired by the nawab. The Holy Qur'an was opened at a particular passage, and prayers were then recited because it was considered auspicious to ring in the new year by reciting prayers. The whole family rose, embraced one another and offered salaams to the elders.

Shab-i Baraat is the Persian title for the fifteenth day of the lunar month of Shabaan, which in Arabic is the night of the middle of Shabaan. The belief was that the God records all the actions that mankind is to perform during the year, and all the children who are to be born or to die in the year are also recorded. Therefore, the Prophet enjoins Muslims to stay awake and pray through the night. However, typically, there is great rejoicing and firework displays. People usually visit graveyards and distribute food among the poor and the needy. This occasion has been very popular among major Muslim sects.

## Customs Associated with the Household in Awadh

Mirza Jafar Husain has given a detailed description of houses in the Awadh era in his famous book *Qadeem Lakhnau Ki Akhiri Bahaar* (*The Last Spring of Bygone Lucknow*, 1981). He mentioned that the residences of the moneyed classes were classified into three types:

a) Mahal, a grand, imposing mansion, comprising one single large unit;

b) Mahalsara, a large building with several segments, with separate areas for males and females; and

c) Deorhi, literally threshold or entrance, which was for persons of royal family or for those who had inherited a royal legacy.

Meanwhile, a good description of the women's apartments in a Muslim household in Lucknow is recorded by Mrs Hassan Ali. As per her, these houses were quadrangular in structure. Three sides were taken up by residential buildings and the fourth side by the kitchen and other rooms, leaving an open courtyard in the middle. Such apartments were divided into halls with small rooms in the corners for keeping stores. The rooms had neither doors nor windows, and privacy was ensured by hanging thick curtains across the openings between pillars. The curtains, made of coarse calico, were generally of two colours in a patchwork design. In addition, blinds made of thin, painted bamboo strips, called chilmans or chiks, were used. These blinds kept out flies and insects but admitted air and provided shade from the extreme glare.

The bedsteads were placed in a row at the back of the halls during the day. The frame of the bed was laced with thick cotton tape (niwar). The legs of the bed sometimes had silver gilt work or were painted with enamel. Mrs Hassan Ali has reported that mattresses were seldom used. However, a sozini (quilted or embroidered coverlet) was spread on the bed and over this was placed a sheet, tied at each corner of the bed with cord, and this comprised the bedding. There were several thin pillows of beaten cotton. In winter, a muslin sheet and a thick razai (quilt) or lihaaf (very thick quilt) served as the covering for the sleeper. The concept of a nightdress did not exist, and the same suit was worn by the lady during the day and night, unless a change was warranted.

The floors of the halls were first covered with palm-leaf matting over which were spread shatranjies, or chequered cotton carpets. A white calico carpet was spread on the shatranjies and it was on this that the females sat. When the ladies were assembled in their colourful dresses, brilliant jewels and glittering drapes, accompanied by their female attendants and children of all ages, the barren look of the unfurnished halls changed and became attractive.

The mistress of the house usually sat on a cushioned sheet or masnad; no other person could sit on it. The masnad was made from several varieties of fabric, according to the taste of the lady. It was spread on the floor, preferably near a pillar at the centre of the hall. The masnad was considered to be a seat of honour and when an honoured guest paid a visit, the seat was given to her with the lady of the house humbly sitting on the edge of the carpet.

The use of the fan (punkah) has been vividly described by Mrs Hassan Ali. The female quarters that she had seen did not have fixed punkahs pulled manually with strings. The punkahs in use required fanning with the hand. This was done by women employed for this purpose. The men's apartments had punkahs suspended from the ceiling by a rope that passed through a hole in the wall to the verandah. There a man constantly pulled on the rope to move the fan and create a pleasant breeze. The punkah was in use, day and night, for at least eight months in the year. The women pulling the fans were 'tenderly treated' and discharged their duties in rotation.

## Customs of Women in Awadh

Mrs Hassan Ali has described the make-up, embellishments and ornaments of Lakhnavi women. Every married woman of class was expected to use missi for her lips, gums and teeth. According to Platts' Dictionary, missi is a powder composed of, among other things, yellow myrobolan, gallnut, iron filings and vitriol, and is used for tinting the teeth and lips a deep black. This, according to Mrs Hassan Ali, was in contrast to the coral hue favoured by ladies of the West. When using missi went out of fashion after the 1930s, the ladies of the erstwhile United Provinces looked down on missi application as it was then confined to the unlettered women of villages.

The eyelids of the ladies were pencilled with kajal, which was lampblack or soot mixed with pure ghee. This kajal was also used as a collyrium for the eyes. Sometimes, instead of kajal, ladies used surma, a compound of antimony in powdered form. The surma was applied to the eyes by means of a salai, a large metallic needle, which was taken out of the surmadan (receptacle for surma) and slid gently across each eye with the eyelid closed. The surma was so drawn with the salai that it left a small tailpiece at the extremity of each eye towards the ear, and this was called the dumbala.

Women applied mehndi or henna to their hands and feet to colour them with a reddish hue. The powdered leaves of the henna shrub were mixed with catechu and made into a paste, which was applied on different parts of the body and then washed off once it dried, leaving a red stain.

A nose ring (nath) signified the married lady. Married women did not remove the nath until widowhood or during the mourning month of Muharram. Mrs Hassan Ali describes the nath in so many words:

…made of gold wire, the pearls and ruby between them are of great value, and I have seen many ladies wear the nuth as large in circumference as the bangle on her wrist, though of course much lighter; it is often worn so large, that at meals they are obliged to hold it apart from the face with the left hand, whilst conveying food to the mouth with the other.

The hair underwent the ceremonies of washing, drying and oiling with sweet, scented oil. It was drawn back from the forehead and twisted into a plait, which often reached below the waist. The ends were tied with coloured ribbons.

According to Mrs Hassan Ali, the pyjamas worn by the ladies of the gentry were made of rich satin, gold cloth (gulbadan), mashru (a striped silk from Benaras), fine English chintz and gingham (lightweight, woven cotton cloth, typically chequered). The pyjamas were full length and the feet were covered by their fullness. The waistband of the pyjama featured a cylindrical passage of cloth through which passed the izarband (the cord used to tie the pyjama at the waist). The two ends of the izarband had rich tassels of gold and silver and dangled in front.

The angia or mahram was a form of bodice or bra. It was worn by women to fit the bust and fastened at the back with strong cotton cords. The cups were of gauze, net or muslin and it was agreed that the more transparent the texture, the more agreeable it was. The bodice sometimes had very short and tight sleeves. The angia or mahram was not removed even at night.

Over the angia was worn a kurti, usually of transparent or semi-transparent cloth, which reached the waistband of the pyjama but did not fully cover it.

Mrs Hassan Ali has described the dupatta (the mantle of two folds) as 'the most graceful part of the whole female costume'. She has stated that the dupatta '…is worn with much original taste on the back of the head, and falls in graceful folds over the person; when standing, it is crossed in front, one end partially screening the figure, the other thrown over the opposite shoulder.'

The ladies never wore socks with their shoes. The shoes had generally sharp, pointed toes curling upwards and were flat like slippers. They were often embroidered, sometimes with beads or with gold or silver spangles. She has described a pair of shoes with silver embroidery, neatly made with pointed toes and having small silver bells fastened round the instep, which jingled gently while walking.

As to the disposition of well-bred women, she has remarked that '...they are naturally gifted with good sense and politeness, fond of conversation, shrewd in their remarks, and their language is both correct and refined.'

She observed that when meeting with distinguished guests, the ladies rose and arranged their drapery, advanced a few steps from their place, embraced their visitor thrice and ended by salaaming, with the head bowed towards the ground and the open hand raised to the forehead, three times in succession.

As far as participation in the kitchen was concerned, ladies of the gentry did not hesitate to assist or single-handedly prepare a dish. When a lady sent her friends a tray of delicacies made by her own hands, it was considered a high form of favour.

Regarding food in the households, Mrs Hassan Ali found that there was no provision for breakfast. After the morning prayers, the ladies chewed pan and smoked hookahs. The morning repast comprised dried fruits, confectionary, carrots, radishes, etc. The first substantial meal was around ten or eleven o'clock in the morning, which was followed by a long gap before dinner.

Mrs Hassan Ali has observed that there was no roast or boiled joints, but the stews and curries were innumerable. Small lean steaks, seasoned and covered with spices and condiments, were grilled or roasted on a charcoal fire and were called kebabs. For large gatherings, food was prepared by a nanbai or a bazaar cook. All meals were served on the floor on a table-spread called the dastarkhwan. Before the meal commenced, each lady washed her hands and rinsed her mouth. Although no spoons or forks were used, the food was conveyed to the mouth with the fingers in such a delicate manner that not a grain of rice soiled the fingers or the dress. After the repast, a lota (jug) with water and a chilamchi, silafchi or silapchi (a round bowl which is used to collect water when the water is poured from the jug for washing hands) were passed around and each lady washed her hands with chickpea flour (besan).

Mrs Hassan Ali's reminiscences also record the customs relating to the birth and management of children. The birth of a boy was greeted with 'the warmest demonstrations of unaffected joy' while there was less rejoicing when a female child was born. The mothers of affluent families seldom breastfed infants, who were reared by wet nurses, usually poor women. A wet nurse was prohibited from eating meat during the first month and good quality food was provided to her for at least two years.

On the fourth day after the birth of a son, the relatives and friends of the maternal and paternal sides were invited for a joyous gathering which was 'a noisy assembly of singing-women, people chattering, smell of savoury dishes and constant bustle'. On the ninth day, the infant was bathed and oiled.

The first nourishment comprised ghutti, a medicine made up of aloes, amaltas (cassia), a purgative, a vegetable aperient, sugar and the extract of aniseed mixed in water. This was to clear out the meconium of infants and was given for three days. Astonishingly, Mrs Ali mentions that after the third day, a little opium was given to the child daily until the child was three or four years old. The birthday of each son or daughter was regularly observed. For a boy, a knot was tied in a string for each year, and this string was kept by the mother. For a girl, a silver loop or ring was added for each year to a dhaaga (string) on the neck.

**Health-related Customs**

Mrs Hassan Ali has also enumerated several categories of street vendors and persons claiming to offer various services, some of which were as follows:

1. Cupping, both dry and moist, was performed by men and women who traversed the city, carrying their instruments. They were known as seengiwala or seengiwali and cupping was called seengi lagana. A heated, hollow horn was applied to the skin and allowed to cool. This caused the swelling of the tissues beneath and an increase in the flow of blood in the area. This was thought to draw

out harmful excess blood from diseased organs and to promote healing. In wet cupping, the skin was cut so that the blood would actually flow into the horn and thus be removed.

2. Using leeches for bloodletting was a popular medical practice and was called jonk lagwana. Women applied leeches to their skin to suck blood. After they had had their fill, the engorged leeches would fall off. Pressure was applied on the leeches, which discharged the sucked blood. The leeches were then kept in fresh water and could be used again if required. Bloodletting was a physical means to bring down blood pressure.

3. The cleaning of ears was done by a man called kaan saf karnewala. The ear canal was scraped with metallic probes and besides a small amount of dirt, earwax was also unnecessarily taken out, causing harm to the ears.

4. Mrs Hassan Ali has observed that all classes treated themselves to massaging and shampooing. She wrote that '...the comfort derived from the pressure of the hands on the limbs, by a clever shampooer, is alone to be estimated by those who have experienced the benefits derived from this luxurious habit, in a climate where such indulgences are needed to assist in creating a free circulation of the blood.'

5. Slaked lime (chuna) was applied to wounds, which were then wrapped up for a few days. It was also used as a remedy for burns and scalds, where lime was mixed with water and a little oil and then applied. According the Mrs Hassan Ali, this cure seldom failed.

## Ceremonies

### Religious Ceremonies

Badshah Begum, the chief wife of Ghazi-ud-Din Haider, ruler of Awadh (1814–27), can be credited with initiating a few ceremonial rituals, even as the worthiness of some of them can be debated.

Badshah Begum's biography, *Tarikh Badshah Begum*, written by

Abdul Ahad, tells us that she was strict in religious observances and formalities. She was also fond of introducing innovations in religion, a practice frowned upon by Muslims in general. Since she was the favourite wife of the ruler, she was not questioned. Following are some of the innovations she introduced as part of her religious practices.

Badshah Begum initiated the celebration of the chhati ceremony of Imam Mahdi, the twelfth Imam, in which both the mother and the child are bathed on the sixth day after the birth of a child. She commemorated this event in the Muslim lunar month of Shabaan. Large sums of money were spent and the Begum watched every item of the programme.

Nasir-ud-Din Haider, the son of Badshah Begum, also performed several ceremonies to cater to his mother's fancies. He, in fact, introduced a few more, which he himself had innovated. For example, on the day of the birth of each of the imams, he would pretend that he was suffering from the pains of childbirth. A doll studded with jewels was kept on his lap to represent the child. The ladies who were playing the parts of the wives of the eleven imams were also given dolls and they too pretended to go through childbirth.

On the sixth day, Nasir-ud-Din Haider took a bath, in accordance with the custom of chhati. On the night following the chhati, he would dress in female attire, and with the doll in his lap, go through the ceremony of sitarabini, or looking at the stars with the Qur'an placed upon his head. The doll-child was kept in a magnificent bed and nazar (a gift of money) was given to it with all marks of respect. This was followed by grand feasting.

Meanwhile, beautiful girls from Syed families were kept in the palace as the wives of eleven of the twelve imams (excluding Hazrat Ali who, along with his wife Hazrat Fatima, was held in too much respect to allow the mimicking of his personality). Each girl took the name of the wife of one of the eleven imams. The eleven girls were called 'achhooti', that is, they were pure and virgin. Every achhooti was provided with three female attendants and was given expensive clothing and delectable food. The Begum ensured that she saw the face of one of the achhootis first thing in the morning as she considered it to be a good omen. The Begum did not favour the marriage of the achhootis and believed it to be sacrilegious. There was also a custom of 'achhootas', the male counterpart of the achhootis. However, not much is known about them except that a room was designated for the celebration of the birthdays of the imams with full pomp.

The achhootis got their freedom after the death of Haider and many were able to get married and live normal lives. Incidentally, there is a narrow, dilapidated lane in the Chowk area of Lucknow connecting Chawal Wali Gali (where several shops sell sheermal) and Ghulam Husain Ka Pul (where many potters sell their wares), which was originally called Achhootion Ki Gali. In the 1920s and 1930s, the lane was known as Janab Wali Gali after the famous Mujtahid-ul-Asar Maulana Muhammad Nasir (d. 1940), who resided in the vicinity. Later, the lane was renamed as Bhand Wali Gali, after the mimes and jesters who had settled there.

## Marriage Ceremonies

The pomp and etiquette of Lakhnavi weddings have not been adequately described in any worthwhile non-fiction work. The main reason for this could be that the ceremonies do not have religious sanction under Islam. A Muslim marriage is not a religious ceremony but a contract between the parties, involving an offer and acceptance, and thus called Nikahnama. However, despite Islamic injunctions for a simple service, weddings were often celebrated with much pageantry, spectacle and extravagance. Many classic tales and dastans in Urdu and Persian written in India have mentioned the grandeur and pomp associated with marriages.

The 1969 edition of Mirza Rajab Ali Baig Suroor's famous nineteenth-century book *Fasana-i Ajaib* depicted marriage ceremonies which was a reflection of the culture of Awadh at that time. It includes an appendix describing Muslim marriage ceremonies in Lucknow, and revelry and enjoyment of royal stature. Written by Athar Parvez, the appendix pointed out that customs have a close connection with the community; and several traditions and conventions have local origins. It adds that there were efforts to remove these customs because they were contrary to religion, but remained unsuccessful.

The marriage ceremonies were spread over many days, sometimes nine or even eleven days before the nikah (nuptials). They began with the practice of confining the bride to maanjha or maayon. From that day she wore yellow clothes and did not leave her room except for basic necessities. The word maanjha probably comes from the Punjabi meaning a bed or a cot. Everyday her body was cleansed with ubtan (a paste of ground grain or pulse with turmeric, oil and perfume). The ubtan was applied to soften the skin and make it glow. The whole body was depilated. The ubtan for the first day along with henna was taken in a procession to the groom's home along with pindias (laddoos) made of toasted and browned flour, ghee and nuts.

According to Abdul Halim Sharar, a prolific Urdu writer and author of *Guzashta Lakhnau*, the yellow dress for the maanjha and a painted, low pedestal were taken in a procession accompanied by musicians. The younger sisters of the bride proceeded in palanquins or sedans along with female singers. On reaching the house of the bridegroom, seven pieces of pindias and seven portions of sugar candy were forced upon the groom. The day the bride sat in maanjha was also generally the day when the bridegroom was confined to the maanjha. Girls and sisters sang marriage songs. A particular ittar, known as suhag ka ittar (the perfume of good luck or wedlock), was applied on the bride and bridegroom. The fragrance is very soft, lingering and sensuous, and lasts for many days. The main purpose of the maanjha, it is speculated, was to encourage the bride and bridegroom to think of one another and thus come together in thoughts. In fact, in the bride's house songs were sung praising the qualities of the groom.

Another important practice during the nuptials was the saachaq. The word is said to have come from the Turkish and was probably brought by the Mughals. In this, wedding clothes were presented by the groom's family to the bride along with the sahra (wreath and veil worn on the head by the bride at the wedding), a gold ring, a silver ring and those ornaments that the bride will don when she departs from her parents' home to live with the bridegroom. The clothes and ornaments were accompanied by a quantity of sugar and dried nuts. The gifts were taken in procession, which usually included a large number of painted earthen pots mounted on festooned bamboo structures. Ahead of the pots was carried a small silver pot containing curd, around the neck of which were tied one or two small fish. The symbol of a pair of fish was an emblem of the kingdom of Awadh. Even now the state government of Uttar Pradesh uses this logo. Fish are thus considered a symbol of good luck.

On the day following the saachaq, the bride's family took ground henna in a procession to the bridegroom's house. The suit of clothes that was to be worn by the bridegroom at the nikah was also given on that day. In traditional times, the clothes were of courtly nature and usually comprised a robe (khilat), the embroidered end of a turban (shamla), an ornament of precious metal worn at front of the turban (sarpech), an aigrette or a plume (kalghi), a pearl necklace, silken pyjamas, a ring and the ornamental head and face cover (sahra) for the bridegroom.

The nikah took place on the day following the henna ceremony. The groom's procession (baraat) wended its way to the bride's house with pomp and ceremony. In *Guzashta Lakhnau,* Sharar has remarked that earlier the usual time for the marriage procession was at about three o'clock in the morning, but it was later advanced to nine or ten in the morning. It is said that this was started in the time of Wajid Ali Shah, whose baraat started late, when the day had already dawned. People then gradually adopted this later time, especially as holding the procession in daylight reduced expenses. This led to the practice of a morning baraat followed by the solemnization of the marriage at about midday. The marriage procession proceeded to the accompaniment of a live band, which played music on large drums, cymbals, organs, etc. Usually the groom sat on a horse or an elephant and his position was that of a 'king' for the day, which is why the groom was referred to as the naushah (new king). The famous Urdu poet Mirza Ghalib (d. 1869) had the appellation of Mirza Naushah.

The procession was welcomed at the bride's home by a big crowd. The bride had already bathed in water that had been kept for seven days, and this water was thrown beneath the feet of the groom's horse or elephant. The groom was then taken to the female section of the house. According to Sharar, at that time the bride had not yet donned her bridal attire and was thus wrapped in a large sheet. A piece of sugar candy was kept in the palm of the bride, which was then fed to the groom. Sisters-in-law, boisterous young ladies and professional female singers of the dom caste (domnian) teased the groom.

After registering his presence in the female apartments, the groom was brought to the male section of the bride's house, where the marriage contract (nikah) would be finalized. The groom usually sat on a platform or dais, typically with his head bent, his headgear so laden with flowers that it was difficult to see his face. The nikah differed only slightly among Sunnis and Shias. In the Sunni nikah, two relatives or friends of the bride acted as witnesses and the person (qazi) conducting the marriage contract ascertained the amount of the dower (mehr) from the groom's side. The witnesses testified to the offer of wedlock by the groom and the acceptance by the bride and this was done three times orally. Among the Shias, there were two mujtahids who served as agents of the bride and groom and bore witness to the offer and acceptance of the groom and bride respectively. Usually, the certificate of marriage (nikahnama) was signed by both the bride and the groom and the witnesses. This tied both of them in matrimony. This was followed by the distribution of dates and sweets among the guests, after the practice of the Prophet.

After the nikah the groom was taken to the women's quarters where his sisters-in-law and young girls teased him while marriage songs were sung. There was a well-established custom in Awadh that bawdy songs relating to the samdhan and the samdhi were sung by domnis. The samdhans are the mothers of a bride and bridegroom while the samdhis are the fathers of a bride and bridegroom. The point to note is that in the early twentieth century and even before, girls who had just reached puberty and were between ten to fourteen years old became brides. The mothers of these girls would sometimes be in their twenties and therefore in the bloom of youth. The samdhan songs targeted these young mothers-in-law and humorously attributed licentious and lustful behaviour to them. The songs were a licence to utter profanities in poems. They were mostly folk songs with plenty of fervour and zest and have been largely lost. This author has in his collection an Urdu and Persian compilation titled *Diwan-i Ghazalhai Samdhanwa Jawab-i Samdhan*[2], by

---

[2]This collection is appended to *Kulliyat-i Jafar Zatalli* from pages 96 to 108, published by Matba Muhammadi, Delhi, in 1289 AH./1872-73.

Rai Tota Ram Aasi Lakhnavi. Aasi ('s' being the letter saad) was a sahib-i diwan poet of Lucknow.

This was followed by the aarsi-mushaf ceremony. The aarsi is a mirror and the mushaf is the Qur'an. The bride and the bridegroom sat opposite each other with the Qur'an and a mirror on a stand (rehl) between them. According to Sharar, the bride was wrapped up like a bundle, reminding one of a non-working clock. The mirror reflected the face of the bride, who kept her eyes closed; this was supposed to be the groom's first glimpse of the bride. However, before the groom saw the bride, he was supposed to read or recite Surah al-Akhlas (Purity of Faith), the 112th chapter of the Qur'an. The women entreated the bride to open her eyes and after numerous pleas, the bride opened her eyes for moment, had a quick look at the groom's face and shut her eyes again. This marked the end of the aarsi-mushaf ceremony.

The next step was to bedeck the bride for the rukhsati (departure of the bride from her home to the groom's home as a legally wedded wife). Domnis sang rukhsati songs, while the vestments, utensils, furniture, jewellery and other paraphernalia that the bride was taking with her as dowry were put on display.

The groom's party, along with the bride, proceeded to the groom's home with much pomp and show. Upon arrival, the bride was taken inside and the groom offered a prayer of thanks (namaaz-i shukrana) on the long skirt (daaman) of his bride's dress.

The next ceremony was the roonumai (beholding the face of the bride). The bride, whose face was covered with a veil or ghunghat, was surrounded by the groom's female relatives, who, one by one, lifted the veil to see her face and made an offering of money, jewellery or gifts.

The first night spent by the bride in her new house was the takht ki raat or suhaag raat and was the night when the marriage was supposed to be consummated. The next day the brother of the bride or her close relations visited the groom's house with sweetmeats and took the bride back to her parents' home. Traditionally, she took with her seven kinds of vegetables and seven kinds of sweets.

On the fourth day after saachaq, or the day following the arrival of the bride at the groom's house, the chauthi ceremony was held at the bride's house when the bride and the bridegroom visited the bride's family as a newly married couple. After feasting, there was a show of belting and beating with flowers and vegetables between both the families. The shoes of the bridegroom were hidden by the young companions of the wife, which were returned only after a handsome amount was given to them by the groom. As part of the chauthi ceremony, the bride donned a new set of clothes, which was often more splendid than the bridal suit.

Two to four days after the chauthi ceremony, four chaalas were usually observed. The word chaala indicates setting out. It was the ceremony of the wife going to and returning from her parents' home. Her aunts usually invited her turn by turn and the bride went with her husband to their homes, where they were given presents.

## Manners

### Etiquette of Meeting

An interesting book called *Kitabein Apne Aaba Ki* (*Books of Our Ancestors*), by journalist and writer Raza Ali Abdi, discussed Maulavi Abul Hasan's book *Nuzhat al-Naazir*[3] (*Purification of the Viewer*). The book provides a glimpse of the etiquette, conventions and manners of Awadh as they existed after the Uprising of 1857. It was written at a time when the traditional code of Awadhi behaviour was disintegrating and a different culture was in the making. Some guidelines for civility and courtesy are quite interesting and mirror the politeness and affability that were the hallmarks of the Awadhi lifestyle:

1. When you are in the company of respectable people, wish them loudly and make sure that you bow slightly and touch your forehead with your right hand. This should not be done in a perfunctory manner.
2. In an assembly, if someone asks you how you are, give your thanks or say that God be praised.

---

[3]Published by Naval Kishore Press, Lucknow, 1876.

3. In a gathering, do not sit with your back to someone. If you do so accidentally and then realize your mistake, apologize to the person concerned.

4. Do not talk loudly in company and also do not roll with laughter. Do not chuckle or giggle over a small matter. If you do so it shows that you are not a person of gravity. However, if the matter calls for laughter, do so in a restrained manner and do not go into stitches.

5. If a hookah or paan is offered by a person elder to you, then accept it with grace by half rising and stepping forward to take it.

6. In a congregation, talk in a mild tone and use everyday words without sounding pompous or extravagant. Do not use pedestrian, banal and dull language.

7. In a musical sitting or in a poetry symposium, do not be carried away by ecstatic responses. Shower praise where it is deserved. Applaud in the right place and do not make a laughing stock of yourself.

8. While eating in company, do not rush to consume your meal. Give preference to others and begin eating when others start. Do not show your craving for a victual no matter how much you long for it.

## Hospitality

In Hindu culture, providing food and shelter is the traditional duty of the householder. It is enjoined that an unexpected guest (atithi) be treated as God. Atithi means 'without time'. The Bible mentions partaking of food together as a token of friendship and commitment. Among the Sikhs, the food provided and eaten in the langar is a sign of brotherhood. In Islam, hospitality (mehman nawazi) is a great virtue. Societal ties can be strengthened by being hospitable to guests and neighbours. The Qur'anic verse 59:9 highlights importance of hospitality to a guest, citing example of Abu Talha and his wife Umm Sulaima who had little to eat themselves but still fed their guest well. The hosts only pretended to eat by dim candlelight.

In addition to providing food and drink, Muslim culture requires that the host should treat guests with dignity and respect. Helping out a person in time of need is also hospitality. There is grace in food being shared, and breaking bread together is a matter of goodwill. In the culture of Lucknow, hospitality is a sign of conviviality, cordiality and socialness. It is a part of waz'adari or goodness of form and manner. A recent book titled *Hospitality and Islam: Welcoming in God's Name* makes the first major contribution to the understanding of hospitality within Islam and beyond.

**Salutations**

The most accepted, recognized and customary salutation among Muslims is the Arabic greeting '*as-salamoalaikum wa rahmatullahi wa barakaatuhu*', which means 'peace, mercy and blessings be upon you'. The 'you' in the greeting is plural. It is usually shortened to '*as-salamoalaikum*' (peace be with you). The response to the greeting is '*wa-alaikum as-salaam*' (and upon you the peace). The greeting, although in second person plural, is also used to address one person, similar to the use of vous (you) in French.

Tradition says that one should say salaam when joining a gathering and when leaving. As to who should say the salaam first, the practice, especially among Indian Muslims, including those in Awadh, is that the greeting should be made by the person who first sees the other person. There is no difference in the greeting offered by an elder or younger person. It is a matter of 'first seen, first greeted'. It is also in the Qur'an (24:61) that upon entering the house, one should salute the others with a greeting.

In the Indian subcontinent, greeting may be followed by the shaking of the right hand and is often accompanied by a hug, but only between those of the same gender. The greeting is often accompanied by the raising of the right hand to the chest or to the forehead and the uttering of 'aadaab' or 'aadaabarz', which means 'regards' or 'respect'.

In Awadh, particularly in Lucknow, in keeping with the elegance of its culture, the gesture of salaam has traditionally been endowed with polish and gracefulness. The head is lowered a little, the right hand is slightly cupped (with fingers together), raised gently and shaken a few times just inches below the chin.

When one leaves, the traditional salutation is 'Khuda hafiz' (God protect you). With perhaps the increasing Wahhabi influence, people, particularly in Pakistan and to some extent in India as well, have substituted it with the less secular 'Allah hafiz'. Another phrase used when departing is 'fi amaillah' (I leave you in the protection of God).

## Traditions

### Fairs

The melas (fairs) in Awadh used to be elaborate affairs and would draw huge crowds. Not many of the old fairs have survived, although they have been mentioned in the prose and poetry of the eighteenth and nineteenth centuries. Khwaja Abdur Rauf 'Ishrat' Lakhnavi wrote an article on the royal fairs of Awadh in the July 1926 issue of the monthly *Zamaana* of Kanpur and the article has been reproduced in the book *Lakhnau-Tarikh: Adab aur Muasharat* (*Lucknow: History, Literature and Society*).

The following fairs of Lucknow have been mentioned by Ishrat:

*Aishbagh Fair:* According to Ishrat, the foundation of the Aishbagh area of Lucknow was laid by Nawab Asaf-ud-Daula when he came to Lucknow in 1775. It was the locality where the Nawab took his morning ride. A grand day-fair was held on four Fridays of the Hindu month of Shravana (which begins on July 23). Later, Saturdays were also included as fair days. Visitors included the aristocracy and rich Hindu traders who came in their carriages. The common people—greengrocers, butchers, washermen, cotton carders, weavers, etc.—also visited the fair. Stalls were set up to sell popular eatables like dahibara, pera, gulab jamun, balushahi, jalebi, imarti and dalmoth. Swings were strung from strong branches of trees and songs of the monsoon were sung. There were snake charmers, bear and monkey dance shows and displays by acrobats. Food vendors brought cauldrons of qorma, pulao and qalia. There were shops selling toys. Paan and hookahs were dispensed by attractive women dressed in their finery.

Cannabis and opium addicts indulged freely in their drugs. Whores and prostitutes in their trinkets and frippery went about attracting prospective clients. All around, people sat with family and friends on carpets, leisurely eating, smoking and conversing. Mushairas (poetry symposiums) were also held under the auspices of Munshi Shiv Prasad, manager of *Awadh Akhbaar* and a disciple in poetry of Khwaja Mirza Asad Aftab-ud-Daula 'Qalaq' (d. 1879). Invitation cards were issued in advance. On the day of the mushaira, a white sheet was spread on a carpet under a canopy and the invitees were entertained with hookahs and dalmoth.

Besides the Shravana mela described above, the fair of Tar was also held in Aishbagh, a day after the festival of Eid al-Fitr, which is celebrated on the first day of the Muslim month of Shawwal, after the month of Ramadan. It was marked by gaiety and merrymaking. It had a special attraction for opium addicts and prostitutes.

*Gudion Ka Mela* (Dolls' Fair): This was held in the Gungani Shukal Ka Talab area of Lucknow, a little beyond Aminabad in the east, in the Hindu month of Shravana. Parents gave their married daughters presents. In the evening, girls beat dolls made of rags and cotton and threw them out of the house. Young boys battered the dolls with coloured sticks. This fair was more like a village fair and the usual footpath stalls were set up. There were also wrestling matches. The fair is still held, but at a far lower key.

*Athon Ka Mela* (Fair of the Eighth): This fair was held on the eighth day of Chaitra, the first month of the Hindu calendar, which begins on 21 or 22 March, at Raja Tikait Rai Talab. This was a typical village fair. The venue also had a temple dedicated to Shitala Devi, the goddess of smallpox.

*Aliganj Ka Mela* (Aliganj Fair): This fair was held near the Hanuman temple at Aliganj in Lucknow. Devotees, clad in red loincloths, would crawl to the temple. This popular fair is still held in the city.

*Chhariyon Ka Mela* (Fair of Sticks): This fair was also held in the month of Shravana and was also known as the fair of Zahir Pir. Although essentially a fair for sweepers, people from various communities also visited the fair. Devotees of the Pir carried large sticks wrapped in red cloth and tied around with locks of hair, with two to four coconuts hanging from them. The sticks were buried in the earth. There was group singing expressing the piety of the Pir. Entertaining shows and spectacles were held. According to Ishrat Lakhnavi, it was a magnificent fair and was held in the new Chowk area of Lucknow.

*Alaule Ka Mela* (Transgender's Fair): This fair was held in Mukarim Nagar in Lucknow, where eunuchs and transgender people resided. This was their fair. They sang and danced in the typical fashion of eunuchs in India. There were competitions among groups in which speeches loaded with double meaning and puns were made. Foul language and profanities were frequently exchanged for fun. No respectable men or women visited this fair. Only persons who wanted to savour obscenity made the trip.

*Satrikh Ka Mela:* Satrikh is a town in the Barabanki district, adjacent to Lucknow district, in Uttar Pradesh. Muslims are said to have settled in Satrikh around 1030 CE, when it was invaded by Syed Salar Dawood Ghazi and his son Syed Salar Masud Ghazi (whose tomb is at Bahraich). The tomb of Syed Salar Dawood Ghazi is at Satrikh and it is also called Buddhe Baba Ka Mazaar (Tomb of the Grand Old Man). A fair is held during the full moon of the month of Jyaistha (which begins on May 22).

# Some Characteristics of Lakhnavi Urdu and Culture

## Lakhnavi Urdu

There was always a conscious effort to make Urdu mellifluous, soft and soothing. A smattering of words of Persian origin were also in use. The profusion of public recitals of Urdu elegies and dastans made the literary language comprehensible to the masses, including the unlettered. One of the gifts of Lakhnavi Urdu was that it enabled uneducated and unschooled persons to become poets. This was possible because these unlettered persons kept the company and companionship of the cultivated and the erudite. Many such poets like Nanhu Sahib 'Shafiq' Lakhnavi of the early twentieth century published their diwans (collection of poetry). Such poetry, though not of the first order, was certainly appreciable.

Qasbas, which were sizable villages or small towns and were sometimes the dwelling places of the landed gentry, had societies that closely imitated those of the larger cities. Poetry symposiums (mushairas), recitations of dastans and sometimes even literary discussions, were held in these suburbs or qasbas. During Muharram, elegies (marsiya) written by master poets were narrated. To cater to the village audience, religious poems composed in Awadhi were also in fashion. These small places had an Islamicate culture of their own, which was a direct reflection of the urban setup, and the language in use was simple and direct.

The Urdu spoken in Lucknow up to the nineteenth century had the consciousness and sensitivity of the times with the tone, accent and understanding typical to the language. At that time there were differences in the Urdu spoken in Delhi and Lucknow, so much so that these two cities became rivals in a way. For example, the words 'qalam' (pen) and 'dahi' (curd) were masculine in Lucknow but feminine in Delhi. Lakhnavis believed that the guarantors of the language could only be the 'ahal-i-zaban' (the people of the language), only the born natives of Lucknow. Many skilled poets of standing who were born elsewhere and settled in Lucknow had to suffer the ignominy of not being 'ahal-i-zaban' and their speech or writing was seldom considered taksaali (having true ring or genuine). For example, Mirza Wajid Husain Yas 'Yagana' Changezi (1884–1956) was born in Patna but settled in Lucknow. He was a poet of renown but was rarely treated at par with even the less talented native poets of Lucknow.

By the 1930s, this bigoted view of Lakhnavi Urdu had finally faded and the forced compartmentalization of Urdu disappeared. There was no longer a distinction between Lakhnavi or Dehalvi Urdu. Later, with the Partition of India in 1947, the language lost ground in India. This was unfortunate and Urdu became branded as a language of Muslims, receiving the almost reluctant support of the government. This was besides the fact that the language was extensively used, particularly in literary works and films by a multitude of talented non-Muslims. Urdu speakers felt that an unfair prejudice had developed against their language. A sop soon came and bodies like Urdu Akademies were created to 'further' the cause of Urdu. However, they were manned by politicos who had little or no connection with language or literature, which proved ruinous for the language.

The contribution of Lucknow to Urdu cannot be doubted. This was the city where forms (uslub) and shapes of the language were polished and crystallized. This led to the writing of books on various subjects and the notion that creativity in the language was only ornamental or skin-deep was largely wrong. There was a cultivated sense of literature. Literary debates were held and disputed facets of the language were decided, which helped in enrichment and promotion of Lakhnavi Urdu.

## Islamicate Culture

The term 'Islamicate' was coined by Marshall Goodwin Simms Hodgson (1922–1968), the great scholar of Islamic culture. He was the author of the three-volume *Venture of Islam: Conscience and History in a World Civilization*. In the first volume of this book he defined Islamicate as something that 'would refer not directly to the religion, Islam, itself, but to the social and cultural complex historically associated with Islam and the Muslims, both among Muslims themselves and even when found among non-Muslims'. Therefore, Islamicate culture is one associated with a region in which Muslims are or were culturally dominant, and where their culture has impacted the lifestyle of non-Muslims as well, without the adoption of Islam by others.

In Awadh, the contact between Muslims and Hindus resulted in the birth of a composite culture. Both communities took customs, traditions, etiquette, fashion, observances and practices from one another. This, by and large, resulted in harmony and consonance. People who live together, side by side, do not exist in a vacuum, and one's traditions impinge constructively on the other. This is also the basic requirement of a plural society, much needed in the present social milieu and environment.

## Caste System

In the nineteenth and early twentieth centuries, Awadh was plagued by the caste system among Muslims. Many persons claimed aristocratic heritage for their families. Whatever the nature of one's profession, people exulted in claiming falsely a rich ancestry, even asserting that they were descendants of the erstwhile nawabs of Awadh. This led to discrimination and in some instances, honour killings.

Gradually, the illogical and unwarranted division of Indian Muslim society on the basis of 'aristocracy' versus working class is disappearing with the promotion of education, especially liberal education, among boys and girls. Professor Masood Alam Falahi has written a comprehensive book in Urdu against the Muslim caste system, titled *Hindustan Mein Zaat Paat Aur Musalman* (*Muslims and Caste Divisions in India*), published by Ideal Foundation, Mumbai (second edition, 2009). He has earned many bouquets for his venture but there have also been brickbats from among the conservative diehards. As in most other communities, caste and gender inequalities have not vanished, but they have certainly lessened. As social norms are heavily loaded in favour of patriarchy, discriminatory customs persist. Nonetheless, voices are being raised to correct the picture. Increasingly, marriages are not based on the merits or demerits of the genealogy of the parties concerned.

## Ganga-Jamuni Culture

Ganga-Jamuni culture is the culture of the plains of northern India, especially the Doab region of the Ganges and Yamuna rivers, regarded as the cradle of the fusion of Hindu and Muslim cultures. It is a region lying between and reaching to the confluence of two rivers (especially that between the Ganges and Jumna/Yamuna). This expanse has an area of about 60,500 square kilometres[4]. Awadh is considered to be the nerve centre of this composite culture which is an example of unity-in-diversity. While the *diversity* came with the migration of different groups who settled in this region, the *unity* came from the peaceful coexistence of these varied communities and cultures. There are no fault lines and the mixed social fabric is not brittle or fragile. The Ganga-Jamuni culture was one of interaction and acceptance of the best in other cultures. Festivals were shared and there was mostly an atmosphere of conviviality. There were no

[4]Source: https://www.britannica.com/place/Ganges-Yamuna-Doab

sharp dividing lines, and whenever any detestable notion was attempted, it was largely abhorred and rejected. It typifies religious tolerance and multiculturalism. The Ganga-Jamuni culture or tehzeeb can be seen in the daily lives of the people in Lucknow, Kanpur, Gorakhpur, Sitapur, Benaras, etc., in Uttar Pradesh (including Awadh) and can also be glimpsed in places like Rampur, Bhopal and Hyderabad.

There is a short account of India's composite culture since the first arrival of Muslims in India in AD 712 in the book *Ganga Jamuni: Silver and Gold, A Forgotten Culture* by Naz Ikramullah. It describes how the cultures of the Muslims were polished by the Mughals and their successors in the fields of architecture, music, art, literature and cuisine, and this was the result of contact with Hindu culture. The Perso-Arabic script was adopted and used by both Muslims and Hindus. The local dress and jewellery were modified. The sherwani and the shalwar were adopted by both communities. Besides Persian, the local vernaculars were developed. The Sufis used Braj Bhasha as well as Awadhi and Urdu/Hindavi became the lingua franca. Local customs were adopted and modified by Muslims. The marriage rituals followed by Muslims in India were quite different from those of their counterparts in other countries. The most striking example of composite culture was the milieu of Urdu marsiyas (elegies) on the martyrdom of Imam Husain. Although the locale of these elegies was Karbala in Iraq, and the characters were Arabs, in the Urdu marsiyas, particularly those written in Lucknow, the events seemed to have taken place in Lucknow on the banks of Gomti River. For example, on the dying of the major characters, the women of the house broke their bangles as a sign of widowhood. This is an Indian custom and does not exist in the Arab world. This is the reason why the elegies have been so popular and loved.

# 2.

# Dastangoi: The Art of Storytelling

The tradition of dastangoi or oral storytelling can be traced back to the times of the Mughal Emperor Akbar when the language in use was Persian. Dastangoi, a Persian word, is a compound of the words dastan (story) and goi (to narrate a story). Although it is not certain when the narration of tales started in Urdu, educated guesses place the emergence of this tradition in the beginning of the nineteenth century. Delhi is often associated with the beginning of dastangoi, which later spread to Faizabad, Rampur and Lucknow. In Urdu literature, dastangoi has been set down in writing as a cycle of lengthy tales, called dastans, often published in multivolume series. Loose plotlines and verbosity are some of the defining characteristics of dastans.

Hamid Dabashi, an author and Professor of Iranian Studies and Comparative Literature at Columbia University in New York City, has stated that '[...] what in Urdu is called dastan is a mode of storytelling that combines popular fantasies and literary tropes to produce highly readable and entertaining stories. These stories give an account of heroic deeds [...] whose very out-of-the-ordinary flamboyance place them on the two extremities of legendary lives and thus mark their heroes from mere mortals [...]'

The Urdu dastans are a precious heritage and a gem among them is the *Dastan-i Amir Hamza*, which was composed in Lucknow in forty-six volumes in the late nineteenth and early twentieth centuries. However, at the time when the Naval Kishore Press of Lucknow started printing

*Dastan-i Amir Hamza*, the Western form of the novel was also gaining a following in areas where Urdu was in use. Though the dastan was not abruptly replaced by such novels, readers were gradually moving away from the dastans.

The eminent Urdu critic Shamsur Rahman Faruqi[5] of Allahabad has stated that a dastan is a narrative that is created for listening, irrespective of whether it is spontaneous or has been composed thoughtfully. In contrast to a novel, the oral storyteller can see his audience and can assess whether it is paying attention or becoming jaded. He has suggested that reading the cycle of dastans should have a significant gap between volumes so that immediate overlapping does not take place. Oral narrative can also be great literature. Homer's Illiad and Odyssey and Valmiki's Ramayana were conceived by tellers and singers of tales.

Although single-volume dastans and even a few volumes of the *Dastan-i Amir Hamza* could be found in personal libraries, the entire forty-six-volume opus of Amir Hamza did not exist in any private or public library. It was only in the 1970s that the significance and relevance of the dastans in Urdu literature were realized. There was then a scramble to pick up stray volumes of *Dastan-i Amir Hamza* to form complete sets, but very few people were able to acquire all forty-six volumes. Faruqi was one such rare person. He diligently pieced together the lost and abandoned volumes to complete his set. There is perhaps only one library, in the United States, which has the complete *Dastan-i Amir Hamza*, besides Faruqi's personal collection. Also, he seems to be the only person to have read all the volumes.

The world of the dastan is not related to our world but is a realm where there is enchantment, magic, sorcery and wizardry. The Urdu dastan's domain is similar to that of Sir Thomas Malory's *Le Morte D'Arthur* or J.R.R. Tolkien's *The Lord of the Rings*. Like the two aforesaid English fantasy books, the dastans have their own invented methodology, mainly borrowed from earlier tales, but made fascinating by the innovative, ingenious and gifted narrator. Characters seesaw between the real world and the world of enchantment. Strictly, the cosmos of the dastan is

---

[5]I am indebted to Shamsur Rahman Faruqi for most of the material in this chapter.

teleological, the regulations and criteria are governed by the purpose they serve rather than by postulated causes. The voluminous *Dastan-i Amir Hamza* does not have any punctuation. Indeed, punctuation in early Urdu printing was limited to a small dash, which signified the full stop. Traditional Urdu presses in the nineteenth century, particularly in prose, never bothered to put even a full stop or divide the printed form into paragraphs. One may well feel that reading a work lacking any punctuation or delineation would be difficult. However, once one starts reading it, the cadence, rhythm and intonation of the words work out naturally, and the reader is astonished by the swing and flow of the language. This prose is akin to reading poetry where the meaning and the subtlety of the language acquaint you with the pauses, intervals and flow of the language in all its richness and solemnity.

## The Origin

The writers of several volumes of the *Dastan-i Amir Hamza* have repeatedly claimed that what they were presenting was a translation of the Persian original. While it is true that such dastans existed in the Persian language, the chronicle and fictional account proffered in Urdu was original and conceived in India, mostly in Lucknow. This is supported by the fact that till date there has been no evidence of the survival of the so-called Persian 'original'. The published dastans, particularly *Amir Hamza*, are local creations, not translations, although inspiration or our concepts may have been taken from older texts or oral histories of folk origin.

The geographical features described in a dastan are quite unconventional, unusual and sometimes quite puzzling. The story can start from two places or two countries at the same time and the locales keep changing as the story progresses. There are several areas of action; some of them are discrete while others intersect. The narrator is free to change or add locales and they are not confined to any known map or design. He takes pains to tell the listener that the creator or creators of the dastans were different from the narrator and what is being told is old history and not his invention. The actual authorship of the dastan is not given any importance but the reciter revels in the delusion that what is being presented is of antiquity and belongs to olden times. According to Shamsur Rahman Faruqi, the author of the dastan abstains from claiming authorship, not out of any sense of inferiority, but for the demands of the dastan, which is passed off as being of yore, with roots in the past.

## The Art of Dastangoi

There is an impression that the Urdu dastan was a precursor of the Urdu novel and that it was a rough or primitive form of the novel, but it is wrong to say so. In this debate we sometimes overlook the fact that the dastan is an oral narrative, no matter if it is written or printed many times. The dastan came into existence for recital and hearing. Even if the dastan was printed, it retained its original form. The novel, as we all know, is structured as a written work.

The novel is written and before that it is not narrated, nor is it composed for recitation. On the other hand, the dastan is primarily performed. Although the basic story remains the same, the dastan is altered, amended, modified and sometimes reshaped in oral renderings. On the other hand, because a novel is a written form that is meant to be read, no matter how many times it is read, the text remains the same, unless it is altered by the author in subsequent editions. In the novel there are only two factors, namely, the text and the reader, and there is nothing in between. However, in a dastan, the performer is the middleman between the creator of the dastan and the audience.

Dastan narratives do not describe events as they have occurred, rather, they remodel the incidents afresh. Some happenings may occur simultaneously, but they are narrated in such a way that they occur in different places. In dastangoi, the intricate workings of the characters' minds are seldom described; such descriptions are a technique of the novel. However, every occurrence is stated openly. Often, the happenings of the future are disclosed briefly in advance and these events are described later in detail. The suspense we are used to in fiction does not exist in the dastangoi. The narrator of a dastan or dastangoi is called a dastango. The dastango assumes that there is an audience that wants to hear the narrative and that is how rapport is established. In a dastan, there is total agreement between the narrator and the listener/reader.

The four constituents of the dastan are battle and combat (razm), assembly and entertainment (bazm), enchantment and magic (tilism), and craftiness and knavery (ayyari). The entire story is woven around these components. The element of enchantment is given more importance in the Lucknow dastans. All things present in the fantastic world and all affairs that may happen are powerful, strong and highhanded, exceedingly splendid and exceptionally beautiful or ugly. This attitude underlines the fiction of oral narration. If a city is depicted, its beauty, lustre and elegance are beyond description; gardens are such that the historical gardens of the past are deserts; the women surpass houris in their comeliness; the men put the legendary heroes of the past to shame. The knave is more nimble, smart and cunning than the devil, and the magician beats the sorcerers of bygone days. The dastan thus does not relate the reality of this world. Further, there are descriptions of so many real and imaginary countries that a particular dastan can seldom be positively related to a particular land or time. The dastango derives his inspiration from different streams, uses his genius to remould, creates plots and plots within plots. However, new events, incidents and happenings find place spontaneously, without any laboured ceremony.

Some of the characteristics of the dastan in Urdu literature that have been mentioned by literary critics are as follows:

i. It mirrors the social conditions of the times.

ii. It reflects Indian culture, including customs, modes of dressing and items of food and drink that are essentially Indian.

iii. The narration contains interesting and astonishing events and even humorous incidents.

iv. It provides escapist entertainment, a means to forget the stresses of daily life.

v. It contains a huge number of unconventional words and phraseology.

vi. There is a grand presence of characters as well as absorbing and intriguing events.

vii. There is conflict between truth and falsehood and the tussle is between good and evil. Ultimately, truth and goodness are victorious.

viii. A dastan, like that of Amir Hamza, is an extraordinary creative effort in which attempts are made to reach great heights in the use of language and narration; to a large extent, the endeavours have been successful.

ix. The forty-six volumes of the *Dastan-i Amir Hamza* are the last grand example (and in the case of Urdu the first) of oral narrative taken to almost the pinnacle.

x. The *Dastan-i Amir Hamza* volumes give the worldview of the Indo-Islamic universe.

The dastan has often been criticized for being long-drawn and for the repetition of similar happenings. However, Shamsur Rahman Faruqi insists that these are the requirements of the genre and are indications of the strength of the dastan. The dastan announces that it is unreal and anti-mimetic. The basic characteristics that Amir Hamza and his followers adhere to are manliness, bravery and courage and a firm belief in the oneness of God. Despite these values, the good characters are not presented as examples of high character as they have all the trappings of worldliness and are absorbed in affairs of the world. They do not resort to deceit, but their cunning and sly opponents freely resort to lies, deception, duplicity and fraud. Although there is mention of Islam in many places, the powers that the good characters have achieved are not because of their religion but are mainly unearned. Sexual morals are also quite free and profuse. Petting and necking are common, but matters sometimes go farther and there are even instances of incest and homosexuality.

We must not forget that at the time the Urdu dastans were composed in the nineteenth century, it was the text that was important and the name of the creator held very little fascination for the reader. This was unlike the allure of a poet, whose creation was related to his name and stature. The flexibility and elasticity of the dastan tradition was the result of innumerable tellings and the established text only crystallized after it took printed form. Later, in the printed dastans, there was noticeable effort by the reciter to claim authorship.

The methodology of composing the dastan has never been clarified: how the dastango created or narrated the dastan, whether the dastan was recited or whether it was recorded as if it was being narrated. One Amir Hasan Noorani, an elderly employee of the Naval Kishore Press of Lucknow, claimed that old employees of the press had shared with him that some dastangos would first dictate the tale to scribes, but it is difficult to prove the truth of this averment. However, it is to be noted that in certain printed dastans there are typographical errors that appear to have crept in because of the faulty hearing of the scribes. We can assume that the dastango learnt the important and popular portions of the dastan by heart and during recitation, he enriched and garnished the story and added details to enhance appreciation and for the entertainment of the audience. It was the custom to commit to memory the basic dastan, and it was not possible to become a dastango merely by reciting the dastan many times.

## The Artistes

Dastans were narrated by dastangos (narrators). They were intelligent and capable storytellers. The many incidents described in the dastans were gleaned from different places because of the very nature of the dastan and were skilfully amalgamated and integrated to give an ingenious, almost unified structure. Despite borrowings, the matchless and unparalleled elegance and grace of the oral narrative remains, as it was never treated as an inferior, low or secondary form. A good memory was an essential quality of a storyteller, but far more important was his inventiveness, innovation and the resourcefulness of his imagination.

The profusion of incidents in the narrative is a prominent quality of the dastan. Every recitation brings in changes, no matter how small. If nothing else alters, the body language of the narrator—his gestures, eye movements and pauses—keeps changing. In other words, you never step into the same river twice. An oral narrative could leave aspects of the tale incomplete as, by its very nature, the dastan is prone to being open-ended. In fact, there is no surprise ending and the listeners are more or less aware of the conclusion. There is no unity or tautness in the plot as this cannot be expected from a narrative of such extraordinary length. It is the characters who alone keep a semblance of wholeness and connectivity in a dastan.

The dastango keeps telling the listener/reader what is going to occur and nothing is held back. It is a mark of the consummate skill of the narrator that he is able to present anticipatable incidents in interesting ways. The inception and resolution of characters in dastans are seldom dramatic, striking or vivid. The brave, the pious and the truthful meet success, and evil characters, despite their machinations, face collapse and downfall. This is the grand design of dastans. There is a lot of bloodshed, killing, butchery and brutality in the *Dastan-i Amir Hamza,* but the dastango usually does not linger over such details. Rather, the dastango dwells on the positive aspects of the story and relishes happy meetings, marriages, fairs, souks (bazaars) and even battles, happenings that bring elation and rapture to the reader or listener. Tragic flaws of character and distressing failures are not part and parcel of the dastan.

In India, and also in the Islamic world, there is a strong tradition of remembering texts by rote. The Hindus have a custom of memorizing works such as the Ramayana, Bhagwad Gita and the *Ram Charit Manas,* while the Muslims have an established practice of memorizing the Qur'an. In a similar vein, the dastango kept in mind the bare outline or skeleton of the tale and while reciting it before his audience, he would embellish and clothe the account, using his masterly ingenuity.

One of the characteristics of the oral dastan is that there is always a profusion of lists of attributes, peculiarities and traits. These have no direct relevance to the story, but they add dignity and grandeur to it. While describing a battle, for example, a long list of weapons may be given and different manoeuvres may be described. While mentioning adornment, assorted dresses, ornaments and items of make-up would be listed.

The dastango sees everything afresh, in a new light and with a creative fervour. The dastans, like the external world, have contest and conflict, friendship and infidelity, raillery and obstinacy, meanness and eminence, selfishness and sacrifice, humour and obscenity, ribaldry and sexuality, enchantment and miracles, austerity and deceit and other facets of life.

This may give the impression that the dastan is a reflection of life, albeit in an exaggerated and amplified form. However, the reader/listener of a dastan doesn't mistake the tale for reality and there is no participation as in a live world. In fact there is a deliberate attempt to demolish reality and make it hollow.

## Popular Dastans

### Dastan-i Amir Hamza

This resplendent epic originated somewhere in Middle East, perhaps in the ninth century, though some of its origin myths place it even earlier, while some date it to later times, especially to the time of Mahmud of Ghazni, in the eleventh century. The chief personage in this dastan is Hazrat Hamza ibn Abdul-Muttalib, the paternal uncle of Prophet Mohammed, who was an adherent of Islam and was martyred in a battle in AD 625 during the Prophet's time. The dastan recounts the adventures and heroic deeds of Amir Hamza, his companions and his successors in their fight against the enemies of Islam. Amir Hamza is described as Sahibqiran (Lord of the Auspicious Conjunction). It is a staus conferred by God to whom He decides to desrve it. There can be only one Sahibqiran at one time. Occasionally, Hamza himself bestows the Sahibqirani to a suitable candidate, but even this has to be confirmed by God through His signs and omens. The rivalry among Hamza's blood descendants for the Sahibqirani is an interesting side-plot of the huge dastan.

The dastan originally arrived in India in the Deccan around 1590. It was in Persian and was at that time called *Rumuz-i Hamza* (Mysteries of Hamza). The dastango (narrator), one Haji Qissa Khwan Hamadani, impressed the king so much with the originally quiet dastan that he ordered him to prepare a summary of it. This Hamadani did, calling it *Zubdatur Rumuz* (The Cream of the *Rumuz*). Only one copy exists now. It is in the Khuda Bakhsh Libray in Patna, and even this copy is missing many pages. The dastan duty eventually arrived in the Court of Akbar who liked it so much that he had large miniatures, 140 in number, painted by his court painters. (Only about twenty such paintings are extant today, none in India.)

From these beginnings, the dastan grew and grew, as is the chief characteristic of all oral narratives. In due course, many smaller versions, and some not so small, also arrived in India. The longer version, and the shorter version, continued to be recited in Persian when a short, one-volume version was translated from the Persian into Deccani in the first quarter of the eighteenth century. This version remained unknown in the north. The shorter version must have been more popular, because Khalil Ali Ashk, a 'moonshie' at the College of Fort William, produced an Urdu version in 1802. The Persian original of Khalil Ali Ashk's version has not been identified so far. Over the nineteenth century, many editions of the Ashk version became popular and, also, a short Persian version and a much longer Persian version. This longer Persian version was read and much enjoyed by Ghalib in the latter half of the nineteenth century. Some form of the Urdu version was among the popular recitals in and around Delhi, especially the Jama Masjid, as testified by Mirza Sangin Baig in 1822, and later by Ghalib, and still later by Syed Ahmad Khan. From Delhi, the dastan travelled to Rampur and became extremely popular with the ruling nawabs there. Many dastan reciters of great power and originality became active there. These included a son of Emperor Bahadur Shah, Mir Ahmad Ali, and Munshi Amba Prasad Rasa. By this time, the dastan had swollen into a huge ocean, full of all kinds of wonders and variety. The dastan seems to have reached Lucknow during the first quarter of the nineteenth century.

In Lucknow, the popularity of the dastan of Amir Hamza exceeded all bounds. Munshi Naval Kishore took it up for publication around the 1880s and finally, forty-six volumes were published in Lucknow or Cawnpore (Kanpur) by the Naval Kishore Press. It is perhaps the longest work of oral romance in world literature. The complete dastan has 42,226 pages, or an average of 918 pages per volume. Although the *Dastan-i Amir Hamza* is now recognized as a landmark of Urdu literature, till the 1970s not much notice was taken of this masterpiece of literary imagination and inventiveness. Shamsur Rahman Faruqi has written a pioneering work on this dastan. His four-volume study, *Sahri, Shahi,*

*Sahibqirani: Dastan-i Amir Hamza ka Mutalia*, published in 1999, 2006 and 2011 by the National Council for Promotion of Urdu Language (New Delhi), is a seminal work, full of insight and erudition.

In a span of twenty-six years, between 1883 and 1909, forty-five of the forty-six volumes of *Dastan-i Amir Hamza* made their appearance. The most prolific of the writers was Ahmad Husain Qamar, who contributed as many as nineteen volumes. The second most productive dastango was Shaikh Tassaduq Husain, who composed fifteen volumes. He may have collaborated with other dastangos in as many as seven volumes. These persons were dastango (Dastan reciter), not authors. It is not clear if they actually wrote the volumes, or reproduced what they had learnt from their teachers, or composed extemporaneously, or dictated from memory. All such possibilities are equally plausible.

An eminently readable, complete and unabridged translation of a one-volume version, produced in 1871 by one Abdullah Bilgrami (itself based on a one-volume version made by Ghalib Lakhnavi in Calcutta in 1855) has recently appeared as a Modern Library edition, an imprint of Random House, New York, and its Indian reprint is *The Adventures of Amir Hamza: Lord of the Auspicious Planetary Conjunction*, by Ghalib Lakhnavi and Abdullah Bilgrami. The translator is the Pakistani-Canadian novelist Musharraf Ali Farooqi.

According to Shamsur Rahman Faruqi, the theme of *Dastan-i Amir Hamza* revolves around four functions:

1. *Sahiri* (Magic and sorcery, the magician claiming direct, godlike powers over all material things): The Magician-King exercises absolute domination over the immediate environment, bringing about a direct change in the circumstances. It includes leading a charmed life, enjoying pleasures and delights and not being subject to any moral law except the canons of occultism. The advantages of necromancy encompass long life or claims of divinity.

2. *Shahi* (Kingship and Temporal control): This requires having full control over what has been achieved by conquest and ruling over the subjects of the country who practise the religion of Magic, or un-Islamic beliefs. Among the Magician-Kings, there are many religions

and numerous gods, including the Magician-King himself, who claims to be God. Reaping the delights of life includes ruining the enchanters with the help of brave warriors who fight in the name of the One and Only God.

3. *Sahibqirani*: Chosen by God, the Sahibqiran ranks superior to the King, though does not himself. He possesses miraculous gifts from God and is practically invincible. He has extraordinary valour and power. The Sahibqirani may pass from father to son, but not always. The Sahibqiran is the ideal of valour, gallantry, generosity and kindness. But he can be harsh, even cruel, if the occasion demands. He acts always through or under divine inspiration.

4. *Ayyari*: The Ayyar is a secret agent, a friend of the Prince, has extraordinary powers of endurance and is highly intelligent. He knows many languages, is a musician of surpassing merit, is extremely loyal to the Prince to whom he is attached. He can perform uniqe feats of physical prowess. He does not practise magic and can only kill a magician by using his own skills and physical powers. The Chief Ayyar in the dastan is Amar, who was born the same day as Hamza, and evinced qualities of cleverness, trickery and deceit from the day he was born.

Khalil Ali Ashk identified the four elements described above as the main components of a dastan. Ghalib Lakhnavi, writing in 1855, added that Magic and the Magician-King were present in early version of the dastan too, but they gained full fruition in India.

## Qissa-i Mahr Afrozwa Dilbar

One of the first dastans to be written in Urdu in prose was *Qissa-i Mahr Afrozwa Dilbar* by one Iswi Khan Bahadur, perhaps a native of Delhi and about whom almost nothing is known. According to Masud Husain Khan, who edited and published the only existing manuscript of the dastan in 1966, it was probably composed between AD 1732 and 1759. The language of the dastan appears to be an improved form in which the effects of Punjabi and Haryanvi have almost disappeared. The expressions are more progressive than the language of *Bikat Kahani* by Afzal (who lived in the time of the fourth Mughal Emperor Jahangir, who ruled from 1605 till 1627) and there is very little effect of Braj Bhasha. Iswi Khan was probably well versed in Sanskrit and Braj Bhasha and lived in the eighteenth century.

## Nau Tarz-i Murassa

The most important precursor of the *Dastan-i Amir Hamza*, in terms of its emphasis on wonder and magic, etc., was *Nau Tarz-i Murassa*, a comparatively short romance which was written by Mir Muhammad Husain Ata Khan Tehsin, son of Muhammad Baqir Khan Shauq, a respected poet of Awadh. It was edited by Syed Noorul Hasan Hashmi, and published by Hindustani Academy, Allahabad, in 1958. It was composed in about 1775 when prose writing in Urdu was finding its feet. The author Tehsin probably hailed from Etawah in Uttar Pradesh and had lived in Calcutta, Patna and Faizabad. In his introduction to *Nau Tarz-i Murassa*, Tehsin writes that on a journey by boat to Calcutta, a co-passenger was whiling away the time by narrating various tales and one day he related the basic theme of *Nau Tarz-i Murassa*. Tehsin thought that he could turn the story into ornamental and rhyming prose. He presented a few portions of the tale before Nawab Shuja-ud-Daula, who liked them. But before he could complete writing the story, the Nawab passed away. Ultimately, the book was presented to his successor, Nawab Asaf-ud-Daula.

*Nau Tarz-i Murassa* is based on the famous tale of the four dervishes, which was first written in Persian in India by Hakeem Muhammad Ali alias Masoom Ali Khan. The story was later the basis of a better-known prose romance titled *Bagh wa Bahar*, composed by the famous Mir Amman of Delhi. He was one of the Urdu 'moonshies' appointed by the English to teach Urdu to English officers at the Fort William College in Calcutta. Mir Amman served from May 1801 to June 1806. The text of *Bagh wa Bahar* was composed during 1801–02 and was printed at the Fort William College in 1804.

Some scholars have asserted that the Persian original of *Nau Tarz-i Murassa* was first picked up by an obscure writer (maybe a schoolteacher) who described himself as 'Ahmad Ali, son of Shah Muhammad'. Nothing is known about him, but in any case, his work was produced *after*, and not *before* the *Bagh wa Bahar*, so that translation is not important to the history of the development of Urdu prose in the nineteenth century. For many reasons, its limpid style not the least important among them, *Bagh wa Bahar* became very popular and remains in print today. The *Nau Tarz-i Murassa* is better known for its Persiate style and can be described as the last great example of Persianate prose in Urdu. Tehsin's style was influenced by the Persian prose of that time; it had several archaic words and showed an artificial tone, quite distinct from the simple and flowing expression of Mir Amman in *Bagh wa Bahar*.

### Gulshan-i-Nau Bahar

Another significant dastango of Lucknow was Shaikh Muhammad Bakhsh 'Mahjoor', whose first book was titled *Gulshan-i-Nau Bahar* (*The Garden of the New Spring*). This tale was composed in about 1805 and was first published in Lucknow in 1846. It was again published in Lucknow in 1985, edited by Syed Suleiman Husain.

Mahjoor was a native of Fatehpur Hanswa, but he later settled in Lucknow. In poetry, his teacher was the famous poet Qalandar Bakhsh Jurat, an Indian poet of the Lucknow school (d. 1809–10).

The story revolves around a prince, Mahr Afrzo, and his quest for his beloved, Princess Mah Parvar. The search goes through many ups and downs before the lovers are finally united with the death of the demon, Aqrab.

### Fasana-i Ajaib

Another dastan that was probably written in Lucknow and which continues to draw attention is the *Fasana-i Ajaib* by Mirza Rajab Ali Baig Suroor. His exact date of birth is not known but is believed to be around 1785–86. He belonged to Lucknow and died in 1869. Suroor was a disciple of the poet Nawazish, whose couplets he has quoted extensively in his dastan. *Fasana-i Ajaib* was completed in 1824–25, during the reign of Ghazi-ud-din Haider (d. 1827). Suroor had before him the model of Mir Amman's *Bagh wa Bahar*, which used idiomatic but everyday Urdu. On the other hand, Suroor's dastan was a real mirror of the standard language of Lucknow and its affirmation. Suroor related to Lucknow and Mir Amman to Delhi, and they were the two stalwarts who put the Urdu dastan on a high pedestal and became the benchmarks for the genre.

*Fasana-i Ajaib* was the first work of prose that Suroor composed, at about the age of forty, after dabbling with poetry. The popularity of *Fasana-i Ajaib* was such that in the introduction to *Guldasta-i-Panch* (edited by Pandit Kishan Prasad Kaul), Pandit Brij Narain Chakbast Lakhnavi (an eminent Urdu poet) wrote that Suroor received unprecedented eminence and esteem because of *Fasana-i Ajaib*.

*Fasana-i Ajaib* narrates the story of Prince Jaan-i Alam, who set out on a journey with the son of his wazir to seek out the beautiful Anjuman Ara, who had been abducted by a magician. During his journey, he meets another beautiful princess, Mahr Nigar. He rescues Anjuman Ara and marries both the beautiful girls. However, the story doesn't end there. The father of Mahr Nigar had taught Jaan-i Alam the secret of changing hearts. The wazir's son, who fell for Anjuman Ara, had deceit in his heart and one day he persuaded Jaan-i Alam to share with him the secret of changing hearts. When Jaan-i Alam put his soul into the body of a dead monkey, the wazir's son transferred his own spirit into the lifeless body of Jaan-i Alam. How Jaan-i Alam returns to his own body forms another major sub-plot of the story. Although *Fasana-i Ajaib* contains numerous plots, sub-plots and incidents, it is able to sustain the interest of the reader and despite the passage of so many years, the popularity of the tale remains, which can be seen from the numerous editions the book has gone through. Among the short dastans, *Fasana-i Ajaib* remains a favourite and has received acclaim from connoisseurs of Urdu literature.

Others popular dastans include Faqir Muhammad Khan Goya Lakhnavi's (d. 1849–50) *Bustan-i Hikmat* (*The Garden of Wisdom*), an Urdu version of the Persian *Anwaar-i Suhaili* by Mulla Husain Wa'iz Kashifi (d. 1505), which in turn was a translation of the famous *Panchatantra*.

## The Decline and Recent Revival

Among the last of the great dastangos who rose in the middle of the nineteenth century was Mir Baqir Ali Dehalvi (1850–1928). He recited and published short humorous tales. His short dastans were recited on rooftops, in the light of a wick lamp. The listeners would often give small donations. Mir Baqir Ali himself marketed his printed tales. A few of them have survived, but many of them are untraceable. Recently, a recording of Mir Baqir Ali, incoherent in form, was located in London and was brought to India. Mir Baqir Ali's body of work comprises about twenty-one small books. His notable short tales include the following:

1. *Bahadur Shah Ka Maula Bakhsh Hathi* (*Bahadur Shah's Maula Bakhsh Elephant*)
2. *Garhay Khan aur Malmal Jaan Ki Jung* (*The Quarrel between Garhay Khan and Malmal Jaan*)
3. *Garhay Khan Ka Dukhra* (*The Sufferings of Garhay Khan*)
4. *Garhay Khan Ki Dhakawali Se Mulaqat* (*Garhay Khan's Encounter with the Woman from Dhaka*)
5. *Garhay Khan Ne Malmal Jaan Ko Talaaq Di* (*Garhay Khan Divorces Malmal Jaan*)

His compositions are amongst the last remains of a glorious era of dastangoi in Lucknow and Delhi.

Dehalvi's only daughter is said to have left for Karachi, Pakistan, and died in about 1952. Her husband, Syed Zameer Hasan, in 1960 established Idara-i Dastan, or Urdu College, in Karachi. The first and perhaps the only book brought out by the Idara was a reprint of the first part of *Khalil Khan Fakhta* (which is in two parts). The Idara has since disappeared with no trace. Not many booksellers in India and Pakistan, or for that matter, librarians, are even aware of Mir Baqir Ali. Most of his tales and other books, including one on an unlikely subject like firearms (*Araradhoon*), were printed as chapbooks. They were brought out privately and hawked by Mir Baqir Ali himself in the streets of Delhi.

It is not essential for a dastan to be lengthy. There were several popular dastans that were in one volume and ran between just fifty to three hundred pages. The reason for the decline of the dastan was not its length but the rise of new avenues of entertainment, such as novels, the theatre and cinema. What perhaps steered the reading public away from the dastan was that, with the introduction of Western education, there grew a general dislike for fantasies with detailed descriptions and the leisurely unwinding of action. No matter how engrossing the dastango's art, there was a notion that dastangoi took a lot of time. Also, the tales in the dastans were not in sync with the evolving way of life. After the 1930s, there was no significant following for dastans. They simply went out of fashion.

Unlike the novelist, the dastango is never alone and has a discernable listening audience. The breaking of the link between the dastan and the listeners in later years led to the misunderstanding that the dastan was an unsophisticated, childish and unrefined style of storytelling and that what was narrated was fanciful and illusive. With the end of the era of the Muslim ruler and nobility, the popularity of the dastan waned. The moneyed elite, many of whom were lovers of tales and whose patronage had nurtured the dastangos, was on the decline. The general and ordinary people unfortunately did not have the wherewithal to support the dastangos. The taste for the Persian language had diminished and familiarity with Urdu had also waned, and as a result, the conventional terminology of the dastan started to appear alien. As the elite gradually left the dastan out in the cold, the common man also followed suit.

Recently, the tradition of reciting dastans has received a fillip with the increasing awareness that Indian performing arts which have sunk into oblivion need to be recognized, appreciated and revived. Many Indian languages have a custom of oral storytelling. One person who has been instrumental in breathing new life into dastan recital is Mahmood Farooqui, the nephew of Shamsur Rahman Faruqi. He held the first recitation of a portion of *Tilism-i Hoshruba* at the India International Centre in New Delhi in May 2005. Historically, the dastan was recited by a single person, but Mahmood Farooqui introduced an innovation whereby the recitation is done by two persons, one after another, like characters speaking in a play. This saves the bother of learning a long portion of the dastan by rote, and two different voices appeal to the audience.

Such events have not only been held in India and Pakistan but also in other countries. Some of the reciters speak only Hindi, but their interest has made them learn passages of chaste, high-flown and, sometimes, very descriptive and flowery Urdu. Mahmood Farooqui, along with Muhammad Qasim, brought out an Urdu book titled *Dastangoi*, which was published in 2011. This book describes the coming into fashion of dastan recital and contains a few vivid passages from *Tilism-i Hoshruba*. The book also has a newly composed contemporary dastan on the Partition of India.

Mention may also be made of the Pakistani miniature painter Ustad Allah Bakhsh (d. 1978), who captured the 'magic and dense storytelling' of *Hoshruba* in his painting *Tilism-i Hoshruba*, which hangs in the Lahore Museum.

Dastangoi is as much a living tradition convention as any other performing art. Although new dastans are not being written in Urdu, the corpus of classical Urdu literature has thousands of pages of memorable, stirring and dramatic pieces full of graphic and intense imagery. The important thing is that in modern dastan recitals, the audience is not only confined to the Urdu-knowing public but a large percentage of non-Urdu speakers are also entranced by the dramatic and colourful renditions of the reciters.

# 3.

# Muharram and Marsiya in Awadh

## Muharram

After Prophet Mohammed passed away in 632 CE, his succession became a bone of contention. The splintering of Islam into the Sunni and Shia sects was primarily due to the dispute over the succession after the demise of the Prophet, although the successor was not expected to be vested with any prophetic or oracular qualities and abilities. Whereas the Sunnis (comprising the majority of the Muslim population) averred that the first four caliphs after the Prophet were the rightful successors, the Shias believed that only members of the family of 'Ali (ahl al-bayt) had the sole and unshared right to the caliphate. Therefore, according to them, the first three caliphs were usurpers.

Later, the martyrdom of Imam Husain, the grandson of the Prophet Mohammed, in 680 CE in Karbala (detailed in the annex) became the cornerstone of the spirit of resistance in Islamic history and, throughout the Muslim lands, between Sunnis and Shias.

In the Islamic ethos, the life of Imam Husain depicting his ordeal and physical sufferings has become a reference point for high character and lofty ideals. Indeed, the first month of the Muslim lunar Hijri calendar is Muharram (which means 'forbidden' or 'secret'), and is a month of remembrance and mourning for Imam Husain and his supreme sacrifice. Although the ardour and intensity of remembering the grief is far more pronounced in the Shia Muslim sect, the solemnity of the month is respected and venerated among the Sunni Muslims also. All Muslims, irrespective of denomination, feel the pain and grief of the tragedy of Karbala, particularly in the first ten days of the month of Muharram. The tributes to the great Imam translate into emotions empathizing with his suffering, anguish and torment. Muharram is the only occasion in the Muslim calendar when a festival is not celebrated; rather, it is a period of commemoration, a time to look back and call to mind the sacrifice made by the beloved grandson of the Prophet on the path of truthfulness and pure uprightness.

In the Persian book *Manshur-i 'Aqayid-i Imamyyiia* by Ayatollah Ja'far Sobhani, which has been translated into English as *Doctrines of Shi'i Islam* by Reza Shah-Kazemi, the importance of Muharram has been summed up as follows:

> In addition, mourning for those martyred in the path of God has a 'philosophical' underpinning: maintaining the grandeur of such persons is a means of preserving their school of thought, thereby upholding the perspective which is founded upon sacrifice for the sake of religion, and upon the ideal of refusing to submit to humiliation and disgrace. The logic of this perspective is summed up thus: 'A red death is better than a humiliating life.' The word 'ashura means 'ten' and refers to the tenth day of the month of Muharram in 60 AH/680 CE when Imam Husain was martyred. In every gathering of 'ashura, the tenth day of the month of Muharram, commemorating the martyrdom of Imam Husain, this logic is revived, and entire nations have learnt and continue to learn a great lesson from his supreme act of self-sacrifice.

The observance of Muharram among Muslims in Indian cities with a sizable Muslim population is a regular feature and a part of the Muslim cultural heritage. Awadh, which had a significant Shia Muslim population, was ruled up to 1856 by a series of culturally edifying nawabs and kings of Shia denomination who patronized, encouraged and promoted customs and rituals of a unique nature. Many of these customs have survived and are a reflection of the multicultural aspects of the Awadhi Ganga-Jamuni ethos (composite culture) to which both Hindus and Muslims contributed and subscribed. The events and ceremonies associated with Muharram found echoes in the mores and lifestyle of Awadh and spread into its history, literature, art, music and folk culture.

Mrs Meer Hassan Ali, in the first volume of her famous *Observations on the Mussulmauns of India* has described the observance of Muharram in Awadh in the early nineteenth century in so many words:

> [...] the first day of Mahurrum invariably brings to my recollection, the strongly impressed ideas of *The Deserted Village* (Oliver Goldsmith's poem first published in 1770). The profound quiet and solemn stillness of an extensively populated native city, contrasted with the incessant bustle usual at all other times, are too striking to Europeans to pass by unheeded.

The second day of Muharram brought multitudes of people on horseback, in palanquins and on foot out on to the streets, in mourning garments. People visited imambaras and houses of friends to pay respect (ziarat) to tazias that had been set up. The imambara, according to T.P. Hughes, is a building in which services are held to commemorate the martyrdom of Hazrat 'Ali, Imam Hasan and Imam Husain. The tazia, which means a consolation, is a model of the tombs of Hasan and Husain carried in procession during Muharram. The tazia is usually made of a framework of bamboo over which is fastened coloured paper to produce a replica. Tazias have also been made of ebony, ivory, sandalwood and even silver.

Mrs Meer Hassan Ali has vividly described the installation of tazias in the early nineteenth century in Awadh. The tazia was placed such that it faced Makkah and the pulpit (mimber) was located such that the preacher also faced Makkah. The mimber consisted of a flight of steps, usually without a railing to allow the preacher to sit or stand. Banners in many coloured fabrics were arranged along the wall. Several articles, believed to have been used by Imam Husain at Karbala, were placed at the foot of the tazia. These included a turban, a sword, a bow with a quiver of arrows, lights, particularly candles in myriad colours, and incense-burning censers. Mourning assemblies were held in the imambaras twice a day, particularly in the evening. A cleric with a gift of oratory recited before the assembly the tragedy of Karbala, step by step, and enthused the audience with intense fervour and zeal.

This is how Mrs Hassan Ali has described one of the assemblies:

> I have been present when the effect produced by the superior oratory and gestures of a Maulvee has almost terrified me, the profound grief, evinced in his tears and groans, being piercing and apparently sincere. I have even witnessed blood issuing from the breast of sturdy men, who beat themselves simultaneously as they ejaculated the names 'Hasan!' 'Hosein!' for ten minutes, and occasionally during a longer period, in that part of the service called Mortem [*sic*].

The word 'Mortem' used by Mrs Hassan Ali should actually be 'matam', which means 'mourning' and 'matam karna' meaning 'to mourn or lament'.

The assemblies included the recitation of the tragedy of Karbala. Mulla Husain Wa'iz Kashifi (d. 1505), a native of Baihaq, was a preacher who is famous for three Persian books on this subject, namely, *Anwar-i Suhaili*, *Akhlaq-i Muhsini* and *Rawdat al-Shuhada* (*The Garden of Martyrs*). *Rawdat al-Shuhada* was composed around 1502–03 CE and was read extensively in India and Iran in mourning assemblies among the Shia Muslims. It lost its importance in India when the preachings and sermons of the Shia ulama improved and increased. Moreover, *Raudat al-Shuhada* is a lengthy work and reading even one chapter of it in an assembly was not easy, especially when the gathering also listened to the recital of marsiyas (elegies) and nauhas (dirges). People therefore started narrating summaries of Kashifi's book, such as *Khulasa-i Rawdat al-Shuhada* or *Dah Majlis* (*Ten Assemblies*), or *Yazdah Majlis* (*Eleven Assemblies*), or *Dawazdah Majlis* (*Twelve Assemblies*). The summary was eagerly read on the third or tenth day of Muharram. The most prominent Urdu rendition of Muharram recitations was the *Karbal Katha* (*The Karbala Tale*) by Fazl Ali 'Fazli', which was written around 1732–33 CE and revised in 1748 CE. Fazli was probably a native of Delhi and was perhaps born in 1710 or 1711 CE. His book is in Urdu prose with a scattering of poems.

Besides the narration or reading of the circumstances that led to the martyrdom of Imam Husain, his family and kinsmen, the Muharram majlis (assembly) usually included the recitation of marsiyas. The elegies were, more often than not, recited by the author himself. There were also trained and professional marsiya reciters and they carried a basta (cloth bag) containing sheaves of handwritten or printed elegies of one or several authors. The professional marsiya khwan (elegy reciter) was adept at combining stanzas of different poets in the same metre and reading the elegy as one composite production. The literary flavour of the Muharram spirit among the people of Awadh, particularly in the nineteenth century and in the first half of the twentieth century, permeated and touched all levels including the unlettered, so much so that mendicants and beggars solicited by uttering '*Khuda gham-i Husain ke siwa koi gham na de*' (except for the grief of Imam Husain, may God give you no other woe).

Mrs Meer Hassan Ali describes some of the observances of the Muslims, particularly of the Shia sect, during Muharram. Everything that constituted comfort, luxury or convenience at normal times was done away with. Ladies no longer used bedsteads and mattresses and lounged on mats on the floor instead. No jewellery, to which women were so attached, was worn from the time the new moon of Muharram was sighted. Women untied their hair and allowed the tresses to fall in disorder. The colourful attire of the women was replaced by mourning clothes, usually black, especially during the first ten days of Muharram.

The daily diet also underwent a change, with the lavish meals replaced by coarse and simple foods. For the first ten days of mourning, even paan was not consumed; it was replaced by gota, comprising a mixure of dry coriander seed, desiccated coconut, betel nut and sweet fennel. Any form of entertainment, including music, cinema and games, was also avoided.

Families, according to their means, kept tazias in a prominent part of their house. Even today, some families place tazias in their homes from the first to the tenth of Muharram. Assemblies narrating the tragedy of Karbala were held in houses as also in imambaras, where services were held to remember the martyrdom of the imams. In these gatherings, there was no restriction on the entry of people and all were welcome, irrespective of their religion. The imambaras were brilliantly lit. The congregations displayed genuine grief as well as ceremonial and ritualistic demonstration of sorrow. Strict Islamic law prohibits excessive, intemperate and vehement displays of grief. However, the gamut of

Awadhi Muharram ceremonies had a remarkably pronounced emphasis on the outward exposition and manifestation of agony, lamentation, sobbing, wailing and even beating of breasts.

In the chambers where the tazias are kept during Muharram, alams, which are standards or flags, are also displayed. In Lucknow, the practice was that on the fifth day of Muharram, the alams were brought out from various imambaras for consecration at the Dargah Hazrat Abbas in Rustam Nagar. The word 'dargah' means 'threshold'. J.R.I. Cole, in his book *Roots of North Indian Shi'ism in Iran and Iraq: Religion and State in Awadh, 1722–1859*, notes that one Mirza Faqeer Baig returned to Lucknow from the holy city of Karbala in Iraq in the reign of Asaf-ud-Daula (1775–97), bringing with him a metal crest that was claimed to have been mounted on the banner of Hazrat Abbas, the half-brother of Imam Husain, at the battle of Karbala. To house the relic, a dome was built in the home of the owner of the relic. A regular shrine was later built by Nawab Saadat Ali Khan in about 1803. The folk nature of the founding of the shrine was questioned by certain ulama, but the renown and reputation of the dargah among the common people, exhibiting their love for the family of the Prophet, added to its charisma.

The imambara became, for the Shia Muslims, the location and place for open and public mourning for the martyrdom of Imam Husain. The Great Imambara at Lucknow was built by Kifayatullah, an architect from Delhi, in the reign Asaf-ud-Daula and completed in 1791. A series of imambaras sprang up in Lucknow, including Imambara Mir Baqir Saudagar in Jauhari Mohalla, Imambara Agha Ali Khan on Victoria Street (1875) and Imambara Darab Ali Khan in Maulviganj (1891). The Husainabad Imambara in Lucknow was built by Nawab Muhammad Ali Shah in 1838. The Imambara at Shah Najaf was constructed by Nawab Ghazi-ud-Din Haider between 1818 and 1823. Imambara Ghufran Ma'ab was constructed by the eminent Shia cleric Syed Dildar Ali Naseerabadi (1753–1820). Earlier in Lucknow, Muslims of both Sunni and Shia sects offered congregational prayers (namaz) together. After Syed Dildar Ali Naseerabadi alias Ghufran Ma'ab, who was trained in Ithna Ashari theology, the Shias separated from the Sunnis for prayer, and followed Ghufran Ma'ab, who led the prayers on 12 April 1786. At that time, Asaf-ud-Daula was ruling Awadh with his capital in Lucknow.

The observance of Muharram in Lucknow had been institutionalized. The ceremonies, rites and proprieties, though of Shia origin, were embraced not only by Sunni Muslims but also by a significant section of the Hindu population of Awadh. Particularly the ten days of the month of Muharram saw the observance of formal and staid functions, making societal mourning an essential component of the community. Although the intensity and ardour of the solemnities have reduced as compared to the enthusiasim rampant in the nineteenth century, nevertheless, they are still observed, sometimes to the letter.

Azadari is the general term for the practices of mourning and commemoration of the martyrdom of Imam Husain. The imambara is also called azakhana (house of mourning) or aashurkhana (a structure or house for the reception of banners and other such objects used in the Muharram processions). In the context of the events at Karbala, the period of remembrance stretches over about two months and eight days from the evening of 29/30 Dhul Hijja to the evening of 8 Rabi' al-Awwal.

The ritual objects connected with Muharram are as follows:

1.  **Tazia:** A replica of the tomb of Imam Husain at Karbala that is installed during Muharram. It is said to have been introduced in India by Taimur-i Lung (1336–1405) when he invaded India in 1398. The tazia has two parts: the lower portion called the takhta, and the upper portion with two tombs known as the rauzah (literally 'garden').

2.  **Zarih:** This is a modified form of the tazia and is made of silver. It is an imitation of the silver railing fixed around Imam Husain's tomb at Karbala. The zarih has three parts, namely, the takhta or the lower portion, the rauzah in the middle with two tombs, and the gumbad (dome), which is the uppermost part. The difference between the tazia and the zarih is that the former does not have a dome.

3.  **Tabut:** This literally means 'coffin'. In Lucknow, the majority of tabuts are of Imam Hasan (the second Imam), Imam Husain (the third Imam) and Ali Asghar, the youngest son of Imam Husain. The tabut is pierced with an arrow, sword or knife to signify the slaying. A turban on the coffin signifies that it is a bier. Sometimes, the tabut is

sprinkled with red to signify blood. At times the coffins are covered with red or green cloth, the green for Imam Hasan and the red for Imam Husain.

4.  **Alam:** This literally means banner and was an important symbol for the meagre army of Imam Husain. The alam is also known as a nishan. It has two portions—the alam or nishan made of gold, silver, tin or other metals, and the patka (sash of cloth, generally silken), decorated with embroidered borders in gold and silver.

5.  **Duldul:** This was the mule of Prophet Mohammed. It was presented by the Prophet to his son-in-law Hazrat Ali (the first Imam). Hazrat Ali later gave Duldul to his son Imam Husain. It is said that after the martyrdom of Imam Husain, Duldul, with the blood of the Imam on its forehead, conveyed the news of the tragedy to the Imam's followers.

6.  **Zuljinah:** This was the name of Imam Husain's horse. It was so named because its neighing was sweet and also furious. It was gifted by Prophet Mohammed to his grandson Imam Husain, who rode it in the battle at Karbala.

7.  **Buraq:** This literally means 'the bright one'. It is the animal upon which the Prophet sat on the nocturnal journey called the Mi'raj (an ascent), or Isra. According to tradition, the Buraq was a white animal between the size of a mule and an ass, having two wings. The Mi'raj took place in the twelfth year of the Prophet's mission in the month of Rabi' al-Awwal. According to Shia tradition, the name of the horse of the twelfth Imam, Muhammad al-Mahdi, was also Buraq.

8.  **Kalawas:** This is a Hindi word for the band or rope around an elephant's neck in which the mahout secures his feet. In the terminology of Muharram, kalawas are the green and red threads worn round the neck. The green kalawa is for Imam Hasan and the red one is for Imam Husain.

9.  **Mehndi:** The henna plant, the powdered leaves of which are used to colour the hair and decorate the body of the bride and bridegroom during Indian marriages. The ritual of applying mehndi paste on the seventh day of Muharram symbolizes the marriage of Hazrat Qasim, the eldest son of Imam Hasan, to Fatima Kubra, the elder daughter of Imam Husain. Tradition states that the two were married before

the final battle of Karbala and Fatima Kubra became a widow the following day. Hazrat Qasim was in his teens when he became a martyr. His body was in pieces after being trampled by horses. It should be noted, however, that the fact of the marriage of Hazrat Qasim with Fatima Kubra is of doubtful authenticity and is disputed.

10. **Sabeel:** The word means 'way', 'road' or 'course'. In the context of Muharram, it is the place in a locality or on a road where water or sherbet is given to thirsty travellers and passers-by. A sabeel may be kept at any time of the year, but because many of the martyrs of Karbala died of thirst, some people keep a sabeel from the first day of Muharram while others start from the seventh day of Muharram, when the food and water supplies of Imam Husain's men were cut off by al-Hurr's army. Sabeels are also taken out in a procession. Besides water, in Lucknow, a delicious mixture of milk, water and sugar, scented with keora and garnished with slivers of pistachio, is also distributed.

11. **Tabarruk:** The word implies a blessing, benediction or portion of food given or dedicated to a spiritual person. Such food or drink is extended to persons attending different rituals connected with Muharram.

12. **Niyaz:** It is an offering of food or a delicacy dedicated to the martyrs of Karbala as well as other members of the Prophet's family or holy personalities.

13. **Mimbar:** This is the raised pulpit in a mosque from where the preacher (khateeb) delivers his sermon (khutbah). It is usually a wooden structure with several steps, generally three or five. Traditionally, the uppermost step is left vacant and the preacher, while giving his discourse, sits on the steps below it. The mimbar was also used in the times of Prophet Mohammed, who frequently delivered his sermons from it.

Apart from these ritual objects, another element integral to the observance of Muharram is the majlis. A majlis is a congregation, assembly or meeting. In the context of Muharram, the majlis is a congregation where the grief and sorrow of the tragedy of Karbala are recalled. Believers and friends get together in arranged gatherings where people recall the happenings of Muharram and poets as well as professional reciters discuss theological issues deriving from the martyrdom of Imam Husain. Usually in a majlis, religious discourse is supplemented by sozkhwani (dirge chanting), marsiyakhwani (recitation of elegies), matam (ritual lamenting), nauha (threnody by a professional mourner), ziyarat (visit to the tomb of a martyr or saint, from a distance, which may also include a tazia) and tabarruk (a portion of food dedicated to a martyr or saint that is distributed among the believers).

Typically, the majlis is preceded by sozkhwani. The person who chants the dirge is known as sozkhwan and is usually skilled in this art, having learnt it from his forefathers. Sometimes, non-Muslims are also sozkhwans. A soz is not sung but recited in the style of a raga. A soz is usually of four to six verses followed by salaam (a poetic form of salutation to a martyr or a holy person). Normally in a majlis one soz and one salaam are performed.

Sozkhwani is followed by marsiyakhwani. A marsiya is an elegy for a deceased person expressing sorrow at his or her death. However, in the context of Muharram, the elegies relate to the martyrdom of Imam Husain, his family and associates. The Muharram elegies are an important genre of exquisite Urdu poetry and volumes of such poetry have been published extensively.

After marsiyakhwani, a religious discourse is given by a zakir. The speaker is supposed to be well versed in the Qur'an, Hadith and events at Karbala. The zakirs are specially trained for public speaking in Shia madrasas in centres like Lucknow, Meerut and Moradabad. The zakir sits on the mimbar and calls upon the congregation to repeat Sura Fatiha, the first chapter of the Qur'an. The khutbah or sermon is then delivered by the zakir, who uses all his rhetorical and oratorical skills to stir the audience. Towards the end, the zakir recollects and evokes the martyrdom of Imam Husain and his followers.

After the zakir's discourse, the mourners stand up for the matam (ritual mourning). The participants beat their breasts to the accompaniment of nauhas (dirges), which are simple poems recited in a tragic rhythm to draw out tears. The nauhas are declaimed by a group. The leader of the nauhakhwans delivers a line, which is then repeated by the other members of the group. The matam lasts for about twenty minutes.

The ceremony of matam is followed by ziyarat, an incantation that covers the martyrs of Karbala (especially read on every Thursday after prayers), and is an invocation on the tomb of Imam Husain on the tenth of Muharram, and on Chihlum (forty days after Karbala). After reading the ziyarat the mourners disperse and tabarruk is distributed among them.

According to the monograph of the Census of India, 1961, the educational institutions of the Sunnis in Lucknow and Delhi do not have any role in the observance of Muharram. Generally, the educational institutions of the Shias are also not involved in the Muharram ceremonies. However, the Shia religious institutions, such as the Imambara Husainabad Trust, organize majlises during the first ten days of Muharram. There is no public majlis in Lucknow among the Sunnis.

The monograph of the Census of India, 1961, lists the majlises commencing from the first day of Muharram. In general, they cover the following, but this list is not mandatory:

| First day | Men of the tyrant caliph Yazid demand that Imam Husain give his allegiance to Yazid or face death. |
| --- | --- |
| Second day | Departure of Imam Husain for Karbala. |
| Third day | Arrival of Imam Husain at Karbala. |
| Fourth day | Account of Hazrat Hurr who was sent to Karbala to fight Imam Husain, but being convinced of the righteousness of the Imam, he joined him on the last day and sacrificed his life. |
| Fifth day | Account of Ali ibn al-Husain Zain al-Abidin, son of Imam Husain who fell ill in Karbala and could not take part in the battle. |
| Sixth day | Account of Hazrat Ali Akbar, the eighteen-year-old son of Imam Husain, who died valiantly fighting the enemy at Karbala. |
| Seventh day | Account of the martyrdom of Hazrat Qasim, son of Imam Hasan, aged about thirteen years. |

| Eighth day | Account of the martyrdom of Hazrat Abbas, younger brother of Imam Husain by another mother, who was the flag-bearer of Imam Husain's force. He was extremely brave, full of anger, very faithful and skilled in warfare. He managed to reach the banks of the Euphrates and fill his leather bag with water. Not waiting to quench his own thirst, he returned and was surrounded by the enemy enroute. He fought them bravely. He was martyred by the blow of a mace. |
|---|---|
| Ninth day | Account of the martyrdom of Hazrat Ali Asghar, the thirsty infant son of Imam Husain, who was killed by an arrow. |
| Tenth day | Account of the martyrdom of Hazrat Imam Husain. |
| Eleventh day | Account of the tribulations of Ali ibn al-Husain Zain al-Abidin, the only male who survived the Karbala tragedy and became the fourth Imam. |
| Twelveth day | Account of the sufferings of Hazrat Sakina, the youngest daughter of Imam Husain, who was then aged about four years. She is said to have died in prison in Syria. |

In addition to majlises, several processions are also held in Lucknow in connection with Muharram:

1.  Bari zarih processions: A zarih is a wax tazia. The main items carried in the procession are zarih, alams, duldul, mehndi, palna (cradle) and sabeel. The procession is accompanied by drum beaters, who play a mournful tune in a particular rhythm. In Lucknow, the processoin starts in the early evening from the Asafi Imambara, passes through Khun Khunji Road and terminates at the Husainabad Imambara.

2.  Mehndi processions: The mehndi procession is held on the seventh day of Muharram to commemorate the marriage of Hazrat Qasim, son of Imam Hasan, and Hazrat Fatima Kubra, daughter of Imam Husain. The main items carried in the processions are big round trays with henna leaf paste. There are two important mehndi processions held in Lucknow. One is from Imambara Asaf-ud-Daula to Imambara Husainabad and the other is from Imambara Darogha Wajid Ali to

Imambara Nazim Sahib. The first procession commences at about 10.30 p.m., passes through Shah Mina Road, Chowk and Khun Khunji Road, and reaches its destination at about 1.00 a.m. The second procession starts early in the evening and passes through Golaganj, Dr Pyare Lal Road and Shah Mina Road to arrive at Imambara Nazim Sahib after 10.00 p.m.

3.  Alam processions: Numerous alam processions are taken out on the eighth, ninth and tenth days of Muharram, the twentieth day of Safar and the eighth day of Rabi' al-Awwal. The two important processions are the ones held on the eighth and ninth days of Muharram. The one on the eighth day is from Dariyawali Masjid. It begins at about 11.00 p.m., passes through Khun Khunji Road and Chowk, and terminates at Imambara Gufran Ma'ab. The one on the ninth day begins at about 10.00 p.m. from Imambara Nazim Sahib and terminates at Dargah Hazrat Abbas in Rustam Nagar.

4.  Zarih processions: There are a multitude of zarih processions on the tenth day of Muharram. Wax tazias and two alams are borne to the accompaniment of the mournful beating of drums. The members of the processions offer lamentation by beating their breasts. Some stalwarts thrash their backs with bunches of knives tied to iron chains. The painful wounds are soothed with cool keora water.

5.  Chup tazia: This famous procession is taken out on the eighth day of Rabi' al-Awwal. It starts from Imambara Nazim Sahib on Victoria Street and terminates at Karbala Kazimain in Rustam Nagar, where the tazias are buried in the ground. The peculiarity of this procession is that the participants remain perfectly silent. No matam by beating of breasts is performed. Only the names of Imam Hasan and Imam Husain are uttered inaudibly under the breath. The procession includes a horse led by the bridle by a man. Traditionally, this horse is never ridden by anyone. During the chup tazia procession, the person leading the horse recites sawaaris. The word 'sawaari' refers to any horse or animal on which one rides. In the context of the Muharram processions in Awadh, the sawaari is a short, six-line poem in the rhyme scheme *a a a a b b*, and the last line ends with the words *'yeh sawaari hai'* (this is the conveyance). The horse in the procession

represents Zuljinah, the steed ridden by Imam Husain at Karbala.

In addition to majlises and processions, other activities observed in Lucknow during Muharram are as follows:

1.  Fire walking (aag ka matam): This is one of the famous spectacles of Muharram in Lucknow. On the sixth day of Muharram, just a few metres from the steps leading to Imambara Asaf-ud-Daula, a trench about 4 metres long, 1.5 metres wide and about half a metre deep is dug and within it are burnt big logs of wood. By the time of the performance at about 9.00 p.m., the fire pit is aglow with hot embers. A select group of mourners walk through the pit with alams in their hands shouting 'Hai Husain'. The fire-walkers are in a trance and do not get burnt.

2.  Tabut-i Qasim: Observed on the seventh day of Muharram, this revolves around the tabut, or replica of the coffin of Hazrat Qasim, the eldest son of Imam Hasan. He was to be married to Fatima Kubra, daughter of Imam Husain. While it is uncertain whether they got married or not, what is certain is that on the following day, he fought in the battle and was killed, mercilessly trampled by horses. The most famous tabut-i Qasim is held at Imambara Ghufran Ma'ab. The congregation observes matam and the mourners weep ritually.

3.  Illumination: Many imambaras in Lucknow, particularly those of Asaf-ud-Daula, Husainabad and Shah Najaf, are illuminated on the eighth and ninth days of Muharram. This was perhaps started by the nawabs to attract persons to the imambaras.

4.  Final day processions: On the tenth day of Muharram, Roz-i Ashura, the day of the martyrdom of Imam Husain, hundreds of tazias are brought out by the Shia community for burial in various karbalas. Women do not generally participate in the processions, but they are seen lining the roads along with children. Processions also occasionally include displays of martial arts like staff fighting, and the beating of backs with bunches of sharp knives tied to a chain. The processions are quite clamorous, with drums and cymbals being continuously beaten in a martial rhythm. The Talkatora Karbala in the Rajajipuram area of Lucknow is the most important burial ground for

tazias and is used by both Shias and Hindus. Each tazia is dismantled and the pieces are lowered into hollows that have been dug in the ground. The Kalima is uttered and earth is poured over the tazia. Incense and candles are burnt. The burial is similar to the covering of a fresh grave.

The activities of the tenth day as observed in the early twentieth century have been described by the late Mirza Jafar Husain (1899–1989) in an article 'Qadeem Lakhnau Ki Taaziadari' ('Taaziadari in Old Lucknow'), published in the February 1978 issue of the monthly *Aaj Kal*. According to him, the lifting of the tazias from the houses started at sunrise. It was as if a funeral were taking place in the house. In the old city of Lucknow, the tazia processions converged in the Nakhkhas market, from where they proceeded to the 'graveyard' in the Talkatora Karbala where the Shias buried the tazias. The Sunnis had a different 'graveyard' in Badshah Nagar, near Nishatganj. The scenes were more spectacular and eye-catching in the Shia localities. The processions included sozkhwani, nauhakhwani and simple mourning or tear-shedding. Mournful tunes were played on drums and cymbals. There were also roadside displays of martial arts by spirited youngmen wielding maces, clubs or sticks.

Mirza Jafar Husain also tells us that some of the leading courtesans of Lucknow, such as Haider Jaan, the two sisters Badr-i Muneer and Mahr Muneer, Bibban, Mughal Jaan, Najja and Hasso, sometimes accompanied the tazia processions. However, there was no question of the crowd watching the processions harassing or pestering the women. The roads were decked as if for a fair with shops of eatables, although by and large the Shia Muslims avoided eating and drinking on ashura during the day. A simple meal was eaten about two hours before sunset.

In the Lucknow milieu prior to 1947 and up to the 1950s, majlises relating to Muharram mourning were held from the first day of Muharram to forty days later. They were addressed by eminent zakirs. The audience comprised mainly Shia Muslims, but some Sunni Muslims and culturally conscious Hindus also participated. According to Mirza Jafar Husain, in Shia Muslim areas of the city, majlises were held in almost every other house but were so timed that contiguous assemblies did not clash. Further, Mirza Jafar Husain has mentioned that the two largest majlises were in Imambara Syed Taqi Sahib and Imambara Ghufran Ma'ab. One important feature of all majlises was that at the end, eatables of quality were distributed among the audience. They could take the form of bread and meat curry or bread and dal or sweets. This distribution of food was a speical attraction for the impoverished section of the populace.

The Sunnis of Lucknow had a different and less rigorous schedule during the ten days of Muharram. Bayaan (discourse) was organized for each day, which started with the recital of the Qur'an. Some Sunni families also kept tazias, which were also buried on the tenth day of Muharram in Sunni karbalas, the chief of which is on Faizabad Road, near Badshah Nagar.

When the crescent moon of the Muharram month is sighted on the last day of the month of Dhul-Hijjah, traditionally, Shia women take off their ornaments, break the bangles on their wrists and don black or green clothes in remembrance of the martyrs of Karbala. Generally, during the first four days of Muharram, majlis is held in the evening at the domestic imambara (if in existence) followed by matam. The wooden pulpit is clothed in black and alams are displayed. In the family majlises, only women and children participate. Nauhas are declaimed in a melancholic tone. At short intervals, there is a session of breast-beating. Women sob and shed tears. After the first four days of Muharram, the ceremonies with mannat (vow) start. Children are dressed as beggars in fulfilment of a vow, for long life or well-being. The ninth day of Muharram is called Qatl Ki Raat (the night of slaughter) or Shab-i Bedaari (night of the wake). On this night the mourners do not sleep but pray through the night. On the tenth day of Muharram, the tazias are removed from homes and taken to karbalas for ritual burial. The women of the family accompany the tazia to the main gate of their homes, beating their breasts and uttering cries of alvida (farewell to the tazia).

On the tenth day, Shias fast and in the evening the fast is broken by faqa shikani (literally, breaking of fast). Usually, baked grains and water are taken. The majlis on the tenth day of Muharram is also known as Shaam-i Gharibaan (the night when Imam Husain's family was rendered destitute).

There is usually a majlis with matam in some families on the eleventh day of Muharram, but no special ritual is performed. On the twelfth day of Muharram, called tija (the third day after the death), the doors of imambaras, private and public, which were closed on the tenth day of Muharram, are reopened. The ceremony is called shok utarna (cessation of mourning). The females of the house stand and recite marsiya, followed by nauha and matam. Sherbat and elaichidana (sugar-coated cardamom) are offered. In the evening, some members of the family usually visit the karbala where the tazia of the family was interred, and niyaz (dedicated) food is offered and then eaten. Candles or shamas are lit.

The twentieth day of the lunar month of Safar is the fortieth day of the martyrdom of Imam Husain and is called Chihlum. Families that did not bury all their tazias on the tenth day of Muharram hold majlises till all the tazias are finally interred on the day of Chihlum.

After Chihlum, the final important day for public performances connected with Muharram is the eighth day of Rabi' al-Awwal. Shias believe that on this day, Imam Ali ibn al-Husain Zain al-Abidin (the fourth Imam) and other surviving associates of Imam Husain returned to Madina. In Lucknow, the chup tazia procession, described earlier, is taken out.

The grieving period, which starts on the first day of Muharram, finally ends on the eighth day of Rabi' al-Awwal. In traditional and conventional families, normal life is resumed on the ninth day of Rabi' al-Awwal. Eid-e-Zehra is celebrated on the ninth day of Rabi' al-Awwal, the third month of the Islamic calendar, and commemorates the day when Imam Husain's sister, Hazrat Zainab, smiled for the first time after the occurrence of the tragedy of Karbala. So by convention, the stringent period of mourning observed by Shia Muslims lasts for about sixty-eight days. This covers the two lunar months of Muharram and Safar, and eight days of Rabi' al-Awwal. Although all Shia Muslims are respectful of this period, the core period of the Muharram grieving is confined to the first twelve days of the month of Muharram.

In the cultural framework of Indian Muslims, the events of Karbala have a permanent place and find expression in the creative literature, customs, arts and way of life. Indeed, the rituals, ceremonies, rites and protocol connected with Muharram in Awadh—and by and large in other cities with Islamicate culture in India—have been almost completety indigenized and Indianized. The essence of Muharram is the remembrance and honouring of the martyrdom of Imam Husain and members of his family, but the observance and rites are Indian in their flavour. Arab society did not have elaborate conventions of mourning. However, in India, the tragedy is evoked through numerous practices and observances, which is alien to the strict Arab/Islamic experience. It is perhaps this Indianization that affects the Indian audience with intense emotion and endears the various practices, thereby striking a familiar chord among Indian Muslims (particularly Shias) who are, after all, Indians.

However, the observance of the rituals of Muharram has sometimes engenderd sectarian conflicts between Shia and Sunni Muslims, particularly in Awadh and notably in Lucknow. One of the causes of such friction was the recitation of tabarra among the Shia Muslims. Tabarra is the vilification of the first three caliphs before Hazrat Ali—Hazrat Abu Bakr, Hazrat Umar and Hazrat Uthman—done because according to the Shia belief, the first three caliphs were usurpers. Sunni Muslims find tabarra offensive as they revere all the four caliphs (including Hazrat Ali). J.R.I. Cole, in his book *Roots of North Indian Shi'ism in Iran and Iraq: Religion and State in Awadh, 1722–1859*, has given a brief account of the Sunni-Shia issues in Awadh from 1827 to 1847. The Shias have always acknowledged the ijtihad[6] of their mujtahids (those who strive). After the rise of an almost independent Shia kingdom in Awadh after 1819, the mujtahids became increasingly insistent on tabarra against the first three caliphs. There were even allegations that the Nawabi government persecuted Sunnis. This led to an increase in militancy among the Sunnis. Mrs Hassan Ali mentions in her book that such quarrels between the two sects took place in many major cities in India and led to bloodshed. Cole recounts an incident that took place in 1828, during Muharram. The

---

[6]Ijtihad literally means 'exertion', and refers to the effort of personal reasoning and reasoning by qiyas (analogy) on questions of Islamic law that have not been provided for in the Qur'an and Hadith.

Nawab, Nasir-ud-Din Haider, issued an order enjoining those who could not passively listen to tabarra to either quit the city or confine themselves to their homes. A riot broke out between Shias and Sunnis, leaving six dead and nine wounded.

In the twentieth century, Sunni dissent over the recitation of tabarra by Shias found voice in the polemics of Maulana Abdul Shakoor Farooqi (1877–1962), a Sunni from the qasba of Kakori on the outskirts of Lucknow. Maulana Abdul Shakoor fanned the flames of discord by introducing certain practices in the ashura. The Sunni tazias and banners were inscribed with the names of the chaar yaar (the first four caliphs) in contradistinction to the Shia panjtan (the Prophet, Hazrat Fatima, Hazrat Ali, Imam Hasan and Imam Husain). Maulana Abdul Shakoor, along with a few other maulavis, asserted that the keeping of tazias was permissible only if accompanied by the recitation of madh-e-sahaba (praise of the Companions of the Prophet). The introduction of madh-e-sahaba was meant to counteract the open recitation of tabarra. In the words of Justin Jones,

> [...] the routinization of the madh-i-sahaba interpolation effectively transformed Muharram among many Sunnis from a moment of remembrance for Husain into, effectively, one for the valorization of the Sunni Caliphs. In contrast to earlier Sunni exaltations of the glories of Husain, a new and innovative genre of Sunni elegiac poetry in praise of the Caliphs emerged and was 'published, sold, distributed, read and recited publicly everywhere'.

A Shia-Sunni riot broke out in 1908 when it was alleged that a procession of Shias was attacked by some Sunnis. The then British government appointed a committee under Justice T.C. Piggot of the Oudh Chief Court to look into the matter. The recommendations of the committee in 1909 that the organized recitation of the madh-e-sahaba be prohibited on three days, namely, the tenth of Muharram, Chihlum (the fortieth day of ashura) and the twenty-first day of Ramadan, and that there should be a restriction on the recital of tabarra, were accepted by the government.

In 1935, some Sunnis defied the government order and recited madh-e-sahaba on Chihlum, leading to skirmishes between the two Muslim communities. The British government constituted the Allsop

Committee under Justice Allsop. This committee in 1938 stood by the recommendations of the earlier Piggot committee. By this time, more Sunni maulavis had jumped into the fray. Maulana Abdul Shakoor Farooqi began to hold narrations of the achievements of caliphs Abu Bakr and Umar during the first ten days of Muharram and these bayaans were held right next to the Shia Madrasat al-Wa'izin in Lucknow, which lay on the route of the tazia procession.

The then Congress government had in its communiqué of 31 March 1939 permitted the recital of madh-e-sahaba by Sunnis in Bara-Wafat (the twelfth day of the month of Rabi' al-Awwal, observed as the birthday of the Prophet) processions. This led to discontent among the Shias, who felt that this was an unnecessary privilege granted to the Sunni Muslims. In 1940, the Lucknow district authorities banned both madh-e-sahaba as well as tabarra in meetings and processions.

The tensions between the Shias and the Sunnis, particularly in the old parts of Lucknow city, continued to simmer. The ban on azadari in 1977 led to peaceful demonstrations by the Shias. After a series of agitations, the Shia community took out their first azadari procession in January 1998 in the lunar month of Ramadan. Processions have been permitted under tight security and minor riots take place now and then in the old city. These frictions appear to have been ignited by political parties to make petty gains in the vote bank. Both Sunnis and Shias have to rein in provocation and practise restraint.

The volatile issue of the sucession after the Prophet has been the almost cataclysmic bane of Muslim individuals and societies throughout history, jeopardizing the peaceful coexistence among the different sects. The rift was evident while the Prophet was alive and the polarization was completed with his passing away. The Sunnis argued that the Prophet's successor should be chosen by the community, while the Shias asserted that the successor should carry the divine spark of the Prophet through his daughter Fatima, and since Fatima was married to Caliph Ali, he should have been the natural successor to lead the community. The Shia cited two instances to support their claim that the Prophet himself wanted Hazrat Ali to be his spiritual and worldly heir. At the water tank called Khum-i Ghadir, the Prophet made his famous observation: Those who count on me as their Master today will count on Ali as their Master tomorrow. The second instance advanced by the Shia is that once the Prophet, when he was critically ill, wanted to dictate guidelines for the future. The Sunni argued that the Prophet was in delirium and there was no need for instructions when the Qur'an expressly states that it will be the definite counsel for all future matters. This debate accentuated the schism in the then Muslim society.

As long as there is organized religion, divisions, sects, schools of thought and splinter groups will persist. All adherents cannot be expected to toe a single line. Differences will have to be recognized and respected. Sain Zahoor, Pakistan's unlettered mystic of music and living repository of the Punjabi poetry of Baba Bulleh Shah (1680–1757), on being asked about the sectarian violence in Pakistan, made the following observation in the 2012 summer issue of the bi-annual journal *Sufi* (London): 'We are here for a short time, ultimately we are going to meet the dust. When our souls fly off, what will count is our deeds, not the differences between us.'

The desire for amity among the different Muslim sects has always been felt. Wajid Ali Shah, the last Nawab of Awadh, is quoted by Abdul Halim Sharar as saying the following: 'Of my two eyes, one is Shia and the other is Sunni.'

## The Evolution of the Urdu Marsiya in Awadh

*Woh kaun hai duniya mein jise gham nahin hota?*
*Kis ghar mein khushi hoti hai, matam nahin hota?*
*Kya surma bhari ankhon se aansu nahin girte.*
*Kya mehndi lage hathon se matam nahin hota?*

Who, in one's span of life, has not suffered pangs of grief?
Which house has seen only happiness, but no affliction?
Do tears not well up in kohl-smeared eyes?
Do henna-stained hands not rise for breast-beating?

—Syed Riyaz Ahmad 'Riyaz' Khairabadi (1852–1934)

Urdu literature has many genres of poetry and the general impression is that the ghazal in self-contained couplets is the most captivating and engaging mode of poetic expression in that language. However, another significant form of Urdu poetic composition is marsiya (elegy), articulating the grief on the death or loss of a person. As in other world poetry, these elegies comprise individual examples of anguish at a bereavement or deprivation.

*The Encyclopedia of Poetry and Poetics,* edited by Alex Preminger, defines elegy as 'a lyric, usually formal in tone and diction, suggested either by the death of an actual person or by the poet's contemplation of the tragic aspects of life [...] this emotion, originally expressed as a lament, finds consolation in the contemplation of some permanent principle.' Maulana Altaf Husain 'Hali' (1837–1915), in his famous book *Muqaddima Sher Aur Shairi* (*Introduction to Poetry*), has stated that a qasida (panegyric ode) is in praise of a living person while a marsiya is the declaration of sorrow and regret for a dead person. There is a noteworthy and sizable corpus of Urdu elegies on the martyrdom of Imam Husain at Karbala.

How well the calamity of Karbala has carried a message for all right-thinking Muslims has been put in a brilliant couplet by Maulana Muhammad Ali 'Jauhar' (1878–1931):

*Qatl-i Husain asl mein marg-i Yazid hai*
*Islam zinda hota hai har Karbala ke baad*

Not Husain, but the slayer Yazid was in disdain
Who imagined he had scored as Husain lay slain
Not realizing Karbala made it doubly sure
That Husains and Islam will rise again and again

The tragedy of Karbala has inspired poets and sermonizers to compose elegies and lectures elaborating on the circumstances and depicting the moral and didactic aspects of the heartbreaking event. Elegies on the calamity have been penned in almost all the languages of the Islamic world. However, elegies on Imam Husain feature extensively in Urdu literature, and are characterized by refined verses and highly ethical and high-minded poetry.

Like other facets of Urdu poetry, early examples of the elegy developed mainly in the Deccan, starting from the time of the Bahmani

Sultanate in South India, which flourished from 1347 to 1527. As its rulers were Shia, there was considerable contact with Iran. It was natural that this association brought many influences, including the ceremonies connected with azadari. After the collapse of the Bahmani Sultanate, five distinct territories were formed with seats of power at Bijapur, Golconda, Ahmednagar, Bidar and Berar. Marsiya writing had already started and the first efforts were with stanzas of three lines, which later progressed into four-line stanzas, then five-line stanzas and finally, six-line stanzas. The early Urdu marsiyas flourished under the Adil Shahi dynasty (1490–1687) of Bijapur and the Qutub Shahi dynasty (1518–1687) of Golconda.

In Delhi, the marsiya flourished along with other genres of Urdu poetry. Dargah Quli Khan (1708–1766), an Iranian who wrote his famous travelogue on Delhi in Persian, stated that in those days there were many ashurkhanas in Delhi where majlises were held. He has praised Miskeen, a marsiyago of Delhi. Delhi poets like Mir Taqi Mir (b. 1723–24; d. 1810) and Mirza Raf'i 'Sauda' (b. 1706–07; d. 1781) not only wrote ghazals, masnavis (long poems in rhyming couplets) and qasidas but also composed marsiyas that merit attention. The marsiyas of Mir Taqi Mir dwell upon the larger purpose of shahdat (martyrdom). He has stressed the religiousness and piety of Imam Husain, his love for peace and his indifference to worldly honours.

## Prominent Elegy Writers of Awadh

In 1775, Asaf-ud-Daula moved Awadh's seat of governance from Faizabad to Lucknow. As the ruling class was predominantly Shia, the observance of Muharram ceremonies gained ground. There were a good number of poets in Lucknow who lived in the eighteenth century and have left behind numerous marsiyas, most of which are in manuscript form, but a few have found their way into anthologies. Two of the greatest Urdu marsiya writers, namely, Mirza Salamat Ali 'Dabir' and Mir Babar Ali 'Anis', lived in Lucknow in the nineteenth century. They took elegy writing to unsurpassed heights. Two other poets of note were Mir Khaleeq and Miyan Dilgir. Besides these four, there was also one Mirza J'afar Ali 'Fasih', whose published marsiyas are extremely rare and are said to have been published from Lucknow in two volumes. He was born in Faizabad in 1781 and died in Makkah sometime between 1846–47 and 1852–53. In poetry, Fasih was a disciple of Shaikh Imam Bakhsh 'Nasikh' (d.1838), and had relations with the royalty in Awadh including Nawab Ghazi-ud-Din Haider, Nawab Muhammad Ali Shah and other noblemen.

In addition to the profusion of gifted Muslim marsiya writers in Lucknow, there was also a host of meritorious Hindu marsiya writers. In his book *Hindu Marsiyago Shuara*, Dr Akbar Hyderi Kashmiri has given biographical sketches and critical assessments of fourteen marsiya poets. Among those who were connected with Awadh was Zaheen Lakhnavi, who was probably born around 1790. Although no printed marsiya of this poet has so far surfaced, Dr Kashmiri has claimed to have seen twenty-two marsiyas of Zaheen in manuscript form.

Another Hindu poet was Maharaja Balwan Singh 'Raja', the son of Raja Chet Singh of Benaras. He was probably born in 1799. He is said to have compiled his diwan of ghazals, which has not been traced. One of the raja's marsiyas along with some rubais and a salaam were published from Agra around 1869–70.

Raja Ulfat Rai 'Ulfat' was connected with the Awadh army in the times of Nawab Wajid Ali Shah. He was born in 1819–20 and died in 1854 at a very young age. He was famous for his marsiyas; although they were never printed, they are available in manuscript form in the library of the Aligarh Muslim University. Raja Dhanpat Rai 'Muhib' was the son of Raja Ulfat Rai 'Ulfat' and died in 1854. Forty of his marsiyas exist in manuscript form.

Shah Abdul Latif Bhittai (1689–1752) is considered to be the greatest of all Sindhi language poets. His poetry is steeped in mystical themes and is often compared to that of the Persian poet Jalaluddin Rumi (d. 1273). His poetry dwells in the literary consciousness of both Muslim and Hindu Sindhis. One portion of his collected poetry *Shah Jo Risalo* is called *Sur Kedaro* and recounts the martyrdom of Imam Husain. Thus, besides superb elegies in Urdu, the tragedy of Karbala has also been depicted in languages like Sindhi and Kashmiri.

Following are some of the famed marsiya writers.

## Mir Mustahsin 'Khaleeq' (b. 1768–69; d. 1844)

He was among the first extensive writers of marsiya in Awadh. Also known as Mir Khaleeq, he had a distinguished lineage. He was the son of Mir Ghulam Hasan 'Hasan' Dehalvi, who was famous for his masnavi *Sahr ul-Bayan (The Enchantment of Narration)*, and grandson of Mir Ghulam Husain 'Zahik'.[7] Thirty-four marsiyas were collected and edited for the first time under the title *Maraasi-i Mir 'Khaleeq'* by Dr Akbar Hyderi Kashmiri and published by Marsiya Foundation in Karachi, Pakistan, in 1997. The marsiyas of Mir Khaleeq are powerful in expression and diction. Although he used metaphors, at the same time his language was plain. One of his contemporaries stated that whatever Mir Khaleeq learnt was from his father Mir Hasan, and his writings were a certificate for the correct usage of the Urdu language.

One of his marsiyas describe the imprisonment of the ladies of the house of Imam Husain after his martyrdom. Yazid, the tyrannical ruler, held them in custody in Syria. The separation of the martyred Imam Husain was greatly felt by his daughter Sakina, who did not know of her father's death. She considered the jail to be her home and wept ceaselessly for her father. One night, Sakina, in the process of weeping, fell asleep in her mother's lap. She dreamt of her father and complained to him of being parted from him. This story has been aptly turned into fine verse by Mir Khaleeq.

## Mir Muzaffar Husain 'Zameer' (b. around 1777; d. 1855)

Mir Zameer was another significant marsiyago. He died in Lucknow during the reign of Wajid Ali Shah. He elaborated on the structure of the elegy, which included some of the following elements:

a) Chehra (countenance): This covers features like scenes of mourning, the state of the night, the impermanence of life, relations between a father and son, the travails of travel, the poet praising his own poetry, hymns to Allah, poetic praise of the Prophet, glorifying the Prophet or his companions and prayers, etc. These features are some standard introductions to the elegy.

[7]He was a contemporary of the famous Urdu poets Sauda and Mir, and was renowned in Delhi for his satire and humour in poetry.

b) Sarapa: This is a complete description of the hero, including his physical qualities, his pre-eminence and stately position. The hero is he who does good in the narrative. With reference to Muharram, the heroes were typically Imam Husain's companions.

c) Rukhsat: Here, the hero seeks permission to depart for battle and takes his leave from his friends and relatives, especially from Imam Husain. This is a very trying time for the hero, and emotions involving love for parents, brothers and sisters and sons and daughters come into play.

d) Aamad: The hero arrives at the battlefield on his steed, resplendent in his battle gear. Here even the horse of the hero is described and applauded. This is a splendid moment and is portrayed to underline bravery, valour and the demeanour of the warrior, which causes a stir and tumult in the enemy's camp.

e) Rajaz: The hero eulogizes the bravery and exploits of his ancestors and describes his skill in warfare. The poet Mir Zameer, for example, not only dwells on the courage and dauntlessness of Imam Husain but also acclaims the eminence and greatness of the Imam.

f) Jang: The real battle is described, including how the hero faces a tough adversary. Here his horse and sword are extolled. The descriptions also include praise for the discipline of the forces of Imam Husain.

g) Shahdat: The martyrdom of the hero at the hands of the enemy after being wounded in battle is depicted. The essence of the elegy is the martyrdom of the associates of Imam Husain and the great Imam himself.

h) Bain: This is the lamentation by his associates, particularly women, over the body of the hero. This is usually depicted through heart-rending and anguished verses.

Although Mir Zameer left quite a body of elegies, his published marsiyas came to us in a single volume comprising fifty elegies. This volume was published several times by Awadh Akhbar Press, Lucknow, and was finally also brought out by Naval Kishore Press in 1898.

**Lala Chhannu Lal or Miyan 'Dilgir'** (b. around 1780; d. 1847–48)
Another important writer of elegies in Urdu was Lala Chhannu Lal, a
kayasth of Lucknow, who converted to Islam and took the name of Miyan
'Dilgir'. In poetry he was a disciple of the famous Urdu poet Shaikh
Imam Bakhsh 'Nasikh' (1772–1838). It is said that he changed his religion
because of his great devotion to Imam Husain and after that he confined
his poetry to marsiya writing. He was welcomed in the court of Nawab
Saadat Ali Khan (b. 1757–58; d. 1814). After the death of the Nawab,
Chhannu Lal became a Muslim when Ghazi-ud-Din Haider came to the
throne in 1814. Dilgir is among the few marsiya writers of Lucknow
whose collections were published. His works were compiled in six large
volumes, consisting of about four hundred marsiyas, between 1885 and
1897, and published by Naval Kishore Press in Lucknow.

Dilgir's marsiyas contain very realistic descriptions of battles. He
applauds the adroitness of the sword. His scenes of lamentation are
touching. He frequently dwells on the impermanence of the world.
He crafted lines like: '*insaan se hai sibaat ziyad hubab ko*' (a bubble
has more constancy than a man's life), '*aamaal ke siwa nahi kuch sath
jayega*' (it is only your deeds that will go with you from this world)
and '*kitne hi mehr wa mah zamin me nihan hue*' (how many suns and
moons, that is, illustrious people, have finally found refuge under the
earth). Like other marsiya writers, Dilgir placed the characters of the
Karbala tragedy within the context of Lucknow society and the social
customs he described were largely Indianized, with little indication of
their Arab origin.

**Mir Babar Ali 'Anis'** (b. 1803)
Anis was born in the Gulab Bari area of Faizabad, to Mir Khaleeq, who
has been mentioned above. The education of Anis included a reasonable
acquaintance with Arabic, and a thorough knowledge of Persian. Urdu
was his handmaid. Anis was also interested in the Awadhi language and
Indian traditions. He took lessons in horse riding and fencing and was
well versed in the fine practical details of these skills. Mir Anis started
writing poetry at about the age of thirteen and was a disciple of his
father, Mir Khaleeq. Early in his career, he also wrote a few ghazals,
a very small number of which have survived. He composed poems in

verses of six lines to commemorate the sorrowful month of Muharram. According to Naubat Rai Saxena 'Nazar', the famous Lucknow poet of the twentieth century, Mir Anis would take several days to refine his lines of poetry. He took the utmost care to select appropriate words, which involved thoughtful deliberation. Even while Anis was in Faizabad, his elegies were famous in Lucknow and connoisseurs were collecting copies. At that time—during the reign of Nawab Nasir-ud-Din Haider—Lucknow was the nerve centre of azadari and there were stalwarts like Dilgir, Mir Zameer and Mir Khaleeq himself who were the stars of elegy writing and recitation.

The prolific poet Syed Ali Muhammad 'Shad' Azimabadi (1846–1927) of Patna has described a majlis to which Anis had invited the renowned ghazal poet Khwaja Hider Ali 'Atish' (d. 1847). After the recitation, Atish is said to have stood up and praised Anis, calling his compositions the apex of elegy writing, which could not be outdone.

Syed Amjad Ali 'Ashahri',[8] an early biographer of Mir Anis, witnessed the public recitation of an elegy by Mir Anis. He admitted that he had never beheld such felicity of expression. It seemed as if an old enchantress was sitting among young boys, weaving magic at will, capable of shifting moods and making people weep. Syed Farzand Ahmad 'Safeer' Bilgrami (d. 1834–35), a disciple of Mirza Ghalib and a devotee of the elegies of Mirza Salamat Ali 'Dabir', once listened to an elegy by Anis and in the second verse the following lines were declaimed:

*Saton jahannum aatish-i furqat mein jaltein hain*
*Shole tiri talaash mein bahar nikalte hain*

The seven hells burn eagerly in the blaze of separation
The flames leap out searching and seeking you

It is said that Syed Safeer was so absorbed in listening that he actually saw surging flames and it was only when someone cautioned him that he realized that he was at a recital by Anis.

Syed Masud Hasan Rizavi 'Adib' (1893–1975) of Lucknow, the

---

[8]Syed Amjad Ali Ashahri's book, *Hayat-i Anis*, was published by Agra Akhbar Press of Agra in 1924–25.

doyen of Urdu marsiya scholars, who spent a lifetime in the study of Anis, was of the view that Anis excelled in characterization, which was almost non-existent in Urdu. There were feeble attempts to describe distinctive characters in Urdu tales and masnavis, but even the great masnavi writer Mir Hasan Dehalvi, the grandfather of Mir Anis, could not outshine Anis in his characterization. There are certain characters in the tragedy of Karbala who have distinguished qualities and whose deeds and accomplishments have been held as the benchmark for integrity. Anis has highlighted these characters. To show the greatness of Imam Husain, Anis has shown him as an example for the world. While the characters in the elegies are Arab, their portrayal is such that they are neither fully Arab nor totally Indian. They are a combination of the two, where the Indian element is more pronounced. Readers/listeners felt that the Karbala characters were from among them and, though Arab, they were worthy of emulation by Indians.

By and large, Anis in his elegies has tried to present ethical education in a dignified manner. His best characters are never trifling, shallow or frivolous. The poetry of Anis is characterized by simplicity, clarity, fluency and eloquence. He is able to use unadorned and simple language to illustrate the most difficult as well as most elegant ideas.

Anis also had a talent for portraying combat. In his elegies, he has taken pains to describe realistic battle scenes. He presents the ferocity of the warriors, the tumult and uproar upon their arrival, the force and vigour of the combatants, the stratagems and manoeuvres of the armies and vivid descriptions of sword fights, spear combats, the art of the archer and horsemanship. The beauty of horses, their gait and swiftness are repeatedly described by Anis in different ways. Anis used technical and long-forgotten vocabulary of traditional warfare. In the battles of yore, when opposing armies were face-to-face, it was customary for a leading warrior to come forth and recite verses of his exploits and victories in battles. These verses were called rajaz and Anis has used such verses with a lot of flourish.

Anis also excelled at describing farewells and send-offs for righteous warriors. His descriptions are full of pathos. The most heart-rending part of an elegy is the lamentation over the dead and the martyred, which is technically known as bain. In fact, the essence of the marsiya is the bain. However, Anis confined himself to writing short bains and there are few long ones in his elegies. Professor Masud Hasan Rizavi 'Adib' was of the view that the audience of Anis comprised persons with delicate sensibilities, who abhorred protracted expressions of sorrow, grief and mourning. For them, a sigh or a sob was enough to rouse and stimulate them.

A few scholars have even gone to the extent of treating Anis on a par with Shakespeare (1564–1616). In fact, one Syed Ghulam Imam wrote a book *Anis & Shakespeare: A Comparison.* The author draws parallels between the poetry of Anis and Shakespeare on such subjects as remorse and anxiety, womanhood and manhood, honour, faithful and faithless companions, solitude and distress, the spiritual realm, life and death, the omens of disaster, the lamentations of a bereaved mother, homage by tears, a triumphant foe, the taunts of an enemy, descriptions of swords, praise of a horse, horsemanship, physical charm and many other human emotions, traits and feelings.

In 1857, Wajid Ali Shah was banished to Calcutta and soon Lucknow was ravaged by the insurrection (or what the British termed as the rebellion) of 1857. Peace was finally restored in Lucknow on 21 March 1858, but it was not the same city that it was before 1857. Many residents had fled from their homes and there was extensive looting and plunder. Around this period, the death of Mir Anis's daughter Abbasi Begum dealt a terrible blow to him. He also experienced financial difficulties and had to read elegies on invitations in far off cities like Hyderabad and Patna. Mir Anis died on 10 December 1874.

According to the Urdu critic Ali Jawad Zaidi, Anis '[...] universalized the tragic story of Karbala and by his great art had it incorporated into the body of Indian literature [...] The development of narrative, descriptive and reflective poetry after Anis can never be considered independently of the debt these owe to him.'

Anis is among the four great Urdu poets, the others being Mir Taqi Mir, Asadullah Khan 'Mirza' Ghalib and Muhammad Iqbal. He was a poet par excellence who rose from the soil of Awadh and spent most of his life in Lucknow.

**Mirza Salamat Ali 'Dabir'** (b. 1803-04; d. 1875)

The only challenger and competitor of Mir Anis was his contemporary, Mirza Salamat Ali 'Dabir'. His father, Mirza Ghulam Husain, was not a poet. Dabir was born in Delhi, but his family migrated to Lucknow when he was still a child. Tradition has it that when he was about twelve years old, Dabir became a disciple of Mir Zameer. When the master poet asked the child to recite a poem, Dabir declaimed the following qita:

*Kisi ka kunda nagine pe naam hota hai*
*Kisi ki umr ka labrez jaam hota hai*
*Ajab sara hai yeh duniya ki jis mein shaam wa sehr*
*Kisi ka kooch, kisi ka muqam hota hai*

Someone's name is engraved on a gem
Someone's cup of life overflows
This world is a strange inn where morning and evening
Someone gets recognition or someone leaves

Dabir's education was confined to the traditional training of those times. At a very early age, he learnt Arabic and Persian to a high degree of competence. He was very punctual in his routine and offered his prayers without fail. He possessed a prodigious memory. His handwriting was mature, controlled and firm. He was not in the habit of dotting the dotted parts of the alphabet. It has been said that Khwaja Haider Ali Atish, upon hearing Mirza Dabir recite an elegy that had no dotted letters, claimed that only Dabir could handle such a peculiar composition with such command and naturalness. Dabir was a full-time poet. While composing poetry, he would immerse himself in the spirit of the lines. Sometimes, he would go into a trance-like state, swaying from side to side.

Dabir produced almost flawless elegies in the classical style. He was responsible for bestowing marsiya writing with respectability and acceptance. This paved the way for intense and poignant poetry like *Musaddas-i Hali* by Altaf Husain 'Hali' (1837–1915), a disciple of Ghalib, and *Shikwawa Jawab-i Shikwa* by Muhammad Iqbal (1877–1938). Dabir's powerful elegies were the cornerstone for non-ghazal and non-rubai Urdu poetry and provided examples of exalted narrative and descriptive poetry. This type of poetry was quite apart from elegies and included inspirational and love poetry, which brought the diction quite close to the common people.

Dabir was gifted in his ability to play with language and despite his use of unfamiliar metaphors and analogies, his language does not come across as awkward, forced or laboured.

Like Anis, Dabir also wrote elegies on the tragedy of Karbala. Although the Urdu marsiya dwells essentially on the well-known incidents of Karbala, the greatness of Dabir is that there is no repetitiveness or monotony in his poetry. With his intense and powerful imagination, he equips the happenings of Karbala with a new vigour, breathes fresh life into the tragedy and sends waves of anguish through the listeners. Indeed, Dabir is extremely successful in depicting sorrow and mourning because he was wedded to the poetic design in his elegies to influence and affect the mind of a sensitive reader/listener. He plays with emotions and works on them with dramatic effectiveness. There is flexibility in his narration and accounts of praise of characters gradually melt into tragic circumstances, and the tone of the elegy takes a new tinge. In fact, Dabir seemed to imbibe in himself the pathos and poignancy of the great eighteenth-century ghazal poet Mir Taqi Mir.

Another characteristic of Dabir's poetry is that many of his six-line verses are like complete poems in themselves. Perhaps this quality endeared him to the great Urdu poet Mirza Ghalib, who considered Dabir to be the greatest Urdu elegy writer.

Dabir also had a talent for depicting natural scenes. The dry and barren desolation near the Euphreates is described in such realistic detail that one cannot but admire the skill of the poet. The faithful and authentic descriptions of sand particles, thorns and the warm desert air are vividly present in the elegies of Dabir.

One of the weaknesses in the poetry of Dabir is that he was too closely wedded to the Persian tradition, so much so that where everyday common words could be used, Dabir chose uncommon and less familiar words and, unlike Mir Anis, became intricate and laborious in articulation. Nonetheless, the attraction of his poetry was so great that, as in the case of Anis, Urdu-speaking persons of all shades flocked to his recitals.

Dabir attempted to perfect the Urdu marsiya and it was Dabir who took the Urdu elegy to great heights. Dabir was quite apart from other poets and was neither an extention nor just an improvement on his mentor Mir Zameer. His poetic imagery is not ornamental but envisages genuine feelings of pain, sorrow and misfortune. Unlike the major simple and direct compositions of Mir Anis, Mirza Dabir revelled in demanding, perplexing and fastidious creations and these were savoured by connoisseurs and cognoscenti.

Two years before his death, Mirza Dabir suffered tragedy in his life. His young son Muhammad Hadi Husain and his elder brother Mirza Ghulam Muhammad Nazir died. His rival Mir Anis also passed away in 1874, which he mourned. Dabir himself died on 7 March 1875.

## Mir Anis and Mirza Dabir as Contemporaries and Competitors

Elegy writers like Anis and Dabir, who confined the majority of their poetry to the tragedy of Karbala, did not write for the sake of fame and renown. Rather, their poetry provided them with spiritual contentment. Love for the family of the Prophet became a part of their character. Anis and Dabir were writing elegies in Lucknow at the time when Daya Shankar 'Naseem' (1811–45) was honing his skills on his famous masnavi and poets like Khwaja Haider Ali 'Atish' (1768–1847) and Imam Bakhsh 'Nasikh' (1772–1838) were producing the great Lucknow ghazals. So, parallel to the accepted genres of conventional Urdu poetry, a group of religiously driven poets were bringing marsiya writing to the gaze and ears of the discriminating Lucknow public. The poetry of Anis owed much to the virtuosity of Dabir, who had strengthened the foundations of great elegy writing in Urdu. The genius of Dabir lay in his brilliance and flair in composing with minimum trappings. He gave the Urdu marsiya a high literary pitch and character, and to achieve this he devised demanding and intriguing constructions in his poetry that were ingenious and metaphorically vivid. Dabir vividly illustrated that Urdu poetry was not confined to the ghazal, masnavi or qasida.

Anis possessed the delicate mind of a ghazal writer with the talent for giving much in just a few words. The elegies of Dabir had the illustrious and majestic eminence of panegyrics (qasidas). The difference in their style is illustrated by the following:

*Aaj Shabbir pe kya alam-i tanhai hai*
What state of loneliness has engulfed Shabbir

—Anis

*Kis ki zabaan se pyas ne pai hai aabru*
Whose tongue has invested thirst with prestige and distinction

—Dabir

The line by Anis conveys softness and elegance, reminding one of a line of a ghazal, whereas the line by Dabir has the grandeur and solemnity of a qasida. Dabir used poetic beauty to give weight to events and descriptions.

There was an unspoken rivalry between the poetic disciples of Dabir and Anis. Both poets also had droves of admirers, so much so that the appreciative public was divided into two streams. The devotees of Anis were called Anisiyas and the adherents of Dabir became Dabiriyas. The tussle between Anisiyas and Dabiriyas intensified during the lifetime of the poets and ended some years after their death. Of course, there were persons who appreciated both Anis and Dabir. The dichotomy of literary preferences engendered a few interesting Urdu publications, which are mentioned below.

1.  *Tanqida-i Aab-i Hayaat* (*Criticism of Muhammad Husain Azad's Aab-i Hayaat*)
    By Muhammad Riza Zaheer. Urdu Press, Lucknow. Published between 1885 and 1893.
    Zaheer was a senior contemporary of Dabir and knew the poet. The author has refuted some of the accounts of Dabir mentioned in Azad's *Aab-i Hayaat*, a classic literary commentary on development of Urdu poetry in India from sixteenth to the nineteenth century.
2.  *Radd-i Waaqiyaat-i Anis* (*Refutation of the Incidents in the Life of Anis*)
    By Sardar Mirza.
    Asah al-Mataabe, Lucknow. Published after 1908.
    Sardar Mirza counters some of the assertions made by Syed Mehdi

Hasan in his book, *Waaqiyaat-i Anis* (*Incidents in the Life of Anis*), published in 1908.

3. (a) *Hayaat-i Dabir Par Ek Nazar* (*A Look on the Life of Dabir*)
   By Syed Husain Rizavi Merathi
   Mufid-i Aam Press, Lucknow. Published in 1914.

   (b) *Hayaat-i Dabir* (*Life of Dabir*)
   By Afzal Husain Sabit
   Published in two volumes, the first volume in 1913 and second volume in 1915.

   Syed Husain regards Anis to be an outstanding poet, and has criticized the poetry of Dabir, even going to the extent of 'improving' it.

4. *Mir Munis Aur Hayaat-i Dabir Par Muhaqqiqana Rai* (*An Investigative Opinion on Mir Munis and the Biography of Dabir* )
   By Syed Muhammad Abdur Rasul Shaki
   Methodist Publishing House, Lucknow. Published in 1921.
   This small book discusses a salaam (salutation poem) written separately in the same metre by Mir Munis, the younger brother of Mir Anis, and Sultan Aliya Sultan, disciple of Mirza Dabir and daughter of Nasir-ud-din Haider, King of Awadh and Mallika-i Zamania. Mirza Dabir is criticized.

5. *Shikwah-i Shaki* (*The Complaint of Shaki*)
   By Syed Sarfaraz Husain Rizavi Khabeer Lakhnavi.
   Noor al-Matabay, Lucknow. Published in 1340 AH.
   Khabeer was a pupil of Mirza Auj, son of Mirza Dabir. In this work, Khabeer responds to the objections raised by Shaki on the salaam of Sultan Aliya Sultan.

In 1907, *Muaazna-i Anis wa Dabir* (*Comparison of Anis and Dabir*) by the Sunni Muslim religious and literary scholar Shibli Numani (1857–1914), was published by the Mufid-i Aam Press of Agra. This was the first attempt to treat the marsiya purely from a literary angle, without any sectarian or dogmatic bias. Shibli was a trained Sunni Muslim scholar who wrote a well-known biography of the Prophet as well as the biographies of many personalities of Islamic history, philosophy and literature. Shibli's

*Muaazna* covers the works of Anis and Dabir and tries to juxtapose and contrast the two great poets. We can safely say that this book changed the outlook and perspective on marsiya poetry, encouraging conscientious Urdu readers to appreciate the marsiyas of Anis and Dabir, not as forms of Shia Muslim sacred poetry, but as part of the prestigious and subline corpus of Urdu poetry.

However, Shibli's book also drew criticism because the advocates of Dabir felt that the book was partial to Anis and therefore, unfair to Dabir. The critics took the view that Shibli did not have access to the total and best works of Dabir and could therefore not present a fair comparison. This charge may be partially correct as at the time when Shibli wrote his book, the main body of Dabir's marsiyas was not readily available. A series of books criticizing *Muaazna-i Anis wa Dabir* were published, many of which critcized Shibli personally as well. These included *Al-Mizaan* (*The Balance*) by Chaudhary Syed Nazeer-ul-Hasan Fauq Rizavi, which was published around 1914 and is the most voluminous book against Shibli's *Muaazna*.

Despite the competitveness and rivalry between Mir Anis and Mirza Dabir during their lifetime, it is a well-established fact that no indecent, deprecatory or insulting remarks ever passed between the poets against each other. If they happened to meet, they met with openness, candour and warmth. They even detested any unfavourable aspersions in the company of like-minded persons. There is an anecdote that when Anis was once in Kanpur, he was asked about the quality of his elegies versus those of Dabir. Anis is said to have replied that the greatness of Dabir lay in the fact that he had acquired the art by himself whereas, if Anis had any significance in his writings, it was because writing elegies (and poetry) was hereditary and had been practised in his family for many generations.

Both Anis and Dabir, with their groundbreaking marsiyas, made an extraordinary contribution to the enrichment of Urdu literature. In fact, their skill took the marsiya to such heights that it outclassed Arabic and Persian poetry of the same genre. Thanks to these two great poets, the marsiya could compete with the other genres of Urdu shairi, namely, the ghazal and masnavi.

Mir Anis died a few months before Mirza Dabir. It is said that Dabir wept over the body of Mir Anis and stated that after Anis's death, the pleasure of recitation had gone out of his life. Dabir also recited a chronogram in which there was the following couplet.

*Aasman be mahi-i kamil, sidra be ruh al- amin*
*Tur-i sina be kaleem allah wa mimbar be Anis*

The heavens are without the glory of the full moon, the heavenly lote tree is without the angel Gabriel
Mount Sinai has lost Moses and the pulpit is deprived of Anis

## Nauha (Lamentation)

A nauha or buka is a lament. Although a nauha can be written for any distressing incident, more often than not, this versified lamentation is connected with the events of Karbala, and is linked with the marsiya, which is recited especially during Muharram. It is normally a short piece and is not as long as a typical elegy. There is no set pattern for the composition of nauhas. It can be any type of poetry relating to the tragedy of Karbala, usually written with the aim of bringing tears to the eyes of the listeners. The rendering is done by men or women (more often by women) without the accompaniment of any musical instrument. The nauha may be chanted by one person or a group in the style of an elementary raga of Indian classical music. The chanting is seldom based on a complete raga and is semi-classical and simple. While the style of reciting nauhas may have changed over the years, it has always retained the musical beat in recitation. Such taal is necessary for enhancing the pathos and acceptability of grieving. Humans can find it difficult to express personal grief in a very explicit way, except perhaps by weeping; the reciting of nauhas helps to communicate and verbalize extreme grief.

Almost all the great marsiya poets, including Anis and Dabir, produced nauhas. During the reign of Ghazi-ud-din Haider (d. 1827), the most famous nauha poet was Ghulam Murtaza (d. 1841–42). The late Professor Akbar Hydari came across several manuscripts in Hyderabad that either exclusively or partially contained nauhas. One, titled *Safinat al-Aza* (*Ship of Mourning*) was composed during the reign of Amjad Ali Shah and had a good number of nauhas.

In the time of Nawab Asaf-ud-Daula, Agha Muhammad Nadeem was a well-known reciter of nauhas. He compiled a book of nauhas called *Bahr al-Buka* (*Sea of Wailing*). After Asaf-ud-Daula had the Bara Imambara constructed in 1790–91, a mourning majlis in remembrance of Imam Husain was held on every Thursday where Agha Muhammad Nadeem declaimed nauhas. On the death of Nawab Asaf-ud-Daula in 1797, Agha Nadeem composed a chronogram in poetry, which was transcribed and hung on the tomb of the nawab.

Mirza Jafar Husain, in an article published in the February 1978 issue of the monthly *Aaj Kal,* has shared that in Lucknow complete poems were recited as nauhas and each poem was in rememberance of a particular Karbala martyr. These poems were delivered on specific days during ashura.

Though Urdu nauhas have been part of the convention of mourning during Muharram, this type of poetry does not have much literary standing. However, we do find nauhas in the works of some of the eminent writers. For example, the kulliyat of Quli Qutb Shah (1456–1513) of Golconda contains a few nauhas as also the kulliyats of some other Deccan Urdu poets.

## Soz (Dirge)

Soz is a Persian word meaning 'burning' or 'inflaming' and in an extended sense, it also connotes 'ardour' or 'passion'. In connection with elegy writing in Urdu, sozkhwani is the chanting of dirges and one who chants a dirge is known as a sozkhwan.

Usually, sozkhwani is performed by three persons. The lead reciter is assisted by the other members of the group who maintain the swara (note). The soz is recited while sitting on one's knees on a platform or carpet. The book containing the relevant poems is placed on a black pillow before the sozkhwan. The lead reciter sits in the middle and is called the sahib-i basta (the person with the bundle). On his right sits the 'bazu' (the arm) and on his left sits the 'jawaabi' (the responder). All three chant together.

Unlike marsiyas, which are part of the best of Urdu literature, the soz anthologies are not considered to be a very significant part of Urdu literature.

The art of sozkhwani reached its apex during the reign of Nawab Wajid Ali Shah, who came to the throne of Awadh in 1847. This was because not only was he an authority on music, but he was also a writer and reciter of marsiyas. Mahdi Khan Lakhnavi was a famous sozkhwan during the time of Nawab Wajid Ali Shah. His soz chanting had an alluring ornamentation of ragas (gamaka), and such was his use of forceful oscillations between adjacent and distant notes that his weaving of high notes was akin to the 'lighting of many lamps'. Mahdi Khan accompanied Wajid Ali Shah when he was exiled to Calcutta, where, during sessions of sozkhwani, the ex-king wore black garments.

There were also female sozkhwans. The three granddaughters of Mir Inshaullah Khan were employed in the palace of Wajid Ali Shah. They were named (in order of seniority) Manjhli Begum, Muhammadi Begum and Nanhi Begum and were sweet-voiced.

After the nawab was exiled to Calcutta, there was a short lull in the bustle and activity of literary and religious assemblies, and the practitioners of various arts were silenced. However, the activities eventually picked up and nawabs, jagirdars (landowners) and the gentry started patronizing marsiyakhwani, sozkhwani and rauzakhwani. These arts not only kept pace in Lucknow but spread to all regions where Urdu was prominently spoken or used.

The single Urdu book on sozkhwani by Syed Sikandar Agha records in brief the history of soz recital and gives biographical material on the lives and achievements of some sixty-six sozkhwans of India up to the present and includes several female sozkhwans.

# Cuisines, Culture and Crafts

*The region of Awadh is recognized globally for its rich cultural heritage, arts and crafts, and cuisine. Awadh rose to prominence in the middle of the eighteenth century, after the decline of the Mughal Empire in Delhi. It is the nawabs of Awadh who are credited with the evolution of Awadh as a centre of cultural renaissance. Abundance of wealth, a taste for the finer things in life and the availability of time for leisure made the nawabs great patrons of music, poetry, dance, drama and art. Hence, during their rule, Awadh attracted artists, architects, poets, artisans, scholars and khansamas who shaped the rich cultural heritage of the region. This section takes you to that golden era when creativity flourished and innovation was appreciated.*

*The first chapter of the section provides a glimpse of an Awadhi dastarkhwan, literally a tablecloth, used metaphorically to refer to the lavish spread of the Awadhi cuisine, which had a variety of dishes ranging from melt-in-the-mouth kebabs, qorma, pulao and sheermal to the soft and weightless makhan malaai and zarda. The aromatic dumpukht method too was adopted in the kitchens and dishes like shabdeg were produced. The nawabs were great admirers of culinary art and encouraged the cooks to invent unique dishes. Awadh had some famous rikabdars, or master chefs, who created artisanal foods. Skilful cooking and amazing presentation coupled with gracious hospitality defined a typical Awadhi culinary experience. Even today, Awadhi cuisine is recognized globally for its refined taste.*

*The nawabs were connoisseurs of fine fabrics and jewellery as well. They patronized the artisans who were skilled craftsmen and Awadh flourished as a centre for arts and crafts. The second chapter in the section covers some of the famous crafts* of Awadh such as *chikankari*, which is still appreciated and worn with love around the globe, *zardozi* and *kaamdani*. The *ittar* (perfume) industry too developed and a firm, Mohamed Ali, founded by Asghar Ali in 1839, earned all-India recognition for the quality of its perfumes. The chapter mentions other popular industries as well like utensil-making, papermaking and calico printing, to name a few. During their leisure time, the people of Awadh played games like the well-known chess and the lesser-known *pachisi*, *chausar* and *ganjifa*. Outdoor games and sports were played as well, such as swimming, wrestling and archery. Some unique pastimes included rearing of pigeons, cockfighting, quail breeding and kite flying.

After the decline of the Mughal Empire, like other artists, painters too started to migrate to Awadh where they received the patronage of the reigning nawabs, who loved to see themselves depicted on canvas. They not only gathered Indian artists, both Hindu and Muslim, but also brought in a few European talents. The third chapter in the section discusses the evolution of painting in Awadh. Famous painters, their styles and significant works find a place in the chapter. Awadh painting, which was an offshoot of Mughal painting, developed its own style, and was later influenced by the European style. Portraits, manuscript illustrations, nature studies, women, romance and scenes depicting the social life of that era were the favoured topics for paintings. Aquatints too supplemented the art of painting. The chapter also covers lithography in the context of Awadh. In the nineteenth century, photography came to India and gradually the demand for hand-painted portraits diminished. Famous photographers and their work are also discussed in the chapter.

# 4.

# Cuisine of Awadh

The art of cooking received a fillip during the reigns of the nawabs of Awadh, who encouraged the refinement of techniques and the creation of new recipes. Some of the legendary preparations of Awadhi cuisine have been mentioned in Abdul Halim Sharar's *Guzashta Lakhnau* and in Syed Israr Husain's *Qadeem Hunar wa Hunarmandan i Awadh*. Nawab Husain Ali Khan, a nobleman who lived during the times of Nawab Ghazi-ud-Din Haider, was very fond of pulao and at his table would be served tens of varieties of pulao. He was thus nicknamed Nawab Husain Ali Khan Chawal Walay (rice-man). It is said that with high wages as encouragement, the chefs excelled in their skills and invented new dishes. Baqerkhani and sheermal, types of breads that are enjoyed even today, are said to have been invented by Muhammadu, a cook of Nawab Nasir-ud-Din Haider. Shabdeg (made with minced meat balls and turnips) and a type of large bread, weighing about two maunds (about 75 kilos) and prepared with sugar and dry fruit, were innovated during the times of Ghazi-ud-Din Haider. It is said that Prince Azim-ush-Shan, son of the third king of Awadh Muhammad Ali Shah, held a feast in honour of meeting his samdhi (child's father-in-law) at which Nawab Wajid Ali Shah was also a guest. It is reported that there were seventy savoury and sweet dishes, all made out of rice. A cook is said to have created pomegranate pulao in which one half of each grain of rice was a shining ruby red and the other half glistened like glass. When the pulao was served, it appeared as if red and transparent gems were on display.

In a similar vein, nauratan pulao comprised rice grains of nine colours, which glimmered in all their splendour.

Among the legendary cooks of Awadh is Shaikh Haider Bakhsh, who lived in the times of Wajid Ali Shah. He is said to have died in Lucknow at the age of about ninety-five in the early 1930s. He was in the employ of Nawab Mirza Muhammad Baqir Ali Khan Bahadur of Sheesh Mahal. Haider Bakhsh claimed that he could prepare three hundred and sixty kinds of breads. One of them, reminiscent of the ear of an elephant, was made so soft that even a slight touch would break it. He also made thin crisps called tunki out of flour, water and a little sugar.

Shaikh Farhatullah was another cook from the times of Wajid Ali Shah. He lived in the Husainabad area of Lucknow and died in the early 1920s. He was skilled in making luqmi (samosa-like puffs filled with minced mutton). The luqmis were brushed with saffron. The moment a luqmi was popped in one's mouth, it dissolved and slipped down one's throat, such was the quality of his luqmis.

In mohalla Nabehra, adjacent to the imambara of Atiqullah in Lucknow, was the shop of Mirza Kababiya, which was famous for its savoury kebabs, known to be better than the kebabs made in the royal kitchens. Five seers (about 4 kilos) of minced mutton were prepared during the day and the kebab patties were sold in the evening. Each kebab was of about fifty grams, containing, among other things, saffron and fresh ghee, and was only for one paisa (one sixty-fourth of a rupee). Those were the times.

∽

There are no authoritative books on authentic Lucknow cookery. There are some old books, but they are confusing with regard to the weights and measures used. If one were to follow a recipe from one of these books to the letter, the dish would likely turn out to be a disaster. The classic Urdu and Persian cookery books therefore serve as pointers regarding the main ingredients and common sense is required to amend, modify and improve the instructions.

When reading a recipe, the taste, colour and flavour of the final fare should automatically strike the tongue, eye and olfactory functions. Any incongruous or excess ingredient should ring a bell. The overall effect should delicately hint at or suggest aromas without jarring the senses. Understatement is the secret hallmark of many tasty dishes. One should be sure of what one is eating, but it should be difficult to guess what all has gone into a dish.

Mirza Jafar Husain (1899–1989) was a connoisseur of Lakhnavi food. He authored *Lakhnau Ka Dastarkhwan*, first published in Urdu in 1980. Jafar Husain was himself a very good amateur cook, had partaken in many traditional feasts and had witnessed the twilight of Lakhnavi culture during the first fifty years of the twentieth century. He led a Bohemian life and had the good fortune to move in literary and cultured circles.

He has recorded that earlier, the common people ate when they had earned enough to buy food and there was no fixed time for meals. However, the moneyed people had established timings for their meals, although they were not rigid and were fairly flexible. When the dastarkhwan (a piece of cloth or leather spread on the ground upon which the dishes of a meal are placed) was unrolled and the persons had settled down on the floor, they continued to sit throughout the meal in the same posture. No portion of the body moved except the hand and the mouth. Each morsel was to be masticated without making any noise in the chewing.

According to Mirza Jafar Husain, no plates were laid on the dastarkhwan, but for each person food items were placed separately in bowls. However, special items like hot pulao or mutanjan (a kind of sweet and sour pulao) were placed in platters. Each prominent family had its own special dishes.

An earthen tandoor sunk in the ground and fired with burning charcoal was exclusively used for baking different types of breads. There was no tandoori chicken or tandoori mutton leg. These were innovated when the migrants from the North-West Frontier came after the Partition of India.

In affluent households, a lot of importance was given to the management of the kitchen. The superintendent of the kitchen was called the darogha-i-bawarchikhana. Under him were a host of cooks, each specializing in either meats or breads or kebabs or sweet dishes and so on. Besides the employed cooks, there were also cooks available on contract for special occasions. In fact, there were various areas in Lucknow where professional cooks resided in number, such as in Bawarchi Tolanear Agha Mir Deodhi, near Ghulam Husain Pul in Chowk, around Husainabad and in Daliganj.

Indo-Islamic culture, particularly in Lucknow and Delhi, is renowned for its hospitality. In fact, the whole geographical belt from Morocco through India, Pakistan and Bangladesh right up to Xinjiang (Eastern Turkestan, formerly Sinkiang) and then to Malaysia and Indonesia is known for the hospitality, warmth and cordiality of the people. Offering food and inviting people for a meal is a way of life in India, irrespective of religion, sex or age. One feels elated to break bread with another and it is a sign of conviviality. Even persons of poor means show no hesitation in offering the best eatables within their means. There is no flinching or shrinking from offering the best hospitality. In fact, providing food for friends is a source of cheer and joy. Compared to Oriental geniality, Western hospitality is often formal, sometimes cold, and eatables are seldom pressed upon guests. While it may be annoying when a host insists that you partake of something tasty, we must realize that what is being offered is with sincerity and without guile.

The importance given to a guest is illustrated by the fact that dastarkhwans were sometimes embellished with Urdu or Persian couplets, many in praise of guests. Two such couplets are recorded here:

*Shukr bajaaaar ki mehmaan-i to*
*Rozi khudi khurd khwaan-i to*

Accord thanks to your honoured guest
He takes his own sustenance from your tray

*Shukr kar tu apne dil mein amad-i mehmaan par*
*Rizq apna kharaha hai tere dastarkhwan par*

Give thanks in your heart on the advent of a guest
He is eating his own sustenance on your table

Although there was no code for homemakers then, a woman was generally considered an adept and proficient house manager if she could, on her own, accomplish the following simple kitchen tasks:

1. Prepare firmly set yogurt from warm milk with the help of a few spoons of a previously prepared curd.
2. Ferment strong vinegar from sugar cane or jambolina (jamun) juice.
3. Temper (bagharna) various lentils and vegetables.
4. Make well-flavoured tea or the Lakhnavi version of Kashmiri chai.
5. Smoke minced meat for kebabs or other items by placing a small bowl containing ghee and cloves or garlic in the mince, putting a glowing piece of charcoal in the bowl and covering the ingredients with a tight lid for a few minutes to give the dish a smoky aroma.
6. Prepare a tasty qorma, which was light and without heavy spices.
7. Contrive a dish of zarda (sweat saffron rice) in which the rice grains were discrete and separate.

## Basic Differences in the Cuisines of Lucknow and Delhi

The preparation of even ordinary dishes common to Lucknow and Delhi is done with more attention in Lucknow than in Delhi. In terms of the use of spices and chillies, Lakhnavi food is milder compared to that of Delhi, but the curries of Lucknow traditionally have a little more oil.

Lakhnavi food is usually served along with both bread and rice (called khushka in Delhi). The daily Muslim food in Delhi is predominantly eaten with bread, but rice is also consumed on rare occasions. It is typically cooked with green peas and a tempering (baghar) of ghee, green cardamom and clove. The Delhi dastarkhwan was sometimes laid only with rice and no bread when guests were entertained. On such occasions, the menu typically included boiled rice with green mung beans or pea pulao and other savouries.

The meat-vegetable curries of Lucknow, in which meat is cooked with a variety of vegetables, usually have a relatively thin curry that can be conveniently eaten with both bread and rice. The meat pieces are comparatively small. Many Lucknowites prefer boneless meat, or meat with a minimum of bones. Such dishes are not so common in Delhi.

# Popular Dishes of Awadh

## Curries

Instead of eating large pieces of boiled, baked or roasted meat, Indians, particularly in Delhi and Lucknow, prefer to cut the meat into small pieces and then stew them with onions, garlic, ginger and other spices. In fact, the British use the generic word 'curry' for any spicy dish with sauce or gravy. In Lucknow and Delhi and other areas having Muslim culinary traditions, the all-comprehensive word for a meat, fish or vegetable curry is saalan. The word saalan does not have its origin in Arabic or Persian and is used largely in the Urdu language. Hindi-speaking vegetarians are often not familiar with the word; for vegetable curries, the word used for the gravy is rassa. An Urdu speaker, when referring to gravy, calls it shorba (which in Persian means 'broth'). The success of saalan lies in the spices being well-cooked. The dish should have only a thin layer of ghee on top. Two folk sayings are noted here:

> Ghiya banaaye saalna, bari bahu ka naam

> It is the ghee that makes the saalan tasty, but it is the daughter-in-law who gets the credit

A beggar used to chant the following couplet:

> Mung ki daal mujhse khai na jae
> Bakri ka shorba bata do hakimji

> I do not relish mung lentil
> Hakimji prescribe mutton shorba for me

Qorma: According to Mirza Jafar Husain, among meat dishes, qorma is the tastiest, most exquisite and most gratifying fare. However, its preparation requires great skill. He was of the view that if one were to eat good qorma even twice a day for a long period, one would not grow tired of it. He narrates that in 1925, he was able to employ a cook who had worked during the Nawabi days. When he was asked what dishes he could cook, he replied: 'O Miyan! What is there to eat besides qorma and chapati? I will feed you only with qorma and chapati and I do not cook anything else.' The man was employed and he worked for Jafar Husain till 1931, when the cook died. During the five or six years that he was with him, the cook routinely served qorma for lunch and dinner, but Jafar Husain did not tire of it. He longingly remembers the taste of the qorma of his late cook, which he found no parallel for anywhere. Jafar Husain remarks that while many hotels and households claim to cook a dish called qorma, it is rarely the real qorma. The authentic qorma is a very different dish and is difficult to come by.

Jafar Husain treated the cooking of qorma as a very delicate operation. He was of the opinion that a good qorma was best prepared from about half a kilogram or so of shanks. The dry spices should be pounded to a very fine powder, which in the days before the coming of electric grinders, used to be done with mortar and pestle. Some people went to the extent of sieving the powdered spices through a fine cloth.

*Qalia:* According to Platts' dictionary of Urdu, classical Hindi and English first published in the nineteenth century, qalia is broiled meat dressed with anything. In other words, it is a meat or chicken curry with lots of gravy. It goes well with bread and also plain boiled rice. The ideal accompaniment to a dish of qalia and rice is a salad of onion rings, tomato slices, beetroot slices, cucumber/gherkin slices, and carrot and radish pieces in salt, pepper and lime juice.

Qalia should have a watery gravy, which is sufficiently spiced and savoury. It is never thick. The pieces of meat or chicken should be quite tender.

*Meat-Vegetable Curries:* The meat-vegetable curries feature meat cooked with a vegetable like potato, parwal (a species of cucumber), tinda (Indian round gourd or apple gourd), green peas, colocasia (arbi/ghuiyan), banda (large-sized colocasia) or turnip.

The meat-vegetable curries have almost the same basic ground spices—red chillies, dry coriander, turmeric, fried/raw onions, garlic-ginger paste and a final dash of 'hot spices' (garam masala, which typically comprises toasted and ground black pepper, black cardamom, cumin seed, clove and cinnamon). Yogurt is always used as the basic marinade. However, despite the common ingredients, each type of meat-vegetable curry has its own distinct flavour, the diversity in taste being provided by the vegetable used in the curry.

A variation of the meat-vegetable curry features vegetables stuffed with meat. The flesh of the vegetable is partially scooped out and it is then filled with cooked minced meat. The stuffed vegetable is tied together with a thread and fried on a griddle. After frying, these stuffed vegetables are put in a chilli-coriander-turmeric gravy. The vegetables typically used for this dish are karela (bitter gourd), brinjal, green capsicum, tomato, tinda and snake gourd.

There are three basic requirements to make a meat-vegetable curry savoury: first, the raw onion rings (along with ginger and garlic paste) should be fried with a minimum of oil till they turn golden brown and crispy. Second, the meat itself is to be fried in the same oil till it sheds some of its moisture and changes colour. And third, the ground spices are then fried with the onions, ginger and garlic paste, and meat in the remaining oil till the spices (masala) separate from the oil; care must be taken not to burn the spices.

The favoured mutton for meat-vegetable curries is usually of the shoulder (dast, meaning hand in Persian) and the meat surrounding the backbone, called put (actually pusht, meaning back in Persian). For trotter curry, which is comprised mainly of bones, some households also add neck pieces to the curry to yield additional meat and bone juice. The meat of the loins is usually used for steaks and for making mincemeat. Breast pieces have the bones of the ribs, with little meat, which is stuck to a lot of fat. The breast meat was once the preferred meat for pulao/biryani, but with the rise in calorie consciousness, put and dast are now more typically used.

Broadly speaking, up to the 1950s, there was a preference for mutton and beef over chicken in Awadh. Chicken was not commonly eaten. Those households that kept poultry would sometimes make chicken qorma. Even for weddings, dinners or large parties, mutton or beef was predominantly used. It is only now that chicken, particularly Leghorn chicken, has become a common and affordable delicacy for a large number of Indians. While the price of chicken has dropped considerably, the price of mutton has touched a new high.

*Qima/Keema:* Pounded or minced meat called qima (also keema) is a very popular dish in Awadh. In fact, it is popular among all Indian Muslims. Typically, qima is cooked dry and is well-fried, without vegetables. One of the main ingredients of qima of any type is cut green chillies, which add to the piquancy of the dish and lend it a distinct flavour. In quite a few households, besides green chillies, fresh coriander leaves are used as garnish. Fried qima may also be cooked with vegetables. The most popular vegetable used is green peas. Other vegetables used are potatoes (in halves), spinach (palak) and other green leafy vegetables, capsicum, seeds of sem (flat or broad bean), cabbage, cauliflower and fried pieces of colocasia (arbi/ghuiyan), among others. Sometimes, fried qima is garnished with slices of boiled eggs or pieces of omelette. By and large, dry qima is popular. However, when there are guests, prudent housewives can make a little go a long way by adding a little gravy and vegetables, creating a sumptuous dish with many servings.

*Ishtoo:* This is another popular meat dish. A sort of dry stew, it is usually made of mutton or chicken pieces cooked with a lot of onions, red chillies (powdered or broken into pieces), tomatoes, and garlic and ginger paste, and is garnished with cut green chillies and fresh coriander leaves. The name ishtoo suggests that it was not originally an Indian dish, but an Anglo-Indian modification.

*Jhalfrezi:* Indian Christians, particularly in Awadh, have been cooking this dish for decades. It is not mentioned in *Hobson-Jobson* by Yule and Burnell or in *Sahibs, Nabobs and Boxwallahs* by Ivor Lewis or in *Hanklyn-Janklin* by Nigel B. Hankin. However, the word 'jalfrezi' is listed in the

*Concise Oxford English Dictionary* and the ingredients are the same. The etymology of the word is interesting: jhal is 'hot' and parhezi (modified to frezi) in Persian/Urdu means 'fit for one under regimen'. So jhalfrezi was supposed to be a dish suitable for an ailing person on a diet. Lizzie Collingham, in her book *Curry: A Tale of Cooks and Conquerors* states that the British in India sometimes curried cold meat, and this is the original jhalfrezi that appears in Anglo-Indian cookery books as cold meat fried with lots of onions and chillies. Some restaurants serve a garbled style of the jhalfrezi, which includes a variation made only of vegetables.

*Shabdeg:* In his cookery book, Mirza Jafar Husain has described the difficult process of preparing shabdeg. This dish was common in Awadh and used to be cooked in households during winter on at least one or two occasions. The turnips were peeled, halved and rubbed with salt and turmeric powder and kept in the sun. Cooking was started in the evening. Minced meat balls were prepared with spices typically used for kebabs. Onion rings were browned and taken out from the pot, in which the usual chilli powder, turmeric powder, coriander powder, ginger and garlic paste were then fried in the remaining oil till the spices separated from the oil. Steaks were added and fried with the spices. The minced meat balls (kofta) and turnip pieces were also added. Some water was included. The pot was sealed with dough and allowed to cook on a low wood fire throughout the night. Care was taken to ensure that the water did not evaporate completely, leading to burning of the meat. In the morning, fried onions were ground in yogurt and were mixed in the pot with 'hot spices' (garm masala) and mace powder. Lime juice was also sprinkled on the dish.

The cooking of shabdeg is a delicate business, which involves using the dumpukht method. The real taste of shabdeg comes from its prolonged slow cooking and the nurturing of its cooked juices.

*Haleem:* This is also known as hareessa (a kind of thick, well-cooked porridge) or khichra. It is made of meat, wheat, barley, lentils, spices and a little oil and is cooked for several hours to produce a thick, tasty gruel. Haleem is a very old dish and is said to have been a favourite of the Prophet Mohammed. The dish, in one form or another, is common throughout the Muslim world. Each country has its own recipe and accompaniments. According to tradition, the dish was invented by the sixth-century Persian King Khosrow. It is typically eaten during the Ramadan and in winter.

Haleem is also known as khichra, particularly in Lucknow and Awadh, because it has a consistency similar to that of the popular Indian dish khichri made of rice, lentils and spices. Incidentally, the word khichri is the original Indian name of the slightly different Anglo-Indian dish called kedgeree.

Hareessa is similar to haleem and is a porridge-like preparation of wheat, mutton and other grains.

## Kebabs

In Awadh, kebab could refer to chunks of meat, or minced meat grilled on a skewer, or minced meat patties fried on a large, flat hot plate called mahitawa. There is a Persian manuscript titled *Kitab-i Tasavir-i Sheeshagaran Vaghairah Wa Bayan-i Aalat-i Aanha* (*The Illustrated Book about Makers of Glassware, etc. and a Description of the Tools*) by one Ghulam Yahya in the Van Pelt Library of the University of Pennsylvania that has been translated and edited by Mehr Afshan Farooqi as *Crafting Traditions: Documenting Trades and Crafts in Early 19th Century India*. In this book, the following types of kebabs have been mentioned:

*Dumpukht kebab:* Here a small fattened goat with the skin, intestines and offal removed is filled with nuts like almonds, pistachios, raisins, etc. The meat is pricked and curd mixed with ground coriander seeds, garlic, onions, black pepper and other spices is rubbed on it. The meat is then put in a large copper vessel and cooked on a slow fire. When the meat is tender, saffron is added.

*Fish kebab:* Minced fish is combined with cream, roasted chickpea flour, poppy seeds, black pepper, onions, ginger juice and 'other customary spices'. A little saffron is also added. The mixture is divided into round patties, which are fried on a flat griddle (mahitawa). The mixture can also be put on skewers and grilled on a charcoal fire.

*Kofta kebab:* Minced meat is mixed with the usual spices such as onion, coriander seeds and curd. The mixture is shaped into balls and then fried.

*Pasanda kebab:* Steaks are thoroughly pricked and rubbed with curd and ground spices including coriander seeds, chickpea flour, cloves and garlic. To make the kebabs fragrant, hot coals are put along with the marinade between two covered dishes and a few drops of ghee are dropped to smoke the meat. After a few minutes the meat is put on iron skewers and roasted on a charcoal fire with a basting of ghee. The recipe advises that the holes in the kebab made by the skewer should be stuffed with finely ground white cardamom and black pepper.

*Shami kebab:* The literal meaning of shami is 'Syrian'. Shami kebabs are usually made with minced meat mixed with various spices such as red chillies, black pepper, green and black cardamoms, cumin, mace (javatri), cinnamon, clove, along with raw onion rings, garlic and ginger and a few spoons of toasted gram dal. The whole mixture is boiled in water till the minced meat is tender and the water has dried up. No tenderizer like raw papaya or kachri (dried, marble-sized melon) is used as the boiling of the minced meat with spices and herbs is sufficient.

The boiled mixture is then ground and patties are prepared with a filling of raw onion rings, chopped green chilli and a few leaves of coriander or mint. The patties are usually shallow fried and served with chutney.

The process of preparing shami kebabs is described in the book *Crafting Traditions*. The minced meat is first boiled with chickpea pulse. When the meat is tender, the usual spices along with baalai (clotted cream) are added and the mixture is ground. It is then divided into patties. Instead of frying the patties, they are placed in a large copper vessel, the mouth of which is sealed with dough. It is then cooked on a coal fire.

*Gilani kebab:* This is made from the shoulder meat of a goat. Dried figs, ginger and other spices are added to curd to make the marinade. This kebab is roasted on a skewer. The author also recommends serving these grilled kebabs in a gravy prepared from clotted cream, white cardamoms, cloves and other spices.

*Chicken kebab:* In *Crafting Traditions*, this is referred to as murgh kebab. A chicken is stuffed with spices and cooked in the same way as dumpukht kebabs.

*Shahpasand kebab:* Minced meat is mixed with egg whites, black pepper and other spices, ginger paste and toasted chickpea flour. This mixture is divided into patties, which are then fried on a griddle.

*Bandhnu kebab:* These are very similar to shahpasand kebabs, the difference being that the mixture is shaped into balls and stuffed with nuts. Sometimes, these kebabs are stuffed with an egg yolk and fried. They are then called baiza (egg) kebabs.

*Galawati kebabs:* The word 'galawat' means 'melting' or 'becoming very tender'. To prepare this kebab, minced meat is mixed with various spices and herbs, but it is not boiled as in the case of shami kebabs. Rather, ground green papaya is added to the mixture, which is then allowed to sit for a while to make it tender. The patties are then made and shallow fried on a flat griddle. The galawati kebabs are garnished with raw onion rings, pieces of green chilli and fresh coriander or mint leaves. The famous kebab seller Tunda (which means a person with only one arm) of Lucknow popularized the galawati kebab, which had a distinctive aroma. Haji Murad Ali, alias Tunday Kebabi (c. 1877–1967), so called because he had only one arm, migrated from Bhopal and set up shop in Lucknow. The original shop is still in the former red-light area of Chowk, in a narrow lane that connects to Victoria Street. The patrons of the prostitutes would buy the kebabs, which were wrapped in leaf donas (packages), and then go up the dingy staircases to visit the women of the night. In his interesting autobiography *Yadon ki Barat* (1972), the famous Urdu poet Shabbir Hasan Khan 'Josh' Malihabadi (1898–1982) has mentioned the Tunday kebab shop in his reminiscences about old Lucknow. Riaz, the son of Haji Murad Ali, was in his eighties at the time, and presently, the shop is being looked after by his son Muhammad Usman. The recipe for Tunday kebab was patented in 1995. While the shop in the Chowk area of Lucknow is the original one, several outlets were later opened in various parts of Lucknow, including in Aminabad, Kapurthala, Alambagh, Kanpur Road, Telibagh, Rahim Nagar and Saharaganj.

## Other Kebabs Popular in Lucknow

Besides the shami and galawati kebabs, a number of other kebabs are also favoured in Lucknow. There are kebabs that are cooked over hot coals on skewers (seekh) and are a form of shish kebab. Both minced meat and boneless meat pieces, marinated in spices and herbs, are cooked on skewers. There is also thegola (ball) kebab, in which a big ball of spiced minced meat is put on a skewer and tied with a thread to prevent it from falling on the burning coals.

Another type of kebab is the handi (pot) kebab. The spiced minced meat is cooked with a little oil in a pot and fried well till it starts emitting a pleasing aroma and turns reddish-brown. I have not seen this kebab in restaurants, but it is cooked in some households.

Liver is also cooked as a type of kebab. Pieces marinated in spices and a little oil are roasted in very hot ashes. After cooking for a few minutes, the pieces are removed with a pair of tongs and the ash is brushed off before eating.

## Vegetarian dishes

Not all dishes of Lucknow are meat dishes. In fact, a variety of victuals are based on grains or vegetables. Some of these dishes are described below.

*Mungchhi:* Pulse of gram, mung or pea is boiled in water till it becomes tender. It is then ground and mixed with powdered dry coriander and red chilli, onion-garlic-ginger paste and salt along with fried onion rings. Small balls of the mixture are then made and steamed in a piece of cloth kept across the mouth of a pot of boiling water. The steamed mungchhies are cooked in a curry made with various spices including chillies, turmeric, coriander and garam masala. Tempering is done with fenugreek (methi) or kasuri methi.

*Riconch:* Green pulse (mash or urad) without the skin is soaked in water for a few hours and then ground into a paste. The paste is mixed with powdered dry coriander and red chilli, ginger and garlic paste and salt along with onion rings. The mixture is shaped into oblong pieces, which are put in boiling water for a few minutes till they become firm and well-cooked. They are cut into pieces and then cooked in a curry similar to the mungchhies described earlier.

## Breads and Rice Preparations

The Awadhi cuisine, although famous for its qormas and qalias, is incomplete without the humble roti and rice. But the Lakhnavi appetite is seldom satisfied with the regular versions of the same. Thus, they offer a wide variety of options to choose from when one is looking for an accompaniment to go with the delicious curries.

*Khameeri roti:* Bread made in the tandoor/tandur (correct form tannoor) or on a hot griddle is prepared using leaven (a raising agent) made of flour and water in which wild yeasts (khameer) have been encouraged to grow by keeping it warm and allowing it to ferment for a few hours. Leaven is commonly known as sour dough culture. A piece of a previous batch of dough is used to introduce natural yeasts and other microorganisms in a new batch of dough, to raise the dough and flavour it. In this process, the dough turns sour and bread prepared from it is fluffy and very slightly sour in taste. It goes well with red meat and chicken dishes with gravy. Today, what passes for khameeri bread is often not the real thing as typically sodium bicarbonate is used as a raising agent, which often causes flatulence.

*Sheermal and baqerkhani:* Sheermal and baqerkhani are very popular breads of Awadh. Although very similar, there is a difference between the two. Sheermal is prepared with refined flour (maida), milk, a little sugar, ghee and leaven. Baqerkhani is made using almost the same ingredients, except that leaven is not used. Also, baqerkhani is thicker. Both sheermal and baqerkhani rounds are baked in an earthen oven (tandoor). The cooked rounds are taken out and while still hot, saffron mixed with milk and keora water are brushed over the bread. However, baqerkhani is also sometimes cooked on a large flat griddle (mahitawa) placed over hot coals and while cooking, the rounds are pricked with a sharp needle to leave holes. After being cooked, both sides of the baqerkhani rounds are brushed with a mixture of milk, egg white, saffron and keora.

*Taaftaan:* This is similar to sheermal, although it does not have as much ghee as required for sheermal. It is a drier and lighter form of sheermal. At breakfast, taaftaan was the bread for eating with shabdeg or nihari.

*Tandoori roti:* Rounds of wheat dough (mixed with a little khameer, or sour dough, prepared overnight) are placed one by one on a handheld cotton cushion. The baker leans into the hot clay oven (tandoor) and slaps each round of dough on to the heated walls of the oven. A few minutes later, using two long iron rods, he pulls out well-baked, slightly puffed rotis. The bread has the right amount of fresh flavour, char and is slightly sour because of the khameer.

In Lucknow, tandoori rotis were usually prepared by professional bakers of bread called nanbais, who received measured quantities of wheat flour from housewives. While preparing the bread, the nanbais mixed khameer into the dough. In the evening, the housewives would collect the number of tandoori rotis in proportion to the weight of the flour they had sent. This practice does not exist anymore. If tandoori rotis are required, they are purchased from small hotels. Unfortunately, they are now baked using baking soda (sodium bicarbonate) instead of sour dough. There is a world of difference in the taste of tandoori rotis made with khameer and those with baking soda. The khameeri rotis are extremely tasty, especially with qorma and other curried dishes.

*Besani roti (bread made from gram flour):* Besani roti was one of the most popular breads in Awadh. It is said to have been a favourite with Nawab Wajid Ali Shah. It is made with gram flour mixed with wheat flour in the ratio of 3:1. The flour mixture also contains a little salt, onion rings and chopped green chillis. The dough is rolled out into thick circles, which are then toasted slowly on a hot griddle. When the bread is brown and crisp, it is rubbed with a little pure ghee. Some people mix a little ajwain (carom seed) in the dough. Hot besani rotis are sometimes eaten with garlic chutney. The recipe for garlic chutney is very simple: pods of garlic are ground with red chilli and a little salt and water. When the mixture is ready, a little fresh lime juice is added and the garlic chutney is ready to eat.

*Waraqi parathay (layered paratha):* To prepare this, refined flour (maida) is mixed with pure ghee and a little salt. Some milk is then added with a little hot water and the whole is mixed to form a homogeneous dough. When using a kilogram of flour, the dough is divided into four parts and left to rest for some time. Each of the four parts is then further divided into five units, and each is rolled out into a roundel. The five roundels are then placed one on top of the other and rolled into a bigger roundel. Care is taken to ensure that each roundel is sufficiently joined with the other. The roundel is then brushed with ghee and milk and fried in a griddle over a low flame. When it browns on one side, it is turned over and treated in the same way. When taken out of the griddle, the paratha is brushed with a mixture of milk, saffron and keora.

*Birhai parathay (paratha with a pulse filling):* A birhai paratha is a paratha with a filling of mashed green gram or powdered gram pulse mixed with spices. As an alternative, hung yogurt (without water) along with spices can also be used as a filling.

*Biryani:* In Persian, biryan means 'fried'. Biryani is a dish of boiled rice and a thick meat, chicken or fish curry, arranged in alternating layers. The dish is sprinkled with saffron or edible saffron colour, creating a mix of white and yellow grains. According to Alan Davidson in *The Oxford Companion to Food*, it is essential to use basmati rice and to lace the dish with saffron. The use of basmati rice in biryani can be troublesome for some cooks because even a slight over boiling results in the rice grains coalescing or becoming glutinous. Therefore, biryani rice is boiled till it is about three-fourths cooked and after arranging the meat curry and rice in alternating layers, the whole dish is put on dum, that is, the vessel is covered with a lid, which is then sealed with wet dough, and the dish is cooked in its own steam for ten minutes or so with hot coals placed under the vessel and on the lid. Just before eating, the dough seal is broken and the biryani is served piping hot on a wide plate. For commercial purposes, cooks sometime avoid using basmati rice and use a fatter variety of rice called sela. Sela rice grains remain separate after routine cooking, but in Awadh, sela rice biryani is considered inferior to the basmati rice biryani. However, I have found that sela rice is commonly used in households in Delhi for biryani.

# Dumpukht

Dumpukht is a Mughal technique, which implies 'to breathe and to cook'. The Persian/Urdu word 'dumpukht' literally means 'steam-cooked'. It involves finishing the cooking of partially cooked food in steam so that the aromas of the herbs and spices are released into the food and retained. It has been mentioned in Abul Fazl's *Ain-i Akbari*. The following is narrated by Lizzie Collingham in her book on curries:

> In Lucknow, the *nanbais* set up enormous cooking pots filled with meat and vegetables that were sealed with lids of dough and placed on hot coals. In this way the food cooked slowly and hungry labourers could be fed at a moment's notice with tender pieces of meat that fell from the bone. When he went to inspect the work, the nawab is said to have found the smells rising from the steaming pots so inviting that he ordered the palace cook to learn the recipe from the *nanbais*. *Dum pukht* was also applied to good effect to a dish of mutton and turnips that was brought to Lucknow by Kashmiris, looking for alternative sources of employment now that the Mughal court was in decline. The Lucknavi cooks made mutton meatballs which were put in a pot known as a *deg* with the turnips. The pot was sealed with a pastry lid (dumpukht) and cooked on a slow fire throughout the night (*shub*). Lucknavis still eat *shub deg* for breakfast, tender after a long night of slow cooking.

This is one of the best descriptions of dumpukht cooking. There are no separate recipes for this type of cooking. The technique is often used for making biryani, which is steamed in a sealed dish after three-fourths of the cooking process is over.

To explain the process of dumpukht, let us take the example of cooking biryani. The rice is not fully cooked and is a little firm (not quite edible), i.e., three-fourths cooked, when it is layered with the meat curry and other ingredients to compose the final biryani. Before the biryani is served, the pot is covered with a lid, which is tightly sealed with flour dough. The pot is kept on a low flame for five to ten minutes. This results in steam being generated inside the pot. It tenderizes the rice and meat and allows the flavours to impregnate the dish. The biryani is taken out from the pot just before eating and it is this first serving of the biryani that has the best taste. Dumpukht food is tastiest just after the opening of the dumpukht pot. It is thus best consumed immediately after the dough seal has been broken.

However, there are certain dishes that are said to taste better after they have been kept overnight. Examples include head and trotter curry (siripaye), liver curry, brain curry and fish curry. These dishes are said to mature overnight.

*Pulao/yakhni pulao:* This is also a dish of meat and rice, but here the meat is cooked with spices tied in a porous cotton bag (like bouquet garni). When the yakhni (the soup-like liquid with pieces of meat) is ready, raw, washed and soaked rice is added to it and it is cooked till most of the liquid has evaporated. Usually, pulao or yakhni pulao is not coloured with saffron or flavoured with keora. It has its own spicy aroma with a touch of fennel (saunf) and green cardamom.

The typical accompaniment to pulao/biryani is raita (sliced cucumbers or grated boiled water gourd or baked brinjal or sliced onions or even small pieces of pineapple mixed in spiced yogurt). In Delhi, people prefer to eat pulao/biryani with a chilli-garlic chutney.

**Desserts**

While a lot of innovation had gone into the main course dishes of the Awadhi cuisine, attention had also been endowed on the sweet tooth of the nawabs. Some of the classic desserts of Awadh are descried below.

*Kheer:* This is a sweet, thick pudding made of milk and whole rice grains garnished with dried fruits. It is also known as gulatthi.

*Firni:* This is similar to kheer, but the differentiating factor is that the consistency is that of rice paste, rather than whole grains of rice.

*Yaqooti:* A gruel is prepared by boiling very fine flour (maida) in a lot of water; the mixture is stirred till it acquires the consistency of milk. It is then left to rest for about fifteen minutes, allowing the feculent matter to subside. The clear water is then poured off. The residue is called nashasta (thick gruel) and is similar to slaked lime in texture. About 250 grams of nashasta is mixed thoroughly in about 2 litres of milk and heated on a low flame. As the milk mixture starts boiling, it needs to be constantly stirred. Once it thickens, about 250 grams of sugar and a little almond paste are added. Keora or rose water is used for flavouring.

*Muzaafar:* This is made from rice (basmati) of superior quality. The recipe calls for one portion of rice and two portions of sugar. The rice is boiled till it is almost cooked, i.e., the grains remain slightly hard. Sugar syrup is prepared separately with saffron or edible yellow colour. In another pot, sufficient ghee is heated with green cardamom and clove till the spices begin to sputter. The sugar syrup is then poured into the pot. The partly boiled rice is added to the syrup and the whole mixture is cooked in steam till all the syrup has been absorbed by the rice. The finesse in using just the right amount of syrup comes from experience. Too much syrup makes the rice soggy and too little syrup makes the rice stiff.

To make the muzaafar or zarda (sweet yellow rice) rich, sieved clotted cream (baalai) mixed with a little milk may be added to the mixture of syrup and rice and cooked for a few minutes. Finally, keora water is added and the dish is garnished with fine slivers of almond and pistachio.

It is advisable to add a little lime juice to the final zarda. Alternatively, pieces of pineapple or a few pieces of karaunda, a fruit preserve, can also be put in the muzaafar.

Muzaafar is also made from vermicelli (sevian) instead of rice. The recipe is the same as that for rice muzaafar. However, the vermicelli should be toasted before cooking and should be of a very fine variety.

It is to be noted that among Muslim sweet dishes, although the ingredients used to prepare muzaafar are simple, it is one of the most difficult dishes to prepare well. The best muzaafar is when each rice grain or vermicelli strand is well-cooked, firm and separate. The dish should not be soft, soggy or too stiff.

*Shahi tukra (royal morsels):* Originally, this dessert was prepared with pieces of sheermal. Nowadays, slices of bread are used. The bread is fried in ghee, which has been tempered with green cardamom and clove. Care should be taken to lightly brown, and not burn, the bread. Milk is boiled in a shallow pan. The fried slices of bread are then immersed in the boiled milk till almost all the milk has been absorbed by the bread. In a separate pot, sugar syrup is prepared with a touch of saffron or edible yellow colour. When the syrup is of the required consistency, it is poured in the mahitawa (flat griddle) on which the bread has been placed. Sieved clotted cream and khoya (inspissated milk) are then gently spread on the slices and drenched with keora. The mahitawa is kept covered over a low coal fire so the milk and syrup are gradually absorbed completely and the topping of cream and khoya turns a light brown. Garnishing is done with thin slivers of almond and pistachio and keora water is sprinkled over the pieces.

## Special Ingredients in Awadhi Cooking

**Common ingredients**

*Gold and silver foil:* In Awadh, sweet dishes and sweetmeats were decorated with very fine gold or silver foil. It was claimed that eating the foil strengthened one. Nowadays, gold foil is hard to find and silver foil is also not very common. Indeed, people are sometimes hoodwinked into using beaten aluminium foil.

*Rose and keora water:* Keora water is extracted from the screwpine, which is a species of Pandanus odoratissimus. It is found mainly is the Ganjam district in Odisha state. The flowers and roots of this plant are used for making keora water. Keora is used for flavouring both savoury and sweet dishes like biriyani, qorma and zarda (sweet saffron rice).

Typically, rose water is made by soaking rose petals in water, and it is used for sweet dishes exclusively.

**Exotic ingredients**

Mention should also be made here of a few interesting ingredients that are no longer used. In particular, three expensive ingredients of Awadhi food have long vanished because of their cost or restrictions on hunting.

*Amber:* This is fossilized resin, familiar for its use in jewellery, but it used to have a role in food and drink. It was sometimes added, in powdered form, to dishes and beverages not only in Europe but also in Muslim cookery. It was sometimes confused with ambergris.

*Ambergris:* It is an intestinal secretion of the cachalot or sperm whale, sometimes found in the animal itself but more often floating in the sea. It was used in culinary practices for perfuming food, mostly confectionary.

*Musk:* It is the glandular secretion of the musk deer and other animals. It has a strong smell. It was used in discreet quantities or in diluted form to flavour dishes, along with rose water and other flavourings.

*Stale chapati pieces cooked with sugar and ghee (a poor man's sweet dish):* I do not know whether this dish has ever had a name. It was cooked in the days when in Muslim households, thin, large-sized chapatis were cooked over a dome-shaped griddle (tawa). The leftover chapatis of the night before were broken into small pieces. Ghee, along with green cardamom and clove, was heated in a griddle till the spices sputtered. The chapati pieces were put into the ghee and stirred constantly to gradually brown them. After a few minutes, a little sugar was poured into the mixture, and stirring was continued till the sugar caramelized and coated the chapati pieces in a transparent film. When the smell of toasting started coming from the griddle, the dish was ready. A little keora was then added.

*Puris with a filling of sweet potato:* Sweet potatoes (yam), when in season, are boiled and mashed with a little sugar and powdered green cardamom. This is mixed in the wheat dough. Puri roundels are rolled out and fried in oil. These puris are delicious with a cup of hot tea.

*Shakar Amba:* A small amount of refined oil is heated in a large griddle or pot and tempered with green cardamom and clove. To this is added a full measure of toasted semolina (suji) and a half measure of sugar. Sufficient water to make a thick gruel is added and the mixture is cooked on a low fire. After about ten minutes, a few slices of raw mango (without skin) are added. The dish is kept on the fire till the semolina is well-cooked and the mango pieces are tender. The final dish should be a thick, sweet gruel. Finally, keora water is added. Shakar amba is best eaten warm.

Instead of raw mango, any firm and slightly sour fruit like pineapple, apricot, pear or peach can be used.

*Namash:* This is a fluffy, milk-based dessert, quite foamy in appearance, which literally melts in the mouth. It is similar to a light syllabub. It is not very sweet. On a wintery morning, it is a delight to consume. In Lucknow, very few people now refer to it as namash. The hawkers who vend it usually carry a round tray with a large earthen dish containing the namash, which is usually covered with a compartmentalized glass cover. A portion of the cover is open and the required quantity of namash is ladled out into a leaf or earthen cup for the customer. This delicacy can only be prepared during the Awadhi winters and is not available in summer.

Mirza Jafar Husain has described the method of preparation of namash. In the evening, about two litres of good buffalo milk are heated on a low flame, ensuring that it does not boil. For this purpose, the milk is constantly stirred. When a good portion of the milk has evaporated, the pot is removed from the fire and the milk is allowed to cool. However, the milk continues to be stirred so that no layer of cream (baalai) forms on the top. When the milk has cooled sufficiently, it is kept out in the open, covered with a fine cloth, for the whole night, so it can be naturally cooled with the falling dew. Early in the morning, the dew-cooled milk is churned with a little sugar till it become frothy. The froth is removed and kept in an earthen pot. Powdered green cardamom, saffron and keora water are sprinkled on it and the namash is ready for consumption.

Namash is sold by hawkers in Lucknow under the name makkhan malaai (butter cream). In Delhi, it is known as daulat ki chaat (the chaat of wealth). Pamela Timms, in her book *Korma, Kheer and Kismet: Five Seasons in Old Delhi* has this to say about namash: '[it] resembles uncooked meringue and the taste is shocking in its subtlety, more molecular gastronomy than raunchy street food, a light foam that disappears instantly on the tongue, leaving behind the merest hint of sweetness, cream, saffron, sugar and nuts; tantalizing, almost not there.' The season for namash is short, starting when there is perceptible cold in the air and ending well before spring, i.e., the Holi festival.

*Baalai or malaai ka paan:* Another sweetmeat typical of Lucknow is baalai ka paan or malaai ka paan. White sheets of porous, clotted cream (baalai), two to three millimetres in thickness, are cut into palm-sized pieces and brushed with sweetened saffron water. On this are put a few pieces of sugar candy and chiraunji or some other nuts (a few pinches only). The clotted cream wrap is then folded into the shape and size of a paan and is ready for eating. The baalai ka paan is soft, slightly sweet and melts in the mouth. Each paan is usually covered with chaandi ka waraq (silver foil). The hallmark of the Lakhnavi baalai ka paan is that it is light, uncluttered and simple without being overburdened with khoya (inspissated milk) and nuts.

## Popular Drinks

*Aam ka panna (sherbet of raw mango):* Raw mangoes are quite prevalent during the hot summer in Awadh. A savoury drink is made from raw mangoes (kairi).

The raw mangoes are roasted on a wire over the flame of a gas stove till the skin is soft and somewhat burnt and the flesh is pulpy. The skin is then removed and the pulp is mashed; the stone is discarded. Water is then added and the mixture is strained. The other ingredients are added and the mixture is then chilled. When serving, crushed ice and a few drops of lime are added.

*Kashmiri chai of Lucknow:* The Kashmiri tea or chai in Lucknow has little in common with the qahwa of Kashmir, except that the main ingredient is green tea. It is perhaps called Kashmiri chai because it was made by persons of Kashmiri origin in Lucknow. It is a rich, sweet and spicy tea, which goes well with sheermal.

It takes time to prepare Kashmiri chai and normally people do not make it at home. The Kashmiri chai sold in Lucknow on the street corners of Aminabad and Chowk is a very inferior, commercial variety.

## Miscellaneous dishes

*Clotted cream (malaai/baalai):* This cream is prepared by boiling milk continuously on a low flame so that layers of cream form. The cream crust on the top is spooned off or the thin layer of cream is picked up by means of two thin sticks. This is repeated a number of times as the layers keep forming on the milk. The various crusts are kept in a flat dish, one on top of the other, till there is a one or two-inch thick layer of clotted cream. This cream is called malaai or baalai (in Lucknow). It is usually eaten with sweet dishes like zarda (sweetened saffron rice), carrot halwa and shahi tukra, among others. Cream was also sieved and put in qorma, or eaten by itself with certain salty dishes like fried steaks.

The great scholar Rasheed Hasan Khan in his book *Zaban aur Qawaid* devoted a whole chapter to the usage of the words malaai and baalai. According to Rasheed Hasan Khan, Maulana Muhammad Husain Azad in his very interesting history of Urdu literature, *Aab-i Hayaat*, has stated that the common Urdu word for clotted cream, i.e., malaai, was changed to baalai by Nawab Saadat Ali Khan, who reigned from 21 January 1778 to 11 July 1814. The source of this information is not clear. However, all the compilers of the later Urdu dictionaries have mentioned the same thing. Further, Rasheed Hasan Khan has said that in the famous Persian lexicon *Farhang-i Jahangiri* of 1608–09 (in the edition published from Lucknow and edited by Syed Muhammad Sadiq Ali Ghalib Lakhnavi), the Persian word charbak means the same thing as malaai and baalai. However, Rasheed Hasan Khan remarked that all the manuscripts of the Persian dictionary that he had seen contained the word malaai and not baalai. It appears that the older word malaai was treated as chaste and pure Urdu, particularly in areas where the Delhi style of Urdu was spoken. The word baalai gained currency in Lucknow and though not rejected by the Delhi Urdu speakers, it was never really used in Delhi.

Abdul Halim Sharar in *Guzashta Lakhnau* also addressed the controversy regarding malaai and baalai and tried to defend the Lucknow usage. Sharar clarified that Nawab Asaf-ud-Daula of Awadh was very fond of clotted cream and he termed it baalai because it lies on top of the milk, balai meaning 'top'. Sharar claimed that the word baalai gained such popularity that the word malaai was used only by rustics. An erudite scholar of Urdu from Lucknow, Syed Zamin Ali Jalal Lakhnavi (d. 1909) in his Persian book *Ganjeena-i Zabaan-i Urdu* took a contrary view that the word malaai was correct and baalai was wrong.

Mirza Ja'far Ali Khan Asar Lakhnavi was a staunch Lakhnavi and in his dictionary *Farhang-i Asar* opposed Jalal Lakhnavi's view and stated that it was not a question of right or wrong but of usage. In Lucknow, the purists used only baalai and not malaai. At the time of Asar Lakhnavi, the word baalai was in vogue only among Urdu speakers. This controversy sums up the finicky attitude of the Urdu-speaking persons of Lucknow.

*Khagina:* This is a dish of scrambled eggs. The white and yolk of the eggs are beaten together. Onion rings, salt, green chillies, pieces of ginger and a little red chilli powder (if desired) are added. The mixture is poured into a griddle with a little oil and is stirred constantly while being cooked. Khagina is eaten with bread or parathas.

## Rikaabdars of Lucknow

A rikaabdar, according to Platts' Dictionary, was a keeper of the dishes, steward, butler, and a manufacturer and vendor of preserves, pickles and other things. Some of the famous rikaabdars of Lucknow are discussed here.

Nabi Bakhsh Lakhnavi was famous for his raw mango preserve. He prepared a preserve of unripe raw mangoes in which the green peel of the mangoes was retained as is, giving an impression of raw mangoes in syrup.

Peer Ali Lakhnavi lived during the reign Nawab Nasir-ud-Din Haider. He was famous for making a sweetmeat that looked exactly like a real pomegranate—the kernels of the pomegranate, its rind and the membrane between the kernels all looked real. Each seed was made from almond, the red flesh surrounding the seed was made from pear juice while the rind and the membrane were made from sugar.

Shaikh Ikram Ali started working under Nawab Ghazi-ud-Din Haider and worked till the reign of Wajid Ali Shah. For Nawab Ghazi-ud-Din Haider he prepared breads from sugar candy and from almonds. He is also said to have made preserves out of gold and silver coins, which retained the engravings on them and which could be read.

Shaikh Fida Ali was a rikaabdar during the reign of Wajid Ali Shah and lived in Sarai Mali Khan in Lucknow. He once placed a transparent lampshade on a table before a British dignitary. He put a lit candle inside the shade and after a little while, he extinguished the candle, broke a piece off what appeared to be a glass shade and started eating it. It was later learnt that the entire lampshade had been made out of sugar candy.

Nawab Syed Mahmud Husain Khan Bahadur Tabaatabai was a master at peeling raw mangoes in a way that the marks of the knife did not leave any blemish or unevenness on the fruit. The peeled mango was smooth and glossy, and, if placed among eggs, could not be distinguished from them.

Nawab Mirza Mehdi lived during the reign of Nawab Wajid Ali Shah and belonged to the family of Salar Jung. He lived in Musahib Ganj in Lucknow. He would squat on the parapet of a well and peel a plum so expertly that the skin would form a thin strip without a break.

## Sweetmeat Sellers

In Awadh, sweetmeats were typically not prepared at home. Rather, shops specializing in preparing sweetmeats catered to the requirements of the public. These were the original halwais (confectioners). One of the most famous shops, Ram Asray, was located in Baanwali Gali in the Chowk area of Lucknow. It was set up by one Gulabji and named after his son Ram Asray. Among his famous sweets were malaai gilauri, sohan halwa and lal peda. The malaai gilauri was made from small sheets of clotted cream that were folded like a paan, containing a filling of dry fruit. A clove was used as a holding stud. The sohan halwa was a pretext for consuming ghee. As one ate it, the flavour of pure ghee pervaded the mouth. The lal peda was made from khoya, sugar and cardamom powder. The khoya was heated and browned with the sugar till it took on a dark red colour. Ram Asray still has a branch near Hazratganj in Lucknow.

Another well-known sweetmeat seller was Husaini, from the times of Nawab Nasir-ud-Din Haider, renowned for his halwas, particularly sohan halwa and habshi halwa. The latter was of a darkish colour, soft in consistency and laden with ghee. Despite it being heavy in calories, habshi halwa was superb in taste. It is still made in one or two shops in Delhi, Rampur and Lucknow.

Sandila in Hardoi district, close to Lucknow, was famous for its delicious laddoos, which were named after it. The laddoos were created by one Atma, and made by three succeeding generations. The laddoo was made with the flour of chickpea or mung, to which was added sugar, ghee and sometimes nuts, and the dough was shaped into small balls. The balls were then rolled in crystalline sugar. These laddoos continued to be sold till the 1970s in Sandila and at railway stations in the region in earthen pots. They were extremely popular. Sandila laddoos have now more or less disappeared.

## Beliefs and practices associated with food in Awadh

For Muslims, all food is generally permitted, with four exceptions: pork, blood, any animal that has died of itself and any animal that has been slaughtered in the name of anyone other than God.

Further, in India there is a belief that certain things should not be eaten either together or one after the other. These combinations include rice and watermelon, rice and sattoo (roasted flour of parched barley and gram), and fish and milk.

There are several sayings of Prophet Mohammed regarding food, some of which are mentioned here:

1. The stomach is the home of disease and abstinence the head of every remedy. So make this your custom.
2. In the sight of Allah, the best food is a food shared by many.
3. Eat when you desire and refrain when you desire.
4. Allow your food to cool before eating, for in hot food there is no blessing.
5. When you eat, take your shoes off, for then indeed your feet can have some rest.
6. Less food, less sin.

A notable Urdu book on the cuisine of Lucknow is *Pukhtwa Paz* (*Cookery and Cooking*) edited by Shaikh Ahmad Ali, who was the chief chef in the kitchen of Prince Mirza Baqir Ali Khan. The editor provides some necessary instructions at the beginning of the which are listed here:

1. Food, to be nutritious and digestible, should be cooked on a proper flame as cooking speedily on high flame destroys the nutrition value and spoils the taste.
2. Food that tires the teeth in chewing needs to be avoided and should be consumed in small quantity.
3. A light diet should be followed, so as to leave space in the stomach for water and air.
4. It is better to take a few morsels of food to satisfy one's hunger, and the amount of food consumed should be such that it can be digested in about three hours.
5. Breakfast should be of wheat porridge with milk and sugar.
6. Meat should be taken in small quantities and instead soup or meat gravy (shorba) should be preferred.
7. Vegetables cooked with gravy are better and tastier, particularly turnips, lady's fingers and turai (luffa acutangula).
8. Fresh and juicy fruits like guava, pomegranate, apple, grape, mango, orange, banana, etc. should be consumed.
9. The next meal should not be taken unless the previous one has been digested.
10. Whether you are ill or healthy, it is better to treat the body with a proper diet instead of medicine.

11. A slow-cooked meal is better for the body than the consumption of digestives or electuaries.
12. Medicines should be taken only when there is dire necessity. One should regulate one's stomach with the correct diet so that one does not suffer from hypochondria. If one's digestion is proper, one will not fall sick.
13. The kitchen and the pantry should be extremely clean and free from dirt, flies and insects.
14. Utensils should be very clean and the ingredients used should be fresh and of good quality.
15. It should be ensured that food is cooked on coals made from gum acacia (babool), tamarind (imli) or flame-of-the-forest (dhak) wood.
16. A mixture of spices and herbs should be used after three or four hours so that the ingredients have matured and have attained their right temper.
17. After a dish is cooked, the pot should be kept on very low heat and the food should be consumed within three to four hours.
18. The taste of a dish depends upon cooking it on proper flame and heat. A dish can turn out badly because of improper attention during the various stages of cooking.

Some observations on good food according to Lucknowites are given as follows:

1. Tasty food is the result of the right ingredients in the correct portions.
2. Flavours should be suggestive and not too pronounced.
3. The skill of the cook plays a large part in the proper preparation of a dish.
4. Like working on anything else, cooking also requires devotion, dedication and love. Half-hearted labour while cooking seldom yields good results.
5. As the saying goes, too many cooks spoil the broth, so it is advisable that cooking should be done by one person and should be supervised by a single person.

6. It is always better to cherish simple meals, which leave a lasting effect of their taste.
7. Too elaborate a recipe and too many ingredients do not necessarily lead to the creation of an ideal dish.
8. The minimum of ingredients result in some of the best dishes.
9. Recipes should not be copied verbatim from a cookery book and need to be modified according to taste and requirement.
10. Rely on handed-down recipes, but do not depend on them.

Cooking was indeed an art form in Awadh, and Awadhi cuisine is characterized by a very balanced and delicate combination of spices, herbs and condiments.

## In Praise of Awadhi Taste

To attract customers, food vendors would devise rhymes in praise of various food items. Some of these are documented in 'Lakhnau Ke Pheri Wale' by Azhar Masud in the October-November 1994 issue of the monthly *Naya Daur*. A few of them are noted here.

Paan-sellers announce:

*Paan kehta hai ki sookh ke mar jaunga*
*Ai lab-iyaar agar tune na chooma mujhko*

The paan claims that it will wither and die
If it does not touch the lips of the beloved

*Yun to har waqt jaan haazir hai*
*Lekin is waqt paan haazir hai*

My life at all times is at your disposal
However presently, only paan is at your service

*Yaad apni tumhain dilate jayen*
*Paan kal ke liye lagaate jayen*

Let me leave something to remind you of me
I leave paans for the morrow

A vendor claims that nothing is left of his eatables for the next day:

*Na bache na kutta khaye*
*Baasi rahe na kutta khaye*

Nothing is left, not even for the dog
There is nothing to become stale, not even for the dog

A qulfi seller in Lucknow claims:

*Bikti agar footpath par*
*Naam hota 'top' par*

If [my qulfi] was sold on the footpath
My fame would have been on the top

A seller of ice announces:

*Barf hai ya kisi mashooq ke ghar ki silhai*
*Lag ke seene se ye karti hai kaleja thanda*

Is this a slab of ice or a grinding stone of my beloved's house?
It fastens to my chest and keeps my vitals cool and refreshed

A nanbai (bread maker) asserts:

*Ik chapati ke waraq me sab waraq raushan hain*
*Ik rakabi me hamein chaudah tabaq raushan hue*

The thin leaf of a chapati illuminates all leaves
The fourteen vaults [of heaven] lit up in a plate

The kebabi (kebab seller) is not far behind:

*Kebab-isee khhain hum, karwatein harsoo badalte hain*
*Jo jal uthta hai yeh pahlu, to woh pahlu badalte hain*

I am a kebab on a skewer and I keep turning on all sides
If one side starts burning, I roll to the other side

The Lucknow gherkins, which are gathered in the summer, are prized if they are long and thin. They are used in salads or even cooked in a curry with meat. The gherkin sellers cry out:

*Kakriyan le lo. Majnun ki pasli or Laila ki ungliyon ki tarah patli*

The gherkins are as thin as Majnun's ribs or as lean as the [delicate] fingers of Laila

On a shop that avoided giving credit, this couplet was displayed:

*Aap se tark-i muhabbatha mein manzoor nahi*
*Qarz dene ka hamare yahan dastoor nahin*

I detest abandoning my loving ties with you
However it is not our custom to give credit

Lucknow is famous for its nihari, a breakfast curry usually made from trotters and cooked on a slow fire overnight. Even now the most famous nihari shop in Chowk is that of Rahim. A ditty on the shop runs as follows:

*Hazaar niamat-i parwardigaar hain paye*
*Purani Dilli se chal karke Lakhnau aaye*
*Janab Hazrat-i Ghalib jab yahan aaye*
*Pakarke baith gaye woh Rahim ke paye*

Trotters are among the thousands of graces of the Lord
They trudged their way from old Delhi to Lucknow
When Hazrat Ghalib [the poet] came here
He sat and caught hold of Rahim's [delicious] trotters

∽

With the generous patronage of the nawabs of Awadh, Awadhi cusine became synonymous with innovation and creativity world over and has over the years fascinated many.

# 5.

# Art, Games, Skills and Pastimes

L ike all centres of culture, Awadh also had its own traditions of arts
and crafts. The nobility and the gentry both patronized artisans and
ingenious and skilled persons, and encouraged the developments
of a variety of arts and crafts, with their associated skills and techniques.
Though low-paid, the handicraftsmen and skilled workmen had no
alternative but to follow the trade that their ancestors had pursued.

Each region had its own speciality in the arts and crafts practised
there. The products were generally the result of the collective efforts
of several persons, or trade guilds, rather than the result of individual
endeavour. Of course, there was a master craftsman who gave the final
touches to the product. Crafting any item was a task of patience and no
effort was spared to bring about a high standard of artistry.

Prior to 1857, Lucknow was a centre for handicrafts and artisanship.
Handmade articles of many varieties were made with skill and finesse.
Embroidery and chikan work was done with expertise. Printed cloth was
also famous—patterns were made on wood blocks, which were carved out
with precision. The printing of the cloth was done in a neat manner with
wooden dies. The darning of shawls was another widespread profession
and so was dyeing. The making of tazias—the replicas of the tomb of
Imam Husain made out of wooden splints and thin, coloured paper—
was a seasonal occupation during Muharram, the Muslim month of
mourning. The ivory work of Lucknow was famous. On smooth, thin
pieces of ivory, coloured paintings in the Mughal style were done.

Not all artefacts were made from costly materials. Everyday articles of utility were produced from humble raw materials. The earthen pots for drinking water were made by ordinary potters. Pots made in winter were more porous and cooled the water most in the dry summer heat. Awadh was also famous for clay reproductions of common fruits, which were so realistic in shape and colour that they could be mistaken for real fruits. The last such artisan of clay fruits closed shop quite recently in one of the by-lanes of Aminabad.

Other articles of common use were also made, such as cane baskets, stools for various purposes, rolling pins and boards, wooden sandals or clogs (kharaun) and twine ropes for weaving beds. Goatskin bags for water carriers and leather buckets for drawing water from wells were articles then in use and were commonly made. Scrubs called jhama, used for cleaning household utensils, were made in Jhawai Tola in Lucknow. The making of firecrackers was another cottage industry.

During the reign of Nawab Ghazi-ud-Din, boats and barges shaped like peacocks, fish and horses were in use. The litters mounted on the backs of elephants were made in such a way that they could be rotated to face the hunted animal. Tents were fabricated in such a way that they could be fixed without the aid of ropes and pegs. A peculiar item in use among the rich was a back-scratcher in the shape of a paw with a handle, which gave solace to itchy backs.

Many bookbinders practised the art of 'chikbandi'. If the edges of the pages of a book had been damaged, but the text was intact, the pages were trimmed, ensuring that the text was aligned in the centre of each page. Then, fresh strips of paper for the four margins were affixed to the page in such a way that it was difficult to tell that the margins had been added to the original page. The book was then bound with the full text and new edges, which merged seamlessly with the old paper. This is now a lost art.

Syed Israr Husain's book *Qadeem Hunar wa Hunarmandan-i Awadh* (*Ancient Crafts and Craftsmen of Awadh*) offers an interesting account of various craftsmen and persons of artistic achievement of Awadh. Unfortunately, the book is now difficult to find and has not been reprinted. Some of the material of this chapter is based on it.

# Popular Crafts of Awadh

## Fashioning of ornaments

Mallika Jahan, the second wife of Nawab Muhammad Ali Shah, had a pa-zeb (an anklet comprising a chain with small bells attached to it) made of pearls and gems. The goldsmith had designed it in such a way that if the ornamental flowers were opened and the metallic threads pulled, the anklet expanded to cover the area of the calf from the ankle to the knee, like a stocking. If a particular nail was removed, then the ornament collapsed to the size of the usual pa-zeb around the ankle.

Mallika Jahan also had a beautiful hookah (hubble-bubble) that was said to weigh the equivalent of 1,700 silver rupees and was made entirely of silver. When it was smoked, a bird on the hookah lifted its neck, flapped its wings and chirruped. The bird sat on a tiny mango tree, also made of silver and embellished with enamelled green mangoes. The base had four figures, one in each corner, and in the centre was a bigger figure, which was holding the hookah. When the pipe of the hookah was kept in the hand of the central figure, it looked as if it was smoking the hookah.

In the soldering and joining of small pieces of jewellery, Babu Bengali of Model House in Lucknow was unequalled. Ashraf of Darzi Baghiya in Jhawai Tola was adept in enamelling. In engraving, the ancestors of the goldsmith Omkar of Raja Bazaar were famous. Muhammad Ismail Khan was renowned for fine and delicate work (sadahkari) in jewellery. Hameed of Kaptaan Kuan, and Muhammad Umar of Sarai Ma'ali Khan, were known for making silver rings.

## Chikankari (chikan embroidery)

According to Sheila Paine, the author of *Chikan Embroidery: The Floral Whitework of India*, chikan '[…] is a type of whitework, that is to say white embroidery on white fabric, with predominantly floral designs executed on fine cotton with untwisted threads of white cotton, rayon or silk. It is embroidery that has evolved over centuries, reaching its peak in the late nineteenth century in Lucknow.'

In old Persian dictionaries, chikan has been described as 'embroidery with gold thread' and later as 'embroidery in various kinds of silk on garments and other items'. The word 'chikan' also appeared in the 1806 edition of *A Dictionary, Persian, Arabic, and English* by John Richardson[9] which gives the definition as 'a kind of cloth worked with the needle in flowers'.

During Nawabi times, chikankari became more popular than jamdani because chikan was within the reach of all. Jamdani is muslin cloth on which flowers and other motifs were woven and not worked. The cloth was extremely fine, soft and delicate and usually the thread was imported. For chikan work, the thread was made in India and the work was done on tanzeb, a cloth of the nainsukh variety, but finer.

Chikan work was once so fragile that it survived only a few washes. Very high quality of chikan was produced in Lucknow in the nineteenth century, and at the commencement of the twentieth century, chikan work was one of the most important industries of Lucknow. According to *Lucknow Gazetteer* (1904) by H.R. Nevill, the chikan industry in Lucknow was in the hands of two firms: Aashiq Ali and Yusuf Ali in Chowk, who had won a medal at the Indian and Colonial Exhibition of 1886.

Sheila Paine points out that chikan embroidery is not done on a frame and the fabric '[...] is stretched taut around the index finger and wedged between the other fingers to hold it in position. The little finger is swung across the palm to restrain the fabric still further. The thumb is free and used to control the progress of the needle.'

Chikan embroidery comprises the following basic stitches:[10]

1. **Tepchi:** A long stitch, which is the basis for further stitches and is used to make the outline of the motif.
2. **Bakhia:** A small stitch worked as a herringbone and used for petals, leaves and flowers. It is of two kinds: ulti (reverse) and sidhi (straight).

---

[9]John Richardson (1740/1741–1795), Orientalist, FAS of Wadham College, Oxford, was the editor of the first Persian-Arabic-English dictionary in 1778–1780.
[10]Details of the different stitches of chikan embroidery can also be found in the book *Romancing with Chikankari* by Veena Singh (New Delhi: Tushar Publications, 2004).

3. **Hool:** An eyelet stitch, which often forms the centre of a flower.
4. **Zanjeera:** A set of chain-like stitches used when long lines are required; it is typically used to outline a petal or a leaf.
5. **Rahet:** It comprises a line of backstitch or stem stitch on the right side of the fabric. It is commonly used in dohra (double) bakhia.
6. **Banarsi:** A twisted stitch used to create a decorative outline for a motif; it is worked on the right side of the fabric.
7. **Phanda:** A millet-shaped stitch for making patterns.
8. **Murri:** A minute stitch, used for creating a small embossed leaf or petal.
9. **Jali:** A minute buttonhole stitch worked by pulling apart the threads of the cloth.

## Zardozi and kaamdani

Average or affluent families typically celebrate occasions like marriages or other festivals for which it becomes necessary to wear clothing that is decorated, embellished or ornamented with costly embroidery. Two centuries ago, a wasteful expenditure of the rich included zardozi work on the screens of palkis, on cushions and couches, floor coverings, pillows, tents and pivilions, curtains and shawls.

Zardozi is embroidery in gold and silver threads on makhmal (velvet), silk or kamkhab (brocade). Kamkhab is a heavy fabric with a pattern of silk, gold or silver threads or their combinations. Colonel Henry Yule's *Hobson-Jobson* gives the name kincob to gold brocade. According to this dictionary, kamkhab in Persian means 'less sleep'; the cloth was perhaps thus called because it is rough to the touch and would therefore prevent one who uses it from sleeping. In her book *Traditional Fabrics of India*, Jaishree Manchanda notes that '[...] in older days, silver and gold wires of such extreme fineness were drawn that the entire fabric could be woven from them, producing literally a cloth of gold. The three main patterns of kamkhab were beldar (scrolled), bootidar (sprigged) and shikargah (hunting scenes).

Zardozi is extensively used to decorate ladies' garments, such as saris, ghararas, kurtas, blouses, etc. In earlier times, and even now, sherwanis, turbans and waistcoats were also decorated.

Initially, zardozi comprised working with gold thread on silk or velvet. Later, badla zari and kalabattun thread came into vogue. Badla zari is flattened gold or silver wire. It is stiff and difficult to weave. Kalabattun is silver thread covered with gold or silver. Today, zardozi work has been modified to include silk thread, plastic and beads, with gold and silver thread being substituted with aluminium thread.

Kalabattun work is easier than badla zari work and is called 'dokht' (sewing). A later development was marori work, which involves twisting the thread. However, the most important innovation in zardozi in India has been salma-sitara embroidery, which comprises small stars between bands of embroidery. Another variation of zardozi work in Uttar Pradesh is banat, which involves gold or silver edging and is called gota or gota-kinari in Awadh. Kaamdani is another type of zardozi work, but from the point of view of craftsmanship, it is more like chikankari. Kaamdani is also known as muqqaish or badla. Badla is a fine wire that is coated with gold or silver and used for embroidery. Weaving on cloth makes the design come up above the cloth. Dots on the cloth with the wire create a beautiful effect. Kaamdani work is also usually done on ladies' garments.

In zardozi work, the pattern is transferred to the cloth and the cloth is fixed and tightened in a wooden frame called karchob by means of cords. The embroidery on the stretched cloth is done with a needle similar to the type used for crochet, and is fixed to a wooden handle.

If one were to walk through the lanes in the old parts of Lucknow, one would see the open doors of rooms where workers are engaged in zardozi work on fabrics stretched within rectangular wooden frames. As in chikan work, here also the workers, mostly male, are semi-literate or illiterate, and are often taken advantage of by the main traders. Although zardozi fetches a decent price in the domestic and international markets, the unorganized artisans earn a pittance. There is no fixed minimum wage. Low wages also affect the quality of work. Designs that are less time consuming to execute are preferred.

## Dyeing of fabrics

As in other parts of India, women in Awadh revelled in wearing colourful clothes. In earlier times, cloth was dyed at home or by professional dyers who were called rangrez or rangsaaz. The skilled dyers not only prepared their own colours but also used mordants to fix the colour to the material so the colour would not fade on subsequent washings.

An Urdu tract titled *Kashf al-Limas fi Sabgh al-Libas* (*The Art of Dyeing Fabrics*) by Khwaja Muhammad Ashraf Ali Lakhnavi contains the ingredients for compounding about thirty-five dyes, all based on herbal and natural products. No chemical dye has been indicated. Some of the colours prepared as a result of the mixing of various components had interesting names, and are listed below:

| | | | |
|---|---|---|---|
| 1. | Surkh (red) | 2. | Anar (pomegranate) |
| 3. | Gulabi (pink) | 4. | Naranji (orange) |
| 5. | Zard (yellow) | 6 | Siyah (black) |
| 7. | Kasni (chicory-coloured) | 8. | Badami (almond-coloured) |
| 9. | Sharbati (pale yellow) | 10. | Firozi (turquoise) |
| 11. | Zamurrad (bright-green) | 12. | Sabz (green) |
| 13. | Kahi (grass-coloured) | 14. | Mongiya (coral-coloured) |
| 15. | Arghawani (crimson) | 16. | Ambwa (unripe mango coloured) |
| 17. | Karanja (light brown) | 18. | Fakhtai (fawn) |
| 19. | Kakrezi (dark purple) | 20. | Tusi (dark brown) |
| 21. | Kishmishi (raisin-coloured) | 22. | Kokai (lotus-coloured) |
| 23. | Unabi (carnation) | 24. | Uda (purple) |
| 25. | Shifalu (peach-coloured) | 26. | Anguri (grape-coloured) |

# Popular Games of Awadh

### Indoor games

*Pachisi:* Pachisi was once 'the national game of India played in palaces, zenanas and public restaurants'. Pachisi is also called pasha. Pachisi is played on a board, and two or four persons can participate in the game. The board is in the shape of a cross and was traditionally made of embroidered cloth. Each arm of the cross is divided into twenty-four squares, i.e., three rows of eight squares.

Each player sits in front of one arm of the cross. In his essay titled 'Notes on "Pachesi" and Similar Games, as Played in the Karwi Subdivision, United Provinces' published in the *Journal of the Asiatic Society* in 1906[11], E. de M. Humphries states as follows:

> [each player's] object is, starting from the centre of the board down the middle and up the left-hand row of his own arm of the cross, to move his four 'men' all round the board, finally bringing them down the right hand side and up the middle row of his own arm and landing them in the triangular space in the centre. The first to do this wins the game.

The game was played with several cowries, which fell with the slit uppermost from a group of seven that were 'thrown from the hand without the use of any dice-box.' Pachisi was played mostly by women.

According to the essay 'The Four-Arm Race: The Indian Game of Pachisi or Chaupar' by I.L. Finkel in *The Art of Play: Board and Card Games of India*, edited by Andrew Topsfield, the origins of the game are obscure and it has been associated with 'courtly circles and the aristocracy'. Two or four persons can play pachisi. William Crooke has written in his book *Things Indian: Being Discursive Notes on Various Subjects Connected with India* (J. Murray, 1906) that 'Pasha is played by two or four players, and in contrast to the decorum of Shatranj, the Pasha board is the scene of noisy vociferation.'

*Chausar:* This is played with dice instead of cowries on a cloth or board. The board is in the form of two long rectangles that intersect at right angles in the centre. The shape of the board is therefore like a cross comprising four rectangles. There are ninety-six squares excluding the large square in middle. Sixteen pieces are arranged on each side of the board and the moves are based on the throwing of dice. Chausar is played mostly by men.

---

[11]The essay was reproduced in *Sedentary Games of India*, edited by Nirbed Ray and Amitabha Ghosh (Calcutta: Asiatic Society, 1999)

*Chaupar:* Chaupar, which is similar to pachisi, has been known from medieval times. However, according to historians, no pre-Mughal chaupar boards have survived. According to an article 'Dice, Chaupar, Chess: Indian Games in History, Myth, Poetry, and Art' by Andrew Topsfield in *The Art of Play: Board and Card Games of India*, chaupar was a favourite board game in the Awadh of the eighteenth century.

Chaupar is played with oblong dice (like chausar) on a cloth board having two transverse bars in the form of a cross. Each arm of the cross is divided into twenty-four squares in three rows of eight each, twelve red and twelve black. In the centre, where the arms meet, is a large black square. The cross is called chaupar, the arms phansa and the squares khana.

*Chess:* There are many legends about the origin of chess. According to David Shenk in his book *The Immortal Game: A History of Chess*, the game '[...] was not invented all at once, in a fit of inspiration by a single king, general, philosopher, or court wizard. Rather, it was almost certainly (like the Bible and the Internet) the result of years of tinkering by a large, decentralized group, a slow achievement of collective intelligence. After what might have been centuries of tinkering, chatrang, the first true version of what we now call chess, finally emerged in Persia sometime during the fifth or sixth century.' Further, Shenk is of the view that chess and Islam came into existence at about the same time and the game became woven into the fabric of Muslim culture.

In an essay 'Morals of Chess' by Benjamin Franklin published in the December 1786 issue of the *Columbian Magazine*, it is opined that by playing chess one may learn foresight, circumspection and caution.

H.G. Raverty, in his article 'The Invention of Chess and Backgammon' (read in March 1802; reproduced in the book *Sedentary Games of India*), has said that the earliest mention of chess in Sanskrit writings was in the first half of the seventh century AD.

More than a hundred years ago, three interesting tracts on playing chess were published in Urdu:

a) *Risala-i Shatranj* (*Tract on Chess*), by Shyam Kishore (Benaras, 1885).

b) *Kitab-i Shatranj* (*Book of Chess*), by Lala Kedar Nath (Moradabad: Shams al-Mataba, 1895–96).

c) *Risala-i Shatranj wa Taash* (*Tract on Chess and Cards*), by Muhammad Abdullah (Kanpur: Islami Press, 1914).

The game of chess is essentially a game of skill without any element of chance. The game, as many know, is played on a square board with sixty-four squares, alternately black and white. The pieces and pawns are thirty-two in number, half of which are black and the remaining white. The moves of the pawns and the other pieces are fixed.

Several words of chess terminology have become a part of our everyday language. 'Checkmate' is a position of check in chess from which a king cannot escape. It also signifies final defeat or deadlock. The word comes from the Persian 'shah maat', meaning 'the king is dead'. 'Stalemate' is a situation in which further progress by opposing parties seems impossible. In chess, 'stalemate' is a position counting as a draw, in which a player is not in check but can only move into check.

The unhurried, relaxed and leisurely culture of Nawabi Awadh was a stimulus and incentive to the widespread adoption of chess as an indoor pastime. The begums played it, the noblemen played it and the common man played it. In areas of old Lucknow, this author had seen till the early 1960s old men passing hours before chessboards. It seemed that the game was a conspicuous feature of their lives. Because the game can go on for hours, family members of those who played chess often found the hobby irksome. It was felt by many that chess was an extravagance and no matter how much it was played, the desire to indulge in it never ceased. Indeed, a book in Urdu titled *Risala-i Shatranj wa Ganjifa: Mausoom Ba 'Ijalah-i Hadiya* (*Treatise on Chess and Ganjifa: A Quick Guide*) by Maulana Hafiz Syed Muhammad Abdullah Bilgrami is a diatribe against chess and ganjifa. It claims that such games give way to betting. Players of these games become so engrossed that they forget hunger and thirst and neglect their daily duties.

This opposition to the playing of chess has been seen in other parts of the world as well. Albert Einstein, although he occasionally played chess, wisely remarked: 'Chess holds its master in its own bonds, shackling the mind and brain so that the inner freedom of the very strongest must suffer.'

In 1774, Colonel Jean-Baptiste Gentil, the French Military advisor to Nawab Shuja-ud-Daula, commissioned an album of illustrations of Indian life by local artists, which included paintings of people enjoying indoor games. Chess is one of the games depicted. There is a painting of noblewomen playing chess in a palace, which is possibly by the well-known Awadhi painter Nevasi Lal. The marked feature of the painting, which depicts several ladies watching two ladies concentrating on a chessboard, is the absorption of the ladies in their game.

The famous short story 'Shatranj ke Khilari' (The Chess Players) by the renowned Urdu and Hindi writer Munshi Premchand (1880–1936) was written in 1924 and is based on two chess-obsessed noblemen of Awadh who were so immersed in the game that they were oblivious to the great political changes happening in Awadh, namely, its annexation by the British. The only Urdu film, *Shatranj ke Khilari*, directed by Satyajit Ray (1921–92), was released in 1977 and was based on Premchand's story. Incidentally, an Urdu play, *Shatranj ke Mohre*, also based on Premchand's story, was written by Habib Tanvir (1923–2009) and was published by Urdu Ghar of Aligarh in 1983.

*Ganjifa:* Ganjifa is a game of cards, and is probably of Persian origin. In Persian, ganj means 'treasure'. The Mughals brought this game to India. Zahir-ud-Din Babur (1483–1530), founder of the Mughal dynasty, mentioned these cards in his memoirs. In 1527, he sent ganjifa cards to a friend in Sindh. The game also reached the Deccan, where rules were framed for eight-suited ganjifa. Although this game originated in Muslim lands, it was also played by the Hindu population.

A pack of ganjifa cards comprised ninety-six cards, i.e., eight suits of twelve cards each. The ashrafi (gold coin) and tanka (silver coin) were two of the suits, which were often designated surkh (gold) and safed (silver) and were also identified with the sun and the moon respectively. Ten cards of each suit were number cards and two were court cards, i.e., the mir (king), generally shown seated on a throne, and the wazir (minister) on horseback. Other cards were ghulam (slave), taj (crown), shamsher (sword), chang (harp), barat (document) and qimash (merchandise). The sequence of each suit was arranged as mir (king) and wazir (minister) and the numbers ace to ten for strong suits and ten to ace for weak suits.

The ganjifa cards were also designed based on the signs of the zodiac.

The ganjifa cards were round, and sometimes rectangular in shape, with lacquered backs. They were handmade and hand-painted and were made of ivory, tortoise shell, mother of pearl, waste paper or cloth. According to the article 'Ganjifa: India's Contribution to the World of Playing Cards' by Jeff Hopewell in the book *The Art of Play: Board and Card Games of India* edited by Andrew Topsfield, ganjifa can be played by three or four persons and '[…] players have to remember what cards have been played, and particular skill is needed towards the end of a game to determine which of the middle-ranking cards may yet be used to win a trick when the higher cards have been played, and which can be discarded.'

Ganjifa playing was more popular in Indian cities with lavish, resplendent and grand cultures, such as Lucknow in Awadh. There were regional variations in the rules for ganjifa. The game has now more or less disappeared and one only comes across ganjifa cards in opulent boxes with antique dealers. From all accounts, ganjifa was a difficult and complex card game and even in its heyday in Awadh, it was not very popular or prevalent.

**Outdoor games**

*Swimming:* Traditional Urdu books on shanawari (swimming) treat the boatman's style of swimming as an initial form of swimming that was copied from the way a frog swims. Various approaches were made popular by master swimmers in Awadh, who not only trained disciples but also held public demonstrations of their skill.

Several books on the skill of swimming were published in Urdu from Lucknow. One such book was *Pairaak* (*The Swimmer*) by Syed Akbar Ali. This book describes the difficult and fine art of swimming along with stunts and stratagems in water and procedures for saving a drowning person. Another book was *Islah-i Pairaak* (*Improvements for the Swimmer*) by Mirza Muhammad Husain. Both books have rough sketches and descriptions of various styles of swimming. The complaint of one of the authors was that with the departure of Wajid Ali Shah from Lucknow, teachers of the art of swimming became highly commercialized.[12]

Some of the persons who made their name in swimming are listed below.

- **Nawab Nasir-ud-Din Haider** was an accomplished swimmer and was a disciple of Ustad Mir Ahmad Anis Sahib alias Mir Machhli. He once ordered a competition between his ustad Mir Machhli and Ustad Mirak Jaan. Both of them competed in jal baank (a curved water manoeuvre). Nawab Nasir-ud-Din Haider sat in his bajra (budgerow, a round-bottomed keelless pleasure-boat) and a crowd had gathered on the riverside to watch the contest between the ustads. The budgerow was moving fast in the water, and the Nawab, waving a bag of one thousand rupees, announced that whoever of the two ustads was able to swim and catch his moving budgerow would be awarded the bag. Mirak Jaan succeded and won the prize.

- **Mirak Jaan or Miran Jaan** was an expert swimmer and was the teacher of Maharaja Digvijay Singh in the times of Nawab Nasir-ud-Din Haider. He was well known for his swimming acrobatics.

- **Maulavi Mirza Mahdi** was another stalwart in swimming. He would challenge a fleet-footed man to race with him on the riverbank while he would swim the same distance in the river. He would invariably leave the runner far behind. He was also gifted in baank (dagger fighting) and lakri (staff fighting). It is said that during the rebellion of 1857, he was shot dead in Mufti Ganj in Lucknow.

- **Mir Safdar Ali** used to teach difficult manoeuvres in swimming to Nawab Wajid Ali Shah. He was a master of aquatic acrobatics and he could tackle eight persons at a time in the river.

- **Shaikh Badlu Lakhnavi** was a barber by profession and also lived during the times of Nawab Wajid Ali Shah. He was renowned for his light and nimble swimming. It is said that he would squat

---

[12]Two other books on swimming are *Risala-i Tairaki* (*Tract on Swimming*) by Maha Narain (Delhi: Matba' Chashma-i Faiz, 1882) and *Risala-i Rahnuma-i Pairak* (*Tract on Guide to Swimming*), anonymous (Lucknow: Nizami Press, n.d.).

cross-legged in the water and propel himself by merely moving his toes. While doing so, he smoked a hookah and carried a baby in his lap. He could also swim upside down, with his body immersed in water from the head to the waist and his legs above the water. He could also swim with a train of twenty-five to thirty persons attached behind him, whom he dexterously pulled along as he swam.

- **Shaikh Abid Ali Lakhnavi** was a pupil of Haji Ahmad Ali alias Nannhay Mirza. It is said that he was so skilled in swimming that his guru made him his successor despite his own sons. He would place a bowl of water on his feet and swim without spilling a drop from the bowl. Shaikh Abid Ali was also adept at rescuing people from drowning, reaching them in no time and plucking them from the water like a flower. In the rainy season, when the current was strong, he would draw a line across his chest and swim erect, as if he were walking in water, the line on his chest untouched by water. He would swim in such fashion from Kankarabad to Kulhiya Ghat.

    Shaikh Abid Ali once navigated a raft of four earthen pots, upon which sat four persons, when the river was in spate. Three of the persons did not know how to swim. The contraption sank near Toota Ghat, but the swimming master managed to save all four persons.

## Some famous sportspersons in other outdoor games

### *Archery and Shooting*

- **Faiz Bakhsh** was a famous archer in the times of Nawab Asaf-ud-Daula. It is said that once, at a sign from the Nawab, he shot an arrow at the father of Mirza Haider with such dexterity that no one saw the archer taking aim nor did Mirza Haider's father realize that an arrow had struck him. It was only when the victim reached his home and opened his taapa (a covering of cloth) that blood spurted from the wound and he died. Nawab Asaf-ud-Daula was himself an expert in archery and gun shooting.

- **Meeran Sahib Pach Bhaiye** lived in the Saadatganj area of Lucknow and till his death served the nawabs of Sheesh Mahal. He was a proficient gun shooter. Such was his skill that he could shoot a bullet through the nose ring of a woman without hurting the woman. It was said that the British would test his skill by placing a lit candle in a glass shade and asking him to extinguish it. He would fire at it and the bullet would extinguish the flame without touching the shade.

- **Jahan Panah Mahal** was a mutaai (temporarily married begum) and died at Matia Burj in Calcutta, after Nawab Wajid Ali Shah. She would ask a man to throw corked bottles into the river and when they popped up, she would aim, shoot and shatter the bottles.

- **Prince Mirza Muhammad Sikandar Qadar Taimuri** was born during the reign of Nawab Amjad Ali Shah and was a tehsildar during the British Raj. He was the maternal grandfather of Syed Israr Husain, the author of *Qadeem Hunar wa Hunarmandan-i Awadh*. The author has recorded that once, Prince Sikandar Qadar went fishing with the British Collector of the region. He shot fish in water and was so adroit that the Collector appreciated him.

- **Hakeem Muhammad Rashid Fatehpuri** was a renowned marksman. He would hang a string and cut it with the first shot. He would place a flower on a glass plate and shoot it such that the flower would be blown away and the bullet would not touch the glass plate.

- **Raja Muhammad Kazim Husain Khan Bahadur** was a past master in military skills. His marksmanship was superb. He would aim four bullets at a marigold flower and would announce in advance which parts of the flower he would blow away.

## Wrestling

Although there were many good wrestlers during the Nawabi era in Awadh, the lives of very few have been recorded. The author of *Qadeem Hunar wa Hunarmandan-i Awadh* has mentioned two names: Bhawani Bakhsh Dariyabadi was a Brahmin famous in the first half of the nineteenth century for defeating a famous wrestler and tearing his jaw off; while Syed

Musharraf Ali alias Jhanda Miyan was another famous wrestler during Nawabi times and, because of his great strength, was known as the second Rustam. Rustam was the hero-wrestler in Firdausi's *Shah Nama*.

Several small tracts on wrestling were published in Urdu:

a) *Gulzar-i Shuja'at* (*The Garden of Bravery*), by Maula Bakhsh.

b) *Bustan-i Shuja'at* (*The Flower Garden of Bravery*), by Sheikh Muhammad Alimuddin (Fatehgarh: Matba Husaini, 1870–71).

c) *Riyazat-i Jismani* (*The Exercise of the Body*), by Sajjad Ali (Lucknow, 1896–97).

d) *Jauhar-i Shuja'at* (*Essence of Bravery*), by Kaleem Sheikh Muhammad Abdur Razzaq (Patna: Union Press, 1889–90).

## *Fencing, spear fighting and javelin throwers*

- **Maharaja Digvijay Singh** was a taluqdar of Balrampur (now a district in Uttar Pradesh). Once he encountered a poisonous snake on a dark night. He drew his sword and severed the snake into two parts, one and quarter elbow-length from the head. The severed snake continued to chase the Maharaja but he deftly killed the snake by cutting it with his sword. **Talib Khan Sher Lakhnavi** was another renowned sword fencer during the Nawabi times.

A few small tracts on fencing were published in Urdu, including the following:

a) *Ma'rka-i Ara* (*The Adorning of the Scene of Fight*), by Muhammad Abdur Rahman (Lucknow, 1850).

b) *Risala-i Ma'rka-i Ara* (*The Tract on Adorning of the Scene of Fight*), by Khwaja Ahmad Ali (Lucknow, 1848).

c) *Kitab-i Talwar* (*The Book of the Sword*), by Captain Muhammad Aijaz Ali (Hyderabad: Shamsul Islam Press, n.d.).

- **Nawab Qaim Khan Bangash** was second to none in spear fighting. Once, a Maratha who was in the service of Baji Rao came from Pune to test the skill of the Nawab. A contest was held between the two at Shikarpur. For a long time, both fought with ability. The Maratha had a handkerchief tied around his arm and the nawab wanted to untie it with the point of his spear. However, due to the profusion of sweat, the knot in the handkerchief had become hard and difficult to undo. Nonetheless, with great skill, the nawab was able to loosen the knot and carry away the handkerchief on his spear-point.

- **Mir Kallu** was a famous javelin thrower in the times of Nawab Burhan-ul-Mulk of Awadh. **Mir Akbar Ali** was also an expert in javelin throw and came after Mir Kallu.

## Other notable sportspersons

- **Ustad Syed Mubarak Husain**: In the Lucknow of the 1940s to the 1970s, there was one Ustad Syed Mubarak Husain who was capable of performing incredible feats of strength (fan-i sipahgari). Niyaz Muhammad Khan 'Niyaz Fatehpuri' (1884–1966), who edited the famous Urdu monthly *Nigaar*, wrote in 1950 that he had seen Syed Mubarak Husain's expertise in stick wielding, baank (dagger fighting), binot, spear fighting, fencing, horse riding, and panjakashi (arm wrestling in which two persons grasp and grapple with their fingers), and found his feats exceptionally impressive. Before his death, Syed Mubarak Husain wrote a book in Urdu, *Fan-i Sipahgari*, in which he gives the details of his accomplishments and how he trained for them. For archery, he used a bag of sand hung from a tree for target practise. He would also hang a wooden board with holes so he could shoot arrows through the holes. In spear fighting, as the aim is to ward off the strikes of the opponent, he stresses that one's eyes must always be focused on the enemy. For fencing, the Ustad describes seven types of swords where the strikes of the opponent's sword are held by the defender without a shield. He stresses that dagger fighting involves quick footwork. The Ustad also describes how to fight with a staff when the opponent is attacking with a sword or with a javelin. Ways to wrest a sword from an opponent are also described. An interesting part of the book relates to dealing with the traditional thug stranglers. Various manoeuvres of wrestling are also spelt out. Finally, the Ustad gives his preferred method of freeing oneself from the stranglehold of a noose round the neck. This is an interesting book in which the traditional martial arts, which are now buried in the past, have been revealed and described.

- **Mir Najm-ud-din** was the master of cudgel playing during the period of Nawab Asaf-ud-Daula. He accepted disciples from respectable families only. From those of the royal family he accepted money, but from persons of good families he accepted donations of sweetmeats only.

- **Gauri Tappaybaz,** the son of Ghulam Rasul, lived during the times of Nawab Wajid Ali Shah and was known as a master of alimad (a peculiar trick in wrestling).

- **Mansur Ali Khan** was adept in dagger fighting and lived in Faizabad during the times of Nawab Shuja-ud-Daula. The Nawab respected his skills.

- **Yahiya Khan** lived in the times of Nawab Asaf-ud-Daula. He won fame in rustamkhwani. He was also a master of dagger fighting.

- **Mir Bahadur Ali** was excellent in dagger fighting. He claimed that if a pigeon were released beneath a bedstead and it escaped from him, then he would forsake his title of master.

- **Mir Ja'far Ali** was the last master of dagger fighting. He accompanied Nawab Wajid Ali Shah to Calcutta when the Nawab was exiled.

- **Mirza Ahmad Baig Katiya Kutiya** was a fencer and lived during the time of Nawab Wajid Ali Shah. He once had an encounter with another fencer in Mohalla Shivpuri, near Husainabad in Lucknow. The two duelled for a while, each expertly attacking and blocking the other. Mirza Ahmad Baig stopped so many swipes of the sword on his chest that the sword-cuts left the design of a necklace across his chest. It was from that day on that Mirza Ahmad Baig was known by the sobriquet of Katiya Kutiya.

- **Mir Vilayat Ali** excelled in staff fighting. No matter how strong the staff of his rival, he would always break it. He was therefore known as Mir Vilayat Ali 'Danda Tor' (staff breaker).

A rare book on cudgel or club fighting was published from Aligarh in 1853 under the titile *Gutka wa Pheri* by Nasrullah Khan.

Two notable tracts in Urdu on dagger fighting are:

a) *Risala-i Razm Ara* (*Tract on Adorning the Combat*), by Khwaja Ahmad Ali, Khalifa Najmuddin Bakait (Lucknow: Naval Kishore Press, 1878).

b) *Risala-i Ma'rka-i Ara Dar Fan-i Baank* (*The Superior Tract on the Art of Dagger Fighting*), by Khwaja Ahmad Ali Lakhnavi.

## Men of Prowess, Daring and Dauntlessness

**Shaikh Ghulam Ahmad Dabaria** was a strongman who lived during the reign of Nawab Shuja-ud-Daula. He could outrun a horse and leap a distance of twenty-three hands, like a deer. It was said that the skin of his body was so hard that the stings of black wasps did not affect him. Even a group of wrestlers could not defeat him.

**Nawab Muhammad Khan Bangash** was from Farrukhabad and lived during the reign of Muhammad Shah of Delhi. He once laid siege to a fort that was surrounded by a deep moat. He swam across the moat and reached the fortress. Fearing for his life, the raja of the fort hid in a small chamber, but the Nawab found him and slew him. The raja's men, finding the Nawab in the chamber, locked him within. The Nawab was almost suffocated in the tiny, airless chamber, but he was able to dislodge a beam with his head and make a hole in the roof. As he was escaping through the hole, the women of the palace saw him and started thrashing him with pestles and utensils. However, he was able to get away and, with the help of an overhanging branch of a tree, jumped into the moat and joined his followers. The Nawab is said to have died at the age of over eighty.

**Mirza Ja'far** was the son of Mirza Yusuf in the reign of Nawab Shuja-ud-Daula. When Mirza Ja'far was about twenty-two years of age, a severe duststorm uprooted many tents in the camp of Nawab Shuja-ud-Daula. During the storm, Mirza Ja'far was in a tent with his three brothers. To save the tent, he asked his brothers to hold on to one of the pegs of the tent while he held fast to the other peg. After the storm subsided, he let go of the peg, fell to the ground and died. His physical efforts are said to have ruptured both his kidneys.

**Muhammad Ghulami Khan** was a famous strongman during the times of Nawab Ghazi-ud-Din Haider. Once, the Nawab released a lion from its cage and invited people to try to subdue the lion with a sword and whip. Muhammad Ghulami Khan controlled the lion by whipping the ferocious animal into obedience.

**Shaikh Zain-ud-Din Haider of Kakori,** a companion of the Raja of Kauria Kasganj, was considered a man of great strength. Once, the Raja's horse escaped and could not be caught. Hearing this, Shaikh Zain-ud-Din lay in wait for the horse on the highway. As it ran by him, he caught one of its legs so firmly that the horse could not escape. He was also a good marksman and could shoot a fly with his bow and arrow.

**Shaikh Aziz-ur-Rahman** was also known as Shaikh Wali Muhammad. He was a wrestler and a courageous man. He was a faujdaar (magistrate) in Paragnah Chail, appointed by Nawab Baqaullah Khan. The fortress there had a stone gateway, through which an elephant with litter and canopy could pass. The gateway had slipped from its place by about a palm-span. Nobody could set it right. He applied his strength and fixed it. On another occasion, a heavy cannon, which was pulled by two oxen, got stuck in the mud and no one was able to pull it free. Not only did he pull out the cannon but he also overturned it. Once, during the reign of Muhammad Shah in Delhi, all and sundry were invited to the Diwan-i Aam on the occasion of Nauroz (the Persian New Year). It was a great day, thick with crowds and it was almost impossible to enter the Diwan-i Aam. Shaikh Aziz-ur-Rahman was able to enter with his friends, carrying two of them on his shoulder and two in his arms.

**Ahmad Ali Khan** was the great grandson of Dilair Khan. His strength was such that in a contest he broke the paws of a lion. He could rub out the engraving on a rupee coin and twist it into a ball.

**Nawab Shuja-ud-Daula** was renowned for his strength. He could sever the head of a buffalo with one blow of his sword. He could rub out the engraving on a coin with his fingers. He could tear a shield apart as if it were a strip of paper. It was said that he could shoot an arrow through the brow of a tiger with such skill and strength that it would exit from its tail. Once, completely clad in his armour, he was hunting tigers in the jungle. A tiger attacked his elephant, which ran towards the river. The Nawab fell into the river Ghagra. He tore off his armour and as he swam towards the bank, a crocodile attacked him. He killed it by tearing apart its jaw and then with one hand, he steered the dead crocodile towards the riverbank and climbed out of the river.

**Shaikh Husain Ali Lakhnavi** lived in the times of Nawab Wajid Ali Shah. He was unparalleled in the use of the baana (a straight, long and broad sword with two edges and a wooden hilt). Although he was thin, he could pick up an ekka weighing about 80 to 120 kilos with one hand.

**Mirza Imdad Husain Lakhnavi** was a kamidaan (captain) in the times of Nawab Wajid Ali Shah. One day, a ferocious butting bull escaped. Mirza Imdad Husain came upon the bull and grasping his shield in his left hand, he held the horns of the bull with his right hand. It butted with all its strength but could not shake off Mirza Imdad Husain, who took out his sword and, with one stroke, severed its head from its body. He was also adept in binot. He died several years after the rebellion of 1857.

**Mirza Qudratullah Baig Lakhnavi** was another man of strength during the times of Nawab Wajid Ali Shah. His strength was such that he could pull out the fibres from a bamboo.

The **wife of Hafiz-ul-Mulk Hafiz Rahmat Khan** was a strong Pathan woman. When she was angry with one of her maids, she would catch her by the neck, lift her up above the ground and threaten to fling her down. Once, she asked her husband Hafiz-ul-Mulk for money. He agreed to give her as much money as she could carry in one go up to the top of the house. It is said that she was able to carry seven thousand rupees in a lagan (deep pan).

**Rasheeda Khanum** lived in the times of Nawab Wajid Ali Shah and was the mother of Nawab Hadi Ali Khan. On one occasion, as the household was asleep in the verandah, a thief entered the house, waking up the family. He tried to run away by leaping over a wall, but Rasheeda Khanum caught the stocking of the thief and gave him such a jerk that his ankle was dislocated.

**Saathka** was famous for long-distance walking. He could cover sixty kos (120 miles/193 km) and return the same day. Dariyabad in Barabanki district is sixty kos from Lucknow and he would go there and return to Lucknow on the same day. He was therefore nicknamed Saathka (of sixty).

**Mirza Ahmad Husain** was a risaldar (commander of troops) of the second order. He was said to be so huge that no horse could carry him. Such was his strength that he could catch the tail of an elephant and hold it immobile.

**Nawab Ghalib Ali Khan** was a contemporary of Mirza Ahmad Husain and in a trial of strength defeated the latter. He would practise using very heavy leaden clubs..

**Meer Lachhchhu Lakhnavi** was a wrestler and trained Nawab Syed Fida Husain Khan Bahadur in wrestling. It is said that he could break a kaitha (wood apple, characterized by a very hard shell) with his head and could strike a wall with such force that marks would be left on it.

**Hakeem Muhammad Raushan** was an expert in military techniques and was employed in the army. He probably lived during the time of Nawab Shuja-ud-Daula. One day, as he lay sleeping on the roof of his house, dacoits entered it. He was awakened by the noise, and the torches carried by the intruders gave him the impression that his house was on fire. He filled an earthen pot with water, came down the stairs and caught the dacoits in the act of stealing his household effects. He flung the water pot at the head of one, splitting his skull. The remaining dacoits attacked him with swords, but he faced them unarmed and made them flee.

**Nawab Mirza Sadiq Ali Khan Bahadur Lakhnavi** alias Nawab Shahenshah Dulah was from the family of Nawab Shuja-ud-Daula. He was in the habit of regularly doing a thousand push-ups in one go. After the exercise, he would consume about 50 grams of arsenic in barfi (sweetmeat made from sugar and inspissated milk). Once, Mirza Sadiq Ali Khan was travelling with some friends in a horse-drawn carriage to a fair in Aishbagh. Near the Moti Jheel in Aishbagh, the horse was disturbed by the noise of the fair and the coach veered towards the pond. Mirza Sadiq Ali Khan leapt out and firmly grasped a spoke of the wheel. The horse could not budge and the occupants of the coach dismounted, unharmed. On another occasion, during the passing of a tazia procession in Aminabad, a British officer lost control of his horse. Mirza Sadiq Ali Khan sprang to the rescue and grasped one of the forelegs of the horse, effectively immobilizing it. A third example of the strength of Nawab Shahenshah Dulah occurred when he fell ill. He was ordered by his physician to bathe in warm water. The water was to be heated in a large cauldron. He asked a few persons to put the water-filled cauldron on the fire, but they were unable to lift it. He then got up, picked up the cauldron and put it on the fire. In doing so he strained himself so much that the stitches of his shoes broke, but he did not even sweat.

# Skills

## Perfumery

Possessing a cultivated and refined lifestyle, the people of Awadh not only indulged in fine clothes and trappings but also had a love for fragrances. Both royal men and women would scent their clothes by the profuse application of ittar (perfume). There were many perfumers in Lucknow itself. But Kannauj—then in Farrukhabad district of Uttar Pradesh—was known for its ittars from Mughal times and is still the fragrance capital of India.

It may be noted that throughout India, the natural ittars were once more popular than Western fragrances. The popularity of ittar over Western-manufactured scents was mainly due to the fact that it is oil-based whereas scents are derived from the mixing of alcohol with floral and chemical fragrance. Muslims generally avoided alcohol-based scents. Further, the scent of ittar lingers longer than the chemical scents. However, while a Western scent can be sprayed without staining one's clothes, ittar has to be used in a slightly different manner. It is smeared and rubbed between the thumb and the index finger and then dabbed on the clothes. This offsets the chances of the clothes being stained.

The oldest Urdu book on perfumery is perhaps *Lakhlakha* (*Unguent Scented Cotton*) by Hasan Mirza 'Qasd', who was a Darogha-i Khushbu (Keeper of Fragrances) in the government of the Nizam of Hyderabad. This extremely rare book has the recipes for making various ittars, and lists the measures in the traditional tolas and mashas. Another useful Urdu book on perfumery is *Risala-i Sakht-i Itr* (*Treatise on Preparing Perfumes*) by Rai Sri Krishan Chand 'Qaisar' (Lucknow: Matba Qaisar al-Mataba, 1883). It gives recipes for itr-i ambar, itr-i gulaab, itr-i fitnah (mischief—concocted from mimosa and acacia flowers), itr-i khass (vetiver) and itr-i argaja (a mixture of ingredients like sandalwood, rosewater, camphor, musk, etc.).

In addition to using ittar, the buring of joss sticks (agarbattis) was also very popular. The base for this type of incense is 'ud (an Arabic word meaning 'wood'), also known as aloes wood or agar (the Sanskrit word 'agaru' means 'heavy'). The evergreen tree Aquilaria malaccensis, native to forests from India to Indonesia, is prone to infection by the fungus Phialophora parasitica. An infected tree secretes an aromatic resin and it is this resinous wood, known as aloes wood, that is the basic ingredient for the world's most valuable incense. The best grade of aloes wood is 'hard, nearly black and very heavy'. It sinks in water.

Another aromatic substance, costly and rare, is musk. It was also used as a fixative. It is known as mushka in Sanskrit, from the word for 'testicle', and kasturi in Hindi. The Persian word is mushk. Natural musk is black and has a penetrating odour. It is obtained from the glandular secretions from the musk deer.

The Awadhi perfumes, as also other ittars of India, were graded according to seasons. Shamaamat al-'ambar, which is still made but not necessarily with the original ingredients, has an alluring fragrance. It is mild and its application on clothes gives a semblance of warmth. It is therefore a winter perfume. In Awadh, during the height of winters, this ittar was used to scent quilts to give the feeling of balminess. Similarly, ittar made from khass is extracted from the root of an Indian grass Vetiver. The fragrance of khass is soothing and calming, and therefore it is popular in the summer season.

An ittar called 'itr-i gill (otter of clay) was made from unslaked pieces of clay pots which were drenched with water. It captured the fragrance of earthen pots soaked in water. Naturally, this was the ittar for the monsoons.

### Mohamed Ali—The Story of a Famous Ittar Firm

After Kannauj, Lucknow has been an important centre for the manufacture if ittar. The contribution and journey of a Lucknow firm called Mohamed Ali, founded by Asghar Ali in 1839 and named after his son, is especially noteworthy. It earned all-India recognition for the quality of its perfumes and hair oils. Another well-known and flourishing perfumery business at the time belonged to Muhammad Murtaza Khan and his sons Muhammad Mustafa Khan and Muhammad Istifa Khan (b. 1892) of Kannauj. Istifa learnt Urdu, Persian and English at home and at the age of about eleven, he moved to Lucknow. He was adopted by his childless elder brother Mustafa Khan. Mohamed Ali was also childless, and he adopted his niece. Musfata Khan and Mohamed Ali were of the same age, and became friends.

When Mohamed Ali's perfumery started sinking due to his poor health, he approached his friend to get his niece married to Istifa Khan. In a simple wedding in 1906, Istifa Khan was married at the age of fourteen to Mohamed Ali's niece. Later, he was appointed the successor of his father-in-law's firm, Mohamed Ali, in Lucknow. After Mohamed Ali passed away in 1907, Istifa Khan took over the firm and was able to clear all its debts.

Istifa Khan also had literary leanings and wrote poetry under the guidance of Syed Abdul Hakeem 'Saif Shahjahanpuri', who was a disciple of Jalal Lakhnavi (d. 1909). Five small collections of the poetry of Istifa Khan were published during his lifetime, which included ghazals, rubais, naats and chronograms. A miniature book containing an erotic poem was privately printed and distributed among friends. In 1932, Istifa Khan built a new perfume factory, which also later became his residence. This building, in the heart of the Chowk area in Lucknow, was called Hinna Building after a well-selling ittar.

Istifa Khan was also famous for habitually going on hajj (till 1961, he had gone as many as twelve times), and expertly skating on a long wooden table. Around 1948, he migrated to Pakistan leaving his perfumery to his sons in India. He died in Karachi in March 1963. After his departure, the quality of products suffered and the firm finally closed down on 16 August 1981 without a whimper. The family scattered and the Hinna Building was sold. Unfortunately, the history of the firm, particularly during its halcyon days, was not recorded, except in a small autobiographical piece given in the second volume of his poetic collection *Aeena*, published from Lucknow in 1961.

## Papermaking

The word for paper in Urdu, Persian and Arabic is 'kaghaz' or 'qirtas'. 'Kaghaz' is also commonly used by Hindi speakers; the nearest equivalent in Hindi is 'pattra'. P.K. Gode says in his essay 'Migration of Paper from China to India–AD 105–1500',[13] that paper came to India from China around the year 1000 and was manufactured in Delhi from the middle of the fourteenth century. Jeremiah P. Losty in *The Art of the Book in India* writes that the process of papermaking was learnt by the Arabs from the Chinese after the conquest of Samarkand in 751, and a type of paper typical of the Middle East, manufactured from shredded cloth, came into vogue in India from the thirteenth century. Paper was first imported but was then manufactured in places like Daulatabad, Ahmedabad, Lahore and Kashmir.

According to the book *Gift of Conquerors: Hand Papermaking in India*, by Alexandra Soteriou, '[...] the craft of floating waste in water to create a film atop a reed support that could be dried and used to write on was held a closely guarded secret for centuries' by the Chinese from at least 200 BCE. The craft gradually moved westward along the silk route and the Arabs learnt papermaking from Chinese prisoners in Central Asia.

In India, there were Muslim families of papermakers often with the suffix 'Kaghzi' to their name. Soteriou has described the process of papermaking, as gleaned from the few remaining Kaghzi families in India. Waste cloth was shreded, ground and mixed in water to give a colloidal solution. This solution was put in pit vats to form sheets. Swamp reeds were woven to form the flexible mould for paper sheets. The craftsmen sat in front of the pit vat, dipped the reed mould into the pulp and shook it to even the fibres. The sheet was taken out of the mould and pressed. Sheet drying was done on smooth plaster walls and after they dried, the sheets were peeled off.

Another handmade paper in extensive use for beautiful writing was marble paper or abri kaghaz (abri means cloud-like). Marbling is a method of paper dyeing that has been practised for centuries. Traditionally, gum, okra juice or quince seed was used to increase the density of water. Various colours were then added, which floated in a film on the surface

---

[13]This essay was published in *Studies in Indian History*, vol. 3, 1-12 (Poona: Bhandarkar Oriental Research Institute, 1969).

of the water. Sheets of paper were placed on the surface of the water, and the patterns made by the floating colours was transferred on to the paper; this marbling decorated the paper with light colours, embellishing the paper like wisps of cloud.

In the times of the nawabs of Awadh, papermaking was a home industry. The paper sold in the market was of foolscap size and was typically in thin or rough sheets. Paper was manufactured in many colours and there was also a two-coloured paper. To bring shine to the paper, it was rubbed with cowries (shells). Handmade paper was used extensively up to the middle of the nineteenth century for writing manuscripts, especially the Qur'an. As rag was used instead of wood pulp, the handmade paper was durable and long lasting.

## Calico Printing

William Crooke in the second volume of his book *The Tribes and Castes of the North-Western Provinces and Oudh* has mentioned as under:

> In Lucknow, according to Mr. Hoey, there are three different classes of cotton printers who pass under the same name and use similar dyes. The first class is the stamper of real or imitation gold or silver leaf on coloured cotton fabrics for use as palanquin covers, curtains (parda), bed covers (lihaf), quilts, etc. The process is simple but ingenious. The Chhîpi makes a mixture of gum, chalk and glue. He stamps the pattern on the fabrics with this mixture by means of a wooden die. He then lays strips of silver leaf over the pattern traced in this way, and taps it gently with a pad. The leaf adheres to the gummy lines of the pattern stamped, and comes away from the unstamped surface [...] The second class mark patterns on muslin for embroiderers (chikandoz), and the third prints cotton fabrics in fast colours for use as quilts, sheets, bed covers, table clothes, etc.

The chhîpi was the class of calico printers and chintz stampers and included both Hindus as well as Muslims.

## Fireworks

The bursting of firecrackers (patakha) was a profession in Awadh and firework displays were done on festive occasions. The basic ingredients used to make fireworks were charcoal powder, sulphur and other chemicals. The skill of the demonstrator lay in creating multicoloured fireworks worked out in designs, figures and various configurations. The making of firecrackers was a dangerous occupation as it sometimes involved fatal accidental explosions.

An Urdu book, *Risala-i Aatishbazi* (*Treatise on Firecrackers*) printed in 1899, contains recipes for making fireworks and here again the weights are in tolas and mashas. In India, popular firecrackers have traditionally been named, and several are described in this book, including anaar (pomegranate), bichchu (scorpion), phuljhari (a firework in imitation of a fountain), hawaai (rocket) and rupahli baarish (silver shower), among others.

## Making of Gold and Silver Leaves

The manufacturing of gold and silver leaves was a traditional craft practised in the ground-floor shops of the red-light district of Chowk in Lucknow. Some of the kothas of the courtesans were situated above these shops. Throughout the day could be heard the rhythmic pounding of hammers in a fast and continuous beat. Gold and silver leaves were also made in Delhi, Hyderabad, Bareilly and Benaras.

A thin piece of silver measuring approximately one square centimetre was placed in a book comprising thin leather sheets (usually made in Agra, which had a leather industry). The book was then beaten with a hammer continuously for four to five hours. Because of the malleability of silver, the pounding transformed it into an extremely thin, page-sized leaf of bright silver. This leaf was so delicate that merely moving it caused it to disintegrate and, if touched, the foil would break and stick to the finger.

Silver leaves are said to be edible and not harmful to one's health. Traditionally, they have been used to decorate sweetmeats and desserts.

Gold leaves were made in the same way, although there is now not much demand for them. Gold leaves are used in Indian medicine and for embellishment in traditional Mughal and Rajasthani paintings.

Today, the making of metal leaves is a dying art and only a couple of silver beaters are left in Lucknow.

## Utensil Making

In the old days, copper utensils were used primarily by Muslims and brass utensils by Hindus. Lucknow was a thriving market for copper. Copper sheets came from Delhi, Hapur, Jagadhri (Punjab), Shamli and Mujaffarnagar. Besides large and small cooking pots, copper was used to make household wares like sini (a round tray with low walls), lagan (a large round tray with high walls), kafgeer (a flat, long-handled spoon for stirring and skimming), paandaan (a box for keeping paan), etc. Lucknow was also famous for forging and moulding. The typical Muslim lota (an S-shaped pot with a spout), used for liquids, was elegantly designed. Abdul Halim Sharar, author of the well-regarded book on the erstwhile culture of Lucknow, *Guzashta Lakhnau,* opined that the Lucknow lota was such a robust and beautiful utensil that it could outmatch any other lota of India.

Engraving on utensils was done to create impressions of flowers, leaves and creepers. Meenakari (enamelling) required the use of a wax-like substance, which was typically black, red, blue or green. This substance was rubbed into an engraving, creating designs in brilliant colours. Ganga-Jamuni was another style of enamelling and, usually, silver and gold designs were made side by side.

## Earthenware

Abdul Halim Sharar was full of praise for the earthenware and clay toys made in Lucknow. The earthenware comprised plates and dishes. The simple, unpolished ones were for fruits and sweets. Utensils polished with black lac were for mournful occasions. The smooth, glazed utensils, usually in green, blue, yellow or gold, did not absorb grease. As such, they were used for sending food items like qorma, pulao, kebabs, etc. to the houses of relatives and friends.

Thin-bodied earthen waterpots (surahis) and goblets (aabkhoras), both small and large, were made to keep liquids, including water, cool in summer when there were no refrigerators and ice was a scarce item. The clay used to make these was mixed with a certain amount of sand. Other clay utensils included large waterpots, small waterpots (jhajris), candlesticks, incense vessels and lamps.

## Bidriware

Bidri craft, a metal handicraft, developed in the Deccan city of Bidar in the northern part of Karnataka in the fourteenth century, during the time of the Bahmani sultans, who ruled a Muslim state of the Deccan from 1347 to 1527. Bidri craft also came to Awadh and bidri sazi developed during the reign of Nawab Asaf-ud-Daula (1775–97).

Ashfaq Ahmad Khan, in his book *Glimpses of the Arts of Awadh: A Guide to the Awadh Gallery*, wrote that bidriware '[...] is a kind of damascening which in itself is an art of encrusting one metal on the surface of another soft metal generally in the form of wire which by undercutting and hammering is thoroughly incorporated into the metal which is intended to be decorated through motifs of various designs.' It is thus a type of inlay work. The metal used is a blackened alloy of zinc and copper inlayed with silver sheets or wires.

In the nineteenth century, one Muhammad Ali, a bidar saz, had a workshop for making bidriware in Chowk Sabzi Mandi in Lucknow. He wrote a book, *Risala-i Aain-i Bidar Sazi* (*A Short Treatise on the Skill of Making Bidriware*), which describes how to make bidriware. The appendix includes twenty-nine plates with designs of bidriware, which comprise vases, goblets, the bottoms of hookahs, etc.

Another form of bidriwork to be found in Lucknow is zarbuland, in which ornamental designs are raised above the surface of the vessel.

## Hookahs

Tobacco smoking and consequently cigarettes and hookahs have gone into disfavour with the realization that they are deleterious to health. However, till the 1950s, there was little realization on this count. What is called the sheesha in the Middle East and the hookah in India was fashionable amongst a class of persons who were not necessarily rich and sophisticated. The traditional hookah of Lucknow had three basic parts. The base of the hookah was made either of metal or of strong clay and it tapered upwards, ending in a long tube. At the top end of the tube was the detachable chillum, the clay bowl that contained the tobacco and burning coal. Sometimes, the chillum cover was made of silver, brass or copper. The third portion of the hookah was the naicha, or the stem of the hookah. It was usually made from narkul (the reed from the bulrush) and was connected to the base of the hookah. There were several types of naicha, including long stems, a tapering and flexible tube, and even one that was twisted snake-like. The naicha was covered completely with black or red cotton thread and this was further wrapped with silk thread worked into designs. The hookahs were sometimes given a colourful coating of enamel. Hookahs with bases made of thin clay were also favoured, especially in summer. The smoke through them was said to be sondha (having the highly agreeable smell of a new earthen vessel when first wetted). The tobacco for the chillum was always fragrant, even to a non-smoker, and was kneaded with treacle and mixed with spices and fruits. The smoke of the hookah perfumed the surroundings.

**Footwear**

The ghateela shoe was perhaps invented in Awadh. The toe of the ghateela shoe was long and, according to Sharar, 'shaped like an elephant's trunk, curving over the feet in a large spiral'. Babbar Ali Lakhnavi was a renowned maker of ghateela shoes during the reign of Nasir-ud-Din Haider. Later, the ghateela shoe was worn by women only.

The kafsh shoe, or a sandal with the heel shod with iron, was a durable shoe. The late Syed Agha Mehdi, in his *Tarikh-i Lakhnau* (*History of Lucknow*) published from Karachi, stated that kafsh were worn by old religious people and the shoes had a piping of leather with a velvet top.

Some famous kafsh makers were Allah Rakkhau, Ramazan Khan and Agha Hasan.

The zerpai were slippers and were normally made with brown leather or had tops of yellow velvet. The artisans who won renown for zerpai-making were Zakir Husain and Ramazan Khan. There was also a demand for shoes with delicate embroidery in gold, silver or coloured threads. This was called aughi embroidery. Women also wore tat bani (brocaded) shoes.

## Tailoring

Awadh has been famous for the elegance of the garments worn by its men and women. Some of the typical garments worn in the region included drawers with wide legs, which became the fashion during the times of Nawab Nasir-ud-Din Haider. These gave way to narrow-legged drawers. However, women continued to wear very wide-legged pyjamas, which sometimes ran into many yards. Also during the reign of Nawab Nasir-ud-Din Haider, men started wearing five-cornered caps. Nawab Wajid Ali Shah started the fashion of wearing a court cap, which he called aalam pasand (Jaan-i-Aalam was a sobriquet of Wajid Ali Shah). The Nawab also favoured the pointed cap called dopalli (comprising two parts stitched together in the middle along the line from the nape to the forehead). Dopalli caps are still in vogue and are worn over kurta and pyjamas.

Some famed outfitters of Lucknow are still remembered. Among these is Mukka Darzi, who lived during the reign of Nawab Nasir-ud-Din Haider and was famous for stitching bodices and chemisettes.

Shaikh Ilahi Bakhsh and Shaikh Muhammad Ali were real brothers and were considered master tailors during the time of Nawab Nasir-ud-Din Haider. Once, when the Nawab met with a high-ranking British commander, the former was wearing a coat of green velvet made by Shaikh Ilahi Bakhsh. The gussets of the coat were stitched in such a way that when the Nawab sat on a chair in the direction of the wind, it seemed that there was a small display of shining fireworks. It is said that the same Shaikh Ilahi Bakhsh made dopalli caps for Nawab Wajid Ali Shah, for each of which the nawab gave an ashrafi (gold coin).

Shaikh Muhammad Ali was so skilled that he could stitch an angarkha (a long tunic or coat worn by men) from one single spool of thread. If one end of the thread was pulled, the entire angarkha came undone. He also made angarkhas without joints in the shoulders or in the armpits.

After the fall of Awadh, both the brothers went to the state of Rampur. Shaikh Muhammad Ali died in the early 1930s at the age of almost a hundred.

## Horse Riding

Some famous horsemen of Lucknow are enumerated below:

Nawab Yamin-ud-Daula maintained a stable of several thousand horses, which were fed grass of a superior imported variety. He once made a bet with the general in charge of Fort William (in Calcutta) that he could jump across the moat on his horse. The general lost the wager as the Nawab cleared the moat effortlessly.

The word 'bangash' in the name of Nawab Haider Khan Bangash signifies a dweller of the highlands. This nawab was a native of Qaimganj in Farrukhabad district of Uttar Pradesh. He came to Lucknow with his father and Nawab Yamin-ud-Daula honoured them. Nawab Haider Khan Bangash was such a skilled equestrian that he could control any horse without a bridle.

Nawab Huzur Alam Naqi Khan was the prime minister of Nawab Wajid Ali Shah. He was a skilled equestrian and a master in javelin fighting. After Nawab Yamin-ud-Daula, there was no better horseman in Awadh except Nawab Huzoor Alam. One day, he was sitting in his mansion when a trader, who was himself a good horseman, appeared. The trader sat on his horse and made a circuit before the Nawab and in the second circuit, he showed his expertise by making his horse's hooves fall exactly upon the impressions made by the hooves during the first circuit. The Nawab understood the manoeuvres of the trader, who had trained his horse, and praised him. The Nawab then mounted an unbroken colt, at which the trader pointed out that the beast had not been trained. The Nawab retorted that it did not matter. He took a round on the colt and in the second round, made the colt do exactly what the trader had made his horse do in his exposition.

Shaikh Babar Ali lived in the times of Nawab Wajid Ali Shah. He would ride a horse and in one hand he would carry a bowl full of water. His skill was such that the water would not spill. Another example of his adroitness was that he would sit on a horse, keep the reins in his left hand and with his right hand on the head of a man, would turn the horse continuously in a tight circle, but his right hand on the head of the man would not move.

## A Famous Coachman

Banda Ali Khan was an incomparable coachman in the employ of Nawab Wajid Ali Shah. He drove the carriage with such skill that the wheels of one side could run over a row of rupee coins placed on the road without disturbing them. When the carriage turned at the Qaisar Bagh gate, it would leave a perfect circular trail, which could be traced with a compass. In a four-horse carriage, the horses went at different speeds, yet when Banda Ali Khan was driving it, this difference in their paces did not cause any discomfort to the passenger in the carriage.

## Farriery

Farriery requires precision and experience as even the slightest inattention while shoeing a horse can injure it. In colonial times, besides the British, the landed gentry also owned horses. While farriers were common in Nawabi times, today it is a dying art. In the *Hindustan Times* (Lucknow edition) of 8 February 2015, Oliver Fredrick wrote that one Babu Khan was the oldest farrier (na'lband) in Lucknow and had his makeshift shop near the Asafi Imambara. Babu Khan was said to be in his eighties and came into the trade in the 1940s when he started assisting his father Qayamat Ali. The then British government had hired his father as a farrier for the horses of the mounted police. According to the newspaper report, there were only two ironsmiths left in Lucknow who were making and supplying horseshoes to about five farriers left in the city.

## Some Famous Barbers

Peer Bakhsh was famous for shaving beards so closely that the skin remained smooth for up to three to four days.

Faqir Bakhsh lived during the times of Nawab Ghazi-ud-Din Haider. He would shave a person without wetting their face. He was an expert at shaving a person while they slept such that the customer would not even be aware of the process.

## Bearing the Flagstaff of Muharram Processions

Aghai Mirza Lakhnavi lived during the Nawabi times and was known for his skill in wielding the flagstaff for Muharram processions. He used many parts of his body including his nails and the space at the junction of two fingers for lifting and balancing the flagstaff. He could also balance the flagstaff on the edge of a sword placed between his teeth. He is said to have died of paralysis in October 1928.

## Woodcarving

According to the book *Kanz al-Tarikh* (*Treasure of History*) there lived a skilled woodcarver in Lucknow who made fine spoons, forks and knives. They were popular among the Europeans, who not only utilized them but also put them on display. On account of his proficiency he came to be known as Haji Chamcha (spoon) and all his descendants bore this name.

## Gun-making

One Mirza Abdul Aziz Lakhnavi lived during the reign of Nawab Wajid Ali Shah. He had a shop for making guns in Nazirabad. He once fabricated a double-barrelled gun that he presented to Mirza Zafar Ali Khan of Sheesh Mahal. It was very similar to the European double-barrelled guns. He forged the barrel with his own hands and did the finishing on a machine.

### Folding Betel Leaf for Chewing

William Hoey, in his book *A Monograph on Trade and Manufacturers in Northern India*, tells us that in Lucknow, the main varieties of paan were kapuri, bangla, begami, kalkatiya and desawari.

Regarding paan there was the following saying:

*Bina wasile chaakri, bina dhaal ke jawan, yeh tinon pheeke lagen bina tamaku pan*

Service without a patron, a young man without a shield, and betel without tobacco are all three tasteless

In Lucknow, the preparation and folding of betel leaves for chewing became an art. The betel leaves were buried in the ground till they turned pale. Slaked lime was washed many times before it was applied to the betel leaf. Catechu (kattha), which was also used in the making of a paan, was spread on a piece of cloth, which was kept in a tray full of ash to remove its astringency. The slicing of the betel nut for the paan also acquired a deliberate fineness.

Besides the round paandaans, which were the special metal boxes containing the ingredients for making paan, there were also covered betel boxes called khaasdaans, which contained prepared paans for immediate consumption.

Mention may be made here of the female paan vendors of Lucknow. They were known as panwaarans or tambolans. They often served paan in assemblies of the gentry. Usually, prostitutes who were past their prime and were not financially secure would vend paan in kiosks.

## Popular Pastimes

### Rearing of Pigeons

It is said that pigeon rearing became a skill in Awadh in the reign of Muhammad Ali Shah (r. 1837–42) and was further encouraged in the times of Wajid Ali Shah (r. 1847–56), as the last king of Awadh was fond of keeping pigeons. Ameer Ahmad 'Ameer' Minai (1829–1900), a poetic disciple of Syed Muzaffar Ali Khan 'Aseer' Lakhnavi, was an important Urdu poet of the late nineteenth century. His works include the *Kabutar Nama*, comprising two hundred rhyming couplets. It relates the fondness of Nawab Wajid Ali Shah for pigeons and is said to have been presented to the Nawab. The poem describes twenty-four kinds of pigeons reared by Wajid Ali Shah.

The varieties of pigeons that were bred and trained in Lucknow were shirazi, chup, lotan, khirqa band, laqqa (the fantail pigeon), makkhi, neela, basra and bhola. According to Mirza Jafar Husain, the girahbaz pigeons were high fliers and once in the air, they came down only at their will. On the other hand, the gola variety of pigeons took to the air when driven and came down when called.

There were masters (ustads) of pigeon keeping and flying, who were followed by khaleefas, and then came the apprentices or disciples known as shagirds.

The term 'kabootar laraana' meant trapping the birds of someone else. The convention was that whoever captured another's pigeons, kept them. However, if their relationship was cordial, the birds were returned to the original owner.

It was common to see pigeons being flown from the clustered rooftops of Lucknow. Indeed, in old Lucknow till about the 1960s, the sight of a flock of domesticated pigeons flying overhead and changing directions abruptly upon hearing the sharp whistle of their owner was a regular feature.

### Quail Breeding and Fighting (Baterbazi)

It is said that the art of breeding quails came to Lucknow from the Punjab region. Quail breeding was an activity that required constant attention and application. The fighting quail was made lean, strong and fierce. For this, various herbal medications were administered. In fact, there were experts in this field in Lucknow. Inayat Ali of Chobdari Mohalla and Bismillah Khan of Kashmiri Mohalla were considered masters of this skill. Some of the techniques the breeders used to prepare fighting quails included keeping the bird between their palms so that the heat of the hands could make the bird thin. Also, the fighting quail's beak was made pointed, its feathers were clipped, it was made to endure hunger and trained to stand noise and din. The breeders also dripped red paan juice on the bird's head to colour it.

A twelve-page booklet, *Risala-i Baterbazi* (*A Short Treatise On Quail Keeping*) by Mirza Wazir Baig 'Riyaat', provides information on the different types of quails and gives home remedies for the treatment of quails. It suggests that a good quail should be tall and well built and should have a large head and a big beak. It should have thin feathers. A slightly aged quail was considered to be more experienced in fights as compared to a young one.

Those who undertook quail fights were known as baterbaz. Quail fighting often involved guile and deceit. An experienced rearer, on seeing a good quail belonging to another, would disguise his own ordinary quail to look like the coveted one and would substitute it with his own common quail. He would then compete with the quail and win a round.

Quail fighting did not involve a large area. In fact, it could be done in a room; the floor would be covered with a white sheet and the quails were let out to tackle each other. Because it did not involve much paraphernalia, quail fighting became a popular sport. Usually, the fighting competitions took place in winter and the rest of the months were spent in training and preparation. Each quail fight took twenty to twenty-five minutes. A quail that won for three successive years was retired. A quail that lost a fight and ran away was called a bhagga (runaway). Such runaway birds were considered useless and were usually distributed. There were some people who trained these birds again, which was another skill.

According to Mirza Jafar Husain, there were many large pits (pali) in Baba Hazara Bagh where quail fights took place. There were also similar pits in the residence of Chhotey Agha Sahib in Tirimini Ganj, in the Ahaata of Mirza Ali Khan, and at Ahini Phatak at Patanala, where people gathered to watch quail fighting. Bird fighting (quail and cock) was enjoyed by both the nobility and the common people. The elite did not indulge in direct betting, as gambling was considered unacceptable. Some Europeans in Lucknow also took an interest in the game. Claude

Martin (1735–1800) witnessed cockfighting with Nawab Asaf-ud-Daula.

## Cockfighting

Cockfighting (murghbazi) was more widespread than pigeon rearing and quail fighting. The best variety of cocks was the aseel. Training fighting cocks was a full-time profession for some people. The cocks fought with claws, spurs and beaks, which were sharpened to make the fight savage and violent. During cockfights, if the contesting birds became weary, they were rested for a while and their owners took steps to invigorate them. Therefore, some cockfights continued for many days, with heavy betting. The fight ended when one of the birds was disabled.

There were regular nurseries for hatching fighting cocks. Attention was given to their diet and training. When two cocks meet, they do not start fighting. Making the cock belligerent was thus a skill. Even the muscles of the cock were massaged, its beak was sharpened and grains were fed to it from a soft surface or from the palm.

R.N. Saletore in his book *Indian Entertainment* has stated that fighting cocks were armed with 'cunningly devised' metallic spurs that were slipped over the natural spurs of the birds. These spurs were like miniature knives and were extremely sharp. 'Some cocks in Lucknow were allowed to fight with their natural spurs covered with cloth strappings merely to prolong the fight which sometimes lasted for several days.' Further, Saletore has observed that '[...] the princes in Oudh employed professional cockers to breed and train cocks and 75% of the young ones bred were killed in order to retain only the very best, each one of which was reputed to cost in those days the fantastic sum of Rs. 2000.'

According to an old admirer of Awadh culture, Khwaja Abdur Rauf 'Ishrat' Lakhnavi (1868–1940), cockfighting started in the times of Nawab Shuja-ud-Daula and was further developed by Nawab Asaf-ud-Daula. Ishrat Lakhnavi mentioned that the methods adopted to train the bird were quite cruel. Initially, the trainee cock was cooped up, one of its legs was chained and its beak was tied. In this condition, he was left to engage with a trained cock. The antagonists were required to be of almost the same weight.

The famous oil painting, *Colonel Mordaunt's Cock Match* by Johan Zoffany (1788), which is now in the Tate Gallery in London, depicts Nawab Asaf-ud-Daula and Claude Martin watching a cockfight.

## Parrot Flying

One Meer Muhammad Ali Lakhnavi, who lived during the reign of Nawab Muhammad Ali Shah, would fly parrots like pigeons. It is difficult to train parrots to carry out flying forays. Nonetheless, he could train about ten to twelve parrots to fly in a group; as soon as Meer Muhammad Ali whistled, the parrots would descend and go into their cages.

## Training of Weaver Birds

In the times of Nawab Muhammad Ali Shah there was a person who trained weaver birds (baya). He would toss a neem leaf or a cowrie and the bird would bring it back.

## Kite Making and Kite Flying

Kite flying was called kankauwwabazi in Awadh. It was a cheap, popular and widespread pastime enjoyed by both the rich and the poor. The smaller kites were called patang and the larger ones, which needed expert handling, were known as kankauwwa.

In Lucknow, kites were made in different shapes and sizes with multicoloured paper. Each type of kite had a local name. With the advent of the twentieth century, most of the old varieties of kites disappeared, and Mirza Jafar Husain, the chronicler of twentieth century Awadh, remembered only two names of kites, namely, 'aadam' and 'banchi'. According to him, the aadam variety was shaped like a man and when flown, it resembled the profile of a human being. The banchi was a decorated and delicate kite that women also flew from the rooftops. Dr Naiyer Masud (b. 1936), a Persian and Urdu scholar of Lucknow, compiled a manuscript titled *Lakhnau Ki Patangein*, which includes sketches of hundreds of different types of kites that are now no longer made, along with their names. Some of the types listed by Dr Masud are rangeeniya, baansdar, ik mangi pattidar, maangdar, aasmani, ababiliya, udi, baansdar tauqia, basanti, paandar, pattidar, pichkaridar, jauhar, chand tara, chap, kharbuzia, dulhan, do patti, sulaimaniya, karaundia, glassdar, gullidar and maangdar, to name just a few. A copy of Dr Masud's manuscript can be found in the Kite Museum in Ahmedabad, Gujarat.

In his article 'Qadeem Lucknow Mein Tafrihi Mashaghill' (Pastime Occupations of Old Lucknow), published in the July 1978 issue of the Urdu monthly *Aaj Kal* (New Delhi), Mirza Jafar Husain has mentioned that kites in Lucknow were made with great delicacy and precision in the Nawabi times and sometimes, foreign paper was used. A pattern called 'anaardana' (pomegranate seed) was particularly elegant. He recalled that the best kite-makers in the early twentieth century were in the Agha Mir Deohri locality of Lucknow and in particular, Rais Agha was known for his kites. Kite making was a hobby even among the nobility. Nawab Fazl Husain, the father of the Urdu poet Nawab Ja'far Ali Khan 'Asar' Lakhnavi (d. 1967), is said to have made extremely good kites for his son.

One of the pleasures of kite flying is to entangle a rival's kite and with a flick of the finger, to cut it in the air. This is known as 'pech larana'. The kite flier has in his hands a 'charkhi', or spool, from which the 'saddi' and 'manjha' (kite string that is coated with pounded glass mixed with wax, oil or the white of egg so as to cut the string of another kite) are rolled out as the kite rises in the sky. Usually, a kite-flier has a helper who handles the spool.

Syed Israr Husain in his book *Qadeem Hunar wa Hunarmadan-i Awadh* has mentioned the following famous kite fliers of old Lucknow:

- Maulavi Amdu lived during the times of Nawab Nasir-ud-Din Haider. He flew kites with a very long string.
- Mirza Nazir Ali would use six or seven seers (about 6 kilos) of string when flying kites.
- Vilayat Ali, alias Vilayati, was a master kite-flier during the reign of Nawab Wajid Ali Shah.
- Ilahi Bakhsh Tundey (one-handed), also from the time of Nawab Wajid Ali Shah, became famous after the Nawab was exiled to Calcutta and was considered skilled in long-string kite flying.

Some books on kite flying include the thirty-page Urdu booklet titled *Hawaai Shaghal* (*Windy Pastime*) by one Syed Ahmad (Lucknow: Nizami Press, 1934). A more comprehensive book on kites titled *Patang* (*Kite*) was published in 1998 by one 'Shorish' Siddiqi from Lucknow. The book also contains interviews with some kite-fliers. Mention may also be made of the Urdu book *Patangbazi* (*Kite Flying*) by Nadeem Waheed and Aadam Naiyer.

# 6.

# Painting, Aquatint, Lithography and Photography

## History of Painting in Awadh

The development of Mughal painting was brought about by both Muslim and Hindu painters who collaborated liberally with each other, sometimes in the creation of the same painting. Indeed, watercolour painting in the Mughal style is an important feature of Indian art. However, the later Mughals, after Aurangzeb (d. 1707), weakened due to a variety of political reasons and did not promote the arts to the extent of their predecessors. With the decline of the Mughal Empire, proficient and skilled painters dispersed to the mushrooming smaller states that had the wherewithal to offer patronage, which was fast disappearing in the dwindling and weak Mughal Empire. These small kingdoms included Murshidabad in Bengal, Farrukhabad in Uttar Pradesh, Hyderabad, Ahmadnagar, Bijapur, Patna, the hilly areas of Punjab and, of course, Awadh.

Nawab Shuja-ud–Daula (r. 1753–75) in Faizabad was a contemporary of the later Mughal kings Aziz-ud-Din Alamgir II (r. 1754–59) and Ali Gauhar, also known as Shah Alam II (r. 1759–1806). He showed a keen interest in and appreciation of the works of Mughal artists and many Mughal artists migrated to Faizabad. His patronage helped keep the flickering flame of Mughal painting from being completely extinguished.

Unfortunately, not many papers have been written on painting in Awadh, which, although an offshoot of the established Mughal style of painting, soon developed its own characteristics. One of the very few books available on Awadh painting is *Awadh Ki Chitrakala* (*Awadh Painting*) by Dr Reena Singh. It is a doctoral thesis submitted by the author at the Kashi Hindu Vishwavidyalaya in Benaras and is a good resource on the subject. Some important points from it are discussed in this section.

Abul Mansur Mirza Muhammad Muqim Ali Khan Safdarjung (b. 1708; d. 5 October 1754), the second Subedar Nawab of Awadh, ruled from 19 March 1739 till his death in 1754. He is credited with bringing a proficient painter by the name of Faizullah to Awadh. Faizullah migrated to Faizabad, then the capital of Awadh, with his father Faqirullah Khan, also an accomplished Mughal painter. It is with Faizullah that painting in Awadh generally commenced.

Jalal-ud-Din Haider Abul Mansur Khan Shuja-ud-Daulah succeeded Safdarjung as Subedar Nawab of Awadh in October 1754 and reigned till 26 January 1775. His reign attracted poets and artists to Faizabad, who migrated there in the hope of better prospects. Although the resuscitation of the arts was not of a magnitude comparable to the flowering of Mughal painting, the small efforts of the émigré artists brought new life to the fading art culture. The Faizabad court not only attracted Indian artists, both Hindus and Muslims, but also brought in a few European talents. There was a visible emergence of Western influence on the work of the local artists.

It was in the times of Shuja-ud-Daula that Awadh paintings really started taking shape. The paintings essentially depicted life in those times. Human emotions and relations, especially love, were the basis for a series of paintings. Mulk Raj Anand in his book *Album of Indian Paintings* was of the view that the Awadh school of painting was of a high order and was a revival of the great Mughal school.

Shuja-ud-Daula was succeeded by Muhammad Yahiya Mirza Amani Asaf-ud-Daula (r. 26 January 1775 to 21 September 1797). Asaf-ud-Daula shifted the capital of Awadh from Faizabad to Lucknow in 1775. The poets and artists of his court also gradually moved to Lucknow. The painters took up themes relating to court life, romantic tales, types of women, raagmala (pictures depicting primary and subordinate modes of ragas) and barahmasa (songs of the twelve months).

Although the Awadh school was an offshoot of the Mughal school, it did not develop and spread to the extent that the latter did. Up to the death of Nawab Asaf-ud-Daula in 1797, Awadh painting remained quite local in its techniques and characteristics. By the time of Nawab Yamin-ud-Daula Saadat Ali Khan, the fifth ruler of Awadh (r. 21 January 1798 to 11 July 1814), Awadh paintings exhibited European influences, which became one of their defining characteristics. During the reign of Ghazi-ud-Din Haider, who was last nawab (r. 11 July 1814 to 19 October 1818) and the first king of Awadh (r. 19 October 1818 to 19 October 1827), the Western influence was quite strong in Awadh paintings. During the reign of Nasir-ud-Din Haider, the second king of Awadh (r. 1827 to 1837), the local artists started copying European paintings and picked up many techniques and characteristics from the foreign style. This influence resulted in the breaking away of the Awadh school from the Mughal qalam by the time of Wajid Ali Shah (r. 13 February 1847 to 11 February 1856). Paintings of the Awadh school are typically portraits, imaginary scenes and portrayals of nature. Initially, the portraits were of the men and women of the nobility. Later, the European dignitaries in Awadh spurred and stimulated the Indian artists to make paintings of the common people like maidservants, barbers, sweepers, fruit sellers, servants and even thugs. The Awadhi miniature painters also made ornamental wall paintings and drew on cloth.

During the period from about 1739 to 1856, i.e., about 117 years, Awadh paintings took many forms and styles. At the beginning of the nineteenth century, around the time that the European influence emerged in Awadh paintings, siyahqalam (black brush) paintings also came into vogue. Siyahqalam paintings also existed in the Mughal school during the time of Emperor Jahangir (1605–27). These were basically sketches with thick lines in charcoal or black ink made for study and practise. According to Som Prakash Verma, as mentioned in his book *Interpreting Mughal Painting*, in the technique of siyahqalam, 'the whole drawing is finished with thinly-shaded black lines with minimal of modelling and very limited use of colours'. Besides siyahqalam sketches, another style of Awadh painting was miniature painting in colour. While the European influence was prominent in siyahqalam sketches, the colour miniatures were dominated by the Mughal style. Miniatures were prevalent up to the reign of Nawab Asaf-ud-Daula and can broadly be categorized as northern Mughal style paintings. The third type were paintings in watercolour or in oil, made initially by modest and conventional European artists whose style was imitated by local talent. This style of Awadh painting was prevalent from the time of Nawab Nasir-ud-Din Haider (1827–37) right up to the fall of the Awadh kingdom in 1856.

The portraits in the northern Mughal style were traditional and individuals were depicted standing, showing one eye in profile and with the foot turned in one direction. The portrait of Nawab Shuja-ud-Daula in this style shows one and a half portion of the eyes and the feet are pointing towards the right. This painting is from Faizabad. Another Faizabad painting shows Nawab Saadat Khan Burhan-ul-Mulk (r. 1722–39) and his nephew Safdarjung (r. 1739–54) sitting face to face in profile with a rosary in front. Both have halos around their heads. The practice of surrounding the faces of the nobility with halos started from the time of the Mughal emperor Jahangir (r. 1605–27).

There is a portrait of Bahu Begum, whose real name was Amat-ul-Zohra Begum, wife of Shuja-ud-Daula and mother of Asaf-ud-Daula. She died in 1816. The painting depicts three-quarters of her face.[14] She is sitting against a bolster with her legs crossed. With the right hand she is smoking a hookah while the left hand is placed in front. A diaphanous scarf (dupatta) covers a part of her head. The face and hair are typical of Awadh paintings. In the background is a curtain with a tassel in the middle. While the hands of the lady show the European influence, the creases of the lehnga (skirt) and the fine work on the hair are definitely in the northern Mughal style. The painting was done in Faizabad.

A painting of Nawab Asaf-ud-Daula, done in Lucknow, depicts the rather obese Nawab seated on a chair with his face in profile. The

---

[14]Image can be viewed at: https://commons.wikimedia.org/wiki/File:Bahu_Begum_of_Avadh.jpg

Nawab is clad in a voluminous white muslin angarkha (a long tunic). The painting is in the Awadh style, but the carpet below the arch where the Nawab is sitting is of Western design.

With the establishment of the new capital of Awadh at Lucknow in 1775, Awadh painting underwent a minor transformation at the hands of artists Mihr Chand and Mir Kalan Khan. Mihr Chand's paintings were characterized by trees with thick foliage and copious clouds in the sky. These features were adopted by other artists of Awadh as well. Artists, including the aforementioned, produced paintings on traditional themes but sometimes reworked original European portraits of the nawabs painted by visiting European artists like Johan Zoffany (1733–1810)[15] and Tilly Kettle (1735–86)[16]. These European artists have been classified as 'Company painters', but they were not employees of the Company. These artists were freelancers and received commissions from the nawabs and their courtiers. Between the skilled Indian artists and the capable European artists there was also a group of mediocre professionals who were copyists and presented unsigned paintings.

In the times of Nawab Asaf-ud-Daula, painters drew sketches and painted according to the desires and requirements of European patrons and the subjects were incidents in the lives of common Awadhi Indians. However, from the beginning of the nineteenth century, the Awadh paintings fully incorporated Western influences due to the demands of the foreign patrons. In 1810, a portrait of Mirza Muhammad Qasim was painted with the subject sitting on a chair with a hookah pipe in his right hand. The body is three-fourths turned to the viewer. There are lines on the forehead. Light and shade have been used on the face and neck, which characterize Western style. On the other hand, the dress and postures of the hands and feet are quite Oriental.

Ghazi-ud-Din Haider, last nawab and first king of Awadh, had appointed Robert Home as a court painter. Home (1752–1834) worked

---

[15]Johan Joseph Zoffany was a German neoclassical painter, active mainly in England. He made several visits to India.

[16]Tilly Kettle was a portrait painter and the first prominent English portrait painter to work in India.

in the court of the Nawab up to 1828, when he retired. The portrait of Ghazi-ud-Din Haider[17] in a seated position with a crown upon his head, in royal regalia, sporting a sash across his chest and a wide, precious stone-studded belt, and wearing a serene expression is quite impressive. The portrait is unusual in that it is oval-shaped, as the majority of the royal portraits of Awadh were either square or rectangular.

From the early decades of the nineteenth century, Awadh paintings were essentially portraits of ordinary persons who were neither nawabs nor from the gentry. The British Residents and other British people in Awadh were attracted by the commonplace. To them, everyday life and paintings based on it were uncommon and exotic. They collected such portrayals and sent them abroad as gifts. In the Bharat Kala Bhawan in Benaras, there are paintings of a woman at a spinning wheel, a fruit seller and a domestic servant. These paintings, like the pictures of the gentry, show these ordinary people against a background of a blue sky, with a line of trees and small hedges. In Mildred Archer's *Company Drawings in the India Office Library* there are about fifty drawings depicting workaday persons such as an arrow maker, a leather worker, a hookah smoker, a woman making chapatis, a bow maker, a goldsmith, an ironsmith, a camel rider, a sweeper, a woman tying her hair, a woman doing pooja, a greengrocer, a cloth weaver, a washerman, a water carrier, a farmer, a fisherwoman and so on. In the preparation of these paintings, imagination has been used extensively to render people realistically. Some of these pictures are sketches while the rest are in colour. The influence and impact of the European style is quite evident in these pictures.

Although paintings were done mainly on paper, under the European influence, paintings were also made on thin, finely smoothened sheets of ivory, which could be accommodated in the palm of one's hand. Ivory pieces were cut into rounds, ovals or rectangles, and exquisite paintings were prepared in oil. This tradition of painting on ivory started in Delhi and spread to Awadh as well. However, in Awadh, this style was quite ordinary and was seldom refined. In the Victoria Memorial in Kolkata,

---

[17]Image can be viewed at: http://www.historicalportraits.com/Gallery.asp?Page=Item&ItemID=1480&Desc=King-of-Oudh,-by-Robert-Home-%7C-Robert-Home

there are eleven ivory pieces depicting portraits of the nawabs of Awadh, but they are not of a very high quality.

There are several Awadh paintings in which the nawab is shown riding with his army or in a procession, or are representations of special occasions. There are also portraits showing the nawab lost in Muslim prayers. The nawabs have also been depicted enjoying indoor games like chess. Happenings at the court, which were an important feature of the Mughal paintings from the reigns of Akbar and Jahangir, did not find much place in Awadh paintings. However, there are a large number of paintings showing the rulers of Awadh in romantic scenes. Many also portray spectacles of music and dance, which were of interest in Awadh. There are also paintings of royal feasts with British Residents and other dignitaries being entertained. These were perhaps occasions when the splendour of the Awadh courts could be displayed.

The pleasure-loving rulers of Awadh had a carefree, easy and leisurely lifestyle. Apart from the risk of losing their titular kingdom, there were not many stresses, or occasions of strife, conflict and clashes. The atmosphere of general sensuousness engendered an ambience of erotic listlessness and paintings were generally an appendage to poetic compositions. The erotic sentiment is one of the rasas in Hindu aesthetics. There is a Faizabad painting in which a prince holds his beloved in an embrace while gazing at her face. There are plants and colourful clouds in the background.

The Awadh painters, despite their extensive production of portraits, could not surpass or equal the talent of the Mughal painters. But in imaginative creativity, the Awadh painters had a flair for using myriad colours. They put life in the portrayal of historic happenings, stories from Hindu mythology, ragas and raginis, sports of Krishna, social events, everyday lives of noblemen and noblewomen and erotic subjects. Such paintings were composed throughout the Nawabi period. The nawabs of Awadh were broadminded with regard to different religions. Although Hindu subjects did find a place in Mughal paintings, such representation was more copious among the Awadh painters, many of whom were Hindu.

## Famous Painters and their Prominent Work in Awadh

### Faizullah

The earliest Awadh painter is said to be Faizullah, who was brought to Faizabad from Kashmir by Safdarjung, the second Nawab of Awadh (r. 1739–54). There is a miniature painting attributed to him at Faizabad made between 1765 and 1770. It is titled *A Princess in the Zenana at Night*[18]. It is a gouache heightened with gold on paper. A princess and her trusted companion are sitting on a carpet beneath a night sky. They are drinking from porcelain cups filled by maidservants who stand in attendance. All are listening to a group of four female musicians who are playing by candlelight. Behind them is a pavilion laid down between gold illuminated brown and blue borders on wide gold-speckled margins.

Faizullah had brought some paintings with him to Awadh and he executed new ones by copying Mughal paintings. He also worked on old themes and developed miniature paintings in new ways and manners.

In the British Museum there is the painting *A Reluctant Maiden being Led to an Eagerly Awaiting Prince.*[19] It was probably painted in 1760 by Faizullah. The artist's name is discreetly written above the doorway on the left. Another Awadh painting in the British Museum is *A lady visiting a Saivite shrine*[20] done around 1750, which depicts a Hindu lady wrapped closely in a rather transparent sari, with her hair pulled back into a bun, visiting a Hindu shrine. The woman is barefoot and is shown full length in profile. Watching her is a female ascetic with ashen skin, saffron robes and vermilion marks on her forehead. It is ascribed to Faqirullah Khan, father of Faizullah, and was painted around 1740. Another painting in the British Museum is either by Muhammad Afzal, the grandfather of

---

[18]Image can be viewed at: https://commons.wikimedia.org/wiki/File:Prince_in_his_zenana_during_the_festival_of_Holi_18_cent._Biblioth%C3%A8que_nationale_de_France,_Paris.jpg

[19]Image can be viewed at: http://blogs.bl.uk/asian-and-african/2013/05/mughal-painting-faizallah-acquired.html

[20]Image can be viewed at: http://blogs.bl.uk/asian-and-african/2013/05/mughal-painting-faizallah-acquired.html

Faizullah, or Faizullah himself, and was probably painted in 1740. The title of the painting is *A Lady at the Jharokha* (A lady at the window).

## Nevasi Lal

There is a painting attributed to Nevasi Lal who flourished around 1760–76. The title of the painting is *Noblewomen Playing Chess* and it was painted between 1780 and 1800. It is in opaque watercolour and gold on paper. The painting is now in the Guimet Museum, a museum of Asian art in Paris. This painting depicts two noblewomen playing chess while family members and attendants (who are mainly women) gather to watch and relax during the heat of the day. There are at least two dozen elegant women in the painting. The line work is very impressive. The composition may have been inspired by the British artist Tilly Kettle (1735–86), who visited Faizabad in 1772 and left India in 1776.

## Mihr Chand

Up to the beginning of the nineteenth century, Awadh miniature paintings were largely in the style and manner of north Mughal paintings. The European influence on the paintings was first noted in the paintings of Mihr Chand, who flourished around 1759–86. He was among the finest painters of the court of Nawab Shuja-ud-Daula (r. 1753–75). He first worked in Faizabad and then in Lucknow. Mihr Chand was known for his fine copies of European portraits and for his sensitive original compositions. His portraits show the influence of British artist Tilly Kettle. He also made paintings of nature and this genre was practised by Bahadur Singh later.

Mihr Chand made portraits of Nawab Shuja-ud-Daula and Nawab Asaf-ud-Daula.[21] He used his imagination to make a portrait of a courtesan. She is depicted squatting and facing the viewer with her visage and eyes slightly inclined and her black hair flowing. She is holding her dupatta (scarf) above her head like a canopy and it also frames her body. The margins of the painting are thick with floral design. The painting is titled *Tasveer-i Khayal* (*An Imaginary Portrait*).

---

[21]Image can be viewed at: http://blogs.bl.uk/asian-and-african/exhibitions/page/3/

Another of Mihr Chand's paintings, titled *Colonel Polier Watching a Nautch*[22], was made in Faizabad in 1773–74 on paper with opaque watercolour. Polier is wearing Indian garb and is sitting on a European couch. In his right hand is the stem of a hookah, and he is watching two girls performing an Indian dance. Behind the dancers are three standing musicians. Four lighted candles in glass chimneys are also depicted.

Mihr Chand's *A Female Hermit with Two Ascetics before a Hut* (made c. 1765–73) shows two sitting ascetics, who appear emaciated and famished, their middles covered with loose cloth-sheet. The female hermit is well drawn. She is wearing pale yellow clothes. Her right leg is folded and the left knee is upright, upon which her left arm rests. She is wearing earrings and a small turban covers her head with the end of her hair dangling on her left shoulder blade. All three are under a tree with deep green foliage.[23]

A painting titled *A Partridge and an Iris*[24] is in the style of Mihr Chand. It was painted either in Faizabad or Lucknow between 1765 and 1775. It is an opaque watercolour and gold on paper. This painting was part of an album of Antoine Polier (1741–95). It is now in the Museum für Islamische Kunst in Berlin. The partridge is shown in profile with the left leg raised. There is a white patch below the eye, followed by a black upper neck and red lower neck. The chest is black and the feathers are partly white and pink and the lower portion of the bird is white. Behind the standing bird is a violet iris with a greenish yellow bunch of leaves.

## Bahadur Singh

A contemporary of Mihr Chand was Bahadur Singh who won prominence in the times of Nawab Asaf-ud-Daula. Bahadur Singh flourished between 1760 and 1790. He had worked earlier with Mihr Chand and his style

---

[22]Image can be viewed at: https://en.wikipedia.org/wiki/Antoine_Polier#/media/File:Colpolier.jpg

The same painting is depicted on page 180 of *India's Fabled City: The Art of Courtly Lucknow*, by Stephen Markel and Tushara Bindu Gude (Munich: Prestel Verlag, 2010).

[23]The painting is depicted on page 35 of *India's Fabled City: The Art of Courtly Lucknow*.

[24]Image can be viewed at: https://enfilade18thc.files.wordpress.com/2011/04/press-release.pdf

was similar to the latter's. Many paintings by Mihr Chand and Bahadur Singh are in the British Museum. One of Bahadur Singh's paintings depicts a male, probably of noble descent, embracing a woman who has lifted her face to look at the man. The attire of the male is of pink hue and in the dresses of both there is a profusion of yellow. The painting shows a pond in the foreground and a blue sky above. This painting is a typical example of Awadh painting.

Bahadur Singh also painted a full-length portrait in profile titled *Portrait of a Mufti*[25]. It is a watercolour on paper and is part of the Johnson Album. The Mufti (a Muslim traditional legal expert) is dressed in a voluminous, off-white gown with small designs and with very wide sleeves. He has a small conical black beard and is wearing a huge circular turban, which is several times bigger than his face. In the background is a courtyard with a very low white wall. Beyond the wall there is greenery with small, dark green triangular shapes indicating trees. Two-thirds of the painting from the top is pale blue sky with three wisps of white clouds placed almost symmetrically. The painting is in pleasant colours and is well drawn.

## Uttam Chand

Uttam Chand was a contemporary of Mihr Chand and Bahadur Singh and flourished between 1775 and 1780. His style was derived from the Mughal school. It was the practice of the early Awadh painters to take ideas and themes from Mughal painters of Delhi and improvise on them in the environment of Awadh. One of his paintings depicts a Hindu woman visiting a shrine. It is similar to a painting attributed to Faqirullah Khan, the son of painter Muhammad Afzal, which was made around 1740. The contours of the body of the lady in transparent clothes have been slightly changed by Uttam Chand.

---

[25]Image can be viewed at: https://books.google.co.in/books?id=ong F6dkNKAcC&pg =PA43&lpg=PA43&dq=Portrait+of+a+Mufti+Bahadur+Singh&source=bl&ots=lQ_ RjaTp50&sig=Aq38qzB20_axd62Oy4RIqYJrJJE&hl=en&sa=X&ved=0ahUKEwjSkfPMgo_ RAhWJPo8KHXc2B3sQ6AEINjAM#v=onepage&q=Portrait%20of%20a%20Mufti%20 Bahadur%20Singh&f=false

The painting is also depicted on page 63 of *India's Fabled City: The Art of Courtly Lucknow*.

## Mir Kalan Khan

Mir Kalan Khan was an important eighteenth-century artist of the Awadh school. He worked first at Faizabad and then came to Lucknow, where his work influenced many painters. He did not belong to the Awadh court, but his paintings were found both in Faizabad and Awadh. He was earlier a painter in the Delhi court.[26]

Mir Kalan Khan specifically showed firelight and other light sources in his paintings. One of his paintings, done around 1770, titled *A European Princess*, shows the princess in profile, sitting on an ornamental Western chair with her feet on a footstool. She is wearing a tight gown over her ample, full dress, and a decorated turban with an aigrette. An Indian lady with flowing dress stands before her and is probably handing something to her. Behind the princess is another Indian lady. All three women are in pale green dress and are on a marble terrace against a dark background.

A portrait of a European lady by Mir Kalan Khan made in the Awadh style is quite attractive. The bust of the lady is in an oval enclosure. Three-fourths of the face is visible and the eyes are turned towards the right. The lady is holding a mirror. On the left and right of the oval portrait are depictions of two other ladies, one each in a rectangular enclosure. All three ladies are wearing hats and are accoutred in the same style. There is an impression that the three separate pictures are of the same lady, but on closer scrutiny they are different. Though the subjects of the painting are non-Indian, the painting bears the mark of the Awadh style.

The painting of Mir Kalan Khan showing Nawab Shuja-ud-Daula on a hunt has innumerable figures deployed with a sense of control and depicted naturalistically in real space, diminishing in the European manner as the landscape recedes away from the viewer. There are bullock carts, elephants, camels and horses along with a cheetah and a hunting dog. On the border of the painting are crocodiles and lions, springing on their victims.

There is a painting in the style of Mir Kalan Khan, painted sometime

---

[26]Four of Mir Kalan Khan's paintings are included in *India's Fabled City: The Art of Courtly Lucknow*, *Christ as a Child in the Temple*, c. 1760; *A Drowning Man Saved from Marine Monsters*, c. 1750-60; *Lovers in a Landscape*, c. 1760-70; and *Village Life in Kashmir*, c. 1760.

between 1760 and 1765, titled *European Woman Seated on a Terrace Smoking a Venetian Style Waterpipe*[27]. The lady is sitting on a chair in profile but is looking at the viewer. Her long tresses are open and partially flowing over her shoulders. She is wearing a full-length dark pink dress and over it a gold-speckled gown, which is partly open to display her dress. Her chair is on a yellow carpet with a floral design, which in turn is on a green ornamental carpet with a wide, patterned pink border. In the left section of the painting a building can be partly seen. The rest of the background is pinkish brown.

## Govind Singh

Govind Singh employed many colours in his paintings. He made large strokes in colour and was skilled in angular composition. One of his paintings, titled *A Young Girl*, is included in the book *Indian Miniatures in the India Office Library* by Toby Falk and Mildred Archer. The beauty of the girl has been depicted with astonishing attractiveness. She is sitting against a red cushion on a terrace and is holding a red flower in her right hand. In front of the terrace is a row of flowers.

## Honahar

Honahar was a portrait painter. He had worked in the Mughal court, but the charm of the Awadh court drew him there. The majority of his works are portraits of men. His portrait of Aziz Khan Chaghatta displays his control of strokes and shading.

## Thakur Das

Thakur Das was a painter in the court of Ghazi-ud-Din Haider who ruled as nawab from 1814 to 1818 and as king from 1818 to 1827. Thakur Das worked with watercolours as well as oils and was proficient in both styles. His raagmala paintings drew praise from his European admirers.

---

[27]Image can be viewed at:
https://commons.wikimedia.org/wiki/File:European_Woman_Seated_on_a_ Terrace_Smoking_a_Venetian_Style_Water_Pipe_(huqqa);_Folio_from_an_ Album_Belonging_to_Shuja_al-Daula_of_Oudh_LACMA_M.72.88.5_(4_of_4).jpg
It is also depicted on page 166 of *India's Fabled City: The Art of Courtly Lucknow*.

## Muhammad Ali

Muhammad Ali was a painter in the court of Nawab Muhammad Ali Shah, the third king of Awadh (r. 1837–42). He was given the title of Maani Raqam. (Maani was the founder of Manichaeism, a Gnostic religion, and lived near Iran in the third century CE. According to Muslim tradition, Maani was also a famous painter and his name is used as an epithet for distinguished artists and calligraphers.) One of his paintings depicts the coronation of Muhammad Ali Shah.

## Fazl Ali

Fazl Ali, son of Muhammad Ali, was also a painter and worked in the court of Nawab Wajid Ali Shah (r. 1847–56). He made several portraits of the Nawab and the European influence in his works is quite pronounced. He also made paintings of the ladies of the Nawab's parikhana (designated dancers and singers).

## Mammu Jan

Another famous painter of Wajid Ali Shah's times was Muhammad Jan, popularly known as Mammu Jan. He is said to have come to the Awadh court in about 1850. He accompanied the Nawab when he was exiled to Calcutta. Mammu Jan usually painted on rough paper. He signed his work in English.

One of his paintings shows Wajid Ali Shah sitting on a chair facing the viewer with a stick held upright in his right hand.

Another one of his paintings is of a frightened horse galloping away, and has been executed very deftly. The horse's front legs are about to touch the earth and his hind legs have just left the ground. Gusts of wind have blown the horse's mane back. The tail is lifted.

After the Uprising of 1857, Mammu Jan worked for the British. Two albums of paintings in the Bharat Kala Bhawan in Benaras contain works by Mammu Jan.

✑

Apart from these notable artists, there are a few others who are worth mentioning here. Bulaqi Das was so adept at sketching that he could make a portrait of a person in a few minutes. Dr Reena Singh mentions a painter by the name of Husain Bakhsh, who, after 1857, started making fake stamps.

## Some Famous Awadh Paintings

There are a good number of Awadh paintings of a high order in various museums abroad. Some of these are described here.

### *Shuja-ud-Daula and his Ten Sons*, circa 1815[28]

This famous painting was made in Lucknow by an unknown artist and is a watercolour on paper. There is an inset in the painting showing Tilly Kettle painting a portrait of Shuja-ud-Daula and his sons. This painting is in the Victoria and Albert Museum in London.

### *Preparation for the Nuth Uterwai ceremony at a courtesan's kotha*, late eighteenth century[29]

This painting is an opaque watercolour with gold on wasli, laid down later on thin card. On the terrace of a kotha, where courtesans entertain clients, sits the central figure, a nayika (brothel madam) smoking a hookah. There are two women on her right and another woman sits with her face towards the nayika. Another sits on the left of the nayika. A young woman reclining on the ground and wearing a garland of flowers has her head in the lap of the woman to the left. She is the girl to be deflowered and hence initiated into prostitution. In the background is a covered pavilion with three openings covered with a screen. On either side of the pavilion is a covered window.

---

[28]Image can be viewed at: https://theframedpicturecompany.co.uk/art/shuja-ud-daula-nawab-of-oudh-1754-75-and-his-ten-sons-engraved-by-p-renault-1796-coloured-aquatint-138/

[29]Image can be viewed at: http://www.oldindianarts.in/2013/04/preparation-for-nuth-uterwai-ceremony.html

## Hamida Banu Begum, wife of Mughal Emperor Humayun, late nineteenth century[30]

This is a painting of the Anglo-Indian school at Lucknow and is an opaque watercolour on waraq, laid down later on card. The painting is mistitled *Hamida Banu Begum, zauja (wife) of Shah Jahan Badshah.*

## Muhammad Shah enthroned on a terrace at night with his officers, circa 1735[31]

This is a painting by Nidha Mal, who was active between 1735 and 1775. His name is neatly signed near the pierced balustrade to the left. This is an opaque watercolour with gold on paper and is in the San Diego Museum of Art. The painting depicts Mughal Emperor Muhammad Shah, holding a hookah, on the open terrace in the royal garden at Delhi, engaged in a conference with his inner circle of ministers. The mood in this court scene is sombre.

## Devgandhar Ragini, Faizabad, circa 1780[32]

This is an opaque watercolour with gold on wasli. A bearded Hindu holy man in a loincloth sits on a hide facing two young women sitting together. An attendant of the hol yman stands behind him with a whisk. There is a single tree in the background between the figures and there are some buildings sketched in the distant background. The painting is in sepia tones and has a double border.

---

[30]Image can be viewed at: https://en.wikipedia.org/wiki/Hamida_Banu_Begum#/media/File:Hamida_Banu_Begum,_wife_of_Mughal_Emperor_Humayun.jpg

[31]Image can be viewed at:
http://www.art.com/products/p36987905605-sa-i9612269/nidha-mal-muhammad-shah-enthroned-on-a-terrace-at-night-with-his-officers-c-1735.htm?sOrig    =CAT&sOrigID=0&dimVals=0&ui=C0799F5F79E8411 D9BE0104360AA61B7

[32]Image can be viewed at: http://www.mughalart.net/ragamala-illustration-devgandhar-ragini-mughal-circa-1780.html

### *Portrait of Mughal Emperor Aurangzeb in a Jharokha,* late eighteenth century

This is an opaque watercolour with tooled gold on wasli. The Emperor is shown in profile. In his right hand is a sword in a scabbard, which rests on his right shoulder. The left arm is bent at the clbow at right angles, and the fingers are pointing ahead. The portrait is small and there are at least five floral borders of varying widths.

### *Posthumous portrait of Nawab Saadat Khan of Awadh,* Lucknow, 1760[33]

This is a gouache and gold on wasli. Muhammad Amin Musawi was made the first Nawab of Awadh by the Mughal Emperor Muhammad Shah and was given the title Saadat Ali Khan. He died in 1739 resisting the invasion of Delhi by Nadir Shah.

### *A fairy princess at court flanked by fairies before a prince surrounded by demons,* late eighteenth century

This is a manuscript illustration, probably from the *Gul-i Bakawali.* It is a gouache painting with gold on wasli and is from Awadh. In all likelihood it is based on a popular Indian tale of a prince called Taj-ul-Mulk and a fairy princess called Bakawali. The story possibly originated in eighteenth-century Mughal India and was rendered in Urdu, Persian and Bengali.

### *Lady at her toilette on a palace terrace,* late eighteenth century[34]

It is an opaque watercolour with gold on wasli, laid down later on thin card. The painting shows a voluptuous lady doing her toilette while sitting on a wooden pedestal. She is partly clad in a sari, which covers the left thigh and leg with the knee bared. She is topless and her long hair is

---

[33]Image can be viewed at: http://www.indianminiaturepaintings.co.uk/Awadh_Saadat_Khan_14911.html

[34]Image can be viewed at: http://www.oldindianarts.in/2012/09/lady-at-her-toilette-on-palace-terrace.html

loose. Her face is in profile, turned towards her left.

## Mughal and Awadh Painting: Influences and Deviations

In Awadh paintings, special attention was paid to decoration, adornment and embellishment. This extended to clothing, ornaments, footwear and turbans, and embraced flowers, trees, flower beds, colourful skies and ponds also. The artists were also skilful at capturing the expressions of the characters. Whether they related to fear in the eyes of women at the sight of a snake, or amazement at lightning bursting from thick black clouds, or the romantic feelings aroused in women during a storm, the emotions and expressions have been brought out masterfully in Awadh paintings.

Portraiture was the very foundation of Mughal painting. Faces in profile, with a single eye showing, were common and were slightly raised with about two-thirds of the body depicted. Initially, Awadh painting followed the Mughal model of showing standing human figures in profile with one eye visible. However, there is a slight difference in Awadh paintings, in that the figures are depicted with one and a half or one and three-quarters of the eyes visible. Whatever be the alignment of the eyes in a portrait, the feet are usually turned in another direction. This is common to both Mughal and Awadh paintings.

Bodily appearance and contours of individuals in both Mughal and Awadh paintings are fairly similar. Beauty and excellence in form were the aims of the artists. Wide foreheads, well-defined noses with a slight, parrot-like bend and small, round chins are common. Mughal painters were more proficient in delineating the countenance than Awadh painters as the former did precise work on the face and head. Mughal painters also gave a lot of attention to the hands, whereas the Awadh painters did not. It seems that Awadh artists expended all their energies on faces; and hands and fingers received secondary attention. Eyes were delicately drawn by Mughal painters, but this sensitivity was lacking in Awadh painting. In Mughal paintings, the eyes are natural with a lot of feeling. In Awadh paintings, although the eyes are extra large and beautifully drawn, they lack the intensity and warmth of those in Mughal paintings.

In Awadh paintings as in the Mughal style, portraits showed the figures in profile, either sitting or standing in a conventional landscape. However, Tilly Kettle painted large portraits in natural poses with figures full-face. The Indian painters in Awadh quickly adopted the Western style and copied such paintings in miniatures.

Because of the salience of court life in Mughal paintings, the Mughal pictures were termed 'court paintings'. Such paintings depict the court life of Mughal kings and their personal life. The focus is on the king and the rest of the features orbit round him. Since the king is the central point, the splendour and grandeur of the life shown is in accordance with imperial requirements. Even casual paintings show the king dispensing justice or visible in a window. The domain of Awadh was on a much lower key as compared to that of the Mughal Empire. There are hardly any court paintings showing the resplendence and glory of the Awadh court.

Shikar paintings received a boost in the reign of Ghazi-ud-Din Haider, when the European influence had permeated Awadh paintings. Some paintings depict the Nawab and his British companions hunting on elephant back. Bharat Kala Bhawan in Benaras has in its collection a few siyahqalam pictures depicting hunting scenes. These are charcoal and pencil sketches and in some of them, a single colour has been used sparingly. In this group there is an attractive painting of a nawab accompanied by a group of elephants hunting a tiger. There are also paintings of British Residents chasing shikar on horseback. It should be noted that the nawabs of Awadh delighted in hunting on elephant-back. The shikar paintings of the Awadh school are oriented horizontally, unlike those of the Mughal school, which are oriented vertically.

The Mughals as well as the rulers of Awadh were essentially secular in outlook and celebrated both Hindu and Muslim festivals with verve and exhilaration. There are many Mughal paintings that display splendid celebrations not only of Eid but also of Holi and Diwali. The September 1958 issue of the journal *Marg* (Bombay) carries an image of a Mughal painting from the Chester Beatty Museum in Dublin, which depicts the gaiety of Holi. The king is walking towards his festooned throne with his hands on the shoulders of two beautiful women. A group of delicate women is engrossed in throwing colours at each other.

Merrymaking and exuberance during festivals in the presence of the nawab are also widely depicted in Awadh paintings. However, in Mughal paintings, the king is invariably distant from such merrymakers, who carry on the festivities in separate groups.

There are Mughal paintings with ordinary characters also, but they are few in number. Bazaar scenes have fruit sellers, dyers and common craftsmen. The subjects of the early Awadh paintings, which were a corollary of north Mughal paintings, are rarely ordinary persons, although there are paintings of Hindu and Muslim holy men, mendicants, recluses, yogis and yoginis. However, with the heavy European influence on Awadh painting, ordinary scenes, artisans and common persons were often depicted.

During Mughal times, especially in the reign of Emperor Akbar, the illustration of books was prominently done, particularly for Persian translations of Hindu epics. Mention may be made of the paintings made in the *Razm Nama* (which was the Persian translation of the *Mahabharata*) and in *'Iyar-i Danish*, which was Sheikh Abu'l Fazl's improved Persian version of the Arabic *Kalilahwa Dimnah* by Ibn al-Muqaffa, which in turn was sourced from the Sanskrit *Panchatantra*. However, in Awadh, painters worked separately and independently on such subjects as Baz Bahadur and Rani Roopmati, Laila and Majnun, Shirin and Khusro, and so on. The painting of Baz Bahadur and Roopmati shows both of them on horseback. There is also a poignant Awadh painting on the death of Farhad. Such paintings, according to Dr Reena Singh, were also done after the end of the Nawabi era of Awadh.

The Awadh school also includes several ragamala paintings. A raga is a musical phrase that evokes, according to Indian tradition, an emotion. It appears that the depiction of ragas in painting started around the sixteenth century with the Vaishnava Bhakti movement in Indian literature, when there was an attempt to clothe devotion to God in earthly terms. The paintings of this genre make profuse metaphorical use of the Shiva-Parvati and Radha-Krishna themes. In other words, these paintings are an amalgam of literature and music in colour and form. The Awadh school of painting also incorporated the use of ragas and raginis and, with the help of natural surroundings and everyday life, the pain, longing and vicissitudes of love, ardour and attachment were freely shown, which could be interpreted as divine or profane love.

Between 1780 and 1782, Richard Johnson (1753–1807), the Assistant Resident of the East India Company in Awadh, had a series of ragamala paintings done. In his album no 32, popularly known as the Johnson Ragamala, there are thirty-six ragamala paintings. Each painting includes the raga and the relevant season on the top. Some of these paintings were done by Bahadur Singh, who flourished around 1775, and all these paintings were done in studios in Lucknow. The earlier ragamala paintings were executed by Ram Sahai, Bahadur Singh and Moolchand during the 1760s and 1770s in Faizabad. Other ragamala painters were Udvat Singh and Mohan Singh. Some paintings on ragas were done in Lucknow by Girdhari Lal and Sital Das.

Paintings of the Mughal school were largely confined to portraits, manuscript illustrations and nature studies. This focus was, to a large extent, accepted and appropriated by Awadh painters. If the matter is further examined, it will be seen that the backbone of Awadh paintings lies in its portrait studies and erotic and romantic coverage. Although both Mughal and Awadh paintings covered common subjects, it was the distinctiveness and individuality of the artists that brought out novelty and originality. Mughal portraits are characterized by an awareness of feeling, reality and subtleness. There are a few examples of Awadh paintings that surpass Mughal paintings in genuineness and liveliness, but this is due largely to the European influence.

Awadh painters in portraying nature did not have the range and scope that Mughal painters exhibited, especially during the reign of Jahangir. The Mughal painter Ustad Mansur was famous for his animal and bird paintings, which were exemplary. Mammu Jan of Awadh in the nineteenth century specialized in painting horses, dogs and cats and showed these animals in motion, with their eyes and necks in movement.

The male garments shown in Mughal paintings reach below the knee and the upper garment is quite voluminous, whereas the attires in Awadh paintings are translucent. The main female attire in Mughal paintings is the peshwaz, which is sometimes excessively transparent.

According to Dr Reena Singh, the Lucknow painters used white and gold colours similar to Delhi Mughal paintings, but learnt their application from the Jaipur school. The traditional Mughal style, as practised in Awadh, thrived up to Nawab Saadat Ali Khan (r. 1798–1814) and after him the nawabs were inclined to accept European influences in local paintings. J. P. Losty has pointed out that gradually in Awadh, pure watercolour paintings evolved into the use of gouache as it gave way to bright and heavy colours.

The European influence became pronounced during the periods of Nawab Ghazi-ud-Din Haider (r. 1814–18) and Nasir-ud-Din Haider (r. 1827–37), who were admirers of English customs. However, both styles—traditional and European-influenced—existed side by side.

In Mughal paintings, the margins are usually wide, while early Awadh paintings have insignificant and thin margins with minimal ornamentation. The margins in the Awadh school are only to encompass the main painting. In some paintings, there is no balance or harmony in the narrow borders with flowers and creepers. Occasionally, instead of flowers, peacock feathers are depicted. Slender, triple borders also came into vogue in Awadh paintings. Some of the multi-bordered paintings feature Persian calligraphy. Gold was frequently used in the margins to lend conspicuous decoration to paintings. Gradually, ornamental margins were replaced with thick lines in black, blue, brown or sometimes yellow. With the adoption and acceptance of European influences, the margins almost disappeared in later Awadh paintings. In fact, one of the methods of identifying Awadh paintings is to examine the margins of the paintings.

## Depiction of Nature in Awadh Paintings

One of the characteristics of Mughal painting is the vivid depiction of nature in all its moods and characters. Every painter has attempted to translate nature into his painting to convey man's close relation with the scenery, environment and landscape. As Awadh painting was a modified form of Mughal painting, nature was an adjunct and accessory for the creativity of the painter. The early Awadh paintings portray different forms of natural surroundings worked out by imagination. Later paintings feature more realistic scenes and views. The Indian Muslim rulers had a pronounced love for nature. The gardens they created personified a modest effort to recreate the euphoria of paradise. This was one of the ways to lighten the burden of a rugged and tough life. Although the rulers of Awadh scarcely led a hard life, as an established convention, the natural and peaceful settings of nature were a matter of routine in the art composed.

In the pursuit of representation of nature, the Awadh painters always endeavoured to show the natural environment intensely in the background in portraits. Where this has not been possible, a character in the painting sometimes holds a flower. In scenes depicting the rendezvous of lovers, painters have depicted the longing and elation of the heart with blooming flowers. Where pangs of separation are shown, the forlornness of the situation is emphasized by showing still waters, motionless birds and animals, dry creepers and weeping willows.

All paintings of romantic couples like Laila and Qais (Majnun), Shirin and Farhad, Radha and Krishna and Baz Bahadur and Roopmati have been made against backgrounds of abundant natural surroundings. There is a painting made during the reign of Nawab Shuja-ud-Daula where in the foreground a palace and a garden have been shown but in the background Laila and Majnun are sitting under a willow tree. They are surrounded by bears, leopards and deer. Such depiction of nature in Awadh paintings was prominently visible in the eighteenth century, but in the nineteenth century, under the strong European influence, such representation became rare.

According to Dr Reena Singh, several paintings of beautiful flowers are attributable to the Awadh painters. They were perhaps paintings of the flora of Awadh that were made at the behest of Western enthusiasts for sending to their own country as part of their endeavour to familiarize them with the Indian subcontinent.

## Women and Romance in Awadh Paintings

One striking aspect of Awadh painting is the prolific display of women. Most of them are portraits of princesses, begums and ordinary women in various postures, stances and arrangements. Paintings depict begums strolling on the terrace, smoking the hookah, enjoying music and dance, adorning and beautifying themselves at toilette and spending time in gardens or open terraces. In other words, these paintings show the daily life and activity of women of the noble class.

There is a Lucknow painting in which a girl, angry with her lover, is sitting in a solitary flower bower with scattered hair, watching birds. In another painting, the lady is suffering the pangs of separation and playing the veena. Paintings were also made depicting offended beloveds being wooed by persistent and tenacious lovers. Divine and profane love, including moving portraits of Radha and Krishna, are among the very popular subjects of Awadh paintings.

In the *Critical Catalogue of Miniature Paintings in the Baroda Museum* by O.C. Gangoly, there are about six miniature paintings of the Lucknow school that depict the beloved as unadorned and separated from her lover; subdued colours have been used to heighten the woeful situation.

Wajid Ali Shah is said to have had an abiding interest in beautiful women. Apart from his legal wives, there were several women with whom he entered into a temporary Shia form of marriage, and who were called paris (fairies). Several paintings have been made featuring Wajid Ali Shah and his paris. In one, the Nawab is shown reclining, surrounded by his favourite paris. The Nawab's curls are in disarray. The hairstyles of the paris are of different types. There is another painting in which the Nawab is engaged in romantic dallying with a pari and two other ladies are attending them. However, if we compare the romantic Rajasthani paintings with the Awadh paintings of the same genre, the former are superior to those of the Awadh artists.

In a painting going back to the period of Nawab Shuja-ud-Daula, a prince is shown in full profile standing close to a lady (also in full profile) and gazing into her eyes. He holds a cup of wine and is evidently in a beautiful garden. The couple is under a tree with white and red flowers. The intimacy of the couple seems to have caused the flowers to bloom in a rocky place as if it is spring. In the foreground, a stream is running swiftly, emphasizing the amorous atmosphere. This is a rare Awadh painting in the Mughal style in which emotions have been glowingly and colourfully brought out.

In Mughal paintings, women, like men, were typically shown in profile with only one eye visible. From the beginning of the nineteenth century, portraits of women from the Awadh school were greatly influenced by the European style and attempted to show depth and shading. We may recall the portrait of Bahu Begum that has been discussed earlier. This painting is clearly influenced by European techniques. This sort of depiction was alien to the earlier Mughal paintings. In Mughal paintings, the faces of the women are round and ample and this is because of the impact of Chinese styles of painting. Generally in Awadh paintings, female visages are narrow and long. However, in rendering the face and eyes, the Awadh paintings fail to surpass Mughal paintings. The faces in Mughal paintings are far more powerful and impressive. The attires in Awadh paintings are more transparent than in traditional Mughal paintings and women are depicted in bright colours. The diaphanous dresses have highlighted body contours. In both Mughal and Awadh paintings, the use of pearls by ladies has been emphasized. In Awadh paintings, women are frequently barefoot, but in Mughal paintings, the women are often in embroidered footwear.

Ladies in Awadh paintings are often shown with black, curly hair flowing over their shoulders, or in some instances, their hair is tied in a small knot. Hairstyles in later paintings, however, varied. In the times of Nawab Wajid Ali Shah, the ladies associated with him were often shown with different styles of partings and puffs.

There are several paintings of ladies at their toilette. In one, a begum is being bathed, in another, her hair is being braided, in a third, dye is being applied to her feet and in yet another, a lady is being massaged. In Awadh, there was much appreciation for the beauty, allure and charm of women, and the artists fully exploited this fascination. This was in spite of the rigid seclusion of women and the painters, it must be presumed, utilized their imagination to the largest extent. The sensuousness of women as represented in Awadh paintings was akin to that of the women in Rajasthani paintings.

There is a painting, made in Lucknow, of a lady going to a Shiva temple for worship. The beauty of the woman is shown in full profile.

She is wearing a translucent dress, which gives a glimpse of her well-formed body. Her eyebrows are like stiff bows. Her ornaments enhance her charm. Her feet are very attractive and are in motion. The left foot is on the ground and the right foot is partly raised. The painter has coloured the ground around the feet in dark shades and so has brought out the elegance of the fair feet. This painting supports the view that the best Awadh paintings are as good as the finest Rajasthani paintings.

⁓

After the end of the Nawabi period in Awadh, artists ceased to have a professional social status. With the coming of the British in Awadh, the temper and attitude to life changed. Earlier, artists and craftsmen had excelled in giving aesthetic value and quality to their creations. However, with the withdrawal of the patronage of the nawabs, arts and skills became only a means of earning a livelihood and, to a certain extent, art took a secondary place. The artistic traditions of Awadh were dramatically transformed by the social, political and economic changes that took place with the advent of colonial rule in the nineteenth century. Subsequently, photography came to India and gradually the demand for hand-painted pictures diminished.

## Aquatint and Lithography

In Awadh, the art of painting was supplemented by the production of aquatints and the art of lithography came in later. An aquatint resembles a watercolour and is made by etching a copper plate with nitric acid; resin and varnish are used to produce tonal shading. The introduction of lithography in India resulted in its application for printing books in Persian and Urdu scripts. Lucknow was fortunate to catch the attention of several Western artists who captured the Oriental buildings and scenes in realistic details. Fine prints have come out from the efforts of these artists. We shall take up a few of them who considered Awadh in their works.

Lithography was invented by Alois Senefelder (1771–1834) in 1796. Senefelder was born in Bohemia, then part of Germany, and was a failed actor and playwright. Lithography literally means writing and designing on stone. Usually, two methods were employed. In one, writing or designing was done on a limestone tablet with a steel pen; the writing was done in reverse, while the design was made in the form of a mirror image. Although this was difficult, it gave the best results. In the second method, the writing or design was done on transfer paper in the normal way. It was then transferred to the stone tablet where it appeared in reverse. The writing or design on the stone was retracted with lithographic ink. When the ink was dry, the stone was treated with dilute nitric acid, which ate away the surface of the stone, except in the areas impregnated with ink. In Lucknow, instead of nitric acid, lemon juice was used. A sheet of paper was pressed onto the stone by using a press or a rolling cylinder over the paper. The required number of copies was then printed.

William Daniell (1769–1837), a British painter and engraver, and his uncle Thomas Daniell (1749–1840) both came to Calcutta in 1786. They travelled to many Indian cities including Lucknow. The work done by the Daniells in India resulted in the publication of the *Oriental Scenery* in six volumes from 1795 to 1808. Of these, only the third volume, published in 1801, contained aquatints of Awadh, which were drawn and engraved:

i)   Gate of the 'Loll-Baug, at Fyzabad'
ii)  The 'Punj Mahalla Gate, Lucnow'
iii) 'Palace of Nawaub Suja Dowla, at Lucnow'
iv)  'Lucnow taken from the opposite bank of the River Goomty'

Later on, *The Oriental Annual, or Scenes in India* was published in seven volumes between 1834 and 1840. Only volumes II, V and VI contain engravings of Awadh, which are:

i)   The 'Moah-Pankee at Lucnow' (which was actually a pleasure boat in the shape of a peacock feather, i.e., 'morpankhi') (volume II, 1835)
ii)  Mausoleum at 'Lucnow' (volume II, 1835)
iii) Garden of the Palace, 'Lucnow' (volume II, 1835)
iv)  Part of Oude (volume V, 1838)
v)   A Celebrated Well at 'Lucnow' (volume VI, 1839)

Another British artist by the name of Henry Salt (1760–1827) also made excellent aquatints and travelled in India visiting Benaras, Lucknow and Madras. According to critics, Salt was considered a worthy successor to the Daniells. However, he made very few sketches of Lucknow. Only two have come to the notice:

i) Mosque at Lucknow, hand-coloured aquatint, 1809
ii) A View of Lucknow, hand-coloured aquatint, 1809

Another aquatint artist was George Hunt whose works are quite rare. One of his aquatints was titled 'City of Lucknow, Capital of Province of Oude, on the Goomty River, 1824.'[35]

Clifford Henry Mecham was a lieutenant in the Madras Army. He was responsible for 'probably the most celebrated series of views of the Mutiny, showing in graphic detail the destruction wrought on the 37-acre Residency compound between June and November 1857', including 'tunneling activities, a feature of the Siege'. His works were published as a book, *Sketches & Incidents of the Siege of Lucknow. From Drawings Made during the Defence. With Descriptive Notices by George Couper, Esq., late Secretary to the Chief Commissioner of Oude.* The book has a tinted lithographed title page with vignette and twenty-six fine-tinted lithographed views on seventeen plates, with original tissue guards. Some of the views of the Lucknow Residency in the book are:

i) Front View of the Residency
ii) The Balley Guard Battery and Hospital
iii) Interior of the Residency Billiard Room
iv) Near View from the Highlanders Post
v) Lying in Wait & Sinking a Shaft

John Luard (1790–1875) was an expert lithographer and he is referred to as 'one of the most talented of the amateur artists who depicted India'. One of his colour lithographs of Lucknow made in 1830s is titled 'Roonnee Durwaza, Lucknow', and depicts the Rumi Gate.

One of the outstanding books on lithographs of Lucknow is *General*

---

[35]Image can be viewed at: http://www.asommer.de/en/karte/city-of-lucknow-capital-of-province-oude-on-the-goomty-river/

*Views & Special Points of Interest of the City of Lucknow. From Drawings Made on the Spot by Lieut. Col. D.S. Dodgson, A.A.G. With Descriptive Notices.* It has a lithographed title and twenty-seven tinted lithographed views of Lucknow on eleven sheets with an engraved plan at the end. One of the lithographs in this book is titled 'View from the Iron Bridge'. The iron bridge of Lucknow was built during the reign of Nawab Amjad Ali Shah (r. 1842–47). The iron structure was imported from Britain and the Nawab approached the East India Company for help in building the bridge, which was finally constructed by the Bengal Engineers. The image depicts the view from the iron bridge looking up the river Gomti towards the Chattar Manzil Palace and the Dil Aram Palace.

Another lithograph in Dodgson's book is titled 'Budshur Bagh'. The place referred to is the Badshah Bagh, which was originally a royal garden constructed by Nawab Nasir-ud-Din Haider (r. 1827–37), and according to Dodgson, 'it had a fine open pavilion for cockfights and was surrounded by pleasant walks'. The flower-filled garden and shallow lakes created a sylvan surrounding for the Nawab's harem, which also included European women. After the Uprising of 1857, the Maharaja of Kapurthala acquired Badshah Bagh. The Lucknow University complex now stands in its place. Other lithographs in the book are 'Fortress of Jellalabad', 'Bank's House' and 'Interior of the Compound of Alum Bagh'.

## Photography

There is a great deal of speculation as to who first took photographs in Lucknow or who was the first practising photographer in the city. In her thesis, titled 'Monumental Vision: Architectural Photography in India, 1840-1901', Sophie Gordon[36] mentions a two-part panoramic photograph of the Rumi Darwaza (the gateway into the Asafi Bara Imambara, Aurangzeb Mosque and Bara Imambara complex). The photographs give a confused, unclear and indeterminate view. They were taken by Alexis de la Grange, (1825–1917) and are titled 'The Rumi Darwaza, with

---

[36]In 2010, Sophie Gordon submitted a thesis for Doctor of Philosophy to the Department of History of Art, School of Oriental and African Studies, University of London.

the Asafi Imambara to the right and river Gomti to the left'. These two albumen prints were taken in 1850–51 and are in the Canadian Centre for Architecture in Montreal.

Sophie Gordon writes, '[...] the city of Lucknow [...] became one of the most photographed locations in nineteenth-century India because of the events of the 1857 Uprising.' Further, 'Lucknow attracted a large number of commercial photographers who were drawn by the opportunities offered by a site of such emotional value.' Gordon is of the view that besides Calcutta and Delhi, Lucknow was '[...] photographed repeatedly in the nineteenth century, and which appear over and over again in personal photograph albums, amateur work and commercial stock.'

Donald Horne MacFarlane (1830–1904), a Scottish amateur photographer, visited Lucknow in 1860. MacFarlane exhibited a 'very fine collection of views taken in Lucknow, the North-West and in and about Calcutta.'

The panorama of Lucknow taken by Felice Beato from one the minarets of the Asafi Imambara comprises a sequence of eight views giving a bird's-eye view of the buildings in the area as they existed in 1858. Similarly, a six-part panorama was captured in 1858 from the roof of the Raushan al-Daula Kothi in Qaisar Bagh.[37]

David Harris, in his essay on Felice Beato's photographs of India in *India Through The Lens: Photography 1840-1911*, edited by Vidya Dehejia, has commented that '[...] the historical value of such photographs rests upon their ability to reveal aspects of the inner mechanics of imperialism, and particularly in furnishing an apparently objective, but in reality a highly circumscribed and one-sided record of the contemporaneous events.'

Two other photographs of Lucknow taken by Beato that have found place in *India Through the Lens* also need mention as they have been well produced: 'Tomb of Sa'adat Ali Khan at Qaisar Bagh' (page 140), and 'Exterior of Asaf-ud-Daula's Imambara' (page 145).

---

[37]Both the panoramas have been reproduced in *India's Fabled City: The Art of Courtly Lucknow*.

Mention must also be made of the British husband and wife team who took post-Uprising photographs in Lucknow in 1858. They were Robert Christopher Tytler (1818–72), a soldier, naturalist and photographer, and his second wife Harriet Tytler (1828–1907), who documented the monuments of Delhi and made notes on the 1857 turmoil.

An album of old photographs called the 'Dannenberg Album' of Indian Mutiny sites and buildings was presented to the British Museum in 1967.[38] It contains seventy-one photographs taken by John Dannenberg along with copies of drawings. It includes photographs taken by Beato, which have been copied, trimmed or touched up. The album contains about twelve scenes of the Lucknow Residency and also photographs of several monuments in Lucknow, such as Chhattar Manzil, Khurshid Manzil, Asafi Imambara mosque, Rumi Darwaza, Machchi Bhawan, Qaisar Bagh gate, La Martinière and Begum Kothi in Hazratganj. According to Sophie Gordon, although Dannenberg was in Lucknow before 1857, he was not there at the time of the Uprising of 1857. Dannenberg visited Lucknow again in 1859 and took a series of views in albumen prints. In 1892, Dannenberg reprinted some photographs of Lucknow and published the album under the title *Mutiny Memorials*.

John Edward Saché (1824–82) was another photographer who recorded the monuments of Lucknow, especially after the Uprising of 1857. He was born in Prussia as Johann Edvart Zachert, and then migrated to Philadelphia in the United States. He arrived in Calcutta in late 1864 and began a partnership with W.F. Westfield under the name Saché and Westfield. While still in partnership, Saché opened a studio in Nainital and from there recorded a large part of North India in photographs. His advertisement in 1868 confirmed that he had compiled 'a new and large selection of over 500 10x12 plates of Nynee Tal, Bheem Tal, Almorah, Delhi, Lucknow, Cawnpore, Calcutta and Bengal Views'.

Saché set up a network of studios, including one in Lucknow (from 1871). Lucknow afforded him ample opportunity to record images depicting monuments. An albumen print taken by Saché around 1866–

---

[38]The album details can be accessed at: https://www.bl.uk/catalogues/indiaofficeselect/PhotoShowDescs.asp?CollID=459

67 shows the Husainabad complex, tank, and Satkhanda with the Jama Masjid. This is one of the rare photographs from the nineteenth century that shows the Satkhanda, a four-storey circular building, 67 metres high, built in 1842 by Nawab Muhammad Ali Shah. This photograph was also reproduced in a picture postcard.

P.C. Mookherji, in his book *The Pictorial Lucknow*, states that photography in Lucknow began to flourish from 1850 onwards. He credits Ahmad Ali Khan (Chotay Mian) as the 'designer of Hoseinabad and Kaisarbagh buildings', and tells us that the latter learnt the art of photography from an Englishman. According to Mookherji, Ahmad Ali Khan, having joined the mutineers, 'lost his fortune and name and died a miserable man'. We have no record as to when this photographer died, but Sophie Gordon has added that 'no photographs later than c. 1862 have come to light'. Either Ahmad Ali Khan died after 1862 or he gave up photography. Ahmad Ali Khan was therefore active from the 1850s to 1862.

The next important photographer of Lucknow was Darogha Abbas Ali, a retired municipal engineer. His period of activity was from the late 1860s to around 1880. He was probably the only nineteenth-century Indian photographer to have issued his photographs in book form. There is an interesting article, 'Darogha Ubbas Alli: An Unknown 19th Century Indian Photographer' by Brij Bhushan Sharma, published in the *History of Photography* (Volume 7, Number 1, January 1983). Sharma states that although Raja Deen Dayal seemed to dominate photography, Darogha Abbas Ali ought to be better known for his architectural studies of Lucknow. His album of photographs with notes, called *The Lucknow Album*, came out in 1874. Its full title reads as: *The Lucknow Album. Containing a Series of Fifty Photographic Views of Lucknow and its Environs together with a large sized Plan of the City executed by Darogha Ubbas Alli, Assistant Municipal Engineer. To the above is added a full description of each scene depicted. The whole forming a complete illustrated guide to the City of Lucknow the capital of Oudh.*

The second book by Darogha Abbas Ali was titled *An Illustrated Historical Album of the Rajas and Taaluqdars of Oudh.* The book has 344 photographs, albumen prints, one 5×4 inches and the others approximately

3×2 inches, titled in Urdu. The smaller prints are mounted four per page within ruled borders, each with printed titles in English on mount.

Mookherji asserts that Abbas Ali also published *The Beauties of Lucknow*, containing photographs of dancing girls of the city. Mookherji is the only person to have attributed this album of dancing girls to Darogha Abbas Ali. The book itself does not mention the name of the photographer and is therefore anonymous. The full title of the book is *The Beauties of Lucknow Consisting of Twenty-Four Selected Photographed Portraits, Cabinet Size, of the Most Celebrated and Popular Living Histrionic Singers, Dancing Girls, and Actresses of the Oudh Court and of Lucknow.*

Regarding the photographs in the album, Zahid R. Chaudhary observes: '[...] the photographic portrait (is) in line with the Indian tradition of miniature painting, and the representation of the veil's blankness in a photographic album [...] written on the very surface of the images, overlay the reality effects of photography with more familiar aesthetic tools.'

Many of the singers and dancers in the album are in theatrical costume for the Urdu opera *Inder Sabha* by Syed Agha Hasan Amanat Lakhnavi and a close examination of the bearing and deportment of the women shows that most of them are under twenty years of age.

*The Beauties of Lucknow* is an extremely rare album of old photographs of Indian women. We may also say that this compilation was the first published series of recordings of Indian women in photographs and as such its significance and importance has to be acknowledged.

From 1859, the practice of having 'carte de visites' made came into vogue; the term meant 'visitor card'. The *Photograph Manual: A Practical Treatise*, published in 1862, referred to the 'carte de visite', but acknowledged that the common name was 'card portrait'. G. Thomas, in his article 'Indian Courtesans in Cartes-de-Visite', published in *History of Photography* (Volume 8, No. 2, April-June 1984), observed:

> Cartes-de-visite of the nineteenth century covered a wide spectrum of subjects, and were indeed 'an interface between photography and the social scene'. People wanted to have their photographs taken 'to share among friends and to express social standing'; the likenesses were

'inexpensive, easy to look at and easy to care for', and much cheaper than a painter's miniature, providing a commercial application of photography in sales of the object depicted.

Although 'respectable' women in nineteenth-century India shunned their photographs being taken because of the prevalence of the veil, some group photographs were taken, but were not intended for display. However, for courtesans, photographs were a means of publicity. The singing and dancing girls posed in all their finery and sometimes with the musical instruments that they could play.

The last important Indian photographer of Lucknow was Mashkur-ud-Daula, who spelt his name as 'Mushkooruddowlah'. P.C. Mookherji in his book *The Pictorial Lucknow* wrote: '[...] Mushkoor-ud-dowlah was the famous photographer of Lucknow and Oudh. His figures and views are excellent. He had an evenness of tone which common photographers cannot attain. Many of his views are printed in this book. He died a rich man, and is known by the title, which the ex-king of Oudh gave him.'

Dr Naiyer Masud in his book *Anis* has given the full name of the photographer as Mashkur-ud-Daula Haider Jan, and tells us that he is said to have practised photography after 1857.

Joachim K. Bautze in an article in *Prajñādhara: Essays on Asian Art, History, Epigraphy and Culture in Honour of Gouriswar Bhattacharya*, edited by Gerd J.R. Mevissen and Arundhati Banerji, has recorded that some of the portraits taken by Abbas Ali and by Mushkur-ud-Daula in the late 1860s and early 1870s show the same backdrop. It is therefore speculated that perhaps both these photographers shared the same studio. Further, both Abbas Ali and Mushkur-ud-Daula photographed courtesans as well as the male gentry. The photographs taken by Mashkur-ud-Daula had at the back the name 'Mushkooruddowlah' followed by 'Photographer/Lucknow'.

The fourth and last important Indian photographer of Lucknow was Asghar Jan. Not much information on him is available in any of the English publications on Lucknow. However, there is a rare, one-page article, 'Glimpses of Old Lucknow' by Syed Haider Abbas Musavi Safavi, which was published on 22 October 1972 in the now defunct *The Illustrated Weekly of India* (Bombay). According to Safavi, Syed Asghar

Jan, popularly known as Nawab Bannan Sahib, belonged to the family of Insha Allah Khan 'Insha', an eminent Urdu poet. He became interested in photography and travelled to Calcutta, where he probably learnt the art from an English photographer. He returned to Lucknow and opened a studio in Qaisar Bagh, which he probably operated jointly with his 'brother'[39] Mashkur-ud-Daula. It is stated that after some years, the studio was closed by Asghar Jan as the art of photography 'had become commonplace and no longer held any charm for him'. Asghar Jan died in 1910. The negatives of the photographs taken by him were destroyed when his old house collapsed.

The author has a few original photographs taken in the studio of Asghar Jan. They are all of courtesans. Below each photograph is the following printed inscription:

ASGHUR JAN, Photographer, Late
MUSHKOOROODDOULAh'S Firm, Lucknow, Kaisur Bagh.

By 1865, the art of photography was well entrenched in the social life of the people in cities like Lucknow. Commercial studios had sprung up and there was a demand for photographs of people to be taken. Sophie Gordon has given a list of photographers in Lucknow who operated between 1860 and 1901. In 1863, Joseph Johannes was the only photographer in the city and he remained in that position up to 1870. From 1871 to 1878, no photographer of Lucknow is listed in any directory. From 1879 to 1882, J. Saché finds a place. From 1883 to 1899, G.W. Lawrie is listed, with Fry & Rahan being mentioned from 1884 to 1895. Mashkur-ud-Daula is listed in 1895 with a studio in Qaisar Bagh. This must have been Asghar Jan's studio, which was functioning after the demise of Mashkur-ud-Daula in 1871–1872.

---

[39]All along it is seen that Mashkur-ud-Daula has been treated as a 'brother' of Asghar Jan in extant literature. However, whereas Mashkur-ud-Daula, according to the published chronogram, died in 1871-72 CE, Asghar Jan is said to have died in 1910, i.e., almost 38 years after the demise of Mashkur-ud-Daula. This gives rise to the suspicion that both the photographers, who for sometime operated a photographic studio together, could not have been real brothers. Perhaps they were distantly related cousins or half-brothers.

# Society and Women

To understand the life of the people of a particular era, one must delve into the lives of the women, who constitute half of the population of any region. They play various roles from being a wife and a mother to a companion and a mentor. Hence, their beliefs, customs and actions shape the environment and culture of a society.

The first chapter in the section gives an insight into the lives of the Muslim women of Awadh and their rights. The role of a woman was largely limited to running the house. Books such as Fawaid-un-Nissa and Aadaab-I Niswan described the responsibilities and duties of a good woman. Not much emphasis was given to their rights. The practice of purdah or seclusion of women was also prevalent at that time. The ladies were made to believe that purdah was in line with the teachings of Islam and thus they themselves did not want to shun it. While some progressive voices did speak out against the practice, this was not appreciated or reciprocated by the majority of women. Abdul Halim Sharar was an opponent of the purdah system and his writings on the same are relevant even today. Illiteracy among women was the main cause of their ignorance. Social reforms could only be implemented when the women themselves were aware of their rights. To be equal contributors to the progress of society, it was important that women too were educated. Syed Karamat Husain was a pioneer in taking up the cause of women's education in North India and founded the Muslim Girls' College at Lucknow. Though the situation has improved over the years, Muslim women remain behind in terms of equality, education and opportunities.

When one talks of the women of Awadh, one cannot help but mention those who were also an important part of its heritage. The second chapter in the section covers the lives of the courtesans, who still have an aura of mystique around them. 'Sham-i Awadh' was a term coined for the glorious evenings of Awadh spent at the salons of the courtesans, which were a hub for Kathak dance, music and poetry. These courtesans had royal patronage and were well provided for. They were considered to be a symbol of artistic traditions, refined manners and social etiquette. Many of them were proficient in singing and dancing, as well as in the art of conversation. Despite being high earners, they were not given a high status in the society. However, the custom of keeping a courtesan was not frowned upon. The patronage courtesans received in the Nawabi era diminished under the British rule. The successors of the courtesans were reduced to the status of lowly prostitutes. Courtesans have always aroused the interest of men, hence they were the central characters of many novels published in that era. Umrao Jan is the one best remembered of them all. The chapter also mentions some famous courtesans of Awadh.

The last chapter in the section contains miscellaneous information about Awadh and talks about many unique and interesting features of Awadh society. One such was chehra navisi, which was the art of recording the description of the physical attributes of a person or thing. It was used for verification and authentication for official purposes. The chapter describes in detail how descriptions of human beings, animals and inanimate objects were recorded. The chapter also lists some famous Sufi poets of Awadh. Lucknow, being the capital of Awadh, was synonymous with the culture of reading, writing and poetry. It is no surprise that Lucknow thus had several printing presses, publishers and booksellers. The iconic Naval Kishore Press acquired cult status and became the pehchan (identity) of Lucknow. It was opened in 1858 with a hand press and some lithographic stones. Some of the famous booksellers of Lucknow have also been mentioned in the chapter.

# 7.

# Life of Muslim Women and Their Rights

## Behaviour and Conduct

One of the earliest books on the upbringing and training of Muslim women was *Fawaid-un-Nissa* (*Gains to Women*), by Munshi Muhammad Masud Bilgrami. The book was published by Naval Kishore Press of Lucknow in September 1873, and it runs to 188 pages. Some of the important issues discussed in it regarding the lives of Indian Muslim women are as follows:

1. The intention is not to keep women inside their house like prisoners. Confinement of women will not ensure their security and care. It is in the nature of human beings that if a thing is prohibited, then there is always a desire to do what has been forbidden.

2. The Qur'anic injunction for a Muslim man is that he may marry whichever other women seem suitable to him, indeed, as many as two, three or four women. But if he fears that he cannot be equitable to them, he should marry only one (Surah 4:3). It is only a lawfully wedded wife who can pair with her husband and give him comfort, relief and pleasure. Munshi Bilgrami is of the opinion that if a man has more than one wife, it means trouble and cruelty for the women. Even if one of the wives practises

patience, her silent sighs will bring down God's wrath and the husband will suffer sorrow.

3. A woman of good character, who is pious and loves her husband, will never tolerate him being in the arms of another woman. When there is true love between a wife and her husband, there is no reason for the man to have another wife in the lifetime of his first wife. Munshi Bilgrami is of the opinion that polygamy is against the laws of nature and against normal customs and is not in accordance with any sense of religious rationality. Monogamy means relief, comfort and love between the couple.

Another chapter in *Fawaid-un-Nissa* relates to the advantages of knowledge and skill among women. The author states that women by nature are kind-hearted, and quick to accept or reject. Even in appearance, women are soft and tender. It is, therefore, best for women to master a skill that does not involve much physical labour.

Bilgrami continues that since wives are needy, indigent and dependent on their husbands, they are often deprived of their rights because they have failed to learn a suitable skill that could have resulted in their earning independently. This does not, however, mean that having picked up a vocation, the woman should separate herself from her husband. On the other hand, money earned by the wife would make the husband beholden to her.

The author feels that a wife should be obedient and submissive, and ready to serve her husband. She should also be loving and, in all circumstances—even if the husband is bad-tempered, she should carry out his wishes. The only right of the wife over the husband is that he should promptly pay her the dowry (mehar) fixed at the time of marriage.

The author has pointed out that with one's lawfully wedded wife one should make pleasant and ordinary conversation, join in mirth and lead a life of satisfaction and enjoyment. However, in this social intercourse, if the wife jocularly says or does anything that is disagreeable, unpalatable or unpleasant, then the husband should show patience and restraint and should not feel displeased, outraged or offended.

Another small book on the good breeding of women is *Aadaab-i*

*Niswan* (*Etiquette for Women*), by Munshi Muhammad Abdur Rauf Hatif.[40] The first chapter is on chastity, a virtue that the author suggests is an ornament and a personal quality of pious women. A chaste woman is higher in value even if the whole world is given in exchange. Further, it also talks about how a woman should be obedient to her husband, respect him and carry out his wishes. The author sticks to the so-called superior position of the husband and adds that some wives annoy their husbands, which sometimes results in lifelong estrangement.

Munshi Hatif is of the strong view that housekeeping is the primary duty of the wife and the household is her realm. According to him, earning money requires hard work and dedication, but it is more important that the money so earned is spent wisely and with thrift. Among the duties of an efficient housewife the following have been mentioned:

- Keeping an account of daily expenditure.
- Maintaining household effects and important items in orderliness.
- Monitoring the work of the servants.
- Using the summer and winter clothing of the children at appropriate times.
- Turning a disarranged house into a well-appointed one.

It is further mentioned that a wife should smile to express her pleasure when her husband returns from work. A well-disposed and affable wife always uses polite language and never says anything that will hurt or annoy another person. When a wife disguises her anger as a moral discourse, then her anger does not appear as such.

The book also emphasizes that the proper nursing and rearing of children are the basic duties of the wife. She should not feed the child frequently and should not offer heavy or indigestible food. To still the child or make him or her sleep, opium should not be administered, as was the custom in many households during the nineteenth and early

---

[40]The author referred to the sixteenth edition (not dated), which comprises 122 pages in clear large-sized nastaliq (a style of writing, specially used in Persian calligraphy). It was published by the now defunct Azizi Press of Agra, probably in the early part of the twentieth century.

twentieth centuries. Such negligence resulted in the child getting sick, and instead of being treated by a doctor or hakeem, he was needlessly taken to a faqir or a spiritual person for prayers and talismans.

Another hallmark book is Mirza Irfan Ali Baig's *Aadaab-ul-Hind*, where the author lists certain essential instructions on running the household:

- If there is an elderly woman in the house, her directions and advice should be taken.
- It is the responsibility of the husband to ensure that every member of the house is comfortable.
- The housewife should keep items in the house with care so that they are neither damaged nor wasted. Costly articles should be kept under lock and key. Provisions should be stored in such a way that there is no shortage when they are required. Care should be taken to ensure that there is no theft, and grains and pulses are not scattered by children or wasted by rot or pest.
- An account should be kept of the clothes and when they are returned after washing, they should be properly accounted for and stored. Old clothes should be mended as necessary.
- Suitable eatables should be kept for the children to be offered when they feel hungry.
- All meals should be prepared properly and on time. They should have the correct amount of salt and gravy. The amount of food cooked should neither be too much nor too little.
- It should be ensured that servants and caretakers perform their duties properly, are fed sufficiently and are paid their salaries regularly and in full.
- If cattle or livestock are kept, they should be looked after and fed according to requirement.
- No such animal should be kept in the house as would make the surroundings dirty or cause nuisance to neighbours.
- If there is a sick person in the house, the necessary treatment should be ensured and, if required, a caregiver should look after that person.

- The women should wear their ornaments regularly. Ornaments are for adornment and in times of need can be used for finance.

## Seclusion of Women

Purdah or the seclusion of women has been a continuing but disappearing practice among Indian Muslims. Women were supposed to wear a veil covering the arms and the body entirely as well as a veil to cover the face. A woman could go out, but she was, by custom, required to move about with the all-encasing shroud-like covering. No concession was available for hot and sultry weather.

It must be made clear that the veiling of women has nothing to do with Islam. In the context of attire and conduct, the Qur'an follows one basic principle, namely, modesty. Verses 30 and 31 of Surah 24 run as follows:

> [Prophet], tell believing men to lower their eyes and guard their private parts: that is purer for them. God is well aware of everything they do.
>
> And tell believing women that they should lower their eyes, guard their private parts, and not display their charms beyond what [is acceptable] to reveal; they should draw their coverings over their necklines and not reveal their charms except to their husbands, their fathers, their husbands' fathers, their sons, their husbands' sons, their brothers, their brothers' sons, their sisters' sons, their womenfolk, their slaves, such men as attend them who have no desire, or children who are not yet aware of women's nakedness; they should not stamp their feet so as to draw attention to any hidden charms. Believers, all of you, turn to God so that you may prosper.
>
> —*Translation by M.A.S. Abdel Haleem, 2010*

Dr Riffat Hassan, Professor Emeritus at the University of Louisville, in an interesting article[41] in the daily *Dawn* (Karachi, 5 February 2010), explained the concept of 'lowering of gaze' in this way:

---

[41]Source: https://www.oozebap.org/biblio/ISLAM_AND_HUMAN_IN_PAKISTAN.rtf

The Qur'anic injunction enjoining the believers to lower the gaze and behave modestly applies to both Muslim men and women. There are no Qur'anic statements which justify the extremely rigid restrictions regarding segregation and hijab which have been imposed on Muslim women by some societies or groups like the Taliban. If the Qur'an intended for women to be completely secluded and covered from head to foot, why would it command the men to 'lower their gaze'?

The eminent Islamic scholar and activist Asghar Ali Engineer has related that in Madina, when Muslim women passed through the markets, they were harassed by Jews. This was the reason why the following verse 59 of Surah 33 was revealed: 'Prophet, tell your wives, your daughters, and women believers to make their outer garments hang low over them so as to be recognized and not insulted: God is most forgiving, most merciful.' (Translation by M.A.S. Abdel Haleem, 2010.)

In a case before the Supreme Court of India it was argued that asking 'purdah nasheen' women to lift their veil in order to be photographed for a voter identity card would amount to sacrilege. The Hon'ble Supreme Court ruled that 'If you have such strong religious sentiments, and do not want to be seen by members of public, then do not go to vote.'[42]

In the book *The Veil*, edited by Jennifer Heath, there is an essay by Mohja Kahf, an associate professor of comparative literature at the University of Arkansas, which points out that the veiling of women long predates Islam, that Christian women in the Near East wore veils as did Jewish, Roman, Greek, Zoroastrian, Assyrian and Indian women. She also points to statuettes of veiled pagan priestesses dating back to 2500 BCE and to the oldest written literature in existence, *The Epic of Gilgamesh*, written in 2000 BCE, in which the young women are veiled.

Hasan al-Turabi is a Sudanese intellectual who completed his doctoral studies at the Sorbonne in Paris and has been one of world's most visible and well-known Muslim activist intellectuals. When he was asked about the hijab, which is now being worn by many Muslim women as if it were

---

[42]Source: http://timesofindia.indiatimes.com/india/Lift-veil-for-voter-ID-SC-tells-burqa-clad-women/articleshow/5489631.cms

religiously ordained, he replied[43]:

> The word 'hijab' appears in the Qur'an. It refers to a curtain in the Prophet's room. Naturally, it was impossible for the Prophet's wife to sit there, while people entered the room—Muslims who came to ask for rulings, converts to Islam who wanted to ask questions, people of the Jahiliya who wanted to visit—this is impossible, even in modern homes... Allah be praised, today's homes are larger, and there are halls and guestrooms, but back then there was only one room, so they put a hijab so the woman would feel comfortable, and wear whatever she liked. And if we want something from her, we request it from behind the hijab. The Qur'an did not refer to this thing as a hijab. This was called a khimar, and it was worn over the chest only. What they are referring to is the khimar, not the hijab. You keep hearing hijab, hijab, hijab. When these words are distorted they mislead people.

Syed Mumtaz Ali (1860–1935), a writer, publisher, editor and champion of women's rights, wrote and published *Huquq al-Niswan* (*Women's Rights*) in 1898. Mumtaz Ali also discussed purdah and 'the deleterious effects of extreme isolation on the women concerned'. At that time, many women wore voluminous pyjamas, which were difficult to manage and crippled easy movement. Mumtaz Ali therefore made a plea to modify female dresses so they would not hamper the movement of women and compel them to confine themselves within the four walls of their homes. Mumtaz Ali was also of the view that women in purdah did not get fresh air and sunshine, were denied any experience of the outer world and if they fell ill, they could not see or be seen by a doctor. He wanted women to be able to leave their homes to visit public places and shops along with their husbands.

Dr Kalbe Sadiq, a Shia luminary, has stated that while a woman should be modestly dressed, nowhere in the Qur'an is it stated that a woman should be in purdah and must cover her face. It must be

---

[43]Source: *https://www.memri.org/reports/sudanese-scholar-islamist-leader-hassan-al-turabi-al-arabiya-tv-women-should-cover-chest-0*

remembered that in the precinct of the Kaaba at Makkah in Saudi Arabia, women are not supposed to cover their faces.

An assertion of religious identity and a claim of modesty have made some young Muslim women in India (including in Lucknow) adopt different styles of coverings for the body in addition to normal clothes. Some of these apparels are listed below:

- **Burqa:** It is the much-maligned Muslim woman's veil through which only the eyes are visible. It is a loose, head-to-toe covering that also conceals the face of the woman wearing it, leaving a net screen to see through. This uncomfortable and unpleasant attire is fortunately on the way out.

- **Niqaab:** It is a woman's veil for the face that leaves the eyes and the upper portion of the nose open. A soft and thin piece of cloth is worn as a mask. The niqaab is generally combined with a headscarf.

There are also some accoutrements worn by Indian Muslim women that are not strictly veils and are not meant to conceal the face of the woman. These are:

- **Hijab:** In Arabic the world 'hijab' means modesty, bashfulness or concealment. It implies covering in general. Imam Ayatollah Ruhollah Khomeini (1902–89) became the supreme religious leader of the Islamic Republic of Iran in 1979. Through his diktat in 1981, hijab became compulsory not just for Iranian Muslim women but also for Iran's religious minorities. The hijab became embodied in Iran as a chador (a large piece of cloth that is wrapped around the head and the upper body of a woman, leaving only the face exposed). The Iranian revolution of 1979 roused, stimulated and amazed Muslims all over the world. Muslim women in other parts of the world also took their cue from Iran and tried to redefine their identity, femininity and Muslimness. Although the Iranian chador did not find acceptance in other Muslim countries, the headscarf took the form of hijab and became the rallying point to assert the identity of a large number of Muslim women vis-à-vis other women.

- **Square hijab:** It is a two-piece covering for women including a close-fitting cap and a cylindrical scarf that covers the neck but leaves the face uncovered. The form is similar to the Indian 'monkey cap' or balaclava, but the main difference is that it is made of a thin fabric, such as cotton, instead of wool.
- **Abaaya:** In Arabic, 'abaaya' means wrapping or a cloak. It is a loose, full-body covering and is typically combined with the hijab.
- **Khimar:** In Arabic, khimar means 'headgear of a woman'. It is a long cape that covers the head, neck and shoulders of a woman, leaving the face uncovered.
- **Kaftan:** It is a Turkish word and refers to a front-buttoned overdress usually reaching up to the ankles. It may be sleeveless or with loose sleeves.

In India, a small section of the women who want to practise hijab adopt one or more of the above additional attires. By and large, Muslim women in India, when in public, cover their head either with a dupatta (long scarf) or with the loose end of the sari.

Although the thinking of enlightened persons on the seclusion of women in Muslim society has been discussed above, the orthodox and conformist Muslims have always prevaricated on the subject. Almost all books in Urdu on purdah have been in favour of it, portraying it as an article of faith in Islam. The voices against purdah were few and were usually clamped down. However, Lucknow took the lead in condemning purdah and one of the foremost voices against the practice was that of Abdul Halim Sharar, a widely respected author, playwright, essayist and historian. He wrote an anti-purdah book in Urdu, *Purdah*, which was published in the early decades of the twentieth century. The book is extremely rare and, to my knowledge, has never been reprinted. One copy of this book is in the Khuda Bakhsh Oriental Public Library in Patna (Bihar). The book is a compilation of the essays of Sharar taken from the journal *Purdah-i Ismat*, which he edited in 1900.

Abdul Halim Sharar was born in Lucknow in 1860 and died in Lucknow on 24 December 1926. He was a prolific writer in Urdu and published a number of historical novels, along the lines of Sir Walter

Scott's novels, but set in the Islamic context. These novels were once extremely powerful and popular and used to be serialized in Sharar's magazine *Dilgudaz*. Incidentally, Sharar is also the author of the famous book on the erstwhile culture of Lucknow, *Guzashta Lakhnau,* which has also been translated and published in English. Sharar was a scholar of Arabic, Persian and Urdu and was reasonably well versed in Islamic theology. That he took up cudgels against the stifling practice of purdah among Muslim women was a laudable pioneering venture. It was a small but significant and noteworthy step to further the rights of women. It is worth noting that this solitary voice emanated from the orthodox Muslim stronghold of Lucknow and his book was published from a Muslim press in the equally conservative bastion of Delhi. Although there were several women's magazines in Urdu after 1926 that were edited by both men and women and carried articles written largely by women, there was no notable articulation of protest against purdah. The writing in the journals toed the official orthodox line and the reformist vein was confined to female education, hygiene, conduct of domestic affairs and duties of wives. Purdah was taken for granted and, as such, hardly became the subject of disapproval or dissent. It is to the credit of Sharar that he openly broached an area which, though not taboo, was at least severely frowned upon. That an inspiring Muslim trained in the traditional madrassa was able to challenge a long-standing social practice and was able to defy fossilized ideas that had muffled the voice of women and had a stranglehold on them is indeed commendable.

Sharar's book *Purdah* is a landmark in Urdu sociological literature as it made inroads into the bulwark of the long-accepted view that Muslim women should be concealed from head to toe and should neither be seen nor heard by male society. The woman's lot was to be confined within the walls of her home, where she could rule the kitchen and bring up children with her very limited knowledge and education. That Sharar thought strongly on the subject is evident from the fact that he wrote a book of nearly two hundred pages in the first quarter of the twentieth century. Some of his arguments put forth in the book are relevant even today, although some of his reasoning appears puerile and trivial. Sharar was battling with the subject of social reform, which most Indian Muslims were too faint-hearted to tackle. In fact, his book was hardly appreciated, and, till now, it has never been the subject of serious discussion.

In the paragraphs below an attempt has been made to summarize Sharar's arguments against purdah, which he rightly considered as not being a part of Islam.

Sharar begins his book by saying that we should give attention to the rights of women and rub out the ignorance that has made 50 per cent of humankind (i.e., women) quite useless. Well-wishers of the Muslim community agree that before God and the Prophet the rights of men and women are the same. Sharar emphasizes the fact that the custom of purdah is against Muslim law and is quite contrary to reason. Women have been misled into believing that their seclusion is according to the will of God and the Prophet. Sharar states that in worldly affairs if men consider women inferior, then men are perpetrating callousness and cruelty on women. Sharar adds that observance of purdah may or may not guard the chastity of women, but it has certainly pulled the wool over their eyes.

Sharar believed that awakening among Muslims was necessary for national progress, and social reforms were needed. This was dependent on female education, which could take place only if purdah was abolished. Sharar reiterates that he is for that freedom which allows girls to go to school. He says that they should learn culture and propriety from the Holy Book and be given permission to visit mosques and pray there. Sharar argues that girls who are made to observe purdah become weak. Purdah prevents proper education from spreading among them. Muslim boys who are educated seldom tolerate being tied-up with women who are uneducated and can therefore never become good wives. Sharar adds that, in his times, some girls were being educated by female tutors who came to their houses to instruct them, but such tutors were limited to teaching basic Urdu and as such they were not of much benefit.

Sharar mentions that the purpose of writing his tract against purdah was to ensure that the edicts of the Qur'an were followed instead of forcibly imposing the practice of concealing the body on a woman. Therefore, he sought for all men to realize the purport of his arguments and judge it impartially. However, he found that the moment it was made known that a book was against purdah, men closed their eyes and showered the author with abuses. Sharar consoled himself that in opposition lay his success and that all those who desired change had to face humiliating hostility before a social reform was blessed.

It was not only men who opposed Sharar's views. His opposition to the practice of purdah made a begum exclaim that women were sitting in a corner and should remain there and they did not require Sharar's sympathy. Sharar aptly records that the brutal practice of purdah had affected women to such an extent that they did not feel empathy. Sharar likens them to a half-conscious patient who speaks ill of the physician, but the physician realizes that it is not the patient who is blaming them, but the disease that is antagonistic to health and a cure. Women, because of ignorance and on account of indoctrination that had influenced their minds and hearts from their childhood, did not themselves want to escape their confinement, even when convinced. If a bird as a fledgling is kept in a cage continuously, then it loses its ability to leave the cage, he mused.

Sharar points out that very few people know how innocent women, trapped in the purdah system, are left to survive on mere bread while the men go out twirling their moustaches. No one can assess what privations such women face and what cruelty they are subjected to because they are shut up in a place from where their sighs cannot be heard by anyone. Such women can easily leave their houses and do manual and domestic work. By doing so they can at least become independent to some extent, but the practice of purdah fetters them to their own household and unsupported widows and divorcees are at the mercy of a better-off relative.

Sharar states that the custom of purdah had broken the social lives of women to such an extent that even visiting the house of a relative had become a difficult task. He is of the opinion that women become ill-mannered because of purdah as it prevents them from forming a social circle. They can interact with only a limited number of women and, as such, lack the ability to broadly distinguish between good and bad. They do not have the advantage of different companionships, they lack the etiquette of good society and the knack for cultured conversation. Being shut up in their homes leads them to desperation and despair and they do not see any purpose in their life except to manage the kitchen and household and bring up children.

Purdah is also deleterious to the health of women, argues Sharar, as fresh air is necessary for good health. Spending their life within the four walls also has a bad effect on children. Sharar remarks that all steps by the government to propagate cleanliness were confined to the streets and lanes, but there was no interference in the standard of hygiene inside houses and the practice of purdah engendered insanitary conditions. Sharar charges that the purdah system provides little incentive to the women to keep their clothes clean as they rarely intermingle with anyone, at least among their own sex.

Sharar states that whenever purdah was discussed, people, without thinking, remarked that if purdah were to be abolished, then the character of women would be spoiled. But a chaste woman, despite all temptations and no matter how many times she has been out of her home, will never be swayed. It is not possible to tease or accost a virtuous woman or be rude to her. Generally, only those women who are of questionable character from the outset are pestered. Sharar agrees that women who have spent all their lives behind the purdah face some risk when they go out, but the likelihood of anything seriously bad happening is remote because the road is not littered with vicious men. However, if there is any pitfall, it is because purdah-observing women have lost their instinct to protect their independence. Men advocate purdah to prevent women from going astray, but they have not wholly succeeded because several women in purdah have strayed. Sharar cites the example of khangis (prostitutes operating from their houses under the guise of being respectable women), who religiously observed purdah.

The purdah segregates women from men. The male members in the men's portion of the house can do whatever they like. If the women of the house were not in purdah, then they would be in a position to watch over the activities of the menfolk and rebuke and censure them as and when necessary. Women also utilize the purdah system to cover up their shortcomings and these are easily hidden from the husbands. Purdah interferes in the realization of their God-given rights.

Although the Qur'an does not disparage women, the guardians of the moral code seem to make women responsible for all wrongs. Sharar cites a book on ethics that states that the beloved, from fifteen to twenty years, has a simple heart. Then from twenty to thirty years, she is delicate and lovely and praised for her beauty. From the age of thirty to forty, she is fertile and is meant to bear children. From forty to fifty years, she is meant to run the household. But after sixty years, she becomes a dark affliction.

Sharar points out that men are not ashamed to give examples denigrating women at large. Men often claim that women should not be trusted. Sharar rightly questions how one cannot but trust a good woman who has been a companion to her husband through thick and thin.

According to Sharar, men who level the charge of infidelity against women are under the wrong notion that they are the masters of the destiny of women. He thinks that the men have formed this opinion without looking into their own circumstances and morals and have not compared their own doings with those of the erring women; they have taken the examples of some immoral women to generalize and have not looked into their own questionable deeds.

Sharar gives a fine example of misplaced logic. It is the criminal who is responsible for the crime. Yet in the case of women, this logic is turned upside down. The looks of men vis-à-vis women are sometimes ill-intentioned and unclean. To protect women, however, Muslim men, instead of plucking out their own eyes, have wilfully enforced the confinement of helpless women.

Sharar rightly mentions that the custom of purdah had divided Muslim society into upper and lower classes. A poor woman has no choice but to walk to get from one place to another; she cannot hire a palanquin. She is, however, treated as a low-class woman and can seldom dream of marrying into the upper classes or even aspire to associate with respectable daughters and daughters-in-law. This is a contradiction of the tenet of Islam that there is no caste or division in the Islamic social order.

Much before Sharar wrote the book *Purdah,* he had written a novella that was published around 1896 in the monthly *Muallim-i Niswan* from Hyderabad. Titled *Badr-un-Nissa Ki Musibat (The Perils of Badr-un-Nissa),* this novella was also against the prevalence of purdah among

Muslim women. In the introduction[44] to the book, Sharar says that it had never crossed his mind that the public would be so attentive to the book, that it would be printed repeatedly in presses in different parts of India and that people would be eager to buy it. He remarks that the novella often gave rise to debate, with people passing opinions for and against it.

In the same introduction, Sharar records that he had faced many difficulties because of the publication of the novella. He was attacked in newspapers and books, and many Muslims levelled charges against him. He says that he discussed the issues raised in various assemblies that included people learned in religion, but he found that no one could justify purdah on the basis of Islamic stipulations.

*Badr-un-Nissa Ki Musibat* is the story of a young bride, Badr-un-Nissa, who lives in Hyderabad and observes strict purdah. She is married off to her cousin when she is only five years old. When she turns fifteen, her father-in-law comes from Lucknow to take her back with him. During their journey to Lucknow, the father-in-law and Badr-un-Nissa meet another young bride accompanied by her brother-in-law, who are going to Farrukhabad. How the brides are exchanged due to their being fully covered in purdah and what happens when each arrives at the wrong destination, forms the rest of the story. Sharar deplores the fact that due to the system of seclusion of women, the brides suffered deception and misery and ended up as brides in the wrong houses. The meaningless custom of seclusion caused confusion and bewilderment.

We can, therefore, see that the eminent writer Abdul Halim Sharar was a passionate and fervent opponent of the purdah system among Muslim women. It is heartening that this need for social reform among Indian Muslims was heralded by a well-known writer entrenched in Lucknow and conversant with Islam. What impact these two books had on Muslim society is difficult to quantify. Although the book *Purdah* was published only once, the novella *Badr-un-Nissa Ki Musibat* was issued repeatedly and it is one of the books on which Sharar made his name.

With the rise of female education and the rational interpretation of

---

[44]Dated 16 July 1899, the introduction was reproduced in the 1912 edition published by Al-Nazir Press, Lucknow.

Islam, the necessity and importance of purdah is fading not only in India but in other Muslim countries as well, so much so that the rector of Al-Azhar in Cairo proclaimed in a girls' school which he visited that purdah had nothing to do with Islam. In October 2015, a constitutional Islamic body in Pakistan stated that covering the face, hands and feet was not mandatory for women under Islamic laws. It must be remembered that during Hajj and Umrah (a minor non-compulsory pilgrimage undertaken at any time of the year), it is clearly stipulated that women are not to cover their faces and hands.

There is a scathing couplet on the disadvantages of the purdah system by Abid Mirza 'Begum' Lakhnavi (b. 1857) that is worth noting:

*Parde mein tarasti rahi main taazi hawa ko*
*Deewaar mein zindan ki na rauzan na dar tha*

I kept longing for fresh air within the purdah
But there was no door or aperture in the wall of my dungeon

While the purdah system is a prevalent form of seclusion of women in Muslim society, with the woman restricted to the four walls of the house, another measure of confining women in the Muslim household is the concept of the zenana. Predominantly, a Muslim house was typically divided into two parts, the male portion and the female (zenana) portion or zenankhana. Since the home is the only sphere where a woman channelizes most of her energies, there are strict regulations as to entry of visitors and menfolk in their domain. Mirza Irfan Ali Baig's *Aadaab-ul-Hind* lays down some guidance regarding the above concept:

- Not all women should be allowed to enter the female portion of the house. Only those who are of good character and are reliable should be preferred.
- Even the owner of the house, without announcing himself and without expressing his desire to visit the ladies' section, should not try to enter.
- While inside a house, a person should not peep into the women's portion of the house.

## Education

Gail Minault in her book *Secluded Scholars: Women's Education and Muslim Social Reform in Colonial India* has recorded:

> Among sharif women of the nineteenth century, therefore, knowing how to read was unusual enough, but knowing how to write was very rare indeed. The taboo on writing was based on the anxiety that if a girl knew how to write, she might write letters to forbidden persons—defined as any man, related or unrelated, who might be an eligible marriage partner—and thereby violate the rules of purdah and damage family honour. The protection of a girl's chastity, and hence the familiy's izzat or honour, was infinitly more important than the development of her mind.

It was only later that religious and social reformers in the Muslim community established the necessity of education and 'correct religious observance'. Maulana Ashraf Ali Thanvi (1864–1943), a former pupil of the Deoband seminary, cited an oft-quoted tradition of Prophet Mohammed that 'it is a duty of every Muslim man and every Muslim woman to acquire knowledge'. The Maulana wrote the famous *Bihishti Zewar* (*Heavenly Ornaments*), which was probably first published in 1905. This was a thick compendium in Urdu for women to take to learning and to lead a pious life.

Munshi Bilgrami, the author of *Fawaid-un-Nissa*, is of the view that education for women should be quite different from what it was for men. Men had careers to pursue and therefore they had to have sufficient knowledge in subjects like languages and the law. However, a woman had to go to her husband's home after marriage, look after the household and nurture children. Therefore, the author advocates that parents or guardians of daughters should first train women so they were well versed in skills such as sewing, embroidery and designing clothes. Times could change and in adverse circumstances a woman would be able to eke out a living through her acquired skills. Such women were virtuous and accomplished. Women without skills, proficiency and polish were slatterns. The author further observes that women should be able to wield the pen. Proficiency in the use of the pen in the woman's mother tongue could be acquired with ease and no man should prevent this knowledge from women. As they were expected to keep an eye on expenditure, they should be able to do all related calculations on paper. Further, the use of the pen related to the heart and the soul. The author writes that after marriage, girls went to another house and what befell them could not be conveyed to their parents unless they had some degree of literacy. However, while he advocates literacy among women, the author is of the view that respectful women should not read romantic poems or fantasy in prose as, according to him, such books do not build character. Oddly, the author considers creative literature to be fit for courtesans only and even ghazals to be taboo for women.

Maulana Thanvi's book *Bihishti Zewar* includes a short list of leading books of Urdu literature that women should not read. The impression was that romantic creative literature sullied the character of Muslim women. In this way the women of good households were deprived of culture and under the garb of appreciating literature, drove husbands to the boudoirs of prostitutes and courtesans.

Munshi Hatif in his book *Aadaab-i Niswan* does not believe in modern education for women and states that freedom for men, to some extent, is necessary, but when women start sharing this freedom, it meant the 'destruction of men's freedom'.

## Spreading Education among Muslim Women

During the medieval period, the sharif Muslim women were not prohibited or debarred from literacy. The women could read and write and besides various skills, also practised calligraphy. However, the decline of the Mughal Empire in the nineteenth century also had a negative impact on female literacy.

Syed Karamat Husain (1854–1917) was 'an earlier champion of women's education in North India'. He had an Islamic education in Lucknow under the guidance of Syed Hamid Husain, his paternal uncle. He went to England in 1886, where he studied for the Bar. He later became a member of the Muhammadan Educational Conference where the resolution for women's education was proposed and a Women's Education Section was formed. He founded the Muslim Girls' College in Lucknow in November 1912.

The Karamat Husain Girls' College first functioned in rented premises in Lucknow, and in the 1920s was moved to a building in the trans-Gomti area on land donated by the Raja Sahib of Mahmudabad, still functioning from there as a postgraduate institution. Interestingly, the first principal was Amina (Ethel) Pope, a Christian lady who had converted to Islam. She was a Canadian, educated in England, who came to India in 1910 and was a strong advocate for women's education. The Muslim community did not react well to the opening of a girls' school with a boarding house for purdah-nasheen students. However, Karamat Husain bravely stated: 'It is far better that I should be cursed and Muslim women educated, than that I should retain my good name, but Muslim women remain in ignorance.' Karamat Husain, according to Gail Minault, was the inspiration for three major women's educational institutions in Allahabad, Aligarh and Lucknow.

## Growing Awareness for Empowerment of Muslim Women

Generally, under patriarchy, the role of women has essentially been considered to be that of bearing and rearing children and looking after hearth and home. Till recent times, she was unfortunately given a limited role or no role at all outside the home. Men were content to have her within the confines of her home, tied to her various domestic duties. It was only at the turn of the twentieth century that she began to claim her freedom, rights and space.

Realizing that 'Muslim women are the weakest link in the generally disempowered chain of Indian womanhood', the National Commission for Women carried out an investigation into the status of minority women. Syeda Saiyidain Hameed published a report in 2000 titled 'Voice of the Voiceless: Status of Muslim Women in India'. According to the report, Muslim women suffer from double disabilities—they are women in a male-dominated society, and being Muslim, they are in a disadvantageous position in the 'social ladder of society'. To help women overcome the disadvantages they suffer, the report has made several recommendations, some of which are included below:

a) Muslim personal law needs to be codified.
b) Polygamy and the practice of triple talaq need to be abolished along the lines of the personal laws of other communities.
c) All marriages should be subject to compulsory registration.
d) In case of divorce, the right of Muslim women to receive alimony from her husband should not be restricted to only ninety days after the divorce (the period of iddah in Islamic law), as was done in the aftermath of the Shah Bano case. Many high courts have frowned on the Muslim Women (Protection of Rights on Divorce) Act, 1986.

## Behaviour of Men towards Women

An interesting book in Urdu, *Aadaab-ul-Hind*, written by Mirza Irfan Ali Baig, who was a deputy collector and a nobleman of Agra, lays down the conventions of decorum, manners and politeness towards women in various circumstances. The book was selected by the Text Books Committee of North-West Province and Oudh and won a prize for its discussion on domestic etiquette. According to the book, in relation to women, men should observe the following:

- In talking to a young woman, the man must be modest.
- The mother, sister or daughter of another person should be like his own mother, sister or daughter.
- When conversing with a woman of any age, a man should not say anything that is uncivilized or obscene and should not relate any story expressing cruelty or sadness.
- No shameless action should be done in front of a woman.
- While talking to a woman, who is not the man's wife, eye-to-eye contact should be avoided.
- Except for the hands, face and feet (up to the ankles), no other part of the body should be exposed before a woman.

- In front of a woman, who is not the man's wife, a man should neither touch the woman, nor smell her, nor examine her clothes.

The author also gives various reasons for avoiding underage marriages. One such is that the child of such a marriage is seldom healthy and the child-bride suffers during delivery, which gives rise to various ailments.

Regarding the relationship between a husband and wife, the author mentions a few interesting points:

- The husband and wife should respect each other and show character and good breeding in their dealings.
- Just as a woman of bad character is a bane for the husband, so is a wicked husband a calamity for the good wife.
- A wife should not be idle and without work. After she has received basic education, she must learn skills and handicrafts to keep herself busy.
- The best wife is one who supports her husband in overcoming his worries and fulfilling his aims and objectives in life.
- It is the duty of the husband not to get annoyed with his wife for no reason and he should not reprimand her without justification; the same applies to the wife as far as the husband is concerned. The husband should behave in a polite manner and the wife should not lose her temper or be harsh with her husband.

It is evident that the women in Awadh were largely encouraged to stay within the four walls of their home, attending to children and household chores. The literature published, also laid down moral codes of conduct for women and focused on their responsibilities. However, it clearly missed the point that to be able to understand and meet these responsibilities, women must be acquainted with the alphabet, and for this literacy is necessary. Times have changed and women's roles have begun to change too. However, not much has changed when it comes to the lives of the ordinary Muslim women in Awadh and they are still struggling for their emancipation. The need of the hour is to equip them with the tools of modern education and skills that will enable them to have greater control over their lives. Above anything else, women themselves need to realize their true value and potential and the role which they can play in national progress.

# 8.

# Courtesans of Awadh

S aint Thomas Aquinas, one of the most important medieval philosophers and theologians, was of the view that prostitution was a necessary adjunct of morality just as a cesspool was necessary to a palace if the whole palace was not to smell.

William Crooke, the Irish ethnographer in India, wrote about prostitution in India in the fourth volume of his famous book, *The Tribes and Castes of the North-Western Provinces and Oudh*. In it, he defines the class of prostitutes as:

> Tawâif, plural of taifa, 'a troop or company of dancing-girls' […] The term is a general one, but is more generally applied to those who are of the Muhammadan faith. The Hindu branch is often called by the title Pâtar, Patoriva, Pâtur, Paturiya from the Sanskrit pátra, 'an actor'. Kanchan, which is derived from the Sanskrit kanchana, 'gold', is usually regarded as the equivalent of Tawâif. The ordinary prostitute, of whatever religion she may be, is often known as Randi (rânr), Sanskrit randa, 'mutilated', 'a widow', from which class, where widow marriage is prohibited, the class is commonly recruited, or Kasbi (Arabic Kasb, harlotry). The large class who prostitute sub rosá or live as kept mistresses are generally known as Khânagi, 'domestic' (khána, 'a house') or Harjâi, 'a gadabout'.

The word tawaif is used as a singular in Urdu and means 'prostitute'. However, Mirza Jafar Husain, who spent most of his life in the traditional atmosphere of twentieth-century Awadh society, observed that the word tawaif baazi for whoring was never used in Lucknow. The equivalent word 'randi baazi' for whoremongery was current but was considered vulgar. In better society, the expressions employed were tamash bini, which means libertinism or licentiousness, and aiyyashi, or debauchery.

## Courtesans and Prostitutes in Awadh

Such was the fascination with and desire for courtesans in Lucknow that the nineteenth-century rekhtigo poet Mirza Ali Baig 'Nazneen' Dehalvi wrote:

> *Kya jaaniye kya kasbiyon mein shahad ghula hai*
> *Ghar walion se khush koi shauhar nahin hota*

> One does not know what honey pot the prostitutes have
> No husband seems happy with his own wife

Writing about courtesans in nineteenth-century Lucknow, Adrian McNeil of Macquarie University observed that courtesans had royal patronage and were 'well provided for'. Those outside 'were engaged by the households of the wealthy or were employed in kothas (bordellos, salons, brothels) in the bazaar'.

Kothas were of two kinds. The kothas on the peripheries of Lucknow catered to the economically weaker sections and largely had coarse, uneducated and unpolished whores. The better ones entertained the gentry and were serviced by courtesans who were 'sophisticated and refined in manners, conversation and performance'.

In Awadh, every newcomer to a kotha usually acquired a new name. When a prostitute left or died, perhaps the same name would go to someone else. According to Dr Moti Chandra in his book *The World of Courtesans*, 'the names of the courtesans (in ancient times) usually ended in dattā, mitrā and senā'. In northern India, particularly Awadh, tawaifs usually had the suffix 'jan' or 'bai' added to their names as an indication of their professional status.

A kotha worker could rarely run away from the kotha. Musclemen were always stationed outside the kothas and they watched all persons entering and leaving. Every kotha had its malkin (the proprietress), who let out tiny rooms to the sex workers. All prostitutes of a kotha were under the control of a nayika. The money earned by each woman was deposited with the nayika, out of which a portion was paid to the malkin. Most of the prostitutes seldom received sufficient money, but their food, accommodation and meagre medical expenses were taken care of. A man smitten by a particular sex worker had to pay a hefty sum to release the girl. There were many instances in Lucknow where prostitutes left their profession and married into respectable families. There were courtesans who developed liaisons with decent men and became magdalens in due course. Largely, such alliances were discouraged and disapproved, but well-to-do men were generally able to get around the censure. With time, the pasts of such wives were forgotten and the stigma and the slur no longer held sway.

Although many courtesans had only one or two abiding sexual liaisons during their life, these relationships were quite lucrative and profitable. Dr Chandra mentions: 'She is a robber of independent will, bereft of love and has desire for sex. She cares only for her own interest [...] Greed never leaves her even when she is old. She is not interested in love [...] The sex act is for money alone.'

Lucknow's native historian, Veena Talwar Oldenburg,[45] who has done pioneering work on the colonial impact on the Nawabi city, visited the kotha of the courtesan Gulbadan between 1976 and 1986 for her research.[46] She noted from the tax records of 1858 to 1877 that the tawaifs of Lucknow were high earners. This income was from both artistic entertainment as well as social and sexual services provided by them. The money, however, did not give the courtesans high social status. Nonetheless, the courtesans were treated as 'a symbol of culture' and despite limitations, the courtesans did exert their influence and weight in the social sphere.

---

[45]Veena Talwar Oldenburg is Professor of History at Baruch College and The Graduate Center of the City University of New York. She is best known for her widely reviewed book on dowry murder. Oldenburg is a native of Lucknow, India.

[46]Source: http://www.india-seminar.com/2007/575/575_veena_talwar_oldenburg.htm and http://www.columbia.edu/itc/mealac/pritchett/00urdu/umraojan/txt_veena_oldenburg.html

## Sham-i Awadh (Evenings of Awadh)

The noted Hindi writer Amritlal Nagar wrote about the tawaifs, mainly of Lucknow, in his book *Yeh Kothewalian* (1958). Among other things, he has recorded a number of interviews with courtesans, which he conducted in the 1950s. This author has attempted to summarize Amritlal Nagar's description of the courtesans of Awadh here.

In large music and dance mehfils (assemblies), courtesans from seven or eight deras, or sources, displayed their talents. In Awadh, these mehfils usually started with singing of thumri, dadra, ghazal, etc., during which the courtesans supplemented their singing with exhibitions of bhava, or hand and facial expressions and gestures. Sometimes, bhands (jesters and mimics) were also present and innuendoes, banter, stinging allusions and sarcastic observations were exchanged between the cultured courtesans and the bhands, much to the amusement of the audience. After light classical singing and mirth, and when the night had advanced and only genuine connoisseurs were left, the classical singing started. The most famous singer presented her art at the end of the programme. The musical programme also included performances of Kathak dance.

Lucknow was once known for thumri singing. The singers would describe bhava in the songs. Along with thumri, dadra and tappa were also rendered. The courtesans sang the ghazals of Mirza Khan 'Dagh' and Amir Ahmad, Ameer Minai and others who were the writers of fine Urdu ghazals. The ghazal repertoire of leading courtesans was rich and many visited the kothas to hear them. It was these tawaifs who formed part of the Sham-i Awadh (Evenings of Awadh). The well-known saying is: Subh-i Benaras, Sham-i Awadhwa, Shab-i Malwa. The mornings in Benaras, with their crowded bathing ghats, are attractive. The revelries of evenings in Lucknow are well known. And because Malwa has clear and cloudless skies, the nights of Malwa are said to be delightful.

Abdul Halim Sharar, who wrote *Guzashta Lakhnau* in Urdu, has mentioned that in Awadh associations with courtesans started from the reign of Shuja-ud-Daula (r. 1753–74), and it became a tradition that refined and cultivated men should have some liaison with such women. The salons of courtesans became the focal and central point for Kathak dance, music and, to some extent, for the discussion and recitation of Urdu (and Persian) poetry. The kothas thus became minor repositories of a refined lifestyle.

✍

Courtesans, like women in general, liked to beautify and adorn themselves. In classical Indian terminology there are the solah singaar, or sixteen adornments, for a woman and these cover toilette, ornaments and embellishment. These are:

1.  **Daantan** (toothbrush)
2.  **Manjan** (toothpowder)
3.  **Ubtan** (cosmetic paste made of chickpea or barley meal for softening or cleaning the skin)
4.  **Sindoor** (vermilion for parting in the hair)
5.  **Kesar** (saffron for the forehead)
6.  **Anjan** (antimony or collyrium or kohl for the eyes)
7.  **Bindi** (dot mark or spangle for ornamenting the forehead)
8.  **Tel** (hair oil)
9.  **Kanghi** (comb)
10. **Argaja** (perfume)
11. **Paan** (betel to redden the lips)
12. **Missi** (a powder composed of yellow myrobalan, gall-nut and iron filings for tining the teeth, gums and lips black)
13. **Neel** (indigo for tattooing)
14. **Mehndi** (henna for the hands and feet)
15. **Phool** (flowers for the hair)
16. **Alta** (red lac dye for staining the feet red)

Muslim women in Awadh usually did not use sindoor, kesar, neel and alta for their beautification.

A feature of a practising prostitute mentioned by Veena Oldenburg is the woman's nakhra (feminine airs or blandishments), which is indeed her 'secret weapon' by which she coaxes, wheedles and sweet-talks her client into parting with money. She does not bare all in a jiffy but shares herself gradually, in stages, using allure, temptation and enticement. This is how she inveigles money. This artifice is used by all, from the highest paid courtesan to the most wretched and exploited tikahi. The stratagem may take the form of a feigned headache, sulking or pretence of anger in which the brothel keeper may also be the prostitute's ally. The aim is to win the confidence of the man by well-acted sham behaviour and make him pliant. However, it is all a game of pretence and seldom does a prostitute really love a man. The rekhtigo Urdu poet Abid Mirza 'Begum' (1857–1930) of Lucknow has so well portrayed the viewpoint of a sex worker:

> *Khaali kholi tiri gharwali ko ulfat hogi*
> *Hum to randi hain, hamein kya tiri chaahat hogi?*

> Your simple wife may have feeling and affection for you
> I'm a whore, what fondness will I have for you?

Although prostitutes spent a great deal of time and effort in beautifying themselves, and used the art of 'nakhra' to entice men, it was all done for money, not pleasure. The carnal act between a man and a woman, according to Veena Oldenburg, seldom resulted in sexual fulfilment for the sex workers. Lesbianism (chapti bazi) was for some of them the most satisfying relationship. Heterosexual involvement for most of them was a mechanical, lacklustre and spiritless process, which entailed fulfilling a physical demand for money. The often brutal behaviour of men engendered a latent dislike for them. Some prostitutes suffered from misandry and were misandrists.

There were several Urdu and Hindi phrases and sayings on promiscuity that were in use and can be understood even now. Some of these are:

- *Chakmak dida, khaye malida*      Wanton eyes are on dainties fed (said of a harlot)
- *Chhatteesi*      An experienced woman who supposedly knows thirty-six postures for carnal intercourse
- *Chhinal ka beta, babua re babua*      A harlot's child is everybody's darling (many talk with the child for the sake of the mother).

- *Chiraband*     A young would-be whore who has not been deflowered

- *Chor ko pakariye gaanth se, chhinaal ko pakariye khaat se*     Catch a thief by his bundle, and a wanton by the cot

- *Do waraqi*     Literally 'two leaves'; implies vulva

- *Din ko sharm, raat ko baghal garm*     Bashful in the day, and in someone's arms in the night

- *Dekhne mein nanhi, leelne mein dhanni*     Petite in appearance, but capable of swallowing a beam

- *Hansi aur phansi*     Smile and be entangled

- *Jawaan raand, burhe sand*     Young widows and lusty old men

- *Khaampara*     A term of abuse applied to a woman who has been cohabited with before the age of puberty

- *Khane kamane ka thikra*     A young disciple kept by an old prostitute to support her

- *Kothe par baithna*     To become a prostitute (by sitting on the balcony of a brothel)

- *Maan beti mein chhinaala nahin chhupta*     Wanton-eyed mothers and daughters can seldom conceal their licentiousness from each other

- *Paturiya murawwat mein gaabhin ho gai*     The whore in her generosity became pregnant

- *Peru*     Mons Veneris or mons pubis

- *Pesha karna*     To be in the profession of prostitution

- *Roomawali*     The thin line of hair above and below the female navel (frequently mentioned in Sanskrit and Hindi poetry)

- *Thikri*     Mons Veneris

- *Yaar ka ghussa bhattaar par*     Vexation over the paramour descends on the husband

## Types of Courtesans

In Awadh, the prostitutes were broadly classified into two groups—kasbi[47] and khangi. A kasbi is a prostitute, or one who leads the life of a harlot. The kasbis worked openly in brothels. There is an interesting Urdu saying: *Din mein tasbih, raat mein kasbi* (rosary by the day and a harlot by night). The second category, khangi, has been defined by J.T. Platts as a clandestine prostitute.

There was another group of prostitutes who lived securely in houses that functioned as brothels. They had a group leader who was designated as a chaudharain, while the mistress of the brothel or the mother-bawd was called nayika. The gharana (household) of the chaudharain considered itself separate and apart from that of the other nayikas. The nayika usually had a number of young whores (nauchis) under her training who were taught the basics of seduction to amass money. She was usually a retired old prostitute who was no longer in active business. There is an Urdu couplet on old bawds:

> *Buddhi huin nayika iss haal ko pahunchin*
> *Sar hilne laga, chhatiyan paataal ko pahunchin*

The old harlot came to this end
Her head started shaking and her breasts dangled to infernal regions

Then there were the deredar tawaifs. They claimed to comprise the highest class of prostitutes. They maintained salons and held dance and music programmes as also literary mehfils. Other appellations for prostitutes included kanchani, a harlot or dancing girl of a tribal caste, and chunewali, which referred to a common prostitute.

According to Abdul Halim Sharar, the majority of prostitutes in Awadh belonged to the kanchani class. From the time of Nawab Shuja-ud-Daula, they migrated from Delhi and Punjab. In fact, the most famous prostitutes of Awadh were kanchanis. The chunewalis were actually sellers of slaked lime, which was popularly called 'chunam' by the British. These

---

[47]'Kasb karna' means to earn, or to follow a trade or profession.

women later entered the flesh trade and were referred to as chunewalis. In Lucknow, Chunewali Haider was a leading prostitute.

There was another category called nagarnian. These were also common whores, but bore alliance to the kanchanis and chunewalis. Another term current in brothels was nauchi, which referred to a young harlot kept under the tutelage of a madam of the brothel.

Then there was the disparaging epithet for a cheap whore, namely takai, takahi or takili, implying that she was a low-priced whore and would offer her virtue for a taka (two pice or 1/32 part of the old rupee). Such a prostitute was usually dirty, uncouth and was typically with her client for just 'one shot'. The working place of these women was provided with the barest necessities—a bed with a cheap carpet and sometimes a paandaan along with an earthen pot of water. There was also usually a dirty curtain, which was drawn to conceal the activities. Nobody stayed after finishing his business.

Other synonyms for prostitutes in Awadh were qahba and fahisha. The word qahba is derived from the Persian 'qahb', which means 'cough'; the epithet came about as a harlot was supposed to inform others of her profession by coughing. Fahisha refered to a lewd or shameless woman who worked as a prostitute (a fahish is a person who has crossed all limits of shamelessness and indecency).

With the coming of the British in India, there were whores who serviced them and they were called gorekamanewali (whores who earned through the white men). They were the most derided lot. In his memoir *Old Soldier Sahib* (1936), Frank Richards, who served as a regular British soldier in India and Burma from 1902 to 1909, wrote at length about the controversial legalized brothels where Indian prostitutes were made available to the British troops.

History professor Veena Oldenburg, in one of her well-known essays, categorized the sex workers by hierarchy. The tawaif, who could be classed as the courtesan, was above others in the profession. She was above the others because her class, etiquette, ada, proficiency in singing and dancing and love for poetry made her high class, suitable to be the mistress of a noble. She was followed by the randi and then came the takahi or the takili. According to Professor Oldenburg, the randi and the takahi had hardly any cultural function and were engaged only in selling sex. All prostitutes were under the control of a chaudharain, the senior-most prostitute in the establishment. They carried out their business in a kotha (brothel). Although the randi did not have the distinction of being cultured, nonetheless, to an emerging middle class or the fading gentry, she was a saving grace for those who did not have affluence or riches to fritter away. The second-rate prostitute did perform dances and sing in the suburbs of Awadh. In the famous Urdu novel *Umrao Jan Ada* by Mirza Hadi 'Ruswa', first published in 1899, the heroine calls herself a randi and not a tawaif.

## Deredar Tawaifs

These tawaifs considered themselves high up in the hierarchy of courtesans. Unlike the other prostitutes, they did not sit on the balconies of kothas but practised their business in private by being visited by the wealthy. They were considered to be the cream of the practising prostitutes. They functioned from brothels as a group. Sharar has recorded that when Nawab Shuja-ud-Daula travelled, several deredar tawaifs accompanied his camp.

Deredar tawaifs who had their brothels in the Chowk area in Lucknow sometimes owned property in that area. Allah Bandi and Najja stayed in Chawal Wali Gali and had imambaras named after them. Most of the deredar tawaifs assumed professional names and their real names were less known. For example, the real names of the chaudharains Nanhua and Bachua were Badr-i Muneer and Mah-i Muneer, respectively.

Such was the repute and esteem of these women that certain gentry allowed the deredar tawaifs to visit their private chambers and even meet the begums. This was because these women were cultured, disciplined and had a decent deportment. Most of these courtesans had some training in literature and were adept at jesting, repartee and witticisms. They were proficient in the art of conversation. Spontaneous use of clever metaphors and witty comments were their forte. Suitable Urdu couplets were readily on their tongues for different occasions and some of them were even poets themselves. Some of them spent their whole lives in close relationships with only two or three men, without causing any friction among the men. Jafar Husain gives an example of a respectable person who had a relationship with the courtesan Haider Jan for about forty or forty-five years, but was said to have never had a sexual relationship with the woman.

## Khangi

The khangi practised prostitution not from a brothel, but from her house. She kept her lewd life secret and tried to pass off as a respectable woman. Khangis sometimes came from respectable families that had fallen on bad times. In the nineteenth century, driven by straitened circumstances, some women worked as seamstresses, embroiderers or tutors, but secretly also operated as prostitutes. The khangis had very limited customers and did not do any singing or dancing. They entertained men usually in the evening or night and the clients stayed for short periods. Generally, the customers of khangis were young men from good families. Sometimes, these novices in whoring lost their hearts to these women and even married them. Some of these marriages were said to have been reasonably successful.

## Mirasin or Domini

According to Volume III of *The Tribes and Castes of the North-Western Provinces and Oudh* by William Crooke, the mirasi or domis are 'a caste of singers, minstrels and genealogists'. Further, '[...] the Mirasi has two functions—the men are musicians, story-tellers and genealogists; the women dance and sing, but they are said to perform only in the presence of women, and are reputed chaste'. However, Adrian McNeil in his article 'Courtesans, Military Musicians and Shi'a Ideology' writes that '[...] the tawaif sang and danced in front of both men and women while domini performed for women but this difference was not constantly maintained'. McNeil also mentions that 'the term dom appears as an occupational term used to denote both Hindu and Muslim musicians from a range of regional and ethnic backgrounds [...]'

**Dhaarhi**

William Crooke in the second volume of his book on castes stated that the dhaarhi was a musician and singer and appeared at houses on occasions of festivity for gifts and endowments. The women who accompanied the dhaarhis sang and played the dholak, tambura, etc. Earlier, it was said, the dhaarhi also begged and went about with women of 'bad character'. There is an interesting proverb that is noted below:

*Randi ki kamaai, ya khae dhaarhi ya khae gari*

The prostitute's earning go to the pimp or the cabman

⌖

Thus, in North India in the eighteenth and nineteenth centuries, prostitutes did not constitute a single, undifferentiated class. Rather, there were many different types of prostitutes, and they have been labelled as 'a dancing girl, a prostitute, a courtesan, a hetaera, and so on'. However, it is difficult to provide a short definition of a woman who functioned as a prostitute for the wealthy or was a kept woman or simply offered physical pleasure or was a maintainer of cultural traditions in a society where literature and music were respected. Despite the questionable practices of the courtesans and their remaining on the margins of society, they were a part of the realm of the Islamicate culture of North India.

## Nawabi Patronage and Colonial Regulations in Awadh

According to Zoya Sameen,[48] a nineteenth- and twentieth-century South Asian history scholar, Lucknow had a distinctive Indo-Islamic culture, with artistic leanings, and was closely connected with the cultivation and development of the Urdu language: 'The tawa'ifs belonged to a privileged social institution of female courtesans who were upholders of artistic

---

[48]Zoya Sameen submitted a thesis for a Master of Arts degree at the University of Chicago titled 'Prostituting the Tawaif: Patronage and Colonial Regulation of Courtesans in Lucknow, 1847–1899'.

traditions and markers of social etiquette. Renowned for their mastery of music and dance, tawa'ifs were the most popular entertainers in the Nawabi capital and also extended companionship and sexual services to the idle and wealthy noblemen with whom they consorted.'

One of the characteristics of the Nawabi culture of Lucknow was that the gentry followed the custom of keeping a courtesan as a mistress quite openly and spent time with her. In fact, if a nobleman failed to have such a connection he 'was not a polished man'.

During the period of Nawab Wajid Ali Shah, given his penchant for dance, music and women, a lot of women of questionable chastity were enlisted in his parikhana, which was an informal school for singing and dancing. The king entered into muta (temporary marriage according to Shia custom) with dozens of women from whom he elicited artistic and cultural contributions, and also took sexual favours.

With the annexation of Awadh in 1856 by the British, however, the patronage on which the tawaifs largely depended declined and the necessity for brothel prostitution grew. There was an element of criminalization of prostitution by the British regime and the respectability and presentability that the tawaifs had enjoyed were immensely reduced. It was no longer a relationship between the courtesan and the patron but an association between the prostitute and the customer. According to Zoya Sameen, the transition was 'from public performer to mere prostitute'.

## Courtesans in the Raj Era

With the end of the Nawabi era there was a void in the traditional training of courtesans who were supposed to be refined women consorting with cultured and intelligent men. Such women found themselves vulnerable and defenceless in the British era. The thin line between the courtesan and the lowly sex worker gradually started disappearing in the British period, and the practice was shorn of any cultural function and institutionalized through legislation. Zoya Sameen found that in the tax ledgers from 1858 to 1877, the prostitutes were classified as 'dancing and singing women'. The British also questioned and seized the land endowments of the erstwhile courtesans made in the Nawabi era as 'they had no rights vested by treaty, and without the formal protection of the Nawab many experienced severe economic dislocation'.

Sameen tells us that 'the plight of the courtesans was not uniform and we have knowledge that some women fared better than others in the circumstances'. The courtesans of the parikhana of Wajid Ali Shah were privileged, but the conditions of the fictional Umrao Jan Ada in Ruswa's novel were that of the common whore (randi) who was categorized as such after the changed milieu of 1857. Sameen cites the instance of Ameer Jan who had entered Wajid Ali Shah's parikhana at the age of eighteen and ultimately rose to the rank of Mahal, i.e., a wedded wife. After the exile of Wajid Ali Shah, she got divorced on 16 March 1856 with six other wives. She lived in Lucknow, purchased an imambara and continued to receive income from her lands.

Lucknow had the largest number of prostitutes among the districts of the North-West Provinces and Awadh, 'with 853 averaging on the register in 1871'. Prostitutes in Lucknow in the colonial times were mainly native women who hung about the barracks, and European and half-caste prostitutes who lived outside the cantonment. There were native prostitutes who consorted with Europeans and lived in quarters bordering the cantonment in a brothel for the exclusive use of British soldiers.

Regarding the legalized brothels for the British soldiers, Frank Richards wrote in his memoirs:

> [A brothel had] between thirty and forty native girls whose ages ranged from twelve to thirty. This number was considered sufficient for the fifteen hundred white troops that garrisoned Agra. Each girl lived in a separate shack of her own, which was made of plaster and mud with a hard-baked mud floor. The only furniture was a native rope-bed with no bed-clothes, a large earthenware vessel for holding water, and a small wash-hand bowl.

Richards further adds:

> Everything possible was done to prevent venereal disease. Each girl had a couple of towels, vaseline, Condy's fluid and soap; they were examined two or three times a week by one of the hospital-doctors,

who fined them a rupee if they were short of any of the above requisites. If he found that any one of them had the disease he had her removed to the native lock-hospital.

In spite of these precautions, there were outbreaks of sexually transmitted diseases among the British troops and syphilis among the troops was common. This led to the passage of the Cantonment Act, 1864, which provided for '[...] the registration of public prostitutes, the prohibition of public prostitution by unregistered women, the adoption of means for the detection of venereal diseases among registered women, the establishment of lock hospitals for the treatment and detention of women suffering such malady.' Legislation in Lucknow was limited within a four-mile vicinity of the cantonments, but the Chowk district of Lucknow was within this limit. The British considered the prostitutes as the principal carriers of venereal diseases. However, there was no attempt to rein in the sexual activities of the British soldier.

As a large number of prostitutes evaded registration and inspection, the occurrence of venereal diseases decreased statistically, but not in reality. The Contagious Diseases Act, 1868, was therefore introduced. Lock hospitals,[49] which treated sexually transmitted diseases, were set up. Lucknow had two lock hospitals, one in the cantonment and another in the city. The women were subjected to biweekly medical examinations and were also frequently the victims of violence by drunken British soldiers.

Policing prostitution was difficult for the colonial administrators as the provisions of legislation did not cover the different types of prostitutes practising in Lucknow. Mistresses of individual men, who consorted with Indians only, treated themselves as exempt from the restrictions.

The registration fee for prostitutes was discontinued in 1873 and the lock hospital in Lucknow city was closed in 1874 as it was 'of no use to the people of the city' and 'it was unjust to tax the citizens in order that

---

[49]A lock hospital was a hospital that specialized in treating sexually transmitted diseases. They operated in Britain and its colonies and territories from the eighteenth to the twentieth centuries.
Source: https://history105.libraries.wsu.edu/fall2015/2015/08/31/the-industrial-revolutions-ban-on-alcohol-and-its-effects-on-other-countries/

the British soldier should be provided with clean women'.

In her thesis 'Negotiating Respectability: The Anti-Dance Campaign in India, 1892–1920' Zsuzsanna Varga[50] points out that the British reformers considered the nautch girls as immoral. Many of the dancing girls were not only beautiful but also rich. They were also witty and pleasant in conversation. Many of the British found the attires of the dancing girls to be very decent and 'not [in] the slightest revealing'. However, the reformers were of the opinion that 'stripped of all their acquirements, these women are a class of prostitutes, pure and simple'. They were not considered tolerable and decorous because they also offered sexual favours. Varga remarks that the reformers failed to mention that the Europeans themselves were ordering the services of nautch girls for private purposes. Thus, while the dancing women were considered to be the personification of corruption, the dance itself was esteemed and appreciated.

During the British period, the days of the salons of the accomplished courtesans were over. The British were shocked by the open-mindedness and permissive attitude of Indians towards courtesans, so different from the ignoble and lowly position of sex workers in British society. Sameen notes that Lucknow, which prided itself for its largely cultured and gifted courtesans, found that after 1858 the lifestyle of sexual urbanity became degraded, disgraced and abandoned. No longer were these women the embodiment of poetry and culture and they had hardly any intellectual interaction with the gentry. The successors of the courtesans were reduced to the status of common prostitutes or whores.

Veena Oldenburg, who examined the records in the Municipal Corporation during the course of her research, found that the dancing and singing girls were in the highest tax bracket. Some of them owned houses, orchards and retail shops. However, after 1857, their immovable properties were appropriated by the British for the alleged involvement of the women in the Uprising of 1857. Under the heading 'Loot' was a description of the plunder of the Qaisar Bagh Palace where lived the

---

[50]Zsuzsanna Varga submitted her thesis paper in 2013 to the Central European University, Department of Gender Studies in Budapest, Hungary.

women associated with Wajid Ali Shah. The movable items included gold and silver ornaments, brocade, jade goblets and valuable furnishings assessed to be worth nearly four million pounds sterling in 1857.

## Training and Life of Courtesans

The courtesans were broadly divided into two groups, khandani (hereditary) and new entrants. Training in singing and dancing was an important feature of the training of courtesans. Right from the age of six or seven, the girls were made to learn music and dance from ustads. This involved long hours of practise and rehearsal. Most of them enjoyed it. In addition, they cultivated the art of etiquette, good manners, decorum and courtesy. Most important was the knack for conversation, especially with the male clientale, which was to be studded with witticisms, repartees and appropriate use of Urdu (and sometimes Persian) couplets. All this required basic literacy with more than a smattering of bookish knowledge. The aim was that the courtesan should be congenial and pleasing company. She was supposed to be an attraction with fascinating appeal in a mehfil.

While the training of the courtesan included proficiency in the art of being coquettish, she had hardly any training or proficiency in cooking, sewing, cleaning the house and general housekeeping. Domestic helpers were retained to maintain the establishment; they dusted, arranged things and generally ensured an orderly setup. It was a long-standing tradition in brothels that hardly any cooking, except perhaps tea, was done on the premises. Whenever food was required, it was ordered, mostly at the expense of the male client, from the nearby eateries. There was a saying that '*tawaif ka chulha kabhi garm nahi hota*' (the hearth of a courtesan is seldom lit). In Lucknow, there were kothas around the original shop of Tunday Kebabwala in the Chowk area, which was well-patronized by the prostitutes and their clients. Men, before going up to the kotha, would buy a heavy dona (leaf container) of fried kebabs and a few garlands of bela and chameli (jasmine).

The women's attire usually comprised a kameez (shirt) and izaar (drawers). They also wore the lehnga (skirt) with a short blouse called shaluka. With the izaar and lehnga, the scarf (dupatta) or head-shawl (orhni) was a must. For dance, usually peshwaz, a tunic comprising a fitted bodice and skirt reaching below the knee, was worn. The bodice or bra was an item of underclothes. It was called the angiya and myriad descripitions of it in Urdu and Indo-Persian poetry are considered examples of bold eroticism. It is to be remarked that in those days there was no question of wearing the correct size of bra. An undersized bra or bodice was frequently worn to bring out the bosom. Nonetheless, the attire of prostitutes did not provide any unseemly exposure of the female body.

William Crooke in his book *Things Indian: Being Discursive Notes on Various Subjects Connected with India*,[51] wrote the following about the nautch: 'The dress of the nautch-girl is highly decorous but arranged with little elegance or grace. It often consists of skirts of scarlet and gold, spangled sáris, trousers of silk brocade, and they wear masses of jewellery, the anklets of silver or gold with little bells making a soft tinkling as their brown feet move.'

Although the courtesans gave the impression of being indifferent to the gaze of their admirers, they liked to be admired. They loved to shower their smiles, coquetry and blandishments. They derived a lot of pleasure from tantalizing their votaries, as also the libertines and the rakes. Displaying the firmness of their breasts was in their interest, so they ensured that the aanchal or the end of the dupatta or sari kept slipping from their breast, which they would then adjust, thus drawing the man's attention. They rolled their eyes, winked or ogled. Their speech was urbane and, as far as speaking chaste Urdu was concerned, their sheens and qafs (pronunciation) were durust (correct). These were some of the ways that the courtesans practised to fascinate and tempt men and thereby increase their earnings. The unassuming and modest housewife was no match for the wily professional courtesans.

The courtesans generally woke up quite late in the day, after a long night. A belated breakfast was followed by riyaz (practise or rehearsal) of dancing and singing. Then came a tardy lunch and then resting,

---

[51] First published in 1906 and reprinted by Oriental Books Reprint Corporation, New Delhi, in 1972.

generally till the early evening, when the working day of the prostitutes actually commenced. They usually bathed and put on flashy, clean clothes appropriate to their work. It was generally noted that they seldom gave attention to ironing their attire. A long time was taken for make-up and no effort was spared to preen and beautify. The prostitutes were engaged in the trade of selling their favours and thereby making as much money as possible. They were in a sort of seamy show business. Thus the lights, décor and furnishings were seldom refined or elegant. They were all on the garish side, vulgar and brash. It was a world of tinsel and tawdry ostentatiousness. By late evening the prostitute had opened shop. She sat along with other girls either in the main hall of the brothel or, as was the custom, settled down on a cane stool (mondha) on the open balcony, displaying her charms to all the passers-by. Those interested in song and dance would seek such performances and those desiring sexual favours would get them, all of course with ample money. The revelry would go on till the small hours. Those who did little or negligible business would experience the wrath of the brothel keeper.

Sex education was usually gathered from the senior prostitutes or from their peers. Initially, there were no books in the vernacular languages to explain the basics of sexual hygiene and physiology. Even in respectable families, discussion about sex was taboo. Menstruation was considered a subject of utter embarrassment. Few understood why menstruation happens and the explanations were replete with myths. Generally, the girls were frightened at menarche. A majority of women, including courtesans, were not very familiar with feminine hygiene. For a long time there was no knowledge of sanitary towels. Old cloth and rags were used during menstruation and the pads were called haiz ki gaddi, haiz ka latta or kursuf. Probably the first Urdu book on sex education was written by Chaudhary Muhammad Ali Rudaulvi (1882–1959), from Barabanki district in Uttar Pradesh. He was a famous essayist, epistle writer and short-story writer. He published his book *Salahkaar* (*Advisor*) in 1928. It was meant for young boys and girls, and went into several editions. Muhammad Ali Rudaulvi also wrote a tract, *Parde Ki Batein* (*Matters behind the Curtain*), on the rhythm method of birth control. Although it is believed that courtesans in Awadh had no specific handbook or manual on the 'business management' of venery, there were in circulation badly translated vernacular versions of Vatsyayana's *Kamasutra* (c. second century CE), *Koka Shashtra* and *Ananga Ranga* by Kalyana Malla (fifteenth or sixteenth century CE). Slender Urdu books known as *Lazzat al-Nissa* (*The Pleasure of Women*) were also available. They were anonymous publications and were a rehash of the Hindu sexual manuals.

## Sex Techniques of Courtesans

It is said that a courtesan could seduce a man with her mind and her charms, and knew all the latest techniques in bed. They learnt the wiles, seductive practices and enticement techniques not from a textbook, but from a past master, usually a retired whore adept at charming and beguiling men in her heydays. However, most of the charm and allure of prostitutes was based on deception and insincerity. It was make-believe and lasted as long as the money kept coming, or till the prostitute found a richer man.

The normal sexual fare with a courtesan, especially in Awadh, related to genital sex, anal sex and oral sex. In Awadh, oral sex, by and large, was considered embarrassing and irritating. Even in Urdu pornographic poetry there are very few instances of oral sex. Whatever the kind of sexual pleasures available, for men, the enchantment and mystique of the prostitute's body was overpowering and pleasurable. Perhaps the main reason was that the courtesans were uninhibited, unrepressed and not at all constrained. Their own wives were generally shy, modest, prim and sometimes unresponsive.

The courtesans perfected the art of controlling the vaginal muscles. In it 'lies the secret of (the courtesan's) much vaunted piquancy'. N.K. Basu, in his book *The Art of Love in the Orient* writes: 'This "velvety grip" together with the insufficiency of Bartholinian secretion that keeps the parts free from sliminess, forms one of the chief attractions of many a professional fornicatrix and constitutes one of the most fundamental factors in weaning away the husband from his more handsome wife who is otherwise ignorant of this art.'

The risks involved in sex work were unwanted pregnancies and sexually transmitted diseases, formerly called venereal diseases. The rubber condom gained popularity in the middle of the nineteenth century and manufacturing advances were made in the late 1920s. The latex condoms became available in India in the early 1930s, but knowledge about them and consequently their use was limited. The condom ultimately became the basic defence against sexually transmitted diseases. Prostitutes attempted birth control through doubtful methods like withdrawal, the rhythm method and douching. Undesirable pregnancies were therefore common. Many illegal abortions were resorted to with the help of unlettered midwives called dais.

## Some Traditions of Courtesans

Coming of age signifies a young person's transition from being a child to entering adolescence. It is the age of puberty and sexual maturity, but it does not mean that a girl has achieved full mental development. However, for a would-be courtesan, it is the time when she is ready to start her profession. In the nineteenth century, when a girl who was to become a courtesan reached puberty and her breasts began to develop, the rite of the angiya, or the assumption of the bodice, was performed. Another ceremony that was studiously practised among the courtesans of Awadh was the missi or teeth blackening ceremony. A very meticulous paper, 'The Missī-Stained Finger-Tip of the Fair: A Cultural History of Teeth and Gum Blackening in South Asia' by Thomas J. Zumbroich has been published and is available in the e-Journal of Indian Medicine, volume 8 (2015), 1-32.

According to Zumbroich, from about the middle of the sixteenth century, blackened teeth and sometimes gums became a part of embellishment and decoration. This was done through missi, a powder made of iron and copper sulphate, tannins and flavouring. 'Teeth blackening as a life cycle event related to sexual maturity and in its literary portrayals acquired distinct sexual overtones.' It was absorbed into the culture of courtesans and prostitutes, among whom the use of missi signified that a girl was ready to sell her virginity.

For the missi ceremony, the novice girl was adorned and clothed as a bride and her teeth were blackened for the first time with missi under the supervision of the bawd and the senior courtesans. The ritual was an internal and private affair and was not normally open to outsiders, including prospective customers. Celebrations were accompanied by dancing and singing followed by a feast, especially among the kasbis. The missi ceremony did not involve the deflowering of a girl; this was a later observance, which was more of a business venture. According to Zumbroich, the festivities of missi were prominent among the deredar tawaifs of Lucknow in the early nineteenth century. Missi application was also done by respectable women in the nineteenth century, but with changing times and with the emphasis on white teeth, the practice of blackening the teeth became unfashionable and unpopular. Missi is now a relic of the past.

After the coming-of-age ceremony described above, was the coming out of the would-be prostitute, wherein she declared herself as being ready, available and accessible. In North India, the coming out of the neophyte prostitute involved a ceremony called nath utrai, or taking off the nose ring. It was the custom among almost all young girls to wear nose rings on the left side of the nose. The ritual of nath utrai involved removing the nose ring worn by the girl, and usually, her deflowering by a bidder for money. It was an occasion of rejoicing and the bidder paid a heavy amount for the privilege of being the first to consort with the girl. Once the nose ring was removed, it was never to be worn again. It signified that the girl was no longer a virgin. Virgins were thought to be worth more than debauched women. Virgins, even on the threshold of commencing a life of debauchery, were considered attractive and charming and worth much more than practising women. Sometimes a wealthy man became associated with a kotha by bidding for a supposedly virgin nauchi. He made regular contributions in order to have exclusive sexual rights to the deflowered girl.

Vikram Sampath in his biography of Gauhar Jan has cited a chaiti, a seasonal semi-classical song sung in the month of Chait (March–April) when Ram Navami is celebrated. The singer was Rasoolan Bai (1902–74) of the Benaras gharana. The song laments the fact that the lady had lost the pearls of her necklace without a thief breaking in or anyone leaving the house. The words of the songs are an allusion to a young tawaif losing her virginity.

## Courtesans as 'sex educators'

The courtesans were socially accepted as counsellors and mentors for 'the social and sexual education of the sons of the elite [...] providing an education in sensuality, poetry, and the graces of courtly conversation.' According to an essay by Sarah Waheed in *Modern Asian Studies,* the kothas 'served as "finishing schools" for young aristocratic men'. McNeil also remarks that the wealthy 'sent their sons to them in order for them to learn manners, grooming and etiquette'. The libidinous sons of the aristocracy and upper-class society therefore, with parental approval and acquiescence, sowed their first wild oats in the hired wombs of the facilitating filles de joie.

However, the tacit or expressed permission to young men to visit courtesans was not meant to be a licence for licentiousness. The youngsters from good Hindu and Muslim families were supposed to behave in a disciplined manner and not become dissipated. Most of these young men were destined to marry into decent families. Anna Morcom in her book *Courtesans, Bar Girls and Dancing Boys: The Illicit Worlds of Indian Dance* has the following to say about courtesans:

> For men to have relationships with courtesans and other dancing girls and enjoy erotic entertainment was acceptable in feudal society, in which marriage was not seen as the only preserve of sexual pleasure. However, in cases where a man actually fell in love with or wished to marry a courtesan, the public and domestic female roles became blurred. That it was a transgression is exhibited in the numerous cautionary tales for noblemen concerning courtesans.

Nonetheless, many wealthy young men became wayward and inconstant. It was unfortunately accepted that married men who had been initiated into sex by courtesans would still keep mistresses. A regular visit to the courtesan was regretfully not frowned upon. The secluded wife suffered within the four walls of the house and some of her lamentations found their way into the Urdu rekhti poetry of Jan Sahib, Sayyid Insha Allah

Khan 'Insha' and Nawab Saadat Yaar Khan Rangin, among others.[52] This was the consequence of the patriarchal feudal society as it existed in the nineteenth and early twentieth centuries.

While the Muslim community did realize the importance of education for women, the nineteenth century and at least the first quarter of the twentieth century was a dismal period for women. Awadh society, for that matter most of North India, was under the hold and influence of the courtesan culture. The Indian hetaeras had, because of state patronage, carved out a queenly niche for themselves. It was more or less accepted that they were the standard bearers not only for sexual pleasure but also courtly manners, customs, demeanour and deportment. The fleshpots in red-light areas like Chowk in Lucknow had become the social clubs of the elite. The wives of the wealthy were confined to chulha (the hearth), chadar (covering from head to the ankles) and char diwari (enclosure of the house), bereft of learning and enlightenment, while the males romped with women of questionable reputation.

## The Art of Seduction

### Singing and Dancing

The musical and dance assemblies of courtesans were held in a large room or hall, or under a shamiyana. The performance took place on a smooth floor covered with carpets. In the salons of moneyed courtesans were huge

---

[52]While rekhti was initially used to describe homosexual love, or gender-ambiguous passion, Sahib's rekhti came to be more concerned with the domestic environment and complaints about marital life. The rekhti genre disappeared after Sahib.
Source: https://www.cambridge.org/core/journals/modern-asian-studies/article/div-classtitlewomenandaposs-voices-menandaposs-lives-masculinity-in-a-north-indian-urdu-newspapera-hrefafn1-ref-typefnadiv/A757464E653DFCB57E6B94E16F7A46D8/core-reader
Nawab Saadat Yaar Khan Rangin (1757, Sirhind to 1835, Lucknow) was an Urdu poet and prose writer. He is credited with creating a feminist form of Urdu poetry known as 'rekhti', which focused on women's lives and used exaggerated 'female' language, or auraton ki zaban.

mirrors, wall-to-wall qalins and even crystal chandeliers. The invitees or guests were seated on one side. The musical programme usually included classical as well as semi-classical songs and some songs were rendered on request (farmaish) as well. At a point in the singing or dancing where the art of the performer was striking and conspicuous, the members of the audience made offerings of money, which was usually called nazrana or nichhawar.

During the times of Nawab Wajid Ali Shah there was a profusion of thumri, dadra and ghazals in singing sessions. Among the courtesans of Awadh, the famed thumri singers included Haider Jan, Jaddan Bai and Achhan Bai. In the late 1930s, Chhuttan Jan and Babban Jan of Lucknow were also well-known thumri singers. Thumris were composed by Wajid Ali Shah as well as Shaikh Nizami and Hafiz Ashraf. Nawab Alam Mahal, one of the wives of Wajid Ali Shah, also wrote thumris and dadras.

In the book *The Courtesan's Arts: Cross-Cultural Perspectives* by Martha Feldman and Bonni Gordon, the following two aspects of the performance of the courtesans have been mentioned:

a) 'In singing, ghazal, thumri and dadra she utilized chaste Urdu and Braj Bhasha and her dance had both bhava (mime) and nrittya (pure dance).

b) 'In the salon dance audiences at the kotha where the courtesan presided, the patrons were treated with grace, elegance and finesse.'

Further, Feldman and Grodon have stated: '[...] it is the tawa'if's uncencumbered identity as a woman that enabled the courtesan to produce a sensual gendered cultural experience for her male patrons in return for the rewards they offer.'

In 2008, Saba Dewan, while conducting research for her documentary *The Other Song*, learnt that up to the middle of the twentieth century, the tawaifs were the leading professional women singers of India. Their contribution, however, has been largely forgotten. According to an article by Amrita Datta in the *Sunday Express* of 24 May 2009 titled 'For the Record', the entire community of women singers 'was airbrushed out of our musical consciousness'.

It must be remembered that singing by courtesans, before the coming of the gramophone, was the only type of singing in vogue. Housewives and respectable women in Uttar Pradesh (including Awadh) seldom sang or were trained to sing. The only singing done by Muslim women was perhaps during marriage festivities and other family celebrations. During Muharram, women recited nauhas (lamentations) and sozes (dirge) at home and, likewise, respectable Hindu ladies practised bhajan singing at home. However, much of the public recitation of nauha and soz was done by courtesans. In Lucknow, Chunewali Haider, Hasso, Bari Jaddan, Mughal Jan, Nanhi Begum and the Chaudharain sisters made their names in Muharram recitals in the early part of the twentieth century, and male devotees always flocked to such functions.

Here the author would like to comment on the timbre and pitch of the voices of some of the courtesans who were talented singers, which have survived on gramophone records. What strikes one is that a majority of the voices were deep and husky. They were throaty voices, loud and sometimes piercing. It may be that from the first decade of the twentieth century, the courtesans were given to smoking, which was frowned upon in respectable society. Some of these husky-voiced singers included Zohra Bai Ambalewali and Malka Pukhraj. The early singers sang loudly because of the rudimentary and primitive system of recording. The music seldom overwhelmed the voice, and musical instruments used were to the minimum. We have very little audio evidence of what and how the courtesans sang in mehfils. There are just a few surviving gramophone records made during the first thirty years or so of the twentieth century, which can be found in music archives. They give a glimpse of what the courtesans sang and how talented they were in the field of singing.

The earliest singers recorded on the newly invented gramophone were the courtesans, starting with Gauhar Jan of Calcutta. In the early song recordings, at the end of each song, the singer quickly announced in English: My name is, followed by her name. The declaration was for the reference of the technical staff who prepared paper labels for the pressed copies of the records.

Gauhar Jan of Calcutta was born in 1873 and died in 1930. On

11 November 1902, Frederick Gaisberg, American-born musician, recording engineer and one of the earliest classical music producers for the gramophone, recorded a song by Gauhar Jan who sang into a large horn in a room of a hotel in Calcutta. This song was '*Ghoor ghoor barasat meharava, bijuriya chamaki anek baar*' (The lightening flashed many times and the rains poured from the sky). '[...] that Tuesday morning in Calcutta was to place her (Gauhar Jan) forever in the annals of world musical history,' noted Vikram Sampath, in his biography of the courtesan titled *My Name Is Gauhar Jaan: The Life and Times of a Musician*, published in 2010. Sampath further wrote that 'Indian classical music took a giant leap forward. From the confines of the courtesans' salons and the rich man's soirées, it was catapulted right into the homes of the common people.' In the course of her life, Gauhar recorded some six hundred songs in nearly twenty languages.

*Bajanaamā: Study of Early Indian Gramophone Records* by Amar Nath Sharma gives a brief sketch of some of the courtesans who earned a name as singers and had their songs recorded. These include:

- **Khurshid Jan and Jali Khurshid of Lucknow and Khurshid Jan of Kanpur**

  The songs of Khurshid Jan of Lucknow were recorded in six records by George Dillnutt in Lucknow in 1909. Khurshid Jan 'is still remembered for her sweet and melodious voice'. Some songs of Jali Khurshid were also recorded and so were some songs of Khurshid Jan of Kanpur. One of her ghazals that became very popular was '*Main jis par jan deta hun woh mera kyun nahin hota*' (Why does she not become mine even though I am willing to lay my life for her).

- **Shamim Jan of Lucknow**

  Shamim Jan was a contemporary of Allah Rakkhi Bai, Buggan, Jali Khurshid, Babban Bai, Tara Bai, Benazeer Bai and Muhammadi Bai of Lucknow. Her songs were recorded by William Sinkler Darby. One of her thumris was '*Piya bin nahin aavat mai ko chain*' (I do not have comfort without my beloved).

- **Jawahar Bai of Lucknow**

  Songs by Jawahar Bai of Lucknow were recorded in about 1906–07 by the recording team of Gramophone and Typewriter Co. Ltd, which was sent to India and comprised William Conrad Gaisberg assisted by George Dillnut.

- **Azmat Jan of Sandila**

  Songs of Azmat Jan of Sandila in Uttar Pradesh were recorded by Pathé Freres Company, founded in 1896. The records were with the label Disque Pathé.

- **Mohammadi Jan and Wazir Jan of Lucknow**

  Beka Record of Beka-Grand, Berlin, recorded songs of Mohammadi Jan and Wazir Jan, both of Lucknow. According to *Bajanaamā*, Wazir Jan was 'an excellent singer of ghazal and thumri of the Lucknow gharana'.

In addition to singing, some of the courtesans would also dance, with copious small bells (ghungroo) tied around their ankles. Sometimes the musicians also played while standing. The musical instruments were tied to their waists with sashes. Some old picture postcards of dancing women show them in the foreground accompanied by musicians standing in the background, with musical instruments fastened to their waists. These dancing parties also sometimes moved in marriage processions. In royal times, the dancing girls at times performed on a moving wooden platform (takht-i rawaan), which was carried on men's shoulders in cavalcades.

## Mujra

The mujra in Awadh was a performance of dance, typically a loose form of Kathak, and singing done by prostitutes to entertain clients. 'Mujra dena' literally means to pay respects or to salute. When a courtesan sang at a mujra, she was typically seated, and the singing was accompanied by bhava, or gestures, eye movements, blandishments and coquettishness. Musical accompaniment was usually the sarangi, tabla and harmonium. In such musical assemblies, the audience sat comfortably against bolsters and pillows, chewing paan and smoking hookahs. When they departed, they left money tucked among the bolsters. In mujras, the dancing went on for hours and the best girls graced the occasion. The mujra programmes of singing and dancing were always seasoned with wit and humour. The connoisseurs appreciated repartees and biting jests.

However, the customers were not there to appreciate the high points of the art. The aim was titillation and arousal. It was performed so the men could savour young women visually (or physically), achieve pleasure and get gratification. The songs would charm and allure, but it was the sensual persona of the mujra dancer (or dancers) that enraptured and proved compelling. This was despite the fact that the mujra dancer was fully clothed without any palpable display of body parts. The mujra never had any elements of a striptease, or for that matter, of the tawdry performance of bar dancers. The mujra was not wholly an erotic performance but was a choreographic salutation to the audience.

Richard Connerney's book *The Upside-Down Tree*, which was a result of his stay in Lucknow, has nicely summed up the role of the courtesans of Lucknow in so many words:

> Nineteenth-century Lucknow was the home of tawaif, professional, geisha-like courtesans who entertained well-bred men in extravagant brothels (kotha). Men of repute in Lucknowi society would gather for special parties where these highly trained women would sing, recite poetry, dance and play musical instruments. Tawa'ifs were no simple streetwalkers; they were refined women who required months of courting and demanded expensive gifts before granting any man access to their physical intimacies.

The courtesans' skills and training as performing artists led some of them to enter India's fledgling film industry, where they went on to become the leading lights of the film world. As someone observed, ghazals, Muslim socials, Awadh and the tawaif were all instrumental in shaping Hindi cinema as a whole. When Indian cinema took birth in 1913, men acted the female roles as women from respectable families did not act in films. Subsequently, female characters were given to courtesans to play as their own business was suffering. We have had a long list of courtesans-turned-actresses and they include names like Jaddan Bai,[53] the mother of Nargis, and Paro Devi[54].

A few Bollywood films have captured a mujra in all its resplendence such as *Pakeezah* (1972) or *Umrao Jaan* (1981). But in the author's opinion, the best mujra has been shown in the Hindi film *Mahal* (*The Mansion*), released in 1949 and directed by Kamal Amrohi. The film shows a mujra dance by two small-times actresses, Leela Panday and Sheela Naikon, and includes the song '*Yeh raat phir na ayegi*' sung by Raj Kumari (1921–2000) and Zohra Bai Ambalewali (1918–90).

## Courtesans and Literature

Courtesans in Awadh flourished in the eighteenth, nineteenth and early twentieth centuries. They were considered to be the repositories of culture, elegance and refinement, and were trained in good taste to cater to urbane male clients. Many of the courtesans could read and write Urdu and some of them were talented poets in Urdu (and sometimes also in Persian). To hone their skills, they also became poetic disciples of some leading Urdu poets. Their memories were sharp and they could retain couplets for timely recitation and for innuendos and repartees in polished gatherings. Some of the poetic collections of these courtesans were also published. The purpose of the salons was to enable men to gather around a host to heighten their knowledge, hone their taste and indulge in cultured conversation. The hosts were sophisticated courtesans who played a dominant role in attracting well-read and refined clientele. The singing courtesans had their own repertoire of ghazals, thumries, dadras and other songs and they, with the help of their ustads, compiled personal notebooks of such songs, which served as aide-memoire for public rendering. In the nineteenth and early twentieth centuries, there were also in circulation printed booklets and chapbooks, which were

---

[53]Jaddan Bai was an early singer, music composer, actress and filmmaker of Bollywood and one of the pioneers of Indian cinema. She was the mother of well-known actress Nargis, and maternal grandmother of Sanjay Dutt.

[54]According to Saadat Hasan Manto, Paro was a courtesan from Meerut. Source: http://cineplot.com/paro-devi/

compilations of the Urdu, Persian and Hindi songs of eminent writers. Some of them metion that they were in use in music programmes at kothas. This author has in his collection some of these printed anthologies, which give an idea of what was sung and what was popular in those days. Some of these booklets are noted below:

1. *Naghma-i Dilkash* (*Heart-Attracting Songs*), Part One
   Compiled by Ram Prasad 'Aamil'
   (Lucknow: Matba Dabdaba-i Ahmadi, n.d.)

2. *Naghma-i Dilkash* (*Heart-Attracting Songs*), Part Two
   Compiled by Ram Prasad 'Aamil'
   (Lucknow: Dil Pazir Press, n.d.)

3. *Ishq-i Dariya* (*Love of the River*)
   By Jaswant Rai 'Josh'
   (Agra: Matba' Ilahi, 1902)

4. *Raag Saar Sangrah* (*Collection of Essence of Ragas*), Part One
   Compiled by Munni Lal Vaish
   (Lucknow: Matba Aijaz-i Muhammadi, n.d.)

5. *Bazm-i Nishat Urf Song Book:*
   Compiled by Pandit Kunwar Gauri Prasad 'Hamdam' Akbarabadi
   (Agra: Abul Ulaai Press, 1909)

It is interesting to go through these long-forgotten songbooks. Besides Hindi dadras, thumris and holis, there are a good number of ghazals of writers like 'Nasikh', 'Atish', 'Qalaq', 'Rashk', 'Tamanna', 'Shafaq', 'Ufaq', 'Momin', 'Zafar', 'Rangeen', and 'Daagh', among others. What is fascinating is that there are numerous ghazals headed by the name of a prostitute. It is difficult to say without further research whether the ghazal was written by the courtesan herself or was penned by some male poet. Another interesting fact is that the women's names have been suffixed by the word 'tawaif'. Some of the names included are 'Mushtari', Nazir Jan, Biggan Jan 'Zeba', Gauhar Jan 'Gauhar' Lakhnavi, Bi Vilaito, Nanhi Jan 'Nazan', Ajuba Jan 'Qatil' Ferozabadi, Malka Jan Lakhnavi, Umrao Jan, Shirin Jan, Gauhar Jan (Calcutta), Mughal Jan, Baiji (Baroda), Dilbar Jan Farrukhabadi,

Rangili Kanpuri, Najmunnissa (Patna), Munni Jan (Muzaffarpur), Janaki Bai (Calcutta), Ladli Jan Lakhnavi and Ram Pyari (Nainital).

As far as this author is aware, very few courtesans wrote their memoirs in Indian languages. At least, there are none in Urdu, except the autobiography of Malka Pukhraj (1912–2004), the great ghazal and folk singer, who was associated with the court of Maharaja Hari Singh of Jammu. Malka Pukhraj was originally from a kotha. Her original Urdu autobiography has not yet been published, but its English translation is available, *Song Sung True: A Memoir*[55], translated by Saleem Kidwai. Another autobiography is that of Binodini Dasi (1863–1941), titled *My Story and My Life as an Actress*, which was originally published in Bengali in 1913 and its English translation[56] came out in 1998. Nalini Jameela's *The Autobiography of a Sex Worker* was a bestseller in Malayalam and its English translation was published in 2007.[57]

## Courtesans in Novels

*Nashtar:* Courtesans are the subjects of several fine novels in Urdu. One such is *Nashtar* (*The Lancet*), which can be considered to be among the earliest novels on the Indian subcontinent, if not the first.

The novel is claimed to have been written in Persian by Syed Muhammad Hasan Shah and professes to be based on real incidents in the life of the author, which occurred in 1784–85. The Persian original has not been found and was never published.

A young Hasan Shah, who is munshi (clerk) to an Englishman, Ming Saheb, in Cawnpore, falls madly in love with a dancing girl from a touring dancing troupe, Khanum Jan. Hasan Shah and Khanum marry in secret. When the time comes for the troupe to leave, Hasan Shah and Khanum Jan plan to flee, but are unable to do so. Khanum finally leaves Kanpur with her troupe and Hasan follows a few days later. However, the lovers are not destined to unite and ultimately, Khanum dies of grief. No details

---

[55]Published by Kali for Women, New Delhi, 2003.

[56]Published by Kali for Women, New Delhi.

[57]Published by Westland Books, Chennai.

are known of Hasan Shah's life after his stay in Kanpur, except that he had settled in Lucknow.

**Umrao Jan Ada:** Perhaps one of the best-known novels on a courtesan of Awadh is the Urdu novel *Umrao Jan Ada* by Mirza Muhammad Hadi 'Ruswa'.[58]

Mirza Muhammad Hadi 'Ruswa' was born in Lucknow in 1857. He was a poet, fiction writer, playwright and writer on religion, philosophy and astronomy. He was well versed in Urdu, Persian, Arabic and English. He learnt calligraphy from one Haider Bakhsh. He invented Urdu shorthand and the Urdu typewriter keyboard. By all counts, Ruswa was an extremely versatile man. He is, however, particularly remembered for the novel *Umrao Jan Ada*, which gives an intimate and sympathetic peep into the lives of the courtesans of Lucknow and their customs.

It is the story of a girl, Ameeran, who is born into a modest family in Faizabad, where she passes a carefree childhood. However, when her father gives evidence against a local ruffian, he abducts Ameeran in revenge and sells her to a courtesan named Khanum in Lucknow. The girl is given a new name, Umrao, and she is brought up along with other nauchis for blossoming into a courtesan. Umrao is fond of writing poetry and does so under the pen name of 'Ada'. She becomes a famous courtesan of Lucknow. Her encounters with different men, from a nawab to a decoit, form the main body of the story. After many years, she meets her brother in Faizabad; however, he refuses to take her back as he feels that she has disgraced the family. Dejected, she returns to Lucknow.

Other novels by Ruswa include *Afsha-i Raz* (*The Disclosure of Secrets*) and *Junun-e Intezar Ya'ni Fasana-e Mirza Ruswa*.

**Bazar-i Husn:** Another significant novel based on the life of a prostitute

---

[58]It is not known exactly when this novel was first printed. The edition in the British Library collection was published by Rai Sahib, Munshi Gulab Singh & Sons Press, Lucknow, and is presumably the first edition of the book, but it does not include the year of publication. Where the introductory pages end, the printed Urdu endorsement reads 'Lucknow March 1899'. Two English translations of the novel are available. The first was by Khushwant Singh and M.A. Husaini (Delhi: Hind Pocket Books, 1970). The second, done about two and a half decades later, was prepared by David Matthews (Calcutta: Rupa & Co., 1994).

is *Bazar-i Husn* (*The Market of Beauty*) by Munshi Premchand (1880–1936), one of the greatest writers of modern Urdu and Hindi literature. Premchand originally wrote the novel in Urdu, but it was published as *Sevasadan* (*The House of Service*) in Hindi by Pustak Agency, Lucknow, in 1919. The Urdu *Bazar-i Husn* came out from Lahore in 1924.

*Bazar-i Husn* is based in Benaras and is the story of an unhappy housewife Suman. She is married to an older man in peculiar circumstances. Her husband is a clerk. The comeliness of Suman earns her the envy of the neighbourhood and the jealously of her husband. One day, when she returns from visiting a friend, her husband does not admit her in the house. She is forced to become a courtesan and experiences the wretchedness of harlotry. Ultimately, Suman reforms herself and serves as the manager of an orphanage for the daughters of courtesans.

It should be remembered that the courtesans of Benaras had an important role in the cultural, literary and municipal life of the city.

*Bazar-i Husn* was Premchand's first major novel. The English translation is titled *Courtesans' Quarter* and was done by Amina Azfar. The Hindi version *Sevasadan* is also available and was translated by Snehal Shingavi.

*Laila Ke Khutoot:* Another Urdu novel on a prostitute is *Laila Ke Khutoot* (*The Letters of Laila*) by Qazi Abdul Ghaffar (1888 or 1889–1954). Qazi Abdul Ghaffar was an author and distinguished journalist who was born in Moradabad, Uttar Pradesh. He started his career in Hyderabad as an editor of an Urdu paper. His own life was quite tragic. Four of his sons were mentally challenged and died in the lifetime of their father. His wife died in childbirth.

Qazi Abdul Ghaffar was an open-minded person and was against the injustice and repression suffered by women. He fell in love with a courtesan and married her after the death of his wife. However, his family strongly disapproved of his choice of wife.

Qazi Abdul Ghaffar wrote many books, but his most important one is *Laila Ke Khutoot*, which was first published in 1934. This book has also been translated into English with the same title by Scheherazade Alim.

*Laila Ke Khutoot* is an epistolary novel, which examines the hardships suffered by a woman shunned by society. It comprises fifty-two letters written by a fallen woman to a man she respects because of his character. The letters are reflective and meditative in nature. The first man in her life made her into a woman but not into a wife. In a society where man has the upper hand, even respectable women have a difficult time playing second fiddle. The novel, when published in the 1930s, caused a sensation. Through her letters, the woman was not only asserting herself but was also making a positive status statement. It was perhaps the first time in Urdu literature that a female character was boldly declaring that despite her socially debased profession, she could think and even decide for herself. She may not be able to fight her destiny, which had induced in her a sense of helplessness and forlornness, but she was in no way incapable of voicing her views.

Wajida Tabassum (1935–2010) is another author who wrote several novels and short stories in Urdu on the theme of prostitutes. She delved into the lives of the courtesans of Hyderabad. However, Wajida got a lot of opprobrium for her writing. She published novels and collections of short stories with telling titles like *Nath Utarai* (*The Taking Off of the Nose Ring*), *Nath Ka Bojh* (*The Burden of the Nose Ring*), *Nath Ki Izzat* (*The Prestige of the Nose Ring*), *Nath Ka Zakhm* (*The Wound of the Nose Ring*), *Nath Ka Ghuroor* (*The Pride of the Nose Ring*), and *Utaran* (*The Cast-Off Clothes*). Mira Nair's Hindi film *Kama Sutra*, released in 1997, is based in part on Wajida Tabassum's short story *Utaran*.

Nawab Wajid Ali Shah (1822–87) also wrote a piece on a courtesan. This Urdu poem (masnavi) was probably never published. However, this author has a copy of the poem, which is titled 'Masnavi Dar Halaat-i Gunna Tawaif' (Poem about the Particulars of Courtesan Gunna).[59] The poem comprises two hundred rhyming couplets. Although it is not known who this Gunna Tawaif was, Wajid Ali Shah took pains to describe her physical attributes with a lot of tenderness and attention. Her face was

---

[59]The author's copy was once in the collection of the late Professor Masud Hasan Rizavi 'Adib' (1893–1975), a collector of rare books.

pockmarked, but Wajid Ali has described her face as being as radiant as the moon, with the pockmarks being 'stars'. She was one with whom one fell in love with even without seeing her, and if she was seen, she could drive one crazy. She was sweet-voiced and was adept in dancing. She was married but considered her house a prison. The author pined to meet her. She was terribly beautiful and was like an idol made from raw earth. Her breasts resembled apples and her eyes were shaped like almonds. Her sexual attributes have also been mentioned in some couplets.

## Literary Contribution of the Courtesans of Awadh

As mentioned earlier, some of the courtesans composed poetry, and some of their works were also printed. The courtesans ensured that while what they sang could be erotic in nature, it did not transgress the boundaries of decency. That was left to the mirasins, a hereditary class of women singers who danced and sang but usually in the presence of women only. Even now mirasins sometimes sing at Hindu and Muslim marriages, particularly in Uttar Pradesh. They sing extremely obscene songs. However, the tradition of the singing of mirasins is now fading. From an anthropological point of view, these daring and audacious songs should be preserved. So far, not many of them have found their way into print. One or two Urdu manuscripts in one of the government libraries in Hyderabad contain some of these songs.

*Tazkirahs:* A tazkirah is an anthology of the brief notes of poets, with samples of their poetry. Sometimes, short glimpses of the lives of the poets are also given. As several of the courtesans of Awadh were proficient in writing, their names too find a place in the tazkirahs.

There are printed tazkirahs for women poets exclusively, starting with *Baharistan-i Naaz* in Urdu by Hakim Fasihuddin 'Ranj' Merathi (1836–85), a pupil of Mirza Ghalib.[60] This book describes 174 female poets, forty-nine of whom wrote in Persian, including two who wrote in

---

[60]First published by Matba' Darul Uloom, Meerut, 1864. It was reprinted in 1869 and in 1882, also from Meerut. Finally, it was edited by Khalil-ur-Rahman Daudi and published from Majlis-i Taraqqi-i Adab, Lahore, Pakistan, in 1964.

both Persian and Urdu. It includes seventeen women who were said to be prostitutes, but were cultured and aesthetically groomed.

There were many tazkirahs of women poets written by Durga Prasad 'Nadir' Dehalvi and another by Raja Durga Prasad 'Mehar' Sandilvi under the title *Hadiqa-i Ishrat*.[61] A short tazkirah, *Tazkira-i Shamim-i Sukhan*[62] was written by Abdul Hai 'Safa' Badauni. The only tazkirah of female poets written in the twentieth century was by Abdul Bari 'Asi' Uldani (1893–1946), titled *Tazkirat-ul-Khawateen*.[63]

∽

A few courtesans of Lucknow who were talented poets are mentioned below.

- **Ameer:** She was from Lucknow and was alive around 1853–54. She wrote impassioned poetry.

  *Yeh mahv-i deed-i rukh-i gul hai bulbul-i shaida*
  *Nahin khabar ki chaman se bahaar jati hai*

  The bulbul is so possessed of the face of the rose
  That it is not aware that spring is leaving the garden

- **Farhat Bakht 'Farhat':** She was a courtesan of Faizabad and was employed by a nawab. She excelled in classical singing and also wrote poetry. One of her couplets is:

  *Main jalun aur kare ghair se yun garm baghal*
  *Dil mein thandak ho mire tu bhi bane jab mujh sa*

  You keep another person in your arms, which makes me jealous
  It will soothe my heart if you also become like me

- **Wazir Jan 'Husn':** She was a courtesan of Lucknow and lived in the Pata Nala area. She was the daughter of Gauhar Jan. A couplet attributed to her is:

---

[61]Published by Queen Press, Sandila, 1893; Matba' Dabdaba-i Ahmadi, Lucknow, 1898.
[62]Published by Naval Kishore Press, Lucknow, (second edition) 1891.
[63]Published by Naval Kishore press, Luknow, 1927.

*Wasl ki shab bhi na baaz aaya shararat se wo shokh*
*Muskura kar pher li karwat sitam ham par hua*

The sprightly beloved did not desist from mischief even on the night
of union
She practised tyranny on me by smilingly turning her back

- **Biggan Jan 'Mehak':** She was the poetic disciple of Imdad Husain
'Riza' Lakhnavi. The following is a couplet from a literary tazkirah:

*Qatl manzoor agar hai to charhaao abroo*
*Ham to muddat se gale milte hain talwaron par*

Raise your eyebrows if you decide to slay me
I have been for long embracing swords

- **Qamrun Jan alias Manjhu 'Mushtari':** She was from Khairabad in
Sitapur, but her profession as a courtesan brought her to the Chowk
area of Lucknow. She was well versed in music, was a good calligrapher
and a fair poet who composed well. She was the sister of Umrao Jan
'Zahra'. She, like her sister, was the poetic disciple of Agha Ali 'Shams'
Lakhnavi and also wrote in Persian. She compiled her diwan. One
of her couplets is recorded below.

*Iss se to wasl ke arman mein marna behtar*
*Ya Ilahi na kisi se koi mil kar chhoote*

It is better to die than desire union (with the beloved)
O God do not part those who have come together

Her Persian diwan was published in 1881 under the title *Tarana-i
Khayal* (*Song of Thoughts*) from the Matba' Syed Abid Ali. A sixteen-
page booklet of dirges (nauhas) titled *Ganjeena-i Aza*[64] (Treasury of
*Mourning*) bears the name of the author as Manjhu Sahiba 'Mushtari'.

- **Umrao Jan 'Naz':** She belonged to Sandila in the Hardoi district of
Uttar Pradesh, but moved to Khairabad in Sitapur. She was naturally
sharp and clever, but did not possess a high literary aptitude. However,

---

[64]Published by Tasvir-i Alam Press, Lucknow, 1882–83.

she composed poetry quite well. One of her couplets is as follows:

*Kuchh tabassum sa lab-i naaz pe neechi nazrein*
*Kin adaaon se shab-i wasl woh sharmate hain*

A hint of a smile hovered coquettishely on her lips
With what graceful blandishments she was bashful on the night of union

- **Amat-ul Fatima 'Sahib':** She was a famous courtesan of Lucknow. She went to Delhi before the Uprising of 1857. There she fell ill and was treated by the famous Urdu poet Momin Khan 'Momin' (1801 or 1802–1852), who was also a hakim (physician). Momin had a weakness for beautiful women. He treated Sahib and became attracted to her. His published poetical works contain a masnavi on her. In the company of Momin, Sahib developed her poetic craft. Like her mentor's, her poetry had pathos as well as playfulness. The following is a couplet penned by Sahib:

*Guneh kya sanam ke nazzaare mein zaahid*
*Yeh jalwa khuda ne dikhaaya to dekha*

O recluse there is no sin in the sighting the beloved
I saw the manifestation because it was shown by God

- **Sardar Begum 'Sardar':** She hailed from a good family in Lucknow. Being widowed, she left Kanpur after the Uprising of 1857 and went to Kannauj and later to Etawah, where she lived for the rest of her life. She started leading the life of a courtesan and became a deredar tawaif. She even trained her daughter, Kazmi Begum, in the profession. She was illiterate but had a talent for composing poetry, which she dictated to others. A person who met her remarked that even in her wayward life, there was a tinge of decency. The following couplet is an example of her poetry:

*Lagaya gul se jo dil ko tune, samajh le dil mein yeh apne bulbul*
*Hain chand roza bahaar ke din, yeh gul to roz-i khizaan na hoga*

O bulbul understand it well in your heart when you fell for the rose

The days of spring are few and this rose, alas, will not see the autumn

- **Imami Jan 'Sharm':** She was from Lucknow and practised her profession as a courtesan from near Akbari Gate. She wrote poetry occasionally. Her Urdu diwan has been published. One of her couplets is included here.

*Asar khaak-i lahad yeh hai ki chhoo jane se*
*Maraz-i hijr ke beemaar shifa pate hain*

The effect of touching the dust of the grave is
That it heals those sick with the ailment of separation

- **Baiga 'Shirin':** She was a courtesan who lived in the Chowk area of Lucknow. She held a high position among her peers. She was beautiful and had a talent for poetry. She was the poetic disciple of Mir Mohammadi 'Siphar' and later she showed her poetry for correction to the famous Urdu poet Shaikh Imdad Ali 'Bahr' Lakhnavi. She was an expert in attaching a completing hemistich to a given hemistich. She wrote in Urdu as well as in Persian. She was said to be sprightly and coquettish. An example of her poetry is given below:

*Ulfat bhi chahiye pe zara dekh bhaal kar*
*Har shola ru ko chahe to chulhe mein jaye dil*

It is necessary to seek love but it should be with a lot of caution
Be damned if you desire every radiant face

- **Umrao Jan 'Zahra':** She lived in the Chowk area of Lucknow. She was the poetic disciple of Mir Agha Ali Shams Lakhnavi, a pupil of poet Qazi Muhammad Sadiq Khan 'Akhtar'. It was alleged that Shams had relations with Zahra's mother, which is why he took an interest in the daughters, Zahra and Mushtari. This led to quarrels between Shams and his peer poets.

A nobleman of Lucknow with the pen name of 'Makhzum' once visited Zahra and teasingly recited the following lines:

*Sair-i falak ko ham kabhi tanha na jaenge*

I will never go alone to wander the heavens

Zahra immediately replied:

*Zahra ke saath jaenge ya Mushtari ke saath*

Either Zahra or Mushtari will accompany you

It is said that Zahra eventually left her profession and married a respectable man. Two more couplets of Zahra are:

*Sab mira haal sun ke hain pur gham*
*Tu na kuch yaar-i bewafa samjha*
*Main ne wallah di dua tujh ko*
*Tu Khuda jane dil mein kya samjha*

All are in sorrow on hearing my plight
O unfaithful friend, you alas could not understand
By God I prayed for you
God knows what you understood in your heart

- **Biggan 'Zainab':** She was a courtesan of Lucknow, but moved to Calcutta later in life. She was the poetic disciple of Mir Asghar Ali 'Asghar'. One of her couplets is:

*Ham hain nawaaqif na hum se uth saki sakhti-i hijr*
*Tajurba karon se puchho waqt-i mushkil kya hua*

I found it difficult to bear the harshness of separation because
I was a novice
Ask the experienced ones what happens in trying times

Despite her cultural and literary accomplishments, Zainab remained a fallen woman in the eyes of society, although her association with the aristocracy did serve her well as far as material prosperity was concerned.

## Some Famous Courtesans of Lucknow

### The Chaudharains

Among the courtesans of Lucknow at the turn of the twentieth century, the kotha of the Chaudharain family was very famous. This kotha was situated in the Chowk area of Lucknow, opposite the small bookshop of Khwaja Abdur Rauf 'Ishrat' Lakhnavi (1868–1940), which was frequented by Urdu literary luminaries like Muhammad Shibli Nomani (1857–1914) and Niyaz Muhammad Khan 'Niyaz Fatehpuri' (1884–1966). Every year a music programme was held under the auspices of the Chaudharains. A sprawling mansion was borrowed for a few days for the conference. There is a very interesting article titled 'Qadim Lucknow Ki Tawaifein' ('The Courtesans of Old Lucknow') by Mirza Jafar Husain (1899–1989) in the May 1977 issue of *Aaj Kal* (Urdu). The following paragraphs are based on this article.

Mirza Jafar Husain named Mughal Jan of Sabzi Mandi, Haider Jan of Parchewali Gali, Azimun of Sabzi Mandi, Hasso of Aminabad, Buggan of Mohalla Jhaulal, Mushtari of Nakhkhas and Bari Jaddan of Taksaal among the courtesans who stayed in old Lucknow. Allah Bandi and Najja were deredar tawaifs who lived in Chawal Wali Gali. They owned houses and even had imamabaras named after them. Mushtari was another deredar tawaif of that period. Although she was quite ugly and had many children, she was among the leading courtesans of Lucknow, very qualified and competent in singing, witty conversation and etiquette.

Other well-known courtesans were Nazeer Jan, Babban, Noor Jahan, Zahra, Mushtari, Kallan and Jaddan, who were excellent ghazal singers and skilled in demonstrating ragas and raginis. Hasso, Bari Jaddan and Kallan were also skilled in the recital of marsiya (elegy) and soz (dirge). On the day of the burial of tazias, the tenth day of Muharram, these courtesans would accompany the various processions declaiming elegies and dirges.

Among all these courtesans there was coalition, restraint and discipline because of the presence of two sisters, namely, Nanhua (real name Badr-i Muneer) and Bachua (real name Mah-i Muneer), who functioned as chaudharains (an honorific for a head woman of the profession). The Chaudharain sisters exercised significant influence over the deredar tawaifs and their words and instructions were largely complied with.

The Chaudharains were consummate artistes and in dance had been trained by the great Bindadin (1830–1918), the founder of the Lucknow gharana of Kathak. The elder sister Nanhua was heavily built, somewhat fat and extremely fair. Bachua, the younger sister, was also a dancer, but she was known for interpreting bhava (hand gestures, rhythm of the feet and eye movements). According to Jafar Husain, she once sang a line of Ghalib as many as thirty-six times and each time she came up with new bhavas. Badr-i Muneer was childless, but Mahr-i Muneer had a daughter by the name of Rashk-i Muneer. She had inherited all the talents of her mother. The residence of the Chaudharains was in the same area of Chowk where the Hina Building, the sprawling mansion of the perfumers Asghar Ali and Mohamed Ali, was later built. The Chaudharains lived with their dependants, retinue of servants and retainers. The Chaudharains had another sister, Mahr-i Muneer. Mahr-i Muneer authored a novel in Urdu titled *Khoobsurat Kahina*[65] (*The Beautiful Sorceress*). The book also contains five ghazals by her.

The common meeting hall of the Chaudharains was always crowded during the mornings and evenings, like a durbar, and included the gentry and several literary figures and poets. Conversations with the Chaudharains were a matter of enjoyment. The dastarkhwan for lunch and dinner was spread regularly, with twenty to twenty-five persons in attendance.

However, the decline in the fortunes of the gentry impacted the income of the Chaudharains and they began to face serious financial difficulties. To keep up appearances, they continued to provide asemblance of their former good life despite mounting debts. Ultimately, their house was mortgaged. They moved to Calcutta in the hope of reviving their fortunes but failed miserably. The calls for mujras in Calcutta had diminished and the common flesh trade was not palatable to the Chaudharains. They found themselves earning little from their profession and their lifestyle was becoming a burden. Subsequently, their house in Calcutta was also auctioned. Rashk-i Muneer, the daughter of Mah-i Muneer, who was the sole breadwinner for the aging Chaudharains, died in her youth and was buried in Lucknow. In her advanced age, the stout Badr-i Muneer, the eldest Chaudharain, spent her time in bed telling her rosary. When eventually both the Chaudharains passed away, the curtain came down on a celebrated and illustrious era of Lucknow's courtesans.

---

[65]The author's name is given as Miss Mahr-i Muneer Chaudharain Lakhnavi (Lucknow: Hamdam Press, 1922).

## Janaki Bai

A contemporary of the Chaudharains of Lucknow was Janaki Bai of Allahabad. Her date of birth is uncertain.[66] She was born in Benaras where her father owned a sweets shop. She was a courtesan of immense talents. She had a wonderful voice and learnt music from Ustad Hassu Khan of Lucknow. Janaki Bai had been slashed fifty-six ('chhappan' in Hindi) times with a 'chhuri' (a small knife), and hence was called 'Chhappan Chhuri'. She died in 1934. Her Urdu poetry was published as *Diwan-i Janaki*[67] and is now extremely rare.

## Azizun Bai

Firdous Azmat Siddiqui in her book *A Struggle for Identity: Muslim Women in the United Provinces* has pointed out that during the Uprising of 1857, '[…] courtesans and prostitutes were very active in boosting the morale of both sepoys and mutineers. They acted as scouts for the rebels, and paid for their actions after the revolt, when the wrath of the British fell upon them.' According to her, these women were 'affected the most by British policies', as 'at one time they had enjoyed the patronage of many landed and royal families'. The story of Azizun, the daughter of a courtesan of Lucknow, illustrates this. She was probably born in 1832. She was brought up in Lucknow in the house of a courtesan at Satrangi Mahal, but later moved to a street of brothels in Kanpur, where she maintained her kotha.

Andrew Ward in his book *Our Bones Are Scattered: The Cawnpore Massacres and the Indian Mutiny of 1857* has given a short account of Azizun. She joined the Indian rebels in Kanpur and was said to have ridden armed with pistols and sowars in male attire. A group of Indian freedom fighters sacked Kanpur on 4 June 1857; the group was led by Azizun. She made her headquarters in one of the gun batteries. According

---

[66]Sampath has given her year of birth as 1880, whereas Susie Tharu and K. Lalita in *Women Writing in India: 600 B.C. to the Present* (Delhi: Oxford University Press, 1991) have given it as 1889.

[67]Published by Asrar-i Karimi Press, Allahabad, 1931.

to Thomas Smith, Azizun was in the confidence of Tantya Tope, Nana Sahib, Azimullah Shah and others. It is said that on the recapture of Kanpur by the British, Azizun was arrested by Major General Sir Henry Havelock (1795–1857) and offered clemency, but she refused. She faced the firing squad.[68]

## Badr-i Muneer

Amritlal Nagar in his book *Yeh Kothewalian* has devoted a chapter to the dying of Badr-i Muneer, the famous courtesan of Lucknow. She was seduced and brought to Lucknow by a man who kept her in a brothel. She observed that the other girls in the brothel were physically beaten. She took to obeying all instructions and learning what she was supposed to learn. She was then put in another kotha, where Nagar had the occasion to hear her sing in 1935–36. Later, she contracted smallpox and was evicted from her kotha. In 1937, a messenger informed Amritlal Nagar that Badr-i Muneer was very sick and had called for him. He visited her in her dilapidated house outside Akbari Darwaza. In a thatched room walled by sackcloth and lit by a feeble wick lamp, Badr-i Muneer lay on a cot. She was wrapped in a quilt. One hand and her red-blistered, skeleton-like face were visible. She was horrible in appearance. She had contracted syphilis, which had developed quickly. That was how the beautiful Badr-i Muneer came to her end.

## Akhtari Bai aka Begum Akhtar

Few in India who enjoy ghazals, thumris and dadras have not heard of Begum Akhtar. A short biographical article titled 'Begum Akhtar: Ek Haqiqat Jo Sigha-i Raaz Mein Rahi' ('Begum Akhtar: A Truth which Has Remained in the Domain of Secrecy') by Muhammad Abdul Sami appeared

---

[68]Brief accounts of Azizun can also be found in *Traders and Nabobs: The British in Cawnpore, 1765-1853* by Zoë Yalland (Salisbury, Wiltshire: Michael Russell, 1987); and *A Star Shall Fall: India 1857* by P.J.O. Taylor (New Delhi: HarperCollins, 1993). Tripurari Sharma wrote a Hindi play in 1998 titled *San Sattavan Ka Qissa: Azizun Nissa*. It was translated into English by Tutun Mukherjee and A.R. Manzar.

in the 22-28 January 2016 issue of the weekly *Hamari Zabaan*. Akhtari Bai was born around 1914 in the Faizabad district of Uttar Pradesh. Her father was one Asghar Husain, a young lawyer. He fell in love with one Mushtari Bai, who became his second wife. Subsequently, Asghar Husain disowned Mushtari and his twin daughters Zohra and Bibbi (Akhtari).

From a very early age, Akhtari trained under Ustad Imdad Khan, a sarangi player from Patna, and later under Ustad Ata Muhammad Khan of Patiala. When she went to Calcutta, she trained under Muhammad Khan, Abdul Waheed Khan and finally Ustad Jhande Khan (d. 1952).

According to Muhammad Abdul Sami, one Syed Ahmad, son of Syed Muhammad Jan Miyan, a member of the gentry of Rampur, was sent to Hyderabad to train as a pilot. He was fond of music and also played a few instruments. At that time, Akhtari Bai was gaining popularity for her voice and soulful singing. Syed Ahmad met Akhtari Bai and fell in love with her at first sight. The meeting blossomed into marriage. Syed Ahmad's father was furious and after failing to persuade his son to leave her, he disowned him.

After living in Delhi and Hyderabad, the couple went to Rampur, but were refused entry into the ancestral home. Syed Ahmad was also debarred from any claim to the property. However, after his father's death, Syed Ahmad approached his mother and was able to get some money from her. During this time, he had become addicted to liquor and drugs. As a result, both his kidneys failed and he died in 1941. After his death, Akhtari Bai remained in Rampur for about two years and then moved to Lucknow in 1943. She worked briefly in the film industry, acting in the film *Roti,* released in 1942. It was directed by Mahboob Khan and the music was composed by Anil Biswas.

In 1945, she married Ishtiaq Ahmad Abbasi, a barrister of Lucknow, and began to be known as Begum Akhtar.

Begum Akhtar finally devoted herself to singing North Indian light classical music and sang about four hundred ghazals, thumris and dadras. Kundan Lal Saigal (1904–47) and Begum Akhtar are credited with setting a trend in ghazal singing and introducing and popularizing many gems of Urdu literature.

In 1974, while attending a concert in Ahmedabad, Gujarat, she breathed her last. Her body was brought to Lucknow and was buried in Pasanda Bagh in Thakurganj, by the side of her mother Mushtari Bai.

### Zareena Begum: 'The Last Courtesan of Awadh'

Zareena Begum was once the queen of mehfils.[69] She was born in Nanpara in Bahraich district of Uttar Pradesh. She was among the five children of Shehenshah Husain, who worked in the court of the erstwhile Raja of Nanpara. It is said that Zareena's talent for music was discovered by her father. He took her to one Ghulam Hasrat and a singer, Chand Khan, who were her first teachers.

While performing in Bahraich, she was heard by Begum Akhtar, who patronized her. She met the tabla player Qurban Husain, brother-in-law of Munne Khan, and married him. Qurban Husain would accompany Zareena on the tabla.

Zareena performed in various cities including Benaras, Rampur, Calcutta, Moradabad and Delhi. She also sang on the All India Radio. She spent a lot of time in the court of Rampur, where she was asked to perform at family weddings. She was gifted land by the former Raja of Nanpara and she also earned well through her performances. However, with the abolition of zamindari in Uttar Pradesh, her fortunes also declined. According to her, she lost most of her savings to relatives and family members. After her husband died, she was faced with poverty, with little support from any side. In August 2015, Zareena Begum was given the first Begum Akhtar Award of ₹5 lakh by the Government of Uttar Pradesh. At that time, she was living in a dilapidated house in old Fatehganj in Lucknow.

In 2008, a 25-minute documentary, *Zareena*, on Zareena Begum was made by Piyush Pushpak and Suhail Bukhari. It provides a glimpse of the life of the singer and includes excerpts of ghazals and other songs sung by her.

---

[69]On 22 June 2014, *htcity*, the *Hindustan Times* supplement, carried an article by Richa Srivastava titled 'The Last Courtesan of Awadh'.

### Rehana, the Film Actress

Rehana was an actress of Hindi cinema in the late 1940s and early 1950s. Her mother's name was Mushtar Jahan. She was probably born in Lucknow.

She was a sex symbol in films. In dancing, she was famous for her jhatkas (jerks) and was known as the 'Jhatka Queen'. She had a leading role in some popular films like *Shahnai* (1947), *Sajan* (1947), *Khidki* (1948) and *Sargam* (1950). She eloped with her lover to Pakistan where she did a few films.

## The Decline

After 1857, all grades of courtesans were labelled as common prostitutes. They were considered a threat to the widely accepted moral order. They were an example of all that was said to be wrong in society. As a result of Victorian morality, the British condemned the entire sex profession and demolished the thin line between the courtesan and the common prostitute. The Indian public was also not far behind and there was widespread condemnation of fallen women who were said to be deleterious to public morality. Visiting kothas began to be frowned upon. Many pamphlets denouncing whoring were published. Two Urdu booklets of versified polemics against prostitution are *Randibazon Ki Hajaamat* (*Castigation of Whoremongers*) by G.R. Sharma Merathi and *Shaitan Ke Bachche* (*Children of Satan*) by Muhammad Khairuddin Khan.[70]

Faced with a declining clientele and incomes, the courtesans had to seek other means of survival. Some of them became the mistresses of a few of the dwindling members of the landed gentry and were fortunate to pass their lives in anonymity. But a majority of the socially refined courtesans found sanctuary in the brothels, which mushroomed in specific red-light districts.

There were also many courtesans who gave up their profession after forming liaisons with respectable men. Despite family opposition in most cases, the women got married and assumed the role of chaste (parsa)

---

[70]Both are in the personal collection of the author.

housewives. Many of these marriages lasted, and even after the husband died, the wife was accepted and integrated into the larger family.

From the 1920s, an attempt was made to dissociate dance from the realm of the professional prostitutes. However, the prostitutes did not stop dancing, especially those who had the talent and skill. To acquire a veneer of respectability, the former dancing girls attempted to pass themselves off as amateur singing and dancing artistes. The 'bais' and 'jans' became 'devis' and 'begums'. B.V. Keskar, Union Minister of Information and Broadcasting between 1952 and 1962, was reportedly of the belief that Indian music had deteriorated under the Muslims and the British. He fancied that they were responsible for its eroticization and trivialization. Under this pretext, he weeded out Muslim women singers of the classical gharanas who performed on All India Radio, some of whom were earlier courtesans, and even banned the harmonium from its studios.

There were regular drives in major cities of Awadh to depopulate the red-light districts where sex workers plied their trade and the areas where the courtesans, deredar tawaifs and the common prostitutes did their business were 'cleaned'. In the past, these defined areas of ill repute were frequented by those who indulged in libertinism. With the move to 'clean up' these areas, prostitution, far from disappearing, began to be practised in areas that had the veneer of respectability. The sex trade continued to flourish, like the clandestine khangi system. However, there was no longer an aspect of culture attached to this trade.

# 9.

## Miscellaneous Information

### Chehra Navisi

In the days when there were no cameras to record the appearance of a person, the medieval bureaucratic system ensured documentation of the outward characteristics of persons, animals and even material things in official papers through chehra navisi. The term means to record a description of the countenance or visage. This description of the physical attributes of a person, animal, or thing was used for identification, verification and authentication.

Chehra navisi may be regarded as a kind of prosopography, though prosopography in its wider connotation commenced with the British historian Lawrence Stone (1919–99) in 1971. Literature and information on chehra navisi are scant.

Dr Naiyer Masud, the renowned Urdu and Persian scholar and fiction writer of Lucknow, documented chehra navisi and other bureaucratic traditions in two papers:

1. 'Chehra Navisi' published in the *Yaadgar Nama-i Fakhruddin Ali Ahmad* edited by Nazeer Ahmad, Mukhtaruddin Ahmad and Sharif Husain Qasimi (New Delhi: Ghalib Institute, 1994).
2. 'Purana Daftari Nizam' ('Old Bureaucratic Traditions') published in the quarterly *Urdu Adab* (New Delhi: Anjuman Taraqqi-i Urdu [Hind], January-March 2004).

Chehra navisi was done for all employees of the state. The person who recorded the appearance and physical characteristics of an employee was called the naqeeb (agent) and against the recording of the chehra, the name and identity of the naqeeb was also written down.

Dr Naiyer Masud mentions two books, one in Persian and the second in Urdu, in which information is given on chehra navisi. The first is *Insha-i Dilkusha* (*Heart-opening Composition*), which is in Persian. It was written by one Syed Nisar Ali Bukhari Barelvi (place of publication not mentioned, published by Fakhr al-Mutabe', 1853–54). The second is *Muallim al-Hisab ma'ruf ba Maktab Nama*, by an anonymous author (Kanpur: Matba' Wadeedi, 1924). On pages 83 and 84 of the 1924 edition of this book, the anonymous writer has stated roughly as under:

> Details of appearances of humans, horses and elephants etc. are necessary. Whoever is an employee of the state, details of his physical appearance and marks on his face should be written down faithfully. It is not possible to recognize thousands of people without records of their characteristics. If the paymaster or chief officer is not able to accurately identify employees, it would create chaos. A man may die or abscond, and another person could assume his name and those of his forebears and could, without hesitation, wrongfully take the salary of the deceased. Therefore the chehra of persons or things should always be on record so that whoever has not seen a person or thing can correctly recognize by perusal of the chehra.

Below are some examples of the descriptions of persons:

- Mirza Anwar Baig, son of Murad Baig, son of Sardar Baig, of Mughal family (Turkman), resident of Mashhad: wheatish complexion, broad forehead, well-defined and separate eyebrows, sheep-eyed, prominent nose, black beard and whiskers, full height and age twenty-three years.
- Mirza Noor Baig, son of Murad Baig, son of Sardar Baig: wheatish complexion, wide and large forehead, open and well-spread eyebrows, high nose, beginning of growth of beard and moustache, small scar of a wound inflicted by a sharp stone on forehead, two

separate moles on right cheek towards ear, prominent black mole on nose towards left.

The descriptions of persons included numerous details in order to clearly identify individuals. Some of the descriptions that were typically used for various body parts are given below.

i)   Description of the colour of the skin: wheatish, dark, very fair, jet black, ruddy.

ii)  Description of forehead: wide or narrow with details of moles, warts and scars and their positions.

iii) Description of eyebrows: joined completely, somewhat joining or eyebrows cleanly separated; location of moles, warts and scars with their placements.

iv)  Description of eyes: doe-eyed, sheep-eyed, cat-eyed (blue), eyes of a meek cat, blind, cross-eyed or squint-eyed; position of moles, warts and scars with respect to each eye. The colour of the eyes was also specified—dark, bleary, blue, etc., and whether the individual was wide-eyed, narrow-eyed or had drooping eyelids.

v)   Description of nose: aquiline, broad-nosed with wide nostrils or flat-nosed; delineation of moles, warts and scars.

vi)  Description of ears: even-eared, jug-eared, small-eared, average-sized ears, soft-eared or cauliflower-eared; perforated ear or pierced lobe with location and number of holes and their placement.

vii) Description of lips: thin-lipped, thick-lipped, pouty-lipped, wide-lipped, narrow-lipped (akin to a bud), pink-lipped, black-lipped; having a wide space between the tip of the nose and the beginning of the upper lip; the depth and width of philtrum with the location of moles, warts and scars.

viii) Description of chin: full-chinned, small-chinned, double-chinned, drooping-chinned, jutting-chinned, hammer-chinned, lantern-jawed or chin with deep cleft.

Descriptions were not limited to persons but were also used for the identification of animals and things. Chehras were written for animals like the horse, elephant, camel or bull. They were also written for objects such as weapons, including knives, swords, daggers, bows, quivers, arrows, spears, armour, cannons and guns; armour for a horse or elephant; accoutrements of the horse, elephant and camel, etc.; garments, including turban and cap; tents, pavilions and canopies; ornaments and jewellery; books and paintings; and houses, among other things.

Regarding the chehra of inanimate objects, it was said that if one learnt how to describe such things, then the skill would be helpful in arithmetic and reckoning. The goods and materials entrusted to a darogha (keeper) or a diwan (minister or chief officer) were to be listed and described in detail and this description bore the signature of the owner. As and when additions were made to the stock, say fifty swords were purchased on different dates, then all features of the additional accessories were put on record for reference and tally. Cashiers and treasurers in their official capacity were expected to keep details of tangible goods such as ponds, reservoirs, tanks, stones, wood and timber, inlaid or beaten gold and silver, hilts of swords, garments, food covers, coverings of palanquins, covers of litters and sedans (for women), cases of daggers, tents, pavilions, qanats (wall of enclosure around an encampment), long bamboo poles, etc.

Here are a few examples of chehras of animals and inanimate objects:

- A horse: High breed steed with black knees, blue-eyed, has a line above the forehead with two spots over the back and on right back leg.

  A full description of the colours of the horse, limb-wise, was made. The breed of the horse, whether it was Turkish, Arab or Iraqi, was mentioned. Apart from these, there were small-statured horses, which were cross-breeds or mixed-breed. Other breeds of small stature were Sikandari and Chungla.

- A book: Gulistan (with 'Bostan' in the margin), written by Shaikh Sa'di. Paper of different colours; book bound in silk thread covered with gold or silver with silk binding; nastaliq calligraphy embellished with gold; name of calligrapher not given but chronogram gives date of completion of manuscript.

- An inkpot: European origin, strengthened with emerald lining along with qatzan (piece of ivory for cutting and preparing nib of reed pen).
- A mansion: Comprises four rooms, inner courtyard with door, audience hall and cattle shed. Type of roofing specified, appearance of outer and inner walls described with descriptions of windows, skylights and doors.
- A short sword (tegha): Approximate size specified, calligraphic engraving on both sides of the blades comprising nad-i 'Ali in golden letters in the form of a tughra; hilt of foreign origin with no scabbard.
- A doshala (shawl): Main body of pale colour with small roses throughout (with numbers noted), marginal borders in green with pink flowers, signs of darning in two places. (The signs of darning were not treated as a defect and in fact confirmed the antiquity of the shawl, which was preserved as a relic.)
- A bow (tir): Of Lahori origin, greenish, capacity of two tanks (i.e., if a weight of seven seers is hung from the bow, both the ends of the bow would bend to meet, one tank being equivalent to three and a half seers), knot vermilion in colour, bowstring of red and white silk, having elasticity and twisting ability and good grip.
- A quiver (tarkash): Exterior of embroidered leather bordered with pink, red and green in a round shape, the bottom lined with velvet on the outside with leather inside, reinforced with silver wire, of Lahori origin.
- An armour (baktar): Made of iron, collar of red velvet with leather laces, skirt slit from back, weight ten seers.

A very rare Persian publication titled *Siyaq Nama* (*Book of Account-Keeping*) by Munshi Nand Ram was published in December 1879 by Naval Kishore Press, Lucknow. It comprises 309 pages. The book is in nastaliq characters but numerations in several places are in khat-i shikast and siyaq. It is claimed in the book that it was written in the times of Aurangzeb (1658–1707). The *Siyaq Nama* is a record of administrative and bureaucratic practices in North India before the coming of the British. It removes the false impression that during medieval times there was no control or direction in the execution of royal institutions and regulations: Issues were largely decided by traditional systems, usages and well-honed methods. The *Siyaq Nama* gives us a glimpse of the workings of a feudal network in a monarchical realm, which also believed in performance, accomplishment and achievement.

## Sufism

Sufism or tasawwuf is the inner mystical dimension of Islam. It connotes man's yearning for communion with God. Sufi orders trace important precepts to Prophet Mohammed through his actions and utterings or through his cousin and son-in-law Ali ibn Abi Talib and Abu Bakr, the first caliph after the demise of the Prophet. The best of the Urdu poetry of Awadh, as of other regions, has prominent sufistic elements or touches of it. Sufi poets who wrote in Braj and Awadhi also exhibited metaphysical and mystical trends in their poetic writings.

The most prominent Sufi establishments in Awadh were at Kakori, Salon and Dewa. Kakori is 14 km north of Lucknow and is a centre of the Qadiriya Qalandari order. Salon is a tehsil in the Rai Bareilly district of Uttar Pradesh and is 110 km from Lucknow. It is famous for its Khanqah-i Kareemia. The third Sufi centre is at Dewa in the Barabanki district of Uttar Pradesh and lies 40 km from Lucknow. It is the shrine of the great Sufi Haji Waris Ali Shah. He was born in 1822–23 and died in 1905.

Among the famous Sufi poets of Awadh is Shah Turab Ali 'Turab' Kakorvi, who was born in 1767–68 and died in 1858. The *Diwan-i Shah 'Turab'* has been elegantly edited by Shah Taqi Anwar Alavi Kakorvi. It contains many popular ghazals. Some of his couplets have passed into popular language. One such is as follows:

*Shahar mein apne yeh Laila ne manadi kar di*
*Koi patthar se na mare mire diwane ko*

In her city Laila has proclaimed this instruction
Do not pelt stones on my forlorn lover

The father of Shah Turab was Shah Muhammad Kazim Qalandar Kakorvi, who wrote in Urdu, Persian and Awadhi. One part of his very long Awadhi Sufi poem has been printed as *Santras* in the Urdu script.

'Bedam' Shah Warisi (1882–1932), a devotee of Haji Waris Ali Shah, was another great Sufi poet. His ghazals are not only sung by qawwals but have also been recorded on discs. His diwan has been published many times. The copy with this author is titled *Mushaf-i Bedam* (*The Book of Bedam*) and was published by Ali Hujwiri Publishers of Lahore, Pakistan.

Syed Muhammad 'Benazeer' Shah Warisi (1863–1932) was a prolific Urdu Sufi poet. His diwan was edited by Muhammad Akbaruddin Siddiqi and published from Hyderabad in 1958.

Another celebrated Sufi poet of Urdu was Asghar Husain 'Asghar' Gondavi (1884–1936). He was a close friend of 'Jigar' Moradabadi. Not much of his poetry has survived. Two small collections of his work were published under the titles *Sorod-i Zindagi* (*The Song of Life*) and *Nishat-i Rooh* (*Liveliness of the Soul*) and were reprinted by the Uttar Pradesh Urdu Akademi in Lucknow in 1982 and 1983 respectively.

Khwaja Aziz-ul-Hasan 'Majzub' (1884–1944), an inspector of schools, was a follower of the Sufi path and was a devotee of Haji Waris Ali Shah. After his death, a selection of his poetry was edited by Muhammad Raza Ansari and published from Firangi Mahal Kitab Ghar of Lucknow in 1957. A larger selection came out as *Kalam-i Majzub*.

Another prolific Sufi poet was Badruddin 'Aughat' Shah Warisi (1874–1952). His collection of poems titled *Faizan-i Warisi* (*Munificence of Waris*) was edited by Anis Ahmad Warisi. His ghazals are often sung by qawwals.

The last of the important Warisi Sufi poets was Baba 'Riza' Shah Warisi (d. 1954). Some of his poetry is included in an anthology titled *Hadis-i Ma'rifat*, which contains the poems of 'Aughat' Shah Warisi, 'Bedam' Shah Warisi and Baba Riza Shah Warisi.

A comprehensive account of Sufi conventions in Awadh can be found in *Piety on its Knees: Three Sufi Traditions of South Asia in Modern Times*, by Claudia Liebeskind (New Delhi: Oxford University Press, 1998). Here the three different Sufi traditions of Awadh, namely, Dewa Sharif, Kakori and Salon, have been discussed. The long-standing reverence for and devotion to these three traditions among both Hindus and Muslims have continued from colonial times to the present day. These Sufis delved not only into Urdu and Persian but also Awadhi. Shah Qazim Qalandar (d. 1806) wrote the Sufi poem Sant Ras or Naghmaat al-Asrar in Awadhi and a large part of the poem has been published in Urdu. The Khanqah-i Karimiya of Salon, in the district of Rai Bareilly, was established in the seventeenth century by Shah Pir Muhammad, a Sufi of the Chishtiya order. Shah Shabbir 'Ata was another luminary of this Sufi family. He was an Arabic scholar and had a prodigious memory. Always elegantly dressed, he was the epitome of Awadhi culture. Maulana Shah Shabbir 'Ata died in Allahabad on 17 June 2015. He was buried in Salon where thousands paid homage to him. He was yet another example of Ganga-Jamuni tehzeeb.

Filmmaker Muzaffar Ali, in his edited book *A Leaf Turns Yellow: The Sufis of Awadh*, also offers an account of some famous Sufis of Awadh like Haji Waris Ali Shah of Dewa, the unbroken line (silsila) of Sufis of Kakori, the Khanqah-i Karimiya of Salon, the Sufis of Bansa Sharif, the Sufis of Kara-Manikpur and Hazrat Makhdoom Shaikh Sa'd-ud-din of Khairabad, Sitapur, etc. The book also elaborates on qawwali, dastangoi and sufisama.

## Printing Presses

According to Ulrike Stark, printing of books in Lucknow in Urdu, Arabic and Persian started in about 1817 when in the reign of Nawab Ghazi-ud-Din Haider (r. 1814–27), the Matba'-i Sultani (Royal Press) was set up. Printing was done through lithography and this process was later adopted by other upcoming publishers. Between 1839 and 1857 at least twenty new lithographic presses opened in Lucknow. One of the best presses during this period was the Matba'-i Mustafai established in 1851 by Haji Mustafa Khan, son of Haji Raushan Khan.

The lithographic technique, rather than using Urdu type, was preferred for printing in Urdu, as the former was more suitable for nastaliq, which is the preferred style for writing Urdu script as opposed to Arabic and Persian, which use the naskh style. An awkward type for Urdu and Persian was developed, which was more akin to the naskh style of writing than nastaliq. This was adopted with minor modifications by Forte William College of Calcutta in its initial Urdu publications from 1801. However, with the advent of lithographic printing, which was first handwritten by a scribe, printing Urdu in type was not popular because the readers thought it to be a distortion of the nastaliq script, which was more elegant and free-flowing. The Urdu typewriter was invented in 1911, but Urdu typography failed to gain acceptance among the common readers. Modern nastaliq typography began with the invention of Noori Nast'aliq in Pakistan in 1981; the daily *Jung* was the first Urdu newspaper to use computer-based nastaliq composition.

In 1849, Syed Kamal-ud-Din Haider alias Syed Muhammad Mir Zair (1794–1881), who was attached to the royal observatory, caused offence to Nawab Wajid Ali Shah on account of two passages in his work on the history of Awadh. To prevent the publication of the book, printing in Lucknow was forbidden. Some printers moved to Kanpur but a number of them retained a presence in Lucknow. To get around the ban, the books published during the short period of the ban exhibited only the name of the press and not the place of publication.

*Savanih 'Umri-i Akhbaraat – Hissa Awwal: Akhtar-i Shahanshahi* (*The Life Stories of Newspapers – Part One: The Royal Star*) is a rare book that was compiled by Syed Muhammad Ashraf Naqvi and published by Akhtar Press of Lucknow in 1888. It is an index of slightly more than fifteen hundred Urdu printing presses and a few newspapers. A rough count shows that just before 1888, there were about 168 Urdu printing presses, journals and newspapers in Lucknow alone.

Aloy Sprenger (1813–93), an Austrian Orientalist, was directed to prepare a catalogue of the royal library in 1848. Among other valuable works, it contained the whole of the literary treasures of Hafiz Rahmat Khan. Sprenger compiled a catalogue of Urdu, Persian, Arabic and Pushto manuscripts, which he wished to publish in five volumes, but only one volume was published: *A Catalogue of the Arabic, Persian and Hindustany Manuscripts of the Libraries of the King of Oudh, Compiled under the Orders of the Government of India*. Whenever the contribution of Awadh to Urdu literature is discussed, this valuable catalogue is always mentioned.

## The Lucknow Publishing House, Lucknow

The Methodist Publishing House in Lucknow was a Christian missionary institution run by the Methodist Church of India. Among the various books published by the press was *Masihi Geet Ki Kitaab*, a booklet of fifty hymns, issued in 1862. Some of the hymns are still sung. In 1870, Thomas Craven, a missionary, arrived in Lucknow and was appointed to study the languages of the region. He compiled *The Royal Dictionary: In Two Parts – English and Hindustani and Hindustani and English*, which was published in 1893 by the Methodist Publishing House. The press also printed books in Hindi, Roman Urdu and Urdu.

In December 1931, the Methodist Publishing House was renamed as the Lucknow Publishing House. The press continues to function and, over the years, it has been responsible for publishing many Christian religious tracts in various languages, including the Awadhi Bible, which was completed in 2004, and the Braj Bible, which was published in 2007.

## Naval Kishore Printing Press, Lucknow

Perhaps one of the best-known presses of the time, Naval Kishore Printing Press, was set up in Lucknow by Munshi Naval Kishore in November 1858 with a hand press and some lithographic stones. It was initially called the Matba'-i Awadh Akhbar and published the Urdu journal *Awadh Akhbar*. Naval Kishore soon expanded his business and started printing in Urdu, Persian, Arabic, Sanskrit, Hindi and English. According to Ulrike Stark, author of *An Empire of Books: The Naval Kishore Press and the Diffusion of the Printed Word in Colonial India* (2007), by the mid-1860s the Naval Kishore Press became the 'largest privately owned printing and publishing firm in North India'. In 1870, the press was relocated to Hazratganj. The new premises included a retail bookshop and a large warehouse for storing paper and books. The growing business led to the opening of a new printing press in Kanpur in September 1875. A printing press was also established at Gorakhpur in eastern Uttar Pradesh. Sales and distribution depots were opened in Lahore, Faizabad, Delhi and Mujaffarpur (in Bihar).

The Naval Kishore Press issued several thick, combined catalogues of Urdu, Persian and Arabic books. Most of these books are now rare.[71]

It is quite astonishing that in those days, this press was single-handedly responsible for bringing out voluminous books in multivolumes. For example, the forty-six-volume *Dastan-i Amir Hamza* was a daring venture. Had it not been published by the Naval Kishore Press, it is a matter of speculation whether any other Indian publisher would ever have brought it out.

The contribution of the Naval Kishore Press to publishing Urdu, Persian, Arabic, Hindi and Sanskrit works is immense and invaluable. Although the press lacked high editorial competence, this is hardly surprising given that it was established when Indian publishing was in its infancy. What is more important is that it made available the works of writers that could otherwise have been lost forever.

Munshi Naval Kishore died in February 1895 and the flourishing business passed on to his adopted son Prag Narain Bhargava (1872–1916), who was the son of his younger brother Ram Sevak. Under Prag Narain Bhargava, the firm, according to Ulrike Stark, 'continued to prosper for some time'. However, in the first half of the twentieth century, 'the heyday of Northern India's largest publishing house was over'. The '[...] lower public demand for Persian and Urdu literature, increased competition in the publishing trade and adverse political circumstances combined to bring about its slow but steady decline'. After Prag Narain's death, the business went to his son Bishan Narain (1898–1931). He is remembered for bringing out the famous Hindi literary magazine *Madhuri* from 1922. Its editors included Munshi Premchand (1880–1936). Bishan Narain was succeeded by his two sons, Ram Kumar Bhargava (1915–71) and Tej Kumar Bhargava (1919–87). However, there was conflict in the family and the management of the firm came under a Court of Wards. The Partition in 1947 resulted in the loss of the Pakistani market, and the Uttar Pradesh Zamindari Abolition Act, 1952, affected the landed gentry,

---

[71]One comprehensive catalogue that this author has in his collection is *Fihrist-i Kutub Khana-i Tijarati Ma'tba Munshi Naval Kishore Lakhnau wa Kanpur wa Lahore* (*Catalogue of Trade Books of Munshi Naval Kishore Press, Lucknow, Kanpur and Allahabad*). (Lucknow: Naval Kishore Press, 1911).

dealing a further blow to the business. Around 1950, the alienation of the two brothers resulted in the division of the firm into two separate entities, Ram Kumar Book Depot and Tej Kumar Book Depot. Both the firms continued to function, but no new books were brought out.

## Booksellers of Lucknow

Syed Abdul Husain, a bookseller in Mohalla Dargah, Kothi Sardar Bagh in old Lucknow, issued price lists of Urdu, Persian and Arabic books with an emphasis on elegiac poetry and religious books of the Shia Muslim sect. The characteristic of these catalogues was that the compilations of elegy poetry provided the first line of each elegy in the volume. It was Syed Abdul Husain who published the elegies and other poetry of Mirza Salamat Ali 'Dabir' (d. 1875) in twenty volumes (the paper was of poor quality, however, and with time it became quite brittle).

Syed Yawar Husain and Syed Sajid Husain Zaidi, sons of Maulavi Syed Wajid Husain, who were booksellers in Nadan Mahal, also issued similar catalogues.

There was a distinguished seller of rare books, Syed Nadir Agha, who operated from his house in Rustam Nagar, near Dargah Hazrat Abbas. He was the nephew of Syed Abdul Husain and learnt bookselling from him. He dealt not only in printed Urdu, Persian and Arabic books but also occasionally in manuscripts. He would travel the countryside to track down old families in mofussil areas who were willing to sell books collected by their forebears. Over the years he maintained a full record of the books purchased and then sold by him, including their title, author, editor, publisher's name, place of publication, number of pages and a very brief description of the contents. Unfortunately, all these records were stolen by a customer. This author personally observed Syed Nadir Agha weeping over his loss. With the death of Agha Sahib, the business also closed down.

Another bookshop that dealt in old and rare books was Nizami Book Agency, named after its founder Nizami Badauni. It issued catalogues periodically, and there was quite a rush among book lovers to obtain some otherwise inaccessible publications. The bookshop is extant even now, but has lost its collection and thus charm.

Siddique Book Depot in Aminabad Park was established by Muhammad Siddique (d. 1974) in 1915. It once had a large stock of old Urdu and Persian publications. The founder, Siddique Sahib, was in the habit of buying unsold publications en bloc, some of which became rare and significant in later years. The shop eventually began selling religious books and tracts and the old books disappeared. There was also a huge fire in the bookshop, which resulted in the loss of many books. The shop still exists in the old premises, but it has little to offer.

Mention may also be made of the well-run Danish Mahal (Palace of Learning), a bookshop opposite the Amin-ud-Daula Park. It was opened in 1939 and the late Nasim Ahmad was its proprietor. The shop was set up due to the efforts of Urdu stalwarts including Maulavi Abdul Haq (1870–1961), who was connected with the Anjuman Taraqqi-i Urdu, and Qazi Abdul Ghaffar (d. 1966), among others. Nasim Ahmad had a wonderful memory. He had a love for books and he would try to procure them from any place in India. Indeed, he was an expert in tracing long-forgotten books in far-flung cities. In his bookshop one could find Deccani Urdu books published from Hyderabad or Aurangabad, forgotten and unremembered books published from Madras, Bhopal, Calcutta, Rampur or even nearby Rampur or Badaun.

# Annexures

## Chapter 2: Dastangoi

### Detailed description of *Dastan-i Amir Hamza* (Volumes 1–46)

The following are the summaries of the narrative of all 46 volumes of the *Dastan-i Amir Hamza* as prepared by Shamsur Rahman Faruqi.

- **Volumes 1-3**

  The first volume, *Nausherwan Nama,* describes the birth and marriage of Nausherwan, the birth of Amir Hamza, his being transported to Parda-i Qaaf and his getting engaged to the king's daughter. It also relates the birth of Amru 'Ayyar and Amir Hamza falling in love with Mahr Nigar, daughter of Nausherwan. Amir Hamza visits Serendip, making Landhor bin Sadaan submit to Nausherwan. An 'ayyar, according to one version, is a resourceful rogue who is in society in troubled times. He was often admired 'for courage, for standing up to tyrants and protecting the needy'. The first volume also tells of the birth of Amir Hamza's son Amru bin Hamza, the Greek, from the womb of Naheed Mariyam, daughter of the king of Greece.

  The second volume of *Nausherwan Nama* relates the story of Mahr Nigar giving birth to Qabaad Shaharyar and Gardia Bano becoming the mother of Badi-uz-Zaman. Volumes 1 and 2 cover Amir Hamza's eighteen-year stay in Parda-i Qaaf.

Gardia Bano, the mother of Badi-uz-Zaman, gives birth to Amir Hamza's daughter Zubaida Sherdil. Amir Hamza's fairy-like daughter Quraishia Sultan (also named Quraisha Sultan in some places) is born of Asman Pari, the daughter of the ruler of Parda-i Qaaf. Qabaad Shaharyar is slain by treachery and his mother Mahr Nigar, overcome with grief, commits suicide. Amir Hamza is also stricken with sorrow and withdraws from the world, but is captured by his enemies. Facing great difficulties, Amru is eventually able to free Amir Hamza.

*Homan Nama*, the third volume, contains the tales of the death of Qabaad Shaharyar and Mahr Nigar, which are described from a new beginning and with more vividness. In fact, some incidents in the second volume of *Nausherwan Nama* are first introduced in *Homan Nama*.

- **Volume 4**

  The publisher of *Hamruz Nama*, the third volume, points out that the main events described relate to the *Nausherwan Nama*. It continues the tale of the battles between Amir Hamza and Harmuz and Faramurz, sons of Nausherwan. Amir Hamza does not win complete victory. Nausherwan himself dies in the beginning. Laqa alias Zamurrad Shah, who has claimed divinity, and with whom Amir Hamza will engage in several battles later, makes his first appearance in this volume.

  Faruqi has remarked that the conclusion of this volume lacks the smoothness in linking it with other volumes of the dastan.

- **Volumes 5–6**

  Both *Kochak Baakhtar* and *Bala Baakhtar*, volumes 5 and 6 respectively, are in the series of *Homan Nama* and *Harmuz Nama* and the characters Harmuz and Faraamurz are found here. At the end of *Kochak Baakhtar*, Badi-uz-Zaman is about to enter a maze of enchantment and in *Bala Baakhtar*, we see him penetrating it. Laqa's later doings are described in *Kochak Baakhtar* and *Bala Baakhtar*.

  At the end of *Bala Baakhtar* we find Iraj, son of Qasim, son of Rustam Ilm Shah, son of Hamza and Shapur, son of Amru, have been born nine or ten years earlier. When Laqa is defeated, he flees and takes shelter in the false divinity of Zardahasht.

- **Volumes 7–13**

  In these volumes, due to successive defeats, Laqa takes shelter in the country of Tilism-i Hoshruba, ruled by Afrasiab, and seeks the king's help. Amir Hamza, in pursuit of Laqa, arrives near the mountain of Aqeeq Gulzar-i Sulaimani where Afrasiab, while hunting, captures Badi-uz-Zaman, son of Hamza. The king chases a deer, which is wounded with an arrow and slain. The deer is magical. Afrasiab renders Badi-uz-Zaman unconscious and takes him into the precincts of Tilism-i Hoshuba. A look-alike statue of Badi-uz-Zaman is left in the wilderness. Deliberations start, which set Badi-uz-Zaman free. There are combats and encounters between wrestlers and soldiers of both sides. In these contests, magic, enchantment and cunning play a great part. A sub-plot of the tale tells of Amir Hamza's maternal grandson falling in love with Mahjabeen, the niece of Afrasiab, and how both are imprisoned by Afrasiab.

  The two volumes of *Baqia Tilism-i Hoshruba* were written much later by Ahmad Husain Qamar and do not contain a continuous dastan. The events described are episodic and most of them are related to the seven volumes of *Tilism-i Hoshruba*.

- **Volumes 14–18**

  In these five volumes, the various struggles and conflicts between the armies and crafty and artful persons of both sides, namely, Afrasiab/ Laqa and Amir Hamza, are described. In addition, there are details regarding how Kaukab Raushan Zameer, King Tilism-i Nur Ahshan and his daughter Buran Teghzan try to help Amir Hamza, Badi-uz-Zaman and their followers. Afrasiab is finally defeated, being slain by Asad bin Karb, Amir Hamza's maternal grandson.

- **Volumes 19–21**

  In the middle of the seventh volume of *Tilism-i Hoshruba*, death strikes the great magician Nur Afshan, who is the respected teacher of King Kaukab Raushan Zameer. Before dying, he foretells the coming events, that the non-acceptance of the love between the daughter of

Kaukab Raushan Zameer and Iraj bin Qasim would result in civil war and that Amir Hamza would overcome the armies of Tilism-i Nur Afshan. In fact, the events in *Tilism-i Fitna-i Nur Afshan* take place after the adventures in the *Tilism-i Hoshruba* volumes.

- **Volumes 22–24**

  The enchantment in these three volumes is so broad and vast that the palace of King Haft Paikar has seven grades and each grade is equivalent to a country. Two malevolent and wicked kings of Tilism-i Nur Afshan named Misr al-Gharaib and Sahar al-Ajaib are engaged in conflict with Amir Hamza. Sahar al-Ajaib retreats and takes shelter in Haft Paikar. Qasim bin Rustam, Ilm Shah bin Hamza and Landhor bin Saadan are in hot pursuit of him but become captives in Haft Paikar. In the last pages of the third volume of *Tilism-i Fitna-i Nur Afshan*, Saad bin Qabaad quietly goes towards Tilism-i Haft Paikar.

- **Volumes 25–27**

  At the end of the third volume of *Tilism-i Haft Paikar*, Hakeem Khayal-i Sikandari makes his appearance. In the first volume of *Tilism-i Khayal-i Sikandari* we are told that Aristotle had worked up an incantation at the mausoleum of Hakeem Khayal-i Sikandari, which is called Tilism-i Khayal-i Sikandari, and that Hakeem Khayal-i Sikandari would meet defeat at the hands of Nur al-Dahar bin Badi-uz-Zaman.

- **Volumes 28–30**

  Even before Nur al-Dahar is victorious over Tilism-i Khayal-i Sikandari, Asman Pari, the fairy-like wife of Amir Hamza, has him taken to Parda-i Qaaf where Jamshed the Second is ruling. Jamshed the Second has claimed divinity after the death of his father Jamshed and his uncle Saamri and has imprisoned Quraisha or Quraishia Sultan, the daughter of Asman Pari and Amir Hamza. Nur al-Dahar arrives at Parda-i Qaaf, but Asman Pari, in her haughtiness and haste, has not consulted the soothsayers as to who will be victorious over Naukhez-i Jamshedi. It is later revealed that the victor will be Saad bin Qabaad, who is already there and is engaged in battle. Finally,

Jamshed the Second is killed at the hands of Saad.

- **Volumes 31–32**

  In the second volume of *Tilism-i Naukhez*, Jamshed the Second remarks that he is much troubled by Amir Hamza and that he will go to Tilism-i Naukhez, Sulaimani, which has been described in great details in the third volume of *Tilism-i Naukhez-i Jamshedi*. The lord of enchantment there is Shankaal, the nourisher of demons and his death occurs at the end of this dastan.

- **Volumes 33**

  In this volume, Hamza the Second, son of Amir Hamza, makes his appearance. He is gifted with royal heroism. His artful and crafty companion is Amru the Second, who is the son of Amru the Cunning. According to Faruqi, *Sandali Nama* is a watershed in the entire dastan. After completing *Tilism-i Naukhez-i Jamshedi*, Ahmad Husain Qamar started *Tilism-i Zafranzar-i Sulaimani*, but he died in 1901 before he could complete the dastan (he could complete only the first volume and part of the second). It was Shaikh Tasadduq Hussain who finished the second volume. In the meanwhile, Ismail Asar had written *Sandali Nama* in 1895, creating the advent of Hamza-i Sani. In all likelihood, Shaikh Tasadduq Husain took the opportunity to present heroic royalty (sahibqirani) as a future attribute in the offspring of Amir Hamza.

- **Volumes 34–35**

  At the commencement of this dastan it is stated that it is connected to *Sandali Nama*. This dastan is also mentioned in *Iraj Nama*. Here, Badi al-Mulk, son of Badi-uz-Zaman, son of Amir Hamza the First, makes his initial appearance. However, there is hardly any mention of *Turaj Nama*.

- **Volumes 36–41**

  These volumes describe the exploits of Badi al-Mulk (Sahibqiran the Third). Often, the battles are with Akwan Tajdar, who claims divinity, and his brother Aiwan Tajdar, who is the king of enchantment. Akwan is defeated and dies, is then resurrected and causes much killing and bloodshed. Badi al-Mulk leaves his army and most of his close followers in the wilderness and goes to Makkah where he is required by Amir Hamza.

- **Volumes 42–44**

  Here Badi al-Mulk and his companions face tribulations in their struggle against Akwan Tajdar. Then Adil Kaiwan Shikoh becomes Sahibqiran the Fifth and continues his battles with Akwan and Aiwan. Badi al-Mulk is still on his way to Makkah. Hamza the Second, whom we had not seen for a long time, appears again in this dastan; he is bound for Makkah.

- **Volumes 45–46**

  In these volumes, the major characters of *Dasatan-i Amir Hamza* die. Although this dastan is the last of the series, according to Faruqi, some incidents described in *Lal Nama* indicate that all the events in *Aftab-i Shujaat* had not completely taken place and some transactions in *Aftab-i Shujaat*, *Gulistan-i Baakhtar* and *Lal Nama* are synchronous events.

## Chapter 3: Muharram and Marsiya in Awadh

### The Battle of Karbala and the Martyrdom of Imam Husain

The observance and propriety of the month of Muharram, the first month of the lunar Hijri calendar, is based on the martyrdom of the third Imam, al-Husain ibn Ali (Imam Husain). Imam Husain, the younger son of Imam Ali abi Talib by Fatima, the daughter of the Prophet, was born in Madina on 3 Shabaan 4 AH, corresponding to 8 January 626 CE. He was martyred in Karbala on 10 Muharram 61 AH, corresponding to 10 October 680 CE. According to the lunar calendar, the Imam lived for 57 years, or 54 years in keeping with the solar calendar.

After the assassination of Ali abi Talib, Imam Hasan, the elder son of Imam Ali and Fatima, was appointed Caliph by the people of Kufa. Mu'awiya, the son of Abu Sufiyan and Hinda, had become the governor of Syria and this area was almost independent. Mu'awiya, by show of strength, wanted Imam Hasan to come to terms with him. Imam Hasan, living or dead, was a threat to the authority of Mu'awiya. In his correspondence with Imam Hasan, Mu'awiya took the view that as he was more experienced, better in policies and older in age, Imam Hasan should come to terms with him. Ultimately, Imam Hasan had to abdicate the Caliphate and enter into a peace treaty with Mu'awiya.

Mu'awiya proclaimed himself the Caliph in 659 CE. The claim of Mu'awiya went unchallenged and he established his capital in Damascus, where he had served as governor. He started the dynastic principle of sucession by appointing his son Yazid as his successor to the Caliphate. At this time, Husain ibn Ali was living in Madina and did not interfere in the life of his brother Hasan. Mu'awiya died in 680 CE and was succeeded by his son Yazid. Husain ibn Ali refused to acknowledge Yazid, as the followers of Ali abi Talib in Madina and Iraq contested the appointment. Husain was invited by the people of Kufa to take up the Caliphate. Imam Husain sent his cousin Muslim to study the situation in Kufa. From there, Muslim sent word that he wished Husain to join him in Kufa. Ibn 'Abbas, the brother of Husain, tried to dissuade Husain from going to Kufa. By appointing 'Ubaidullah ibn Ziyad as the military governor, Yazid had moved against Kufa. On 10 Ramadan 60 AH (14 June 680 CE), the leaders of Kufa asked Imam Husain to come to Kufa for their rescue. Many people tried to dissuade Imam Husain from going to Kufa. Nonetheless, it is said that between twelve and eighteen thousand supporters had collected behind the Imam. Husain left Makkah on 8 Dhul-Hijja 60 AH (9 September 680 CE) without performing the annual Haj.

The army of 'Ubaidullah ibn Ziyad had blocked the roads leading to Kufa at Qadisiyya. The Imam learnt that his emissary Qays bin Mashar al Saidawi and the Imam's foster-brother 'Abdullah bin Baqtar had been murdered. Imam Husain then told his followers that those who wished to leave were free to do so and, according to Tabari, many persons forsook the Imam. Due to the blockade of the roads leading to Kufa, Imam Husain had to travel along the Euphrates. Finally, on 2 Muharram 61 AH (2 October 680), Imam Husain arrived in Karbala. On 3 Muharram, troops forced Husain and his followers to move their encampment from the Euphrates to a desert bereft of water. From 7 Muharram (7 October CE), the Imam's camp was cut off from water and the agony and suffering induced by thirst commenced. Husain had only a handful of followers left—his family members and his ardent adherents. There were also ladies and innocent children with the Imam.

On 9 Muharram 61 AH (9 October 680 CE), Shamir (Shimr) bin Dhu'l Jawshan came with the orders of ibn Ziyad, governor of Iraq and the East, that Husain must take an oath of allegiance to Yazid, the Umayyad caliph, and if he refused, he was to be exterminated. Husain's male followers at Karbala numbered only seventy-two, which included young boys and old men. Ibn Sa'd assembled the warring troops in battle order but acceded to Imam Husain's request to postpone the battle for one night so they could offer prayers and vigils. From the morning of 'Ashura (10 Muharram 61 AH/10 October 680 CE), which was a Wednesday, Imam Husain's handful of followers fought courageously and boldly against the opposing army of Yazid, which is said to have numbered 10,000. The Imam's followers had also battled with extreme thirst for the previous three days and, with the odds against them, they were massacred. It is said that the last but one martyr was Imam Husain's little son, Ali Asghar, who was suffering from intense thirst, and was killed by an arrow from the enemy's camp. While Husain was offering the late afternoon prayers, Shimr beheaded the great Imam. The heads of the followers of the Imam were severed from their corpses. The tents of Imam Husain were plundered. When people in Damascus heard about the atrocities brought on the family of the Prophet, there was widespread disapproval and condemnation. Yazid died in 64 AH (683 CE).

The martyrdom of Imam Husain and his companions in 680 CE is considered to be the greatest tragedy in Islamic history. The heart-wrenching account of exemplary courage remains immortal for two major reasons. One, the position of Imam Husain being the grandson of the Prophet is sacred, revered equally by both Shias and Sunnis. Two, it also serves as a constant reminder of the brutality and atrocity on blameless and innocent people and sets the highest benchmark of righteousness and valour in the face of tyranny and oppression.

## Published elegies of important marsiya writers

*Mir Anis:* Some of the important versions of the Urdu elegies of Mir Anis have been published as follows:

1. *Maraasi-i Anis Marhum.* Volumes 1, 2, 3 and 4.
   Lucknow: Matba'Tej Kumar, 1958.
2. *Anis ke Marsiye.* Edited by Saliha Abid Husain.
   New Delhi: Taraqqi Urdu Buro, 2 volumes, 1990 (second edition).
3. *Bazm-i Anis (Intikhab-i Maraasi-i Anis).* Edited by Naiyer Masud.
   Lahore, Pakistan: Rahbar Printers, 1990.
4. *Anis: Ghair-i Matbua Marsiya.* Introduction by Shahab Sarmadi.
   New Delhi: Markazi Anis Sadi Committee, 1990.
5. *Maraasi-i Anis.* Edited by Muhazzab Lakhnavi (Vol. 1).
   Lucknow: Muhafiz-i Urdu Book Depot, 1964.
6. *Wiqaar-i Anis.* Edited by Muhazzab Lakhnavi (Vol. 2).
   Lucknow: Muhafiz-i Urdu Book Depot, 1954.
7. *Rooh-i Anis.* Selected and edited by Syed Masud Hasan Rizavi Adib.
   New Delhi: Sahitya Akademi, 2011.
8. *Baqiyaat-i Anis.* Edited by Akbar Hyderi Kashmiri.
   Lucknow: Muhammadi Publishers, 1979.
9. *Tajzia Yadgar-e-Anis: Jab Qata Ki Masafat-e-Shab Aftab Ne.* Edited by Syed Taghi Abedi.
   Canada: Published by the editor, 2002.
   (The book contains the English translation of the marsiya under the title 'The Battle of Karbala' by David Matthews.)
10. *Mir Anis Ka Ek Marsia: Bakhuda Faris-i Maidan-i Tahavvur Tha Hur.* Edited by Timsal Masud. (In Urdu and Hindi scripts).
    Delhi: Arshia Publications, second edition, 2012.

There is also a monograph titled *Mir Anis* by Ali Jawad Zaidi, published in English by Sahitya Akademi, New Delhi in 1986.

*Mirza Dabir:* Some of the important versions of the Urdu elegies of Dabir have been published as follows:

1. *Marsiya-i Mirza Dabir.*
   Kanpur: Naval Kishore Press, 1916. In two volumes. (Originally published in 1875 by the same press, comprising thirty-five elegies in the first volume and thirty-four elegies in the second volume).

2. *Daftar-i Maatam* (*Volumes of Grief*).
   Published by Syed Abdul Husain, Mohalla Dargah, Kothi Sardar Bagh, Lucknow, in twenty volumes. Published in 1896 and 1897. This is the largest collection of the works of Dabir. The first fourteen volumes comprise 366 elegies. Volume 15 comprises a masnavi. Volumes 16, 17 and 18 comprise salaams. Volume 19 consists of khamsas, i.e., stanzas of five lines each, and are tazmins, which is the insertion of a verse or two in one's own poems. Volume 20 is for rubais (quatrains) and qitaas (couplets in which the meaning of each couplet is interconnected).

3. *Sabai Masani* (14 elegies). Edited by Syed Sarfaraz Husain Khabeer Rizavi.
   Lucknow: Nizami Press, 1930.

4. *Maah-i Kaamil* (*The Full Moon*). Edited by Muhazzab Lakhnavi. This is an elegy without dotted letters.
   Lucknow: Muhafiz-i Urdu Book Depot, 1961.

5. *Naadirat-i Dabir* (*Rare Works of Dabir*). Edited by Syed Safdar Husain. This is a collection of five elegies, several rubais and salaam.
   Delhi: Chaman Book Depot, 1977.

6. *Muntakhab Maraasi-i Dabir* (*Selected Elegies of Dabir*). Edited by Zaheer Fatehpuri. This is a collection of twenty elegies.
   Lahore, Pakistan: Majlis-i Taraqqi-i Adab, 1980.

7. *Baqiyaat-i Dabir : Yaani Mirza Dabir Ke Ghair-i Matbua Maraasi.* Edited by Akbar Hyderi Kashmiri. This is a collection of twenty-six elegies.
   Lucknow: Published by the editor, 1994.

8. *Daftar-i Dabir* (*Volume of Dabir*). This is a collection of twenty-five elegies.
   Karachi, Pakistan: Muhammadi Education and Publications, 1995.

9. *Taalai-i Mehr* (*Sunrise*): *Kalaam-i Atila-i Utarid* (*Undotted Poetry*

*of Mercury*). Edited by Syed. Taqi Abidi.
Lahore, Pakistan: Chughtai Publishers, n.d.
Dabir, when writing verse in undotted Urdu letters, wrote under
the pen name Utarid (Mercury). This volume, besides rubais and
salaams, has two elegies of 67 and 101 stanzas, respectively.

# Miscellaneous Information about Awadh

## Rulers of Awadh

- **Nawab Burhan-ul-Mulk Saadat Khan**
  He was born circa 1680 and was the son of Muhammad Nasir Musawi.
  He was in power from 1722 to 1739 as subedar nawab of Awadh.
  He was one of the Mughal generals in the battle of Karnal against
  Nadir Shah. He was captured during the battle and died on the night
  of 19 March 1739. He was buried in Delhi, in the mausoleum of his
  brother Sayadat Khan.
- **Nawab Abul Mansur Mirza Muhammad Muqim Ali Khan
  Safdarjung Nishapuri**
  He was born circa 1708. Burhan-ul-Mulk Saadat Khan was his father-
  in-law and paternal uncle. He reigned as subedar nawab of Awadh
  from 1739 to 1754 and made Faizabad his military headquarters. He
  died on 5 October 1754 at Sultanpur. He was buried in New Delhi,
  in the tomb which is today on Safdarjung Road.
- **Nawab Jalal-ud-Din Haider Abul Mansur Khan Shuja-ud-Daula**
  He was born on 19 January 1732 and was the son of Safdarjung, the
  second ruler of Awadh. Shuja-ud-Daula's main consort was Begum
  Ummat al-Zohra Bano alias Bahu Begum (d. 27 January 1816). Shuja-
  ud-Daula ruled as nawab of Awadh from 1753 to 1775. He died on
  26 January 1775 in Faizabad, which was his capital. He was buried
  in Gulab Bari, Faizabad.
- **Nawab Muhammad Yahya Mirza Amani Asaf-ud-Duala**
  He was born on 23 September 1748 in Faizabad and was the son of
  Shuja-ud-Daula. On the death of his father, he became the nawab of
  Awadh and reigned from 1775 to 1797. In 1775, he shifted the capital

of Awadh from Faizabad to Lucknow. Asaf-ud-Daula was also an Urdu poet and his diwan exists in manuscript form. He died on 21 September 1797 in Lucknow. He was buried in the Bara Imambara in Lucknow.

- **Nawab Asaf Jah Mirza Wazir Ali Khan**

  Nawab Asaf-ud-Daula had no son. Wazir Ali Khan was his adopted son. He was born in Lucknow on 19 April 1780. After the death of Asaf-ud-Daula, he was crowned nawab on 21 September 1797. He reigned as nawab from only 1797 to 1798. He won the displeasure of the British and was removed by Sir John Shore (1751-1834), to be replaced by Saadat Ali Khan. He spent almost seventeen years as a prisoner of the British at Vellore Fort. He died in Vellore on 15 May 1817 and was buried in the Muslim graveyard at Kasi Baghan.

- **Yamin-ud-Daula Nawab Saadat Ali Khan**

  Yamin-ud-Daula Saadat Ali Khan was the son of Shuja-ud-Daula. He was born sometime before 1752. He was crowned nawab of Awadh on 21 January 1798 at Bibiyapur Palace, Lucknow, supported by Sir John Shore. He reigned from 1798 to 1814. The nawab's chief consort was Khursheed Zadi. He died on 11 July 1814 in Lucknow. Khursheed Zadi and he were buried in the twin tombs in Qaisar Bagh, adjoining Begum Hazrat Mahal Park.

- **Nawab Ghazi-ud-Din Rafat-ud-Daula Abul Muzaffar Haider Khan**

  He was born circa 1769. He was the third son of Nawab Saadat Ali Khan. His mother's name was Murshir Zadi. He became nawab wazir of Awadh on 11 July 1814. On 19 October 1818 he declared himself as the independent king of Awadh. He died in Lucknow on 19 October 1827 and was buried in Shah Najaf in Lucknow.

- **Nawab Abul Mansur Qutb-ud-Din Sulaiman Jah Shah Jahan Nasir-ud-Din Haider**

  He was born on 9 September 1803 and was the son of Ghazi-ud-Din Haider. He reigned from 20 October 1827 to 7 July 1837. He was poisoned and died in Lucknow on 7 July 1837 at the age of thirty-four. He was buried in an unfinished mausoleum located near the Daliganj railway station in Lucknow. He lived a flamboyant and carefree life. He also wrote religious poetry and a selection of his Urdu verses was edited by Shah Abdus Salam and published as *Kalaam-i Nasir ud-din Haider Badshah: Shah-i Awadh Nasir-ud-din Haider ke Urdu Manzum Kalaam Ka Majmua* from Lucknow in 1983.

- **Nawab Abul Fateh Moin-ud-Din Muhammad Ali Shah**
  He was born in 1777 and was the son of Nawab Saadat Ali Khan. He reigned as the third king of Awadh from 7 July 1837 to 7 May 1842. He became king at the ripe age of sixty. He died on 7 May 1847 in the Farhat Bakhsh Palace in Lucknow. He was buried in the Husainabad Imambara in Lucknow.

- **Nawab Najm-ud-Daula Abul Muzaffar Musleh-ud-Din Muhammad Amjad Ali Shah**
  He was born before 30 January 1801 in Lucknow and was the son of Nawab Muhammad Ali Shah. He was the fourth king of Awadh. He reigned from 7 May 1842 to 13 February 1847. His main consorts were Malika Ahad Begum and Malika Kishwar. He died of cancer on 13 February 1847 at the Farhat Bakhsh Palace in Lucknow. He was buried in the Sibtainabad Imambara in the western part of Hazratganj in Lucknow.

- **Nawab Abul Mansur Mirza Muhammad Wajid Ali Shah**
  He was born on 30 July 1822 in Lucknow and was the son of Nawab Amjad Ali Shah. His mother was Mallika Kishwar, popularly called Janab-i Aliyyah, who was born in 1803. She died on 24 January 1858 and was buried in the Muslim quarter of the Père Lachaise cemetery in Paris. Wajid Ali Shah reigned from 13 February 1847 to 11 February 1856. The kingdom of Awadh was annexed by the British on 7 February 1856. The British exiled Wajid Ali Shah to Calcutta, where he eventually died on 21 September 1887. He was buried at Matiaburj in Calcutta. Wajid Ali Shah wrote profusely in Urdu, Persian and Awadhi and his works, a majority of which have been published, are on poetry, music and dance.

# Bibliography

*A Brief History of the Fourteen Infallibles.* Tehran, Iran: World Organization for Islamic Services.

Abdi, Raza Ali. *Kitabein Apne Aaba Ki.* Lahore: Sang-e-Meel Publications, 2013.

Achaya, K.T. *A Historical Dictionary of Indian Food.* New Delhi: Oxford University Press, 1999.

Adamec, Ludwig W. *The A to Z of Islam.* New Delhi: Vision Books, 2003.

Adib, Syed Masud Hasan Rizavi. *Anisiyat: Mir Anis Par Mazameen wa Maqalat.* Edited by Sabahuddin Umar. Lucknow: Uttar Pradesh Urdu Akademi, 1976.

Adib, Syed Masud Hasan Rizavi. *Aslaf-i Mir Anis.* Lucknow: Kitab Nagar, 1970.

Adib, Syed Masud Hasan Rizavi. *Lakhnauyat-i Adib.* Edited by Tahir Taunsvi. Lahore, Pakistan: Maghrabi Pakistan Urdu Academy, 1988.

Adib, Syed Masud Hasan Rizavi. *Naqd-i Anis.* New Delhi: Shahid Publications, 2004.

Adib, Syed Masud Hasan Rizavi. *Ruh-i Anis.* Edited by Anis Ashfaq. New Delhi: Sahitya Akademi, 2011.

Adib, Syed Masud Hasan Rizavi. *Urdu Drama Aur Stage: Ibtidai Daur Ki Mufassil Tarikh.* Lucknow: Kitab Nagar, 1957.

Adib, Syed Masud Hasan Rizavi. *Wajid Ali Shah.* Lucknow: All-India Mir Academy, 1977.

Agha, Syed Sikandar. *Soz Khwani: Taarikh wa Tazkirah.* Lucknow: Published by the author, 1999.

Ahad, Abdul. *Tarikh Badshah Begum* (*Waqai Dilpizir*). Translated by Muhammad Taqi Ahmad. Allahabad: Indian Press, 1938.

Ahmad, Mushrif. *Shah Husain Haqiqat Aur Un Ka Khandan.* Karachi, Pakistan: Idara-i Adabiyat-i Pakistan, 1977.

Ahmad, Nazeer, Mukhtaruddin Ahmad and Sharif Husain Qasimi. *Yaadgar Nama-i Fakhruddin Ali Ahmad.* New Delhi: Ghalib Institute, 1994.

Ahmad, Syed. *Hawaai Shaghal.* Lucknow: Nizami Press, 1934.

Akhtar, Wajid Ali Shah. Masnavi Dar Halaat-i Gunna Tawaif (Urdu Manuscript).

Ali, Darogha Abbas. *The Lucknow Album. Containing a Series of Fifty Photographic Views of Lucknow and its Environs together with a large sized Plan of the City executed by Darogha Ubbas Alli, Assistant Municipal Engineer. To the above is added a full description of each scene depicted. The whole forming a complete illustrated guide to the City of Lucknow, the capital of Oudh*. Calcutta: Baptist Mission Press, 1874.

Ali, Darogha Haji Abbas. *An Illustrated Historical Album of the Rajas and Taaluqdars of Oudh*. Allahabad: N-W Prov of Oudh Government Press, 1880.

Ali, Meer Hassan. *Observations on the Mussulmans of India*. London: Parbury, Allen & Co., 1832.

Ali, Muzaffar, ed. *A Leaf Turns Yellow: The Sufis of Awadh*. New Delhi: Bloomsbury, 2012.

Ali, Nadir. *Hindustani Press*. Lucknow: Uttar Pradesh Urdu Akademi, 1990.

Ali, Shaikh Ahmad, ed. *Pukhtwa Paz (Cookery and Cooking)*. Lucknow: Nizami Press, 1935.

Ali, Syed Akbar. *Pairaak*. Lucknow: Nizami Press, 1934.

Allana, Rahaab. 'Aperture and Identity: Early Photography in India.' *Marg* (edited by Pratapaditya Pal, Mumbai, Marg Publications, Sep 2009): 12–15.

Allana, Rahaab. 'Ephemeral Encounter: Three Artistics in India, 1857-59.' *Marg* (edited by Pratapaditya Pal, Mumbai, Marg Publications, Sep 2009): 16–31.

Alloula, Malek. *The Colonial Harem*. Manchester: University of Manchester, 1987.

Ameer, Muhammad. *Jins Aur Zindagi*. Hyderabad: Idara-i Tarbiyyat-i Jinsi, 1948.

Anand, Mulk Raj. *Album of Indian Paintings*. New Delhi: National Book Trust, 1973.

Anonymous. *Muallim al- Hisab ma'ruf ba Maktab Nama*. Kanpur: Matba' Wahidi, 1924.

Anonymous. *Qatra-i Muheet-i Bahr-i Hind*. Lucknow: Mustafai Press, 1885.

Anonymous. *Risala-i Aatishbazi*. Kanpur: 1899.

Anonymous. *The Beauties of Lucknow. Consisting of Twenty-Four Selected Photographed Portraits, Cabinet Size, of the most Celebrated and Popular Living Histrionic Singers, Dancing Girls, and Actresses of the Oudh Court and of Lucknow*. Calcutta: Calcutta Central Press Company Ltd, 1874.

Archer, Mildred. *Company Drawings in the India Office Library*. London: Stationery Office Books, 1972.

Aziz-Ul-Hasan 'Majzub', Khwaja. *Kalam-i 'Majzub'*. Saharanpur: Maktaba Imdad al-Ghuraba, 1964.


Aretino, Pietro. *The School of Whoredom*. London: Hesperus Press, 2003.

Azurdah, Mirza Muhammad Zaman. *Mirza Salamat Ali Dabir: Hayaat aur Karnaame*. Sri Nagar: Mirza Publications, 1981.

Bahadur, Iswi Khan. *Qissa-i Mehr Afrozwa Dilbar*. Edited by Masud Husain Khan. New Delhi: Anjuman Taraqqi-i Urdu, 1988.

Bahtar, Khair-un-Nissa. *Zaiqa*. Lucknow: Maktaba-i Islam, 1984.

Baig Suroor, Mirza Rajab Ali. *Fasana-i Ajaib*. Edited by Athar Parwez. Allahabad: Sangam Publishers. 1969.

Baig Suroor, Mirza Rajab Ali. *Fasana-i Ajaib*. Edited by Rasheed Hasan Khan. New Delhi: Anjuman Taraqqi-i Urdu, 1990.

Baig Riyaat, Mirza Wazir. *Risala-i Baterbazi*. Lucknow: Matba' Aijaz-i Muhammadi, 1888.

Baig, Mirza Irfan Ali. *Aadaab-ul-Hind*. Agra: Akbari Press, 1900.

Bakhsh 'Mahjoor', Shaikh Muhammad. *Nau Ratan*. Edited by Khalil-ur Rahman Daudi. Lahore, Pakistan: Majlis-i Taraqqi-i Adab, 1962.

Baqir 'Shams', Muhammad. *Lucknow Ki Tahzeeb*. Karachi: Baab al-Islam Press.

Baqir, Agha Muhammad. *Shaikh Muhammad Bakhsh 'Mahjoor' Lakhnavi: Hayat aur Karname*. Lucknow: Published by author, 1994.

Barlas, Asma. *'Believing Women' in Islam: Unreading Patriarchal Interpretations of the Qur'an*. Karachi: Sama Editorial and Publishing, 2004.

Barthes, Roland. *Camera Lucida: Reflections on Photography*. New York: Farrar, Straus and Giroux, 1981.

Basu, N.K. *The Art of Love in the Orient*. Calcutta: Medical Book Company, 1947.

Behl, Aditya. 'Emotion and Meaning in Mirigavati: Strategies of Spiritual Signification in Hindavi Sufi Romances', in *After Timur Left: Culture and Circulation in Fifteenth–Century North India*. Edited by Francesca Orsini and Samira Sheikh. New Delhi: Oxford University Press, 2014.

Behl, Aditya. *Subtle Magic: An Indian Islamic Literary Tradition, 1379–1545*. Edited by Wendy Doniger. New York: Oxford University Press, 2012.

Bennett, James, ed. *Realms of Wonder: Jain, Hindu and Islamic Art of India including Nepal and Pakistan*. Adelaide, Australia: Art Gallery of South Asia, 2013.

Bilgrami, Maulana Hafiz Syed Muhammad Abdullah. *Risala-i Shatranj wa Ganjifa*. Kanpur: Naval Kishore Press, 1874.

Bilgrami, Muhammad Masud. *Fawaid-un-Nissa*. Lucknow: Naval Kishore Press, 1873.

Bilgrami, Syed Athar Riza, ed. *Awami Risaai Adab-i Qadeem: Hindi, Awadhi aur Muqami Boliyon Mein*. New Delhi: Maktaba Jamia, 2010.

Bloom, Jonathan M. *Paper before Print: The History and Impact of Paper in the Islamic World*. New Haven: Yale University Press, 2001.

Chand 'Qaisar', Rai Sri Krishan. *Risala-i Sakht-i Itr (Treatise on Preparing Perfumes)*. Lucknow: Matba Qaisar al –Mataaba,1883.

Chandra, Moti. *The Technique of Mughal Painting*. Lucknow: U.P. Historical Society, Provincial Museum, 1949.

Chandra, Moti. *The World of Courtesan*. Delhi: Vikas Publishing, 1973.

Chaudhary, Zahid R. *After-image of Empire: Photography in Nineteenth-Century*. Minneapolis, Madison: University of Minnesota, 2012.

Collingham, Lizzie. *Curry: A Tale of Cooks and Conquerors*. Oxford: Oxford University Press, 2006.

*Concise Oxford English Dictionary*. 11th edition, 2004.

Connerney, Richard. *The Upside-Down Tree: India's Changing Culture*. New York: Algora Publishing, 2009.

Craven, Thomas. *The Royal Dictionary: In Two Parts – English and Hindustani and*

*Hindustani and English.* Lucknow: Methodist Publishing House, 1893.

Crooke, William. *The Tribes and Castes of North-Western Provinces and Oudh.* New Delhi: Asian Educational Services, 1999.

Crooke, William. *Things Indian: Being Discursive Notes on Various Subjects Connected with India.* New Delhi: Oriental Books Reprint Corporation, 1972.

Dabir, Mirza Salamat Ali. *Maah-i Kaamil* (A Marsiya). Edited by Muhazzab Lakhnavi. Lucknow: Muhafiz-i Urdu Book Depot, 1961.

*Mah-i Nau* (Dabir Number), Karachi, Sep-Oct 1975.

Daftary, Farhad and Gurdofarid Miskinzoda, eds. *The Study of Shi'i Islam: History, Theology and Law.* London: I.B. Tauris, 2014.

Daftary, Farhad, Amyn B. Sajoo and Shainool Jiwa, eds. *The Shi'i World: Pathway in Tradition and Modernity.* London: I.B. Tauris, 2015.

Datla, Kavita Saraswathi. *The Language of Secular Islam: Urdu Nationalism and Colonial India.* New Delhi: Orient Blackswan, 2013.

Daudet, Alphonse. *In the Land of Pain.* London: Jonathan Cape, 2002.

Davidson, Alan. *The Oxford Companion to Food.* London: Oxford University Press, 1999.

De Souza, Eunice. *Purdah: An Anthology.* New Delhi: Oxford University Press, 2004.

Dehejia, Vidya ed. *India Through the Lens: Photography 1840-1911.* Washington, D.C: Freer Gallery of Art and Arthur M. Sackler Gallery, Smithsonian Institution, 2000.

Denny, Roz. *Real Food Handbook.* London: Prion Books, 1999.

Dodgson, Lt. Col D.S. *General Views & Special Points of Interest of the City of Lucknow. From Drawings Made on the Spot by Lt Col D.S. Dodgson, A. A. G. with Descriptive Notices.* London: Day & Son, 1860.

Downer, Lesley. *Women of the Pleasure Quarters: The History of the Geisha.* New York: Broadway Books, 2001.

Ewin, Jeannette. *The Plants We Need to Eat.* London: Thorsons.

Falk, Toby and Midred Archer. *Indian Miniatures in the India Office Library.* Sotheby's Publications, 1981.

Faruqi, Shamsur Rahman. *Sahiri, Shahi, Sahibqirani: Dastan-i Amir Hamza Ka Mutalia.* Vol 1: *Nazari Mubahis,* 1999; Vol 2: *Amali Mubahis,* 2006; Vol 3: *Jahan-i Hamza,* 2006; Vol 4: *Dastan-i Duniya* (I), 2011. New Delhi: National Council for Promotion of Urdu Language.

Fatehpuri, Zaheer ed. *Marasi-i Dabir.* Lahore, Pakistan: Majlis-i Taraqqi-i Adab, 1980.

Fazil, Syed Murtaza Husain. *Anis aur Marsiya: Zindagi aur Payaam.* Lahore: Published by Syed Abid Murtaza.

Feldman, Martha and Bonni Gordon. *The Courtesan's Arts: Cross-Cultural Perspectives.* New York: Oxford University Press, 2006.

Fonia, R.S. *Monuments of Lucknow.* New Delhi: Archaeological Survey of India, 2013.

Gangoly, O.C. *Catalogue of Miniature Paintings in the Baroda Museum.* Baroda: Museum and Picture Gallery, 1961.

Ghaffar, Qazi Abdul. *Laila Ke Khutoot.* Translated by Scheherazade Alim. New Delhi: Niyogi Books, 2013.

Gondavi 'Asghar', Asghar Husain. *Nishat-i Rooh.* Lucknow: Uttar Pradesh Urdu Akademi, 1983.

Gondavi 'Asghar', Asghar Husain. *Sorod-i Zindagi.* Lucknow, Uttar Pradesh Urdu Akademi, 1982.

Gordon, Sophie. 'Monumental Vision: Architectural Photography in India, 1840-1901'. PhD thesis, Department of History of Art, School of Oriental and African Studies, University of London, 2010.

Gupta, Damodara. *The Art of the Temptress (Kuttanimatam).* Translated by B.P.L. Bedi and Alexander von Humboldt. Bombay: Pearl Books, 1968.

Gutman, Judith Mara. *Through Indian Eyes.* New York: Oxford University Press in association with the International Center of Photography, 1982.

Hameed, Syeda Saiyidain. 'Voice of the Voiceless: Status of Muslim Women in India'. Report for The National Commission for Women, New Delhi, 2000.

Hankin, Nigel B. *Hanklyn-Janklin.* New Delhi, 1992.

Hansen, Eric. 'The Hidden History of a Scented Wood.' *Saudi Aramco World* (Dhahran, Saudi Arabia, Saudi Arabian Oil Company; Nov–Dec 2000).

*Hareemi Dastarkhwan.* Lucknow: Naseem Book Depot, 1969.

Hasan, Amir. *Palace Culture of Lucknow.* Delhi: B.R. Publishing, 1983.

Hasan, Amir. *Vanishing Culture of Lucknow.* Delhi: B. R. Publishing, 1990.

Hasan, Noorani Amir. *Munshi Naval Kishore Aur Unke Khattat Wa Khushnavis.* New Delhi: Taraqqi Urdu Buro, 1994.

Hasan, Noorani Amir. *Sawanih Munshi Naval Kishore.* Patna: Khuda Bakhsh Oriental Public Library, 1995.

Heath, Jennifer ed. *The Veil.* University of California Press, 2008.

Hinz, Walther. *Islamische Masse und Gewichte: Umgerechnet ins Metrische System.* Leiden: E.J. Brill, 1970.

Hodges, William. *Select Views in India: Drawn on the Spot, in the Years 1780, 1781, 1782 and 1783, and Executed in Aqua Tinta.* London: Published by the author, 1787.

Hodgson, Marshall Goodwin Simms. *Venture of Islam: Conscience and History in a World Civilization.* Chicago: University of Chicago Press, 1975.

Hoey, William. *A Monograph on Trade and Manufacturers in Northern India.* Lucknow: 1880.

Holister, John Norman. *The Shi'a of India.* New Delhi: Oriental Books Reprint Corporation, 1979.

Hughes, Thomas Patrick. *Dictionary of Islam.* Calcutta: Rupa, 1988.

Husain, Mirza Jafar. 'Qadeem Lakhnau Mein Tafrihi Mashaghill.' *Aaj Kal* (New Delhi, July 1978).

Husain, Mirza Jafar. 'Qadeem Lakhnau Ki Taaziadari.' *Aaj Kal* (Lucknow, February 1978).

Husain, Mirza Jafar. *Lakhnau ka Dastarkhwan.* Lucknow: Uttar Pradesh Urdu Akadami, 2004.

Husain, Mirza Jafar. *Qadeem Lakhnau Ki Akhri Bahaar.* New Delhi: Bureau for

Promotion of Urdu Language, 1981.

Husain, Mirza Muhammad. *Islah-i Pairaak*. Lucknow: Al-Waiz Safdar Press, 1936.

Husain, Syed Fida. *Shamim Jan Wafa*. Lucknow: Nusrat Publishers, 1995.

Husain, Syed Mubarak. *Fan-i Sipahgari*. Lucknow: Published by the author, 1974.

Hussain, Syed Israr. *Qadeem Hunar wa Hunarmadan-i Awadh*. Lucknow: Sarfaraz Qaumi Press. 1936.

Hyder, Syed Akbar. *Reliving Karbala: Martyrdom in South Asian Memory*. Oxford: Oxford University Press, 2006.

Kashmiri, Akbar Hyderi ed. *Tazkira-i Qadeem Shairaat-i Urdu*. Srinagar: J&K Academy of Art, Culture and Languages, 1996.

Ikramullah, Naz. *Ganga-Jamuni: Silver and Gold, A Forgotten Culture*. Calgary, Alberta, Canada: Bayeux Arts, 2013.

Jafri, Amir H. *Honour Killing: Dilemma, Ritual, Understanding*. Karachi: Oxford University Press, 2008.

Jafri, S. Husain M. *Origins and Early Development of Shi'a Islam*. Qum: The Group of Muslims.

Jaiswal, Ajaish Kumar. 'Asafi Andaz': A First Ever Exclusive Photo Essay on the Asafi Imambara. Exhibition held at Lalit Kala Akademi, Regional Centre, Lucknow, from 11 to 17 July 2012.

Jaiswal, Ajaish Kumar. 'Asafi Imambara… A Fantasy'. Exhibition held at Lalit Kala Akademi, Regional Centre, Lucknow, 2013.

Jeffery, Patricia. *Frogs in a Well: Indian Women in Purdah*. New Delhi: Manohar Publishers, 2000.

Jones, Justin. *Shi'a Islam in Colonial India: Religion, Community and Sectarianism*. New Delhi: Cambridge University Press, 2012.

Kakorvi, Shah Turab Ali 'Turab'. *Diwan-i Shah 'Turab'*. Edited by Shah Taqi Anwar Alavi Kakorvi. Lucknow: Khanqah-i Kazimiyya Qalandariyya, 2012.

Kanshi, Ram. *Zamindari Hisab*. Ludhiana: Matba' Haqqani, 1892.

Karlekar, Malavika. *Re-visioning the Past: Early Photography in Bengal 1875–1915*. New Delhi: Oxford University Press, 2005.

Kashmiri, Akbar Hyderi. 'Taarikh-i Nauha Goi Par Ek Tairana Nazar'. *Naya Daur* (Lucknow, January 2009).

Kashmiri, Akbar Hyderi. *Hindu Marsiyago Shuara*. New Delhi: Shahid Publications, 2004.

Kazi, Muizza Ebrahim. *Urdu Mein Manzoom Awami Adab aur Loriyan*. Mumbai: Ghazali Typesetters, 2007.

Khan 'Tehsin', Mir Muhammad Husain Ata. *Nau Tarz-i Murassa*. Edited by Syed Noorul Hasan Hashmi. Allahabad: Hindustani Academy, 1958.

Khan, Ahmad. *Urdu Adab Mein Awadh*. Mauza Chitarkoni, Dist Ghazipur, UP: Published by the author, 2010.

Khan, Ashfaq Ahmad. *Glimpses of the Arts of Awadh: A Guide to the Awadh Gallery*. Lucknow: State Museum, 1989.

Khan, Muhammad Khairuddin. *Shaitan Ke Bachche*. Agra: Matba' Akbari.

Khan, Rasheed Hasan. *Zaban aur Qawaid.* New Delhi: Taraqqi Urdu Buro, 1983.

Kishore, Naval. *Tawarikh-i Nadir al Asr.* Patna: Khuda Bakhsh Oriental Public Library, 1990.

Kshemendra. *The Courtesan's Keeper (Samaya Matrika).* Translated by A.N.D. Haksar. New Delhi: Penguin Books India, 2014.

Lakhnavi, Alavi and Muhammad Ghausuddin. *Bahaar-i Awadh.* Rawalpindi, Pakistan: Hamdard Steam Press, 1966.

Lakhnavi, Ghalib and Abdullah Bilgrami. *The Adventures of Amir Hamza: Lord of the Auspicious Planetary Conjunction.* Translated by Musharraf Ali Farooqi. New Delhi: Random House India. 2008.

Lakhnavi, Khwaja Abdur Rauf 'Ishrat'. *Lakhnau – Tarikh, Adab aur Muasharat.* Edited by Mahjabeen Zaidi. Karachi: Qirtaas, 2011.

Lakhnavi, Khwaja Muhammad Ashraf Ali. *Kashf al-Limas fi Sabgh al-Libas.* Lucknow: Matba' Nami, 1888.

Lakhnavi, Maulana Hasrat. *Irani Kok Shastra Ba Tasweer: Hayat-i Shabab Awar.* Delhi: Tajalli Press.

Lakhnavi, Mirza Fida Ali Fida. *Tareeq-i Nasr Khwani.* Lucknow: Matba Nami, 1306 AH/1888–89.

Lakhnavi, Shaikh Muhammad Bakhsh 'Mahjoor'. *Nau Ratan (Ba Tasvir).* Lucknow: Matba' Dabdaba-i Ahmadi, 1894.

Lakhnavi, Shaikh Muhammad Bakhsh 'Mahjoor'. *Nau Ratan.* Bombay: Matba' Barq-I Khatif, 1276 AH/1859–60.

Lakhnavi, Shams and Muhammad Baqir. *Lakhnau Ki Tehzeeb.* Karachi, Pakistan: Bab-ul-Islam.

Lakhnavi, Syed Agha 'Ashhar'. *Tazkiratul Zakireen.* Jhansi: Shamsi Press, 1946.

Lakhnavi, Syed Agha Mehdi. *Tarikh-i Lakhnau.* Karachi: Jamiat-i Khuddam-i Aza, 1976.

Lakhnavi, Hasan. *Abbas Tarikh Ki Roshni Mein.* Lucknow: Abbas Book Agency, 1994.

Lakhnavi, Mirza Ja'far Ali Khan Asar. *Farhang-i Asar.* Lucknow: Sarfaraz Qaumi Press, 1961.

Lakhnavi, Muhammad Istifa Khan 'Istifa'. *Aeena* (Mirror), vol. II. Lucknow: Nami Press, 1961.

Lakhnavi, Syed Zamin Ali Jalal. *Ganjeena-i Zabaan-i Urdu.* Lucknow: Naval Kishore Press, 1880.

Lewis, Ivor. *Sahibs, Nabobs and Boxwallahs.* New Delhi: 1991.

Liebeskind, Claudia. *Piety on Its Knees: Three Sufi Traditions of South Asia in Modern Times.* New Delhi: Oxford University Press, 1998.

Llewellyn-Jones, Rosie ed. *Lucknow: Ctiy of Illusion.* Munich: Prestel Verlag with The Alkazi Collection of Photography, 2006.

Llewellyn-Jones, Rosie, ed. *Lucknow: Then And Now.* Mumbai: Marg Publications, 2003.

Llewellyn-Jones, Rosie. *The Last King in India: Wajid Ali Shah (1822-87).* Gurgaon: Random House India, 2014.

Losty, J.P. and Malini Roy. *The Mughal, Life, Art and Culture: Mughal Manuscripts and Paintings in the British Library*. New Delhi: Roli Books, 2013.

Losty, Jeremiah P. *The Art of the Book in India*. London: The British Library, 1982.

MacLean, Major. *Views of Lucknow: From Sketches Made During the Siege*. London: J. Hogarth, 1858.

Malihabadi, Shabbir Hasan Khan Josh. *Yadon Ki Baraat*. Lucknow: Aina-i Adab.

Manchanda, Jaishree. *Traditional Fabrics of India*. New Delhi: Samkaleen Prakashan.

Markel, Stephen and Tushara Bindu Gude. *India's Fabled City: The Art of Courtly Lucknow*. Munich: Prestel Verlag, 2010.

Martinelli, Antonio (Photographs and text by). *Oriental Scenery: Yesterday & Today* (Exhibition Catalogue). New Delhi: Indira Gandhi National Centre for the Arts, 2011.

Martinelli, Antonio. *Lucknow: an miroir du temps*. Filigranes Éditions, 2011.

Masud, Azhar. 'Lakhnau Ke Pheri Wale.' *Naya Daur* (Lakhnau, Oct-Nov 1994).

Masud, Naiyer. *Anis*. New Delhi: Bureau for Promotion of Urdu Language, 2002.

Masud, Naiyer. *Anis*. New Delhi: Qaumi Counsil Barai Farogh-i Urdu Zabaan, 2002.

Masud, Naiyer. *Marsiya Khwani Ka Fan*. Karachi: City Press Bookshop, 2005.

Matthews, David, trans. *The Book of Karbala: A Marsiya of Anis*. New Delhi: Rupa, 1994.

Mecham, Clifford Henry. *Sketches & Incidents of the Siege of Lucknow. From Drawings Made during Siege with Descriptive Notices by George Couper, Esq., late Secretary to the Chief Commissioner of Oude*. London: Day & Son, 1858.

Mernissi, Fatima. *The Veil and the Male Elite: A Feminist Interpretation of Women's Rights in Islam*. Translated from the French by Mary Jo Lakeland. Reading, Massachusetts: Addison-Wesley Publishing, 1991.

Mevissen, Gerd J.R. and Arundhati Banerji, eds. *Prajñādhara: Essays on Asian Art, History, Epigraphy and Culture in Honour of Gouriswar Bhattacharya*. New Delhi: Kaveri Books, 2009.

Minai, Ameer Ahmad 'Ameer'. 'Kabutar Nama.' *Tahqiq* (six-monthly, Urdu Department, Sindh University, Hyderabad, Pakistan, Jan-June 2010).

Minault, Gail. *Secluded Scholars Women's Education and Muslim Social Reform in Colonial India*. Delhi: Oxford University Press, 1998.

Mirza 'Qasd', Hasan. *Lakhlakha*. Madras: Matba' Mazhar al- Ajaib, 1278 AH/1861–62.

*Moharram in Two Cities (Lucknow and Delhi)*. Census of India, 1961. Monograph Series, Volume I, Part VII B. New Delhi: Office of the Registrar General India, Ministry of Home Affairs, 1967.

Momen, Moojan. *Introduction to Shi'i Islam. The History and Doctrines of Twelver Shi'ism*. Delhi: Oxford University Press, 1985.

Mookerjee, Firoze. *Lucknow and the World of Sarshar*. Karachi, Pakistan: Saad Publications, 1992.

Mookherji, P.C. *The Pictorial Lucknow*. New Delhi: Asian Educational Services, 2003.

Moos, Ardaseer Framjee. *Journal of Travels in India*. Bombay: Education Society's Press, 1871.

Moradabadi, Syed Muhammad Ali 'Joya'. *Sarod-i Ghaibi al-Musamma ba Khayaban-i Tarikh*. Lucknow: Naval Kishore Press, 1881.

Morcom, Anna. *Courtesans, Bar Girls and Dancing Boys: The Illicit Worlds of Indian Dance*. Gurgaon, Haryana: Hachette, 2014.

Nagar, Amritlal. *Yeh Kothewalian*. Delhi: Ruchika Publishers, 1958.

Naqvi, Syed Muhammad Ashraf. *Savanih 'Umri-i Akhbarat – Hissa Awwal: Akhtar-i Shahanshahi*. Lucknow: Akhtar Press, 1888.

Nevile, Pran. *Beyond the Veil: Indian Women in the Raj*. New Delhi: Nevile Books, 2000.

Nomani, Muhammad Shibli. *Muazna-i Anis wa Dabir*. Edited by Syed Mujavir Husain and Syed Ali Haider. Allahabad: Published by the editors, 2010.

*New Publications on Books about Books, Spring 1997*. New Castle, Delaware: Oak Knoll Press, 1997.

Paine, Sheila. *Chikan Embroidery: The Floral Whitework of India*. Aylesbury Buckinghamshire, UK: Shire Publications, 1989.

Pal, Pratapaditya. *Marg*, Vol. 59, No. 4. Mumbai: Marg Publications, June 2008.

Papadopoulo, Alexandre. *Islam and Muslim Art*. New York: Harry N. Abrams, 1994.

Patel, Alka. 'The Photographic Albums of Abbas Ali as Continuations of the Mughal Muraqqa' in *Getty Research Journal*. Los Angeles, 2015.

Paul, Michael. *150 Years of the Lucknow Publishing House (1861-2011)*. Lucknow: The Lucknow Publishing House.

Pinney Christopher. *Camera Indica: The Social Life of Indian Photographs*. Chicago: The University of Chicago Press, 1997.

Pinney, Christopher. *The Coming of Photography in India*. New Delhi: Oxford University Press, 2008.

Pinney, Christopher. *Photography and Anthropology*. New Delhi : Oxford University Press, 2011.

Porter, Yves. *Painters, Paintings and Books: An Essay on Indo-Persian Technical Literature, 12-19th Centuries*. Translated by S. Butani. New Delhi: Manohar and Centre for Human Sciences, 1994.

Posh, Kammal and Yusuf Khan. *Ajaibaat-i Firang*. Lucknow: Naval Kishore Press, 1873.

Premchand. *Bazar-i Husn*. Lahore: 1924. (*Courtesan's Quarter*. Translated by Amina Azfar. Karachi, Pakistan: Oxford University Press, 2003 and *Sevasadan*. Translated by Snehal Shingavi. New Delhi: Oxford University Press, 2005).

Preminger, Alex, ed. *The Encyclopedia of Poetry and Poetics*. Princeton: Princeton University Press, 1965.

Qadeer, Fazl, ed. *Mah-i Nau* (Karachi: Sep–Oct 1975).

Qidwai, Sadiq-ur-Rehman, ed. *Anis wa Dabir: Hayaat wa Khidmaat*. New Delhi: Ghalib Institute, 2007.

Ram, Malik, ed. *Anis Numa* (A Bibliography of Anis). *Tahreer* (April–June 1973).

Ram, Munshi Nand. *Siyaq Nama*. Lucknow: Naval Kishore Press, 1879.

Rasheed, Chandrashekar and Abdur Rasheed. *Fihrist-i Kutub Matba' Munshi Naval*

*Kishore.* Delhi: Dilli Kitab Ghar 2012.

Ray, Nirbed and Amitabha Ghosh, eds. *Sedentary Games of India.* Calcutta: The Asiatic Society, 1999.

Richard, Frank. *Old Soldier Sahib.* London: Faber & Faber, 1965.

Rizavi, Mustafa Hasan and Kazim Ali Khan, eds. *Sarfaraz* (Lucknow: Sarfaraz Qaumi Press, 17 Dec 1976).

Rizvi, Saiyid Athar Abbas. *A Socio-Intellectual History of the Isna 'Ashari Shi'is in India.* Two vols. New Delhi: Munshiram Manoharlal, 1986.

*Roots of North Indian Shi'ism in Iran and Iraq: Religion and State in Awadh, 1722-1859.* Delhi: Oxford University Press, 1989.

Rudaulvi, Ali and Chaudhary Muhammad. *Salahkaar.* Delhi: Jamia Millia Press, 1928.

Rudaulvi, Masud Hasan Rizavi. 'Lakhnau Ki Dastkari.' *Naya Daur* (Lucknow, January 1995).

Ruswa, Mirza Muhammad Hadi. *The Madness of Waiting (Junun-e Intezar Ya'ni Fasana-e Mirza Ruswa).* Translated by Krupa Shandilia and Taimoor Shahid. New Delhi: Zubaan, 2012.

Ruswa, Mirza Muhammad Hadi. *Umrao Jan Ada.* Translated by Khushwant Singh and M.A. Husain. Delhi: Hind Pocket Books, 1970.

Safavi, Muhammad Sadiq. *Dabir Aur Shamsabad.* Shamsabad: Published by the author, 1989.

Said, Edward. *Orientalism.* London: Routledge & Kegan Paul, 1978.

Saletore, R.N. *Indian Entertainment.* New Delhi: Munshiram Manoharlal, 1985.

Sampath, Vikram. *My Name is Gauhar Jaan: The Life and Times of a Musician.* New Delhi: Rupa Publications, 2010.

Sandeelvi, Raja Durga Prasad 'Mahr'. *Bostan-i Awadh.* Lucknow: Matba Dabdaba-i Ahmadi, 1892.

Rizavi, Mustafa Hasan. *Sarfaraz* (Muharram Number, Lucknow, 25 Jan 1978).

Saz, Muhammad Ali Bidar. *Risala-i Aain-i Bidar Sazi.* Lucknow: Matba' Mashriq al-Anwaar.

Shah, Syed and Muhammad Hasan. *The Nautch Girl (Nashtar).* Translated by Quraatulain Hyder. New Delhi: Sterling Publisher, 1992.

Shaman, Muhammad Bin Muhammad al-Shaheer ba. *Saheefa-i Nafhaat: Tarjuma Riasala-i 'Itryaat.* Tonk, Raj: Arabic and Persian Research Institute, 1988–89.

Sharar, Abdul Halim. *Badr-un-Nissa ki Musibat.* Lucknow: Al-Nazir Press, 1912.

Sharar, Abdul Halim. *Guzashta Lakhnau: Hindustan mein Mashriqi Tamaddun ka Akhiri Namuna.* Edited by Muhammad Ikram Chaghtai. Lahore: Sang-i-Meel Publications, 2006.

Sharif, Jafar. *Islam in India or the Qanun-I-Islam: The Customs of the Musalmans of India.* Translated by G.A. Herklots. First pub 1921, new edition revised and rearranged with additions by William Crooke. Delhi: Low Price Publications, 1997.

Sharma Merathi, G.R. *Randibazon Ki Hajaamat.* Meerut: Sadiq Press, 1905.

Sharma, Amar Nath. *Bajanaamā: Study of Early Indian Gramophone Records.* Lucknow: Kathachittra Prakashan, 2012.

Sharma, Tripurari. *San Sattavan Ka Qissa: Azizun Nissa.* 1988.

Shenk, David. *The Immortal Game: A History of Chess.* London: Souvenir Press, 2007.

Siddiqi Dehalvi, Abdullah Bin Muhammad Ashraf. *Tazkirat al-Auzaan.* Translated into Urdu by Muhammad Aamir Khan Irfani Nadavi. Tonk, Rajasthan: Maulana Abul Kalam Azad Arabi and Persian Research Institute, 2001

Siddiqi, 'Shorish'. *Patang.* Lucknow: Published by the author, 1998.

Siddiqi, Monaa. *Hospitality and Islam: Welcoming in God's Name.* London: Yale University Press, 2015.

Siddiqui, Firdous Azmat. *A Struggle for Identity: Muslim Women in the United Provinces.* New Delhi: Foundation Books, 2014.

Singh 'Jauhar', Jawahar. *Dastoor al-Mulaqaat.* Lucknow: Matba' Alavi Muhammad Ali Bakhsh.

Singh, Reena: *Awadh Ki Chitrakala.* Varanasi: Kala Prakashan, 1990.

Singh, Veena. *Romancing with Chikankari.* New Delhi: Tushar Publications, 2004.

Sobhani, Ayatollah Jafar. *Doctrines of Shi'I Islam: A Compendium of Imami Beliefs and Practices.* Translated by Reza Shah-Kazemi. London: I.B. Tauris, 2001.

Soteriou, Alexandra. *Gift of Conquerors: Hand Papermaking in India.* Ahmedabad: Mapin, 1999.

Sprenger, Aloys. *A Catalogue of the Arabic, Persian and Hindustany Manuscripts of the Libraries of the King of Oudh.* Compiled under the orders of the GoI. Calcutta: Baptist Mission Press, 1854.

Stark, Ulrike. *An Empire of Books: The Naval Kishore Press and the Diffusion of the Printed Words in Colonial India.* Ranikhet, Uttarakhand: Permanent Black, 2007.

Stephen, Markel and Tushara Bindu Gude eds. *India's Fabled City: The Art of Courtly Lucknow.* Los Angeles: Los Angeles County Museum of Art and Del Monico Books, an imprint of Prestel Publishing, 2010.

Suhail, Agha. *Dabistan-i Lakhnau Ki Dastani Adab Ka Irtiqa.* Lahore: Maghraibi Pakistan Urdu Academy, 1988.

Surati, Syed Abdul Wali 'Uzlat'. *Raagmala.* Edited by Abdur Razzaq Quraishi. Bombay: Adabi Publishers, 1971.

Suvorova, Anna. *Early Urdu Theatre: Traditions & Transformations.* Lahore, Pakistan: Res and Pub Centre, National College of Arts, 2009.

Swarup, Sushama. *Costumes and Textiles of Awadh: From the Era of Nawabs to Modern Times.* New Delhi: Roli Books, 2012.

Syed, Ghulam Imam. *Anis & Shakespeare: A Comparison.* Lucknow: Zahur Husain, 1950.

*Taalim-un-Niswan.* Naval Kishore Press, 1870.

Taylor, P.J.O. *A Companion to the 'Indian Mutiny' of 1857.* Delhi: Oxford Universitiy Press, 1996.

Taylor, P.J.O. *A Star Shall Fall: India 1857.* New Delhi: HarperCollins, 1993.

Thomas, G. *History of Photography, India 1840–1980.* Andhra Pradesh State Akademi of Photography, 1981.

Timms, Pamela. *Korma, Kheer and Kismet: Five Seasons in Old Delhi.* New Delhi:

Aleph Book Company, 2014.

Topsfield, Andrew, ed. *The Art of Play: Board and Card Games of India*. Mumbai: Marg Publications, 2006.

Trivedi, Madhu. *The Making of the Awadh Culture*. Delhi: Primus Books, 2010.

Tsybulsky, V.V. *Calenders of Middle East Countries: Conversion Tables and Explanatory Notes*. Moscow: Nauka Publishing, 1979.

Uldani, Abdul Bari 'Asi'. *Tazkirat-ul-Khawateen*. Lucknow: Naval Kishore Press, 1927.

Verma, Som Prakash. *Interpreting Mughal Painting: Essays on Art, Society, and Culture*. New Delhi: Oxford University Press, 2009.

Wadud, Amina. *Qur'an and Woman: Rereading the Sacred Text from a Woman's Prospective*. New York: Oxford University Press, 1999.

Waheed, Nadeem and Aadam Naiyer. *Patangbazi*. Islamabad, Pakistan: Lok Virsa Research Centre, 1998.

Ward, Andrew. *Our Bones Are Scattered: The Cawnpore Massacres and the Indian Mutiny of 1857*. London: John Murray, 1996.

Warisi, 'Aughat' Shah. *Faizan-i Warisi*. Edited by Anis Ahmad Warisi. Delhi: S.A. Publications, 2006.

Warisi, 'Bedam' Shah. *Mushaf-i 'Bedam'*. Lahore, Pakistan: Ali Hujwiri Publishers.

Yahiya, Ghulam. *Crafting Traditions: Documenting Trades & Crafts in Early 19th Century North India*. Edited and translated from Persian, *Kitab-iTasavir Sheeshagaran Vaghairah Wa Bayan-I Aalat-I Anha* by Mehr Afshan Farooqi. New Delhi: Indira Gandhi National Centre for the Arts and Aryan Books International, 2005.

Yalland, Zoë. *Traders and Nabobs: The British in Cawnpore, 1765–1857*. Salisbury, Wiltshire: Michael Russell Publishing, 1987.

Yalland, Zoë. *Boxwallah: The British in Cawnpore: 1857–1901*. Wilby, Norwich: Michael Russell Publishing, 1994.

Yule, Col Henry. *Hobson-Jobson*. New Delhi: Rupa, 1986.

Zimmer, Heinrich. *Myths and Symbols in Indian Art and Civilization*. Edited by Joseph Campbell. New York: Torchbooks, 1962.

Zumbroich, Thomas J. 'The Missi-Stained Finger-Tip of the Fair: A Cultural History of Teeth and Gum Blackening in South Asia.' E-Journal of Indian Medicine, Volume 8 (2015), 1–32.

# Index

Lady at her toilette on a palace terrace
Courtesy: Peter Blohm/Indian Miniature Paintings Ltd

Preparation for the Nuth Uterwai ceremony at a courtesan's kotha
Courtesy: Peter Blohm/Indian Miniature Paintings Ltd

Folio from a ragamala series: Marwa Ragini. Signed by Faqirullah
Courtesy: Peter Blohm/Indian Miniature Paintings Ltd

Nazneen, a member of Nawab Wajid Ali Shah's Parikhana
Courtesy: State Museum, Lucknow

Dancing Girl, 1772
Tilly Kettle, 1735–1786, British, active in India (1769–76)
Courtesy: Yale Center for British Art, Paul Mellon Collection

Nawab of Awadh, Saadat Khan Burhan ul-Mulk (r. 1722–39)
Courtesy: Peter Blohm/Indian Miniature Paintings Ltd

Nawab Shuja-ud-Daula with his ten sons

Wajid Ali Shah's Harem

Courtesy: State Museum, Lucknow

Muharram procession
Courtesy: State Museum, Lucknow

Colonel Mordaunt's Cock Match at Lucknow, 1792
Richard Earlom, 1743–1822, British
Courtesy: Yale Center for British Art, Paul Mellon Collection

A Pearl Borer, Lucknow

Dyers, Lucknow

Photo of a lady taken by photographer Asghar Jan in his studio in Qaisar Bagh

Miss Nazir Begum of Lucknow

Two courtesan musicians

A scene of the main road, Lucknow

Hindu bathing ghat along the banks of the Gomti River, Lucknow

Gomti River view, Lucknow

A boat shaped like a peacock (moar pankhee), Lucknow

Bridge Boat, Lucknow

Alambagh, the gateway

View of Qaisar Bagh, Lucknow

Palace of Light, Lucknow

Palace of Nawab Shuja-ud-Daula, Lucknow

Tombs of Nawab Sadaat Ali Khan and his wife, Lucknow

Shah Najaf, the tomb of Nawab Ghazi-ud-Din Haider

New road from Kanpur, Lucknow

Qaisar Bagh, Lucknow

Shah Najaf, Lucknow

Turkish Gate, Lucknow

General view of Husainabad

View of the Husainabad Imambara and surroundings, Lucknow

Imambara, the gateway, Lucknow

Made in the USA
Monee, IL
07 July 2026